Utah Territory Legislative Assembly

Acts, Resolutions and Memorials

Passed at the several annual sessions of the Legislative Assembly of the Territory of

Utah - Vol. 9

Utah Territory Legislative Assembly

Acts, Resolutions and Memorials
Passed at the several annual sessions of the Legislative Assembly of the Territory of Utah - Vol. 9

ISBN/EAN: 9783337182403

Printed in Europe, USA, Canada, Australia, Japan

Cover: Foto ©Suzi / pixelio.de

More available books at **www.hansebooks.com**

RESOLUTIONS AND MEMORIALS

PASSED AT THE SEVERAL

ANNUAL SESSIONS

OF THE

LEGISLATIVE ASSEMBLY

OF THE

TERRITORY OF UTAH.

TO WHICH IS PREFIXED:

THE DECLARATION OF INDEPENDENCE, THE ARTICLES OF THE CONFEDERATION, THE ORDINANCE OF 1787, THE CONSTITUTION OF THE UNITED STATES, AND AMENDMENTS THERETO, THE NATURALIZATION LAWS, AND THE ORGANIC ACT OF UTAH, AND TO WHICH IS APPENDED A NUMBER OF LAW FORMS.

———:0:———

PUBLISHED BY VIRTUE OF AN ACT APPROVED JAN. 19, 1866.

———:0:———

GREAT SALT LAKE CITY:
HENRY McEWAN, PUBLIC PRINTER,
1866.

———:o:———

INDEX TO THE ACTS AND RESOLUTIONS OF THE LEGISLATIVE ASSEMBLY OF THE TERRITORY OF UTAH, NOW IN FORCE, BY THEIR TITLES.

———:o:———

INDEX TO INCORPORATED CITIES.

———:o:———

RESOLUTIONS PASSED AT THE FIFTEENTH ANNUAL SESSION.

———:o:———

MEMORIALS BY THEIR TITLES.

INDEX TO FORMS.

DECLARATION OF INDEPENDENCE.

JULY 4th, 1776.

THE UNANIMOUS DECLARATION OF THE THIRTEEN UNITED STATES OF AMERICA IN CONGRESS ASSEMBLED.

When, in the course of human events, it becomes necessary for one people to dissolve the political bands which have connected them with another, and to assume among the powers of the earth the separate and equal station to which the laws of nature and of nature's God entitle them, a decent respect to the opinions of mankind requires that they should declare the causes which impel them to the separation.

We hold these truths to be self-evident; that all men are created equal; that they are endowed by their Creator with certain unalienable rights; that among these are life, liberty, and the pursuit of happiness; that, to secure these rights, governments are instituted among men, deriving their just powers from the consent of the governed; that, whenever any form of government becomes destructive of these ends, it is the right of the people to alter or abolish it, and to institute new government, laying its foundation on such principles, and organizing its powers in such form, as to them shall seem most likely to effect their safety and happiness. Prudence, indeed, will dictate that governments long established should not be changed for light and transient causes; and, accordingly, all experience hath shown that mankind are more disposed to suffer, while evils are sufferable, than to right themselves by abolishing the forms to which they are accustomed. But when a long train of abuses and usurpations, pursuing invariably the same object, evinces a design to reduce them under absolute despotism, it is their right, it is their duty, to throw off such government, and to provide new guards for their future security. Such has been the patient sufferance of these colonies, and such is now the necessity which constrains them to alter their former system of government. The history of the present king of Great Britain is a history of repeated injuries and usurpations, all having in direct object the establishment of an absolute tyranny over these States. To prove this, let facts be submitted to a candid world:—

He has refused his assent to laws the most wholesome and necessary to the public good.

He has forbidden his governors to pass laws of immediate and pressing importance, unless suspended in their operation till his assent should be obtained; and, when so suspended, he has utterly neglected to attend to them.

He has refused to pass other laws for the accommodation of large districts of people, unless those people would relinquish the right of representation in the legislature—a right inestimable to them, and formidable to tyrants only.

He has called together legislative bodies at places unusual, uncomfortable, and distant from the repository of their public records, for the sole purpose of fatiguing them into compliance with his measures.

He has dissolved representative houses repeatedly for opposing with manly firmness his invasions on the rights of the people.

He has refused, for a long time after such dissolutions, to cause others to be elected; whereby the legislative powers, incapable of annihilation, have returned to the people at large for their exercise—the State remaining, in the meantime, exposed to all the dangers of invasion from without and convulsions within.

He has endeavored to prevent the population of these States—for that purpose obstructing the laws for naturalization of foreigners, refusing to pass others to encourage their migration hither, and raising the conditions of new appropriations of lands.

A

He has obstructed the administration of justice, by refusing his assent to laws for establishing judiciary powers.

He has made judges dependent on his will alone for the tenure of their offices and the amount and payment of their salaries.

He has erected a multitude of new offices, and sent hither swarms of officers to harass our people and eat out their substance.

He has kept among us, in times of peace, standing armies, without the consent of our legislatures.

He has affected to render the military independent of, and superior to, the civil power.

He has combined with others to subject us to jurisdiction foreign to our constitution, and unacknowledged by our laws—giving his assent to their acts of pretended legislation.

For quartering large bodies of armed troops among us;

For protecting them, by a mock trial, from punishment for any murders which they should commit on the inhabitants of these States;

For cutting off our trade with all parts of the world;

For imposing taxes on us without our consent;

For depriving us, in many cases, of the benefits of trial by jury;

For transporting us beyond seas to be tried for pretended offences;

For abolishing the free system of English laws in a neighboring province, establishing therein an arbitrary government, and enlarging its boundaries, so as to render it at once an example and fit instrument for introducing the same absolute rule into these colonies;

For taking away our charters, abolishing our most valuable laws, and altering, fundamentally, the forms of our governments;

For suspending our own legislatures, and declaring themselves invested with power to legislate for us in all cases whatsoever.

He has abdicated government here by declaring us out of his protection and waging war against us.

He has plundered our seas, ravaged our coasts, burnt our towns, and destroyed the lives of our people.

He is at this time transporting large armies of foreign mercenaries to complete the works of death, desolation, and tyranny, already begun, with circumstances of cruelty and perfidy scarcely paralleled in the most barbarous ages, and totally unworthy the head of a civilized nation.

He has constrained our fellow-citizens, taken captive on the high seas, to bear arms against their country, to become the executioners of their friends and brethren, or to fall themselves by their hands.

He has excited domestic insurrections among us, and has endeavored to bring on the inhabitants of our frontiers the merciless Indian savages, whose known rule of warfare is an undistinguished destruction of all ages, sexes, and conditions.

In every stage of these oppressions, we have petitioned for redress in the most humble terms. Our repeated petitions have been answered only by repeated injury. A prince, whose character is thus marked by every act which may define a tyrant, is unfit to be the ruler of a free people.

Nor have we been wanting in attentions to our British brethren. We have warned them, from time to time, of attempts, by their legislature, to extend an unwarrantable jurisdiction over us. We have reminded them of the circumstances of our emigration and settlement here. We have appealed to their native justice and magnanimity, and we have conjured them, by the ties of our common kindred, to disavow these usurpations, which would inevitably interrupt our connexions and correspondence. They, too, have been deaf to the voice of justice and of consanguinity. We must, therefore, acquiesce in the necessity which denounces our separation, and hold them, as we hold the rest of mankind, enemies in war, in peace, friends.

We, therefore, the representatives of the United States of America, in general Congress assembled, appealing to the Supreme Judge of the World for the rectitude of our intentions, do, in the name, and by the authority of the good people of these colonies, solemnly publish and declare that these United Colonies are, and of right ought to be, free and independent states; that they are absolved from all allegiance to the British crown, and that all political connexion between them and the state of Great Britain is, and ought to be, totally dissolved; and that, as free and independent states, they have full power to levy war, conclude peace, contract alliances, establish commerce, and do all other acts and things which independent states may of right do. And for the support of this declaration, with a firm reliance on the protection of Divine Providence, we mutually pledge to each other our lives, our fortunes, and our sacred honor.

The foregoing declaration was, by order of Congress, engrossed and signed by the following members:—

ROBERT MORRIS,
BENJAMIN RUSH,
SAMUEL CHASE,
CARTER BRAXTON,
JOSEPH HEWES,
GEORGE WYTHE,
GEORGE READ,
RICHARD HENRY LEE,
THOMAS HAYWARD, JUN.
THOMAS LYNCH, JUN.
WM. FLOYD,
ABRAHAM CLARK,
PHILIP LIVINGSTON,
WM. WHIPPLE,
GEO. WALTON,
LEWIS MORRIS,
GEORGE ROSS,
ROBERT TREAT PAYNE,
GEORGE CLYMER,
JOSIAH BARTLETT,
WM. WILLIAMS,
RICHARD STOCKTON,
JOHN WITHERSPOON,
WILLIAM ELLERY,
ROGER SHERMAN,
CHARLES CARROLL, of Carrolton;
THOMAS JEFFERSON,
BENJAMIN HARRISON,
JOHN HANCOCK,
ELBRIDGE GERRY,
OLIVER WOLCOTT,
JOHN MORTON,
CÆSAR RODNEY,
JOHN PENN,
THOS. M. KEAK,
WM. HOOPER,
WM. PACA,
F. LIGHTFOOT LEE,
ARTHUR MIDDLETON,
BUTTON GWINNET,
LYMAN HALL,
FRANCIS LEWIS,
SAML. ADAMS,
EDWARD RUTLEDGE,
JOHN ADAMS,
B. FRANKLIN,
JAMES SMITH,
SAML. HUNTINGTON,
MATTHEW THORNTON,
STEPHEN HOPKINS,
FRANCIS HOPKINSON,
JOHN HART,
JAMES WILSON,
THOMAS STONE,
GEORGE TAYLOR,
THOMAS NELSON, JUN.

ARTICLES OF CONFEDERATION.

——:o:——

TO ALL TO WHOM THESE PRESENTS SHALL COME, WE, THE UNDERSIGNED, DELEGATES OF THE STATES AFFIXED TO OUR NAMES, SEND GREETING:

Whereas, the delegates of the United States of America in Congress assembled, did, on the fifteenth day of November, in the year of our Lord one thousand seven hundred and seventy-seven, and in the second year of the independence of America, agree to certain articles of confederation and perpetual Union between the States of New Hampshire, Massachusetts Bay, Rhode Island and Providence Plantations, Connecticut, New York, New Jersey, Pennsylvania, Delaware, Maryland, Virginia, North Carolina, South Carolina, and Georgia, in the words following, viz:—

Articles of Confederation and perpetual Union between the States of New Hampshire, Massachusetts Bay, Rhode Island and Providence Plantations, Connecticut, New York, New Jersey, Pennsylvania, Delaware, Maryland, Virginia, North Carolina, South Carolina, and Georgia.

ARTICLE I.

The style of this confedracy shall be, "The United States of America."

ARTICLE II.

Each state retains its sovereignty, freedom, and independence, and every power, jurisdiction, and right, which is not by this confederation expressly delegated to the United States in Congress assembled.

ARTICLE III.

The said states hereby severally enter into a firm league of friendship with each other for their common defence, the security of their liberties, and their mutual and general welfare; binding themselves to assist each other against all force offered to, or attacks made upon them, or any of them, on account of religion, sovereignty, trade, or any other pretence whatever.

ARTICLE IV.

The better to secure and perpetuate mutual friendship, and intercourse among the people of the different States in this Union, the free inhabitants of each of these States, paupers, vagabonds, and fugitives from justice, excepted, shall be entitled to all privileges and immunities of free citizens in the several states; and the people of each state shall have free ingress, and regress to and from any other state, and shall enjoy therein all the privileges of trade and commerce subject to the same duties, impositions, and restrictions, as the inhabitants thereof respectively; provided that such restrictions shall not extend so far as to prevent the removal of property imported into any state to any other state, of which the owner is an inhabitant; provided also, that no imposition, duties, or restriction, shall be laid by any state on the property of the United States or either of them.

If any person guilty of or charged with treason, felony, or other high misdemeanor, in any state, shall flee from justice, and be found in any of the United States, he shall, upon demand of the governor or executive power of the state from which he fled, be delivered up and removed to the state having jurisdiction of his offence.

Full faith and credit shall be given in each of these states to the records, acts, and judicial proceedings of the courts and magistrates of every other state.

ARTICLE V.

For the more convenient management of the general interests of the United States, delegates shall be annually appointed in such manner as the legislature of each state shall direct to meet in Congress on the first Monday in November, in every year, with a power reserved to each state to recall its delegates or any of them, at any time within the year, and to send others in their stead for the remainder of the year.

No state shall be represented in Congress by less than two, nor by more than seven members; and no person shall be capable of being a delegate for more than three years in any term of six years; nor shall any person, being a delegate, be capable of holding any office under the United States, for which he, or another for his benefit, receives any salary, fees, or emolument of any kind.

Each state shall maintain its own delegates in a meeting of the States, and while they act as members of the committee of the states.

In determining questions in the United States, in Congress assembled, each state shall have one vote.

Freedom of speech and debate in Congress shall not be impeached or questioned in any court or place out of Congress; and the members of Congress shall be protected in their persons from arrests and imprisonments, during the time of their going to, and from, and attendance on Congress, except for treason, felony, or breach of the peace.

ARTICLE VI.

No state, without the consent of the United States, in Congress assembled, shall send any embassy to, or receive any embassy from, or enter into any conference, agreement, alliance, or treaty, with any king, prince, or state; nor shall any person holding any office of profit or trust under the United States, or any of them, accept of any present, emolument, office or title of any kind whatever, from any king, prince, or foreign state, nor shall the United States, in Congress assembled, or any of them, grant any title of nobility.

No two or more states shall enter into any treaty, confederation, or alliance whatever, between them, without the consent of the United States, in Congress assembled, specifying accurately the purposes for which the same is to be entered into and how long it shall continue.

No state shall lay any imposts or duties, which may interfere with any stipulations in treaties entered into by the United States, in Congress assembled, with any king, prince, or state, in pursuance of any treaties already proposed by Congress to the courts of France and Spain.

No vessels-of-war shall be kept up in time of peace by any State, except such number only as shall be deemed necessary by the United States, in Congress assembled, for the defence of such state or its trade; nor shall any body of forces be kept up by any state in time of peace, except such number only as in the judgment of the United States, in Congress assembled, shall be deemed requisite to garrison the forts necessary for the defence of such state; but every state shall always keep up a well-regulated and disciplined militia, sufficiently armed and accoutred, and shall provide and have constantly ready for use, in public stores, a due number of field pieces and tents, and a proper quantity of arms, ammunition, and camp equipage.

No state shall engage in any war without the consent of the United States, in Congress assembled, unless such state be actually invaded by enemies or shall have received certain advice of a resolution being formed by some nation of Indians to invade such state, and the danger is so imminent as not to admit of a delay till the United States, in Congress assembled, can be consulted; nor shall any state grant commissions to any ships or vessels-of-war, nor letters of marque or reprisal, except it be after a declaration of war by the United States, in Congress assembled, and then only against the kingdom or state, and the subjects thereof, against which war has been so declared, and under such regulations as shall be established by the United States, in Congress assembled, unless such state be infested by pirates, in which case vessels-of-war may be fitted out for that occasion, and kept so long as the danger shall continue, or until the United States, in Congress assembled, shall determine otherwise.

ARTICLE VII.

When land forces are raised by any state for the common defence, all officers of or under the rank of colonel, shall be appointed by the legislature of each state respectively, by whom such forces shall be raised, or in such manner as such state shall direct, and all vacancies shall be filled up by the state which first made the appointment.

ARTICLE VIII.

All charges of war, and all other expenses that shall be incurred for the common defence or general welfare, and allowed by the United States, in Congress assembled, shall be defrayed out of a common treasury, which shall be supplied by the several states in proportion to the value of all land within each state granted to or surveyed for any person, as such land and the buildings and improvements thereon shall be estimated according to such mode as the United States, in Congress assembled, shall from time to time direct and appoint.

The taxes for paying that proportion shall be laid and levied by the authority and direction of the legislatures of the several states, within the time agreed upon by the United States, in Congress assembled.

ARTICLE IX.

The United States, in Congress assembled, shall have the sole and exclusive right and power of determining on peace and war, except in the cases mentioned in the sixth article—of sending and receiving ambassadors—entering into treaties and alliances; provided, that no treaty of commerce shall be made whereby the legislative power of the respective states shall be restrained from imposing such imposts and duties on foreigners as their own people are subjected to, or from prohibiting the exportation or importation of any species of goods or commodities whatsoever—of establishing rules for deciding in all cases, what captures on land or water shall be legal, and in what manner prizes taken by land or naval forces in the service of the United States shall be divided or appropriated—of granting letters of marque and reprisal in times of peace—appointing courts for the trial of piracies and felonies committed on the high seas, and establishing courts for receiving and determining finally appeals in all cases of captures: provided, that no member of Congress shall be appointed a judge of any of the said courts.

The United States, in Congress assembled, shall also be the last resort on appeal in all disputes and differences now subsisting, or that hereafter may arise, between two or more states concerning boundary, jurisdiction, or any other cause whatever; which authority shall always be exercised in the manner following:—Whenever the legislative or executive authority or lawful agent of any state in controversy with another shall present a petition to Congress, stating the matter in question, and praying for a hearing, notice thereof shall be given by order of Congress to the legislative or executive authority of the other state in controversy, and a day assigned for the appearance of the parties, by their lawful agents, who shall then be directed to appoint by joint consent commissioners or judges to constitute a court for hearing and determining the matter in question; but if they cannot agree, Congress shall name three persons out of each of the United States, and from the list of such persons each party shall alternately strike out one, the petitioners beginning, until the number shall be reduced to thirteen; and from that number not less than seven or more than nine names, as Congress shall direct, shall, in the presence of Congress, be drawn out by lot; and the persons whose names shall be so drawn, or any five of them, shall be commissioners or judges, to hear and finally determine the controversy, so always as a major part of the judges, who shall hear the cause, shall agree in the determination: and if either party shall neglect to attend at the day appointed, without showing reasons which Congress shall judge sufficient, or being present shall refuse to strike, the Congress shall proceed to nominate three persons out of each state, and the secretary of Congress shall strike in behalf of such party absent or refusing; and the judgment and sentence of the court to be appointed in the manner before prescribed, shall be final and conclusive, and if any of the parties shall refuse to submit to the authority of such court, or to appear, or defend their claim or cause, the court shall nevertheless proceed to pronounce sentence or judgment, which shall in like manner be final and decisive, the judgment or sentence and other proceedings, being in either case transmitted to Congress, and lodged among the acts of Congress for the security of the parties concerned; provided, that every commissioner, before he sits in judgment, shall take an oath, to be administered by one of the judges of the supreme or superior court of the state, where the cause shall be tried, "well and truly to hear and determine the matter in question, according to the best of his judgment, without favor, affection, or hope of reward;" provided also, that no state shall be deprived of territory for the benefit of the United States.

All controversies concerning the private right of soil, claimed under different grants of two or more states, whose jurisdiction as they may respect such lands and the states which passed such grants are adjusted, the said grants or either of them being at the same time claimed to have originated antecedent to such settlement of jurisdiction, shall, on the petition of either party to the Congress of the United States, be finally determined, as near as may be, in the same manner as is before prescribed for deciding disputes respecting territorial jurisdiction between different states.

The United States, in Congress assembled, shall also have the sole and exclusive right and power of regulating the alloy and value of coin struck by their own authority, or by that of the respective states; fixing the standard of weights and measures throughout the United States; regulating the trade and managing all affairs with the Indians, not members of any of the states; provided that the legislative right of any state, within its own limits, be not infringed or violated; establishing and regulating post offices from one state to another, throughout all the United States, and exacting such postage on the papers passing through the same, as may be requisite to defray the expenses of the said office; appointing all officers of the land forces in the service of the United States, excepting regimental officers; appointing all the officers of the naval forces, and commissioning all officers whatever in the service of the United States, making rules for the government and regulation of the said land and naval forces, and directing their operations.

The United States, in Congress assembled, shall have authority to appoint a committee, to sit in the recess of Congress, to be denominated, "a committee of the states," and to consist of one delegate from each state; and to appoint such other committees and civil officers as may be necessary for managing the general affairs of the United States under their direction; to appoint one of their number to preside; provided that no person be allowed to serve in the office of president more than one year in any term of three years; to ascertain the necessary sums of money to be raised for the service of the United States, and to appropriate and apply the same for defraying the public expenses; to borrow money or emit bills on the credit of the United States, transmitting every half year to the respective states an account of the sums of money so borrowed or emitted; to build and equip a navy; to agree upon the number of land forces, and to make requisitions from each state for its quota, in proportion to the number of white inhabitants in such state, which requisition shall be binding; and thereupon the legislature of each state shall appoint the regimental officers, raise the men, and clothe, arm, and equip them, in a soldier-like manner, at the expense of the United States; and the officers and men so clothed, armed, and equipped, shall march to the place appointed, and within the time agreed on by the United States, in Congress assembled; but if the United States, in Congress assembled, shall, on consideration of circumstances, judge proper that any state should not raise men, or should raise a smaller number than its quota, and that any other state should raise a greater number of men than the quota thereof, such extra number shall be raised, officered, clothed, armed and equipped, in the same manner as the quota of such state, unless the legislature of such state shall judge that such extra number cannot be safely spared out of the same, in which case they shall raise, officer, clothe, arm, and equip, as many of such extra number as they judge can be safely spared, and the officers and men so clothed, armed, and equipped, shall march to the place appointed, and within the time agreed on by the United States, in Congress assembled.

The United States, in Congress assembled, shall never engage in a war, nor grant letters of marque and reprisal in time of peace, nor enter into any treaties or alliances, nor coin money, nor regulate the value thereof, nor ascertain the sums and expenses necessary for the defence and welfare of the United States, or any of them, nor emit bills, nor borrow money on the credit of the United States, nor appropriate money, nor agree upon the number of vessels of war to be built or purchased, or the number of land or sea forces to be raised, nor appoint a commander-in-chief of the army or navy, unless nine states assent to the same, nor shall a question on any other point, except for adjourning from day to day, be determined, unless by the votes of a majority of the United States in Congress assembled.

The Congress of the United States shall have power to adjourn to any time within the year, and to any place within the United States, so that no period of adjournment be for a longer duration than the space of six months, and shall publish the journal of their proceedings monthly, except such parts thereof relating to treaties, alliances, or military operations, as in their judgment require secrecy; and the yeas and nays of the delegates of each state, on any question, shall be entered on the journal, when it is desired by any delegate; and the delegates of a state, or any of them, at his or their request, shall be furnished with a transcript of the said journal, except such parts as are above excepted, to lay before the legislatures of the several states.

ARTICLE X.

The committee of the states, or any nine of them, shall be authorized to execute, in the recess of Congress, such of the powers of Congress as the United States, in Congress assembled, by the consent of nine states, shall, from time to time, think expedient to vest them with; provided that no power be delegated to the said committee, for the exercise of which, by the articles of confederation, the voice of nine states, in the Congress of the United States assembled, is requisite.

ARTICLE XI.

Canada acceding to this confederation, and joining in the measures of the United States, shall be admitted into, and entitled to all the advantages of this Union; but no other colony shall be admitted into the same, unless such admission be agreed to by nine states.

ARTICLE XII.

All bills of credit emitted, moneys borrowed, and debts contracted by or under the authority of Congress, before the assembling of the United States, in pursuance of the present confederation, shall be deemed and considered as a charge against the United States, for payment and satisfaction whereof the said United States and the public faith are hereby solemnly pledged.

ARTICLE XIII.

Every state shall abide by the determinations of the United States, in Congress assembled, on all questions which by this confederation are submitted to them. And the articles of this confederation shall be inviolably observed by every state, and the Union shall be perpetual; nor shall any alteration at any time hereafter be made in any of them, unless such alteration be agreed to in a Congress of the United States, and be afterwards confirmed by the legislatures of every state.

And whereas it hath pleased the great Governor of the world to incline the hearts of the legislatures we respectfully represent in Congress, to approve of, and to authorize us to ratify the said articles of confederation and perpetual union, Know ye, that we, the undersigned delegates, by virtue of the power and authority to us given for that purpose, do, by these presents, in the name and in behalf of our respective constituents, fully and entirely ratify and confirm each and every of the said articles of confederation and perpetual union, and all and singular the matters and things therein contained. And we do further solemnly plight and engage the faith of our respective constituents, that they shall abide by the determinations of the United States, in Congress assembled, on all questions which by the said confederation are submitted to them; and that the articles thereof shall be inviolably observed by the states we respectively represent, and that the Union shall be perpetual.

In witness whereof, we have hereunto set our hands, in Congress. Done at Philadelphia, in the State of Pennsylvania, the ninth day of July, in the year of our Lord seventeen hundred and seventy-eight, and in the third year of the Independence of America:—

NEW HAMPSHIRE—Josiah Bartlett, John Wentworth, Jun.

MASSACHUSETTS BAY—John Hancock, Samuel Adams, Elbridge Gerry, Francis Dana, James Lovell, Samuel Holten.

RHODE ISLAND—William Ellery, Henry Marchant, John Collins.

CONNECTICUT—Roger Sherman, Samuel Huntington, Oliver Wolcott, Titus Hosmer, Andrew Adams.

NEW YORK—James Duane, Francis Lewis, William Duer, Gouverneur Morris.

NEW JERSEY—John Witherspoon, Nathaniel Scudder.

PENNSYLVANIA—Robert Morris, Daniel Roberdeau, Jonathan B. Smith, William Clingan, Joseph Reed.

DELAWARE—Thomas M'Kean, John Dickinson, Nicholas Van Dyke.

MARYLAND—John Hanson, Daniel Carroll.

VIRGINIA—Richard Henry Lee, John Banister, Thomas Adams, Jno. Harvie, Francis Lightfoot Lee.

NORTH CAROLINA—John Penn, Cornstable Harnett, John Williams.

SOUTH CAROLINA—Henry Laurens, William Henry Drayton, Jno. Matthews, Richard Hutson, Thomas Heyward, Jun.

GEORGIA—Jno. Walton, Edward Telfair, Edward Langworthy.

AN ORDINANCE,

FOR THE GOVERNMENT OF THE TERRITORY OF THE UNITED STATES, NORTH-WEST OF THE RIVER OHIO.

Be it ordained by the United States, in Congress assembled, That the said territory, for the purposes of temporary government, be one district; subject, however, to be divided into two districts, as future circumstances may, in the opinion of Congress, make it expedient.

Be it ordained by the authority aforesaid, That the estates both of resident and non-resident proprietors in the said territory, dying intestate, shall descend to and be distributed among their children, and the descendants of a deceased child, in equal parts; the descendants of a deceased child or grand child, to take a share of their deceased parent in equal parts among them; and where there shall be no children or descendants, then in equal parts to the next of kin, in equal degree; and among collaterals, the children of a deceased brother or sister of the intestate shall have, in equal parts among them, their deceased parent's share; and there shall, in no case, be a distinction between kindred of the whole and half blood; saving, in all cases, to the widow of the intestate her third part of the real estate for life, and one third part of the personal estate; and this law relative to the descents and dower shall remain in full force until altered by the legislature of the district. And until the governor and judges shall adopt laws, as hereinafter mentioned, estates in the said territory may be devised or bequeathed by wills in writing, signed and sealed by him or her, in whom the estate may be, (being of full age,) and attested by three witnesses; and real estates may be conveyed by lease and release, or bargain and sale, signed, sealed, and delivered by the person, being of full age, in whom the estate may be, and attested by two witnesses, provided such wills be duly proved, such conveniences be acknowledged, or the execution thereof duly proved, and be recorded within one year after proper magistrates, courts and registers shall be appointed for that purpose; and personal property may be transferred by delivery; saving, however, to the French and Canadian inhabitants, and other settlers of the Kaskaskias, Saint Vincents, and the neighboring villages, who have heretofore professed themselves citizens of Virginia, their laws and customs now in force among them, relative to the descent and conveyance of property.

Be it ordained by the authority aforesaid, That there shall be appointed, from time to time, by Congress, a governor, whose commission shall continue in force for the term of three years, unless sooner revoked by Congress; he shall reside in the district, and have a freehold estate therein, in one thousand acres of land, while in the exercise of his office.

There shall be appointed from time to time, by Congress, a secretary whose commission shall continue in force for four years, unless sooner revoked; he shall reside in the district, and have a freehold estate therein, in five hundred acres of land while in the exercise of his office. It shall be his duty to keep and preserve the acts and laws passed by the legislature, and the public records of the district, and the proceedings of the governor in his executive department; and transmit authentic copies of such acts and proceedings every six months, to the secretary of Congress. There shall also be appointed a court, to consist of three judges, any two of whom to form a court, who shall have a common law jurisdiction, and reside in the district, and have each therein a freehold estate in five hundred acres of land, while in the exercise of their offices; and their commissions shall continue in force during good behavior.

The Governor and judges, or a majority of them, shall adopt and publish, in the district, such laws of the original states, criminal and civil, as may be necessary and best suited to the circumstances of the district, and report them to Congress from time time; which laws shall be in force in the district until the organization of the general assembly therein, unless disapproved of by Congress; but afterwards the legislature shall have authority to alter them as they shall think fit.

The Governor for the time being shall be commander-in-chief of the militia, appoint and commission all officers in the same, below the rank of general officers; all general officers shall be appointed and commissioned by Congress.

Previous to the organization of the general assembly, the governor shall appoint such magistrates and other civil officers, in each county or township, as he shall find necessary for the preservation of peace and good order in the same. After the general assembly shall be organized, the powers and duties of the magistrates and other civil officers shall be regulated and defined by the said assembly; but all magistrates and other civil officers, not herein otherwise directed, shall, during the continuance of this temporary government, be appointed by the governor.

For the prevention of crimes and injuries, the laws to be adopted or made shall have force in all parts of the district, and for the execution of process, criminal and civil, the governor shall make proper divisions thereof; and he shall proceed from time to time, as circumstances may require, to lay out the parts of the district, in which the Indian titles shall have been extinguished, into counties and townships, subject, however, to such alterations as may thereafter be made by the legislature.

So soon as there shall be five thousand free male inhabitants of full age, in the district, upon giving proof thereof to the governor, they shall receive authority, with time and place, to elect representatives from their counties or townships, to represent them in the general assembly: Provided, That for every five hundred free male inhabitants, there shall be one representative, and so on progressively with the number of free male inhabitants, shall the right of representation increase, until the number of representatives shall amount to twenty-five, after which the number and proportion of representatives shall be regulated by the legislature: Provided, That no person be eligible or qualified to act as a representative, unless he shall have been a citizen of one of the United States three years, and be a resident in the district, or unless he shall have resided in the district three years, and in either case shall likewise hold in his own right, in fee simple, two hundred acres of land within the same: Provided, also, That a freehold in fifty acres of land in the district, having been a citizen of one of the states, and being resident in the district, or the like freehold and two years residence in the district shall be necessary to qualify a man as an elector of a representative.

The representative thus elected shall serve for the term of two years; and in case of the death of a representative, or removal from office, the governor shall issue a writ to the county or township for which he was a member, to elect another in his stead, to serve for the residue of the term.

The general assembly, or legislature, shall consist of the governor, legislative council, and a house of representatives. The legislative council shall consist of five members, to continue in office five years, unless sooner removed by congress, any three of whom to be a quorum. And the members of the council shall be nominated and appointed in the following manner, to wit: As soon as representatives shall be elected, the governor shall appoint a time and place for them to meet together, and when met, they shall nominate ten persons, residents in the district, and each possessed of a freehold in five hundred acres of land, and return their names to congress, five of whom congress shall appoint and commission to serve as aforesaid; and whenever a vacancy shall happen in the council, by death or removal from office, the house of representatives shall nominate two persons, qualified as aforesaid, for each vacancy, and return their names to congress, one of whom congress shall appoint and commission for the residue of the term. And every five years, four months at least before the expiration of the time of service of the members of the council, the said house shall nominate ten persons, qualified as aforesaid, and return their names to congress, five of whom congress shall appoint and commission to serve as members of the council five years, unless sooner removed. And the governor, legislative council, and house of representatives shall have authority to make laws, in all cases, for the good government of the district, not repugnant to the principles, and articles in this ordinance established and declared. And all bills, having passed by a majority in the house, and by a majority in the council, shall be referred to the governor for his assent; but no bill or legislative act whatever, shall be of any force without his assent. The governor shall have power to convene, prorogue, and dissolve the general assembly, when in his opinion it shall be expedient.

The governor, judges, legislative council, secretary, and such other officers as congress shall appoint in the district, shall take an oath or affirmation of fidelity and of office; the governor before the president of congress, and all other officers before the governor. As soon as a legislature shall be formed in the district, the council and house assembled, in one room, shall have authority, by joint ballot, to elect a delegate to congress, who shall have a seat in congress, with a right of debating, but not of voting, during this temporary government.

And for extending the fundamental principles of civil and religious liberty, which form the basis whereon these republics, their laws, and constitutions are erected; to fix and establish those principles as the basis of all laws, constitutions and governments, which forever hereafter shall be formed in the said territory; to provide also for the establishment of states, and permanent governments therein, and for their admission to share in the federal councils, on an equal footing with the original states, at as early periods as may be consistent with the general interest:

It is hereby ordained and declared, by the authority aforesaid, That the following articles shall be considered as articles of compact between the original states, and the people and states in the said territory, and forever remain unalterable, unless by common consent, to wit:

ARTICLE I.

No person demeaning himself in a peaceable and orderly manner, shall ever be molested on account of his mode of worship, or religious sentiments, in the said territory.

ARTICLE II.

The inhabitants of the said territory shall always be entitled to the benefits of the writ of habeas corpus, and trial by jury; of a proportionate representation of the people in the legislature, and of judicial proceedings according to the course of the common law. All persons shall be bailable, unless for capital offences, where the proof shall be evident, or the presumption great. All fines shall be moderate; and no cruel or unusual punishments shall be inflicted. No man shall be deprived of his liberty or property, but by the judgment of his peers, or the law of the land; and should the public exigencies make it necessary, for the common preservation, to take any person's property, or to demand his particular services, full compensation shall be made for the same. And in the just preservation of rights and property, it is understood and declared, that no law ought ever to be made, or have force in the said territory, that shall in any manner whatever interfere with or affect private contracts or engagements bonafide, and without fraud previously formed.

ARTICLE III.

Religion, morality, and knowledge being necessary to good government and the happiness of mankind, schools and the means of education shall forever be encouraged. The utmost good faith shall always be observed towards the Indians; their lands and property shall never be taken from them without their consent, and in their property, rights, and liberty, they never shall be invaded or disturbed, unless in just and lawful wars, authorized by congress; but laws, founded in justice and humanity, shall from time to time be made for preventing wrongs being done to them, and for preserving peace and friendship with them.

ARTICLE IV.

The said territory, and the states which may be formed therein, shall forever remain a part of this confederacy of the United States of America, subject to the articles of confederation, and to such alterations therein as shall be constitutionally made; and to all the acts and ordinances of the United States in congress assembled, conformable thereto. The inhabitants and settlers in the said territory shall be subject to pay a part of the federal debts contracted, or to be contracted, and a proportional part of the expenses of government, to be apportioned on them by congress, according to the same common rule and measure by which apportionments thereof shall be made on the other states; and the taxes for paying their proportion shall be laid and levied by the authority and direction of the legislatures of the district or districts, or new states, as in the original states, within the time agreed upon by the United States in congress assembled. The legislatures of those districts or new states, shall never interfere with the primary disposal of the soil by the United States in congress assembled, nor with any regulations congress may find necessary for securing the title in such soil to the bonafide purchasers. No tax shall be imposed on lands, the property of the United States; and in no case shall non-resident proprietors be taxed higher than residents. The navigable waters leading into the Mississippi and St. Lawrence, and the carrying places between the same, shall be common highways, and forever free, as well to the inhabitants of the said territory, as to the citizens of the United States, and those of any other states that may be admitted into the confederacy, without any tax, impost, or duty therefor.

ARTICLE V.

There shall be formed in the said territory, not less than three, nor more than five states; and the boundaries of the states, as soon as Virginia shall alter her act of cession, and consent to the same, shall become fixed and established as follows, to wit: The western state in the said territory shall be bounded by the Mississippi, the Ohio, and Wabash rivers; a direct line drawn from the Wabash and Post Vincents, due north to the territorial line between the United States and Canada; and by the said territorial line to the Lake of the Woods and Mississippi. The middle state shall be bounded by the said direct line, the Wabash from Post Vincents to the Ohio, by the Ohio, by a direct line drawn due north from the mouth of the Great Miami to the said territorial line, and by the said territorial line. The eastern state shall be bounded by the last mentioned direct line, the Ohio, Pennsylvania and the said territorial line:—Provided, however, and it is further understood and declared, That the boundaries of these three states shall be subject so far to be altered, that if congress shall hereafter find it expedient, they shall have authority to form one or two states in that part of the said territory which lies north of an east and west line drawn through the southerly bend or extreme of Lake Michigan. And whenever any of the said states shall have sixty thousand free inhabitants therein, such state shall be admitted, by its delegates, into the congress of the United States, on an equal footing with the original states, in all respects whatever; and shall be at liberty to form a permanent constitution and state government: Provided, the constitution and government so to be formed, shall be republican, and in conformity to the principles contained in these articles; and so far as it can be consistent with the general interest of the confederacy, such admission shall be allowed at an earlier period, and when there may be a less number of free inhabitants in the state than sixty thousand.

ARTICLE VI.

There shall be neither slavery nor involuntary servitude in the said territory, otherwise than in the punishment of crimes, whereof the party shall have been duly convicted: Provided, always, that any person escaping into the same, from whom labour or service is lawfully claimed in any one of the original states, such fugitive may be lawfully reclaimed and conveyed to the person claiming his or her labor or service, as aforesaid.

Be it ordained by the authority aforesaid, That the resolutions of the twenty-third of April, one thousand seven hundred and eighty-four, relative to the subject of this ordinance, be, and the same are hereby repealed, and declared null and void.

DONE by the United States, in congress assembled, the thirteenth day of July, in the year of our Lord, one thousand seven hundred and eighty-seven, and of their sovereignty and independence the twelfth.

WILLIAM GRAYSON, Chairman.

CHARLES THOMPSON, Secretary.

CONSTITUTION OF THE UNITED STATES.

———:o:———

COPIED FROM AND COMPARED WITH THE ROLL IN THE DEPARTMENT OF STATE.

———:o:———

WE, the people of the United States, in order to form a more perfect union, establish justice, insure domestic tranquility, provide for the common defence, promote the general welfare, and secure the blessings of liberty to ourselves and our posterity, do ordain and establish this constitution for the United States of America.

ARTICLE I.

SECTION I.

All legislative powers herein granted shall be vested in a Congress of the United States, which shall consist of a senate and house of representatives.

SECTION II.

The house of representatives shall be composed of members chosen every second year by the people of the several states, and the electors in each state shall have the qualifications requisite for electors of the most numerous branch of the state legislature.

No person shall be a representative who shall not have attained to the age of twenty-five years, and been seven years a citizen of the United States, and who shall not, when elected, be an inhabitant of that state in which he shall be chosen.

Representatives and direct taxes shall be apportioned among the several states which may be included within this Union, according to their respective numbers, which shall be determined by adding to the whole number of free persons, including those bound to service for a term of years, and excluding Indians not taxed, three-fifths of all other persons. The actual enumeration shall be made within three years after the first meeting of the Congress of the United States, and within every subsequent term of ten years, in such manner as they shall by law direct. The number of representatives shall not exceed one for every thirty thousand, but each state shall have at least one representative; and until such enumeration shall be made, the state of New Hampshire shall be entitled to choose three, Massachusetts eight, Rhode Island and Providence Plantations one, Connecticut five, New York six, New Jersey four, Pennsylvania eight, Delaware one, Maryland six, Virginia ten, North Carolina five, South Carolina five, and Georgia three.

When vacancies happen in the representation from any state, the executive authority thereof shall issue writs of election to fill such vacancies.

The house of representatives shall choose their speaker and other officers, and shall have the sole power of impeachment.

SECTION III.

The senate of the United States shall be composed of two senators from each state, chosen by the legislature thereof, for six years; and each senator shall have one vote.

Immediately after they shall be assembled in consequence of the first election, they shall be divided as equally as may be into three classes. The seats of the senators of the first class shall be vacated at the expiration of the second year, of the second class at the expiration of the fourth year, and of the third class at the expiration of the sixth year, so that one third may be chosen every second year; and if vacancies happen by resignation or otherwise, during the recess of the legislature of any state, the executive thereof may make temporary appointments until the next meeting of the legislature, which shall then fill such vacancies.

No person shall be a senator who shall not have attained to the age of thirty years, and been nine years a citizen of the United States, and who shall not, when elected, be an inhabitant of that state for which he shall be chosen.

The vice-president of the United States shall be president of the senate, but shall have no vote, unless they be equally divided.

The senate shall choose their other officers, and also a president pro tempore, in the absence of the vice-president, or when he shall exercise the office of president of the United States.

The senate shall have the sole power to try all impeachments; when sitting for that purpose, they shall be on oath or affirmation. When the president of the United States is tried, the chief justice shall preside; and no person shall be convicted without the concurrence of two-thirds of the members present.

Judgment in cases of impeachment shall not extend further than to removal from office, and disqualification to hold and enjoy any office of honor, trust or profit under the United States; but the party convicted shall nevertheless be liable and subject to indictment, trial, judgment and punishment, according to law.

SECTION IV.

The times, places and manner of holding elections for senators and representatives shall be prescribed in each state by the legislature thereof; but the Congress may at any time by law make or alter such regulations, except as to the places of choosing senators.

The Congress shall assemble at least once in every year, and such meeting shall be on the first Monday in December, unless they shall by law appoint a different day.

SECTION V.

Each house shall be the judge of the elections, returns and qualifications of its own members, and a majority of each shall constitute a quorum to do business; but a smaller number may adjourn from day to day, and may be authorized to compel the attendance of absent members, in such manner, and under such penalties as each house may provide.

Each house may determine the rules of its proceedings, punish its members for disorderly behavior, and, with the concurrence of two-thirds, expel a member.

Each house shall keep a journal of its proceedings, and from time to time publish the same, excepting such parts as may in their judgment require secresy; and the yeas and nays of the members of either house on any question shall, at the desire of one-fifth of those present, be entered on the journal.

Neither house, during the session of Congress, shall, without the consent of the other, adjourn for more than three days, nor to any other place than that in which the two houses shall be sitting.

SECTION VI.

The senators and representatives shall receive a compensation for their services, to be ascertained by law, and paid out of the treasury of the United States. They shall in all cases, except treason, felony and breach of the peace, be privileged from arrest during their attendance at the session of their respective houses, and in going to and returning from the same; and for any speech or debate in either house they shall not be questioned in any other place.

No senator or representative shall, during the time for which he was elected, be appointed to any civil office under the authority of the United States, which shall have been created, or the emoluments whereof shall have been increased during such time; and no person holding any office under the United States, shall be a member of either house during his continuance in office.

SECTION VII.

All bills for raising revenue shall originate in the house of representatives; but the senate may propose or concur with amendments as on other bills.

Every bill which shall have passed the house of representatives and the senate, shall, before it becomes a law, be presented to the president of the United States; if he approve he shall sign it, but if not he shall return it, with his objections, to that house in which it shall have originated, who shall enter the objections at large on their journal, and proceed to reconsider it. If after such reconsideration two-thirds of that house shall agree to pass the bill, it shall be sent, together with the objections, to the other house, by which it shall likewise be reconsidered, and if approved by two-thirds of that house, it shall become a law. But in all such cases the votes of both houses shall be determined by yeas and nays, and the names of the persons voting for and against the bill shall be entered on the journal of each house respectively. If any bill shall not be returned by the president within ten days (Sunday excepted) after it shall have been presented to him, the same shall be a law, in like manner as if he had signed it, unless the congress by their adjournment prevent its return, in which case it shall not be a law.

Every order, resolution, or vote to which the concurrence of the senate and house of representatives may be necessary (except on a question of adjournment) shall be presented to the president of the United States; and before the same shall take effect, shall be approved by him, or being disapproved by him, shall be repassed by two-thirds of the senate and house of representatives, according to the rules and limitations prescribed in the case of a bill.

SECTION VIII.

The Congress shall have power to lay and collect taxes, duties, imposts and excises, to pay the debts and provide for the common defence and general welfare of the United States, but all duties, imposts and excises shall be uniform throughout the United States;

To borrow money on the credit of the United States;

To regulate commerce with foreign nations, and among the several states, and with the Indian tribes;

To establish an uniform rule of naturalization, and uniform laws on the subject of bankruptcies throughout the United States;

To coin money, regulate the value thereof, and of foreign coin, and to fix the standard of weights and measures;

To provide for the punishment of counterfeiting the securities and current coin of the United States;

To establish post offices and post roads;

To promote the progress of science and useful arts, by securing for limited times to authors and inventors the exclusive right to their respective writings and discoveries;

To constitute tribunals inferior to the supreme court;

To define and punish piracies and felonies committed on the high seas, and offences against the law of nations;

To declare war, grant letters of marque and reprisal, and make rules concerning captures on land and water;

To raise and support armies, but no appropriation of money to that use shall be for a longer term than two years;

To provide and maintain a navy;

To make rules for the government and regulation of the land and naval forces;

To provide for calling forth the militia to execute the laws of the Union, suppress insurrections and repel invasions;

To provide for organizing, arming and disciplining the militia, and for governing such part of them as may be employed in the service of the United States, reserving to the states respectively the appointment of the officers, and the authority of training the militia according to the discipline prescribed by Congress;

To exercise exclusive legislation in all cases whatsoever, over such district (not exceeding ten miles square) as may, by cession of particular states, and the acceptance of Congress, become the seat of the government of the United States, and to exercise like authority over all places purchased by the consent of the legislature of the state in which the same shall be, for the erection of forts, magazines, arsenals, dockyards, and other needful buildings;—And

To make all laws which shall be necessary and proper for carrying into execution the foregoing powers, and all other powers vested by this constitution in the government of the United States, or in any department or office thereof.

SECTION IX.

The migration or importation of such persons as any of the states now existing shall think proper to admit, shall not be prohibited by the Congress prior to the year one thousand eight hundred and eight, but a tax or duty may be imposed on such importation, not exceeding ten dollars for each person.

The privilege of the writ of habeas corpus shall not be suspended, unless when in cases of rebellion or invasion the public safety may require it.

No bill of attainder or ex post facto law shall be passed.

No capitation or other direct tax shall be laid, unless in proportion to the census or enumeration hereinbefore directed to be taken.

No tax or duty shall be laid on articles exported from any state.

No preference shall be given by any regulation of commerce or revenue to the ports of one state over those of another, nor shall vessels bound to or from one state be obliged to enter, clear, or pay duties in another.

No money shall be drawn from the treasury, but in consequence of appropriations made by law; and a regular statement and account of the receipts and expenditures of all public money shall be published from time to time.

No title of nobility shall be granted by the United States; and no person holding any office of profit or trust under them shall, without the consent of the Congress, accept of any present, emolument, office, or title of any kind whatever, from any king, prince, or foreign state.

SECTION X.

No state shall enter into any treaty, alliance, or confederation; grant letters of marque and reprisal; coin money; emit bills of credit; make anything but gold and silver coin a tender in payment of debts; pass any bill of attainder, ex post facto law, or law impairing the obligation of contracts, or grant any title of nobility.

No state shall, without the consent of the Congress, lay any imposts or duties on imports or exports, except what may be absolutely necessary for executing its inspection laws; and the net produce of all duties and imposts laid by any state on imports or exports shall be for the use of the treasury of the United States; and all such laws shall be subject to the revision and control of the Congress.

No state shall, without the consent of Congress, lay any duty of tonnage, keep troops, or ships-of-war in time of peace, enter into any agreement or compact with another state, or with a foreign power, or engage in war, unless actually invaded, or in such imminent danger as will not admit of delay.

ARTICLE II.

SECTION I.

The executive power shall be vested in a President of the United States of America. He shall hold his office during the term of four years, and, together with the vice-president, chosen for the same term, be elected as follows:

Each state shall appoint, in such manner as the legislature thereof may direct, a number of electors, equal to the whole number of senators and representatives to which the state may be entitled in the Congress; but no senator or representative, or person holding an office of trust or profit under the United States, shall be appointed an elector.

The Congress may determine the time of choosing the electors, and the day on which they shall give their votes; which day shall be the same throughout the United States.

No person except a natural born citizen, or a citizen of the United States at the time of the adoption of this constitution, shall be eligible to the office of president; neither shall any person be eligible to that office who shall not have attained to the age of thirty-five years, and been fourteen years a resident within the United States.

In case of the removal of the president from office, or of his death, resignation, or inability to discharge the powers and duties of the said office, the same shall devolve on the vice-president, and the Congress may by law provide for the case of removal, death, resignation or inability, both of the president and vice-president, declaring what officer shall then act as president, and such officer shall act accordingly, until the disability be removed, or a president shall be elected.

The president shall, at stated times, receive for his services, a compensation which shall neither be increased nor diminished during the period for which he shall have been elected, and he shall not receive within that period any other emolument from the United States, or any of them.

Before he enters on the execution of his office, he shall take the following oath or affirmation:—"I do solemnly swear (or affirm) that I will faithfully execute the office of president of the United States, and will, to the best of my ability, preserve, protect and defend the Constitution of the United States."

SECTION II.

The president shall be commander-in-chief of the army and navy of the United States, and of the militia of the several states when called into the actual service of the United States; he may require the opinion, in writing, of the principal officer in each of the executive departments, upon any subject relating to the duties of their respective offices, and he shall have power to grant reprieves and pardons for offences against the United States, except in cases of impeachment.

He shall have power, by and with the advice and consent of the senate, to make treaties, provided two-thirds of the senators present concur; and he shall nominate, and by and with the advice and consent of the senate, shall appoint ambassadors, other public ministers and consuls, judges of the supreme court, and all other officers of the United States, whose appointments are not herein otherwise provided for and which shall be established by law; but the Congress may by law vest the appointment of such inferior officers, as they think proper, in the president alone, in the courts of law, or in the heads of departments.

The president shall have power to fill all vacancies that may happen during the recess of the senate, by granting commissions which shall expire at the end of their next session.

SECTION III.

He shall from time to time give to the Congress information of the state of the Union, and recommend to their consideration such measures as he shall judge necessary and expedient; he may, on extraordinary occasions, convene both houses, or either of them, and, in case of disagreement between them with respect to the time of adjournment, he may adjourn them to such time as he shall think proper; he shall receive ambassadors and other public ministers; he shall take care that the laws be faithfully executed, and shall commission all the officers of the United States.

SECTION IV.

The president, vice-president and all civil officers of the United States shall be removed from office on impeachment for and conviction of treason, bribery, or other high crimes and misdemeanors.

ARTICLE III.

SECTION I.

The judicial power of the United States shall be vested in one supreme court, and in such inferior courts as the congress may, from time to time, ordain and establish. The judges, both of the supreme and inferior courts shall hold their offices during good behavior; and shall, at stated times, receive for their services a compensation which shall not be diminished during their continuance in office.

SECTION II.

The judicial power shall extend to all cases in law and equity arising under this constitution, the laws of the United States, and treaties made, or which shall be made, under their authority; to all cases affecting ambassadors, other public ministers and consuls; to all cases of admiralty and maritime jurisdiction; to controversies to which the United States shall be a party; to controversies between two or more states, between a state and citizens of another state, between citizens of different states, between citizens of the same state claiming lands under grants of different states, and between a state or the citizens thereof and foreign states, citizens, or subjects.

In all cases affecting ambassadors, other public ministers and consuls, and those in which a state shall be a party, the supreme court shall have original jurisdiction. In all the other cases before mentioned the supreme court shall have appelate jurisdiction, both as to law and fact, with such exceptions, and under such regulations as the congress shall make.

The trial of all crimes, except in cases of impeachment, shall be by jury; and such trial shall be held in the state where the said crimes shall have been committed; but when not committed within any state, the trial shall be at such place or places as congress may by law have directed.

SECTION III.

Treason against the United States shall consist only in levying war against them, or in adhering to their enemies, giving them aid and comfort. No person shall be convicted of treason unless on the testimony of two witnesses to the same overt act, or on confession in open court.

The congress shall have power to declare the punishment of treason, but no attainder of treason shall work corruption of blood, or forfeiture, except during the life of the person attainted.

ARTICLE IV.

SECTION I.

Full faith and credit shall be given in each state to the public acts, records, and judicial proceedings of every other state. And the congress may, by general laws, prescribe the manner in which such acts, records and proceedings shall be proved, and the effect thereof.

SECTION II.

The citizens of each state shall be entitled to all the privileges and immunities of citizens in the several states.

A person charged in any state with treason, felony, or other crime, who shall flee from justice and be found in another state, shall, on demand of the executive authority of the state from which he fled, be delivered up, to be removed to the state having jurisdiction of the crime.

No person held to service or labor in one state, under the laws thereof, escaping into another, shall, in consequence of any law or regulation therein, be discharged from such service or labor, but shall be delivered up on claim of the party to whom such service or labor may be due.

SECTION III.

New states may be admitted by the congress into this Union; but no new state shall be formed or erected within the jurisdiction of any other state; nor any state be formed by the junction of two or more states, or parts of states, without the consent of the legislatures of the states concerned, as well as of the congress.

The congress shall have power to dispose of and make all needful rules and regulations respecting the territory or other property belonging to the United States; and nothing in this constitution shall be so construed as to prejudice any claims of the United States, or of any particular state.

SECTION IV.

The United States shall guaranty to every state in this union a republican form of government, and shall protect each of them against invasion; and on application of the legislature, or of the executive (when the legislature cannot be convened) against domestic violence.

ARTICLE V.

The congress, whenever two-thirds of both houses shall deem it necessary, shall propose amendments to this constitution, or, on the application of the legislatures of two-thirds of the several states, shall call a convention for proposing amendments, which, in either case, shall be valid to all intents and purposes, as part of this constitution, when ratified by the legislatures of three-fourths of the several states, or by conventions in three-fourths thereof, as the one or other mode of ratification may be proposed by the congress; provided, that no amendment, which may be made prior to the year one thousand eight hundred and eight, shall in any manner affect the first and fourth clauses in the ninth section of the first article; and that no state, without its consent, shall be deprived of its equal suffrage in the senate.

ARTIÇLE VI.

All debts contracted and engagements entered into before the adoption of this constitution shall be as valid against the United States, under this constitution, as under the confederation.

This constitution, and the laws of the United States which shall be made in pursuance thereof, and all treaties made, or which shall be made under the authority of the United States, shall be the supreme law of the land; and the judges in every state shall be bound thereby, anything in the constitution or laws of any state to the contrary notwithstanding.

The senators and representatives before mentioned, and the members of the several state legislatures, and all executive and judicial officers, both of the United States and of the several states, shall be bound by oath or affirmation, to support this constitution, but no religious test shall ever be required as a qualification to any office or public trust under the United States.

ARTICLE VII.

The ratification of the Conventions of nine states shall be sufficient for the establishment of this constitution between the states so ratifying the same.

Done in Convention, by the unanimous consent of the states present, the seventeenth day of September, in the year of our Lord one thousand seven hundred and eighty seven, and of the Independence of the United States of America the twelfth. In witness whereof we have hereunto subscribed our names.

GEORGE WASHINGTON, PRESIDENT, and
Deputy from Virginia.

NEW HAMPSHIRE.

John Langdon, Nicholas Gilman.

MASSACHUSETTS.

Nathaniel Gorham, Rufus King.

CONNECTICUT.

William Samuel Johnson, Roger Sherman.

NEW YORK.

Alexander Hamilton.

NEW JERSEY.

William Livingston,
William Patterson,
David Breardly,
Jonathan Dayton.

PENNSYLVANIA.

Benjamin Franklin,
Robert Morris,
Thomas Fitzsimons,
James Wilson,
Thomas Mifflin,
George Clymer,
Jared Ingersoll,
Governeur Morris.

DELAWARE.

George Reed,
John Dickinson,
Gunning Bedford, jun.,
Richard Bassett,
Jacob Broom.

MARYLAND.

James M'Henry,
Daniel of St. Thomas Jenifer,
Daniel Carroll.

VIRGINIA.

John Blair, James Madison, jun.

NORTH CAROLINA.

William Blount,
Richard Dobbs Spaight,
Hugh Williamson.

SOUTH CAROLINA.

John Rutledge,
Charles Pinckney,
Charles C. Pinckney,
Pierce Butler,

GEORGIA.

William Few, Abraham Baldwin.

Attest, WILLIAM JACKSON, Secretary.

AMENDMENTS

TO THE CONSTITUTION OF THE UNITED STATES, RATIFIED ACCORDING TO THE PROVISIONS OF THE FIFTH ARTICLE OF THE FOREGOING CONSTITUTION.

ARTICLE I.

Congress shall make no law respecting an establishment of religion, or prohibiting the free exercise thereof; or abridging the freedom of speech, or of the press; or the right of the people peaceably to assemble, and to petition the government for a redress of grievances.

ARTICLE II.

A well regulated militia being necessary to the security of a free state, the right of the people to keep and bear arms shall not be infringed.

ARTICLE III.

No soldier shall in time of peace be quartered in any house, without the consent of the owner, nor in a time of war, but in a manner to be prescribed by law.

ARTICLE IV.

The right of the people to be secure in their persons, houses, papers, and effects, against unreasonable searches and seizures, shall not be violated, and no warrants shall issue but upon probable cause, supported by oath or affirmation, and particularly describing the place to be searched, and the person or things to be seized.

ARTICLE V.

No person shall be held to answer for a capital, or otherwise infamous crime, unless on a presentment or indictment of a grand jury, except in cases arising in the land or naval forces, or in the militia, when in actual service in time of war or public danger; nor shall any person be subject for the same offence to be twice put in jeopardy of life or limb; nor shall be compelled in any criminal case to be a witness against himself, nor be deprived of life, liberty, or property, without due process of law; nor shall private property be taken for public use, without just compensation.

ARTICLE VI.

In all criminal prosecutions, the accused shall enjoy the right to a speedy and public trial by an impartial jury of the state and district wherein the crime shall have been committed, which district shall have been previously ascertained by law, and to be informed of the nature and cause of the accusation; to be confronted with the witnesses against him; to have compulsory process for obtaining witnesses in his favor, and to have the assistance of counsel for his defence.

ARTICLE VII.

In suits at common law, where the value in controversy shall exceed twenty dollars, the right of trial by jury shall be preserved, and no fact tried by a jury, shall be otherwise re-examined in any court of the United States, than according to the rules of the common law.

ARTICLE VIII.

Excessive bail shall not be required, nor excessive fines imposed, nor cruel and unusual punishments inflicted.

ARTICLE IX.

The enumeration in the constitution, of certain rights, shall not be construed to deny or disparage others retained by the people.

ARTICLE X.

The powers not delegated to the United States by the constitution, nor prohibited by it to the states, are reserved to the states respectively, or to the people.

ARTICLE XI.

The judicial power of the United States shall not be construed to extend to any suit in law or equity commenced or prosecuted against one of the United States by citizens of another state, or by citizens or subjects of any foreign state.

ARTICLE XII.

The electors shall meet in their respective states and vote by ballot for president and vice-president, one of whom, at least, shall not be an inhabitant of the same state with themselves; they shall name in their ballots the person voted for as president, and in distinct ballots the person voted for as vice-president, and they shall make distinct lists of all persons voted for as president, and of all persons voted for as vice-president, and of the number of votes for each, which lists they shall sign and certify, and transmit sealed to the seat of the government of the United States, directed to the president of the senate; the president of the senate shall, in the presence of the senate and house of representatives, open all the certificates, and the votes shall then be counted;—the person having the greatest number of votes for president shall be the president, if such number be a majority of the whole number of electors appointed; and if no person have such majority, then from the persons having the highest numbers, not exceeding three on the list of those voted for as president, the house of representatives shall choose immediately, by ballot, the president. But in choosing the president the votes shall be taken by states, the representation from each state having one vote; a quorum for this purpose shall consist of a member or members from two-thirds of the states, and a majority of all the states shall be necessary to a choice. And if the house of representatives shall not choose a president whenever the right of choice shall devolve upon them, before the fourth day of March next following, then the vice-president shall act as president, as in the case of the death or other constitutional disability of the president. The person having the greatest number of votes as vice-president shall be the vice-president, if such number be a majority of the whole number of electors appointed; and if no person have a majority, then from the two highest numbers on the list, the senate shall choose the vice-president; a quorum for this purpose shall consist of two-thirds of the whole number of senators, and a majority of the whole number shall be necessary to a choice. But no person constitutionally ineligible to the office of president shall be eligible to that of vice-president of the United States.

NATURALIZATION OF ALIENS.

:o:

SECTION I.

Any alien, being a free white person, may be admitted to become a citizen of the United States, or any of them, on the following conditions, and not otherwise:

First—That he shall have declared, on oath or affirmation, before the supreme, superior, district, or circuit court, of some one of the states, or of the territorial districts of the United States, or a circuit or district court of the United States, or before the clerk of either of such courts, two years at least, before his admission, that it was bonafide his intention to become a citizen of the United States, and to renounce forever all allegiance and fidelity to any foreign prince, potentate, state, or sovereignty whatever, and, particularly, by name, the prince, potentate, state or sovereignty whereof such alien may, at the time, be a citizen or subject.

Second—That he shall, at the time of his application to be admitted, declare on oath or affirmation, before some one of the courts aforesaid, that he will support the Constitution of the United States, and that he doth absolutely and entirely renounce and abjure all allegiance and fidelity to every foreign prince, potentate, state, or sovereignty whatsoever, and particularly, by name the prince, potentate, state, or sovereignty whereof he was a citizen or subject; which proceedings shall be recorded by the clerk of the court.

Third—That the court admitting such alien shall be satisfied that he has resided within the United States five years at least, and within the state or territory where such court is at the time held, one year at least; and it shall further appear to their satisfaction, that during that time he has behaved as a man of good moral character, attached to the principles of the constitution of the United States, and well disposed to the good order and happiness of the same: Provided, that the oath of the applicant shall, in no case, be allowed to prove his residence.

SECTION II.

Any alien who was residing within the limits and under the jurisdiction of the United States before the twenty-ninth day of January, one thousand seven hundred and ninety-five, may be admitted to become a citizen, on due proof made to some one of the courts aforesaid, that he has resided two years at least within and under the jurisdiction of the United States, and one year at least immediately preceding his application, within the state or territory where such court is at the time held; and on his declaring on oath, or affirmation, that he will support the constitution of the United States, and that he doth absolutely and entirely renounce and abjure all allegiance and fidelity to any foreign prince, potentate, state or sovereignty whatever, and particularly, by name, the prince, potentate, state or sovereignty whereof he was before a citizen or subject; and, moreover, on its appearing to the satisfaction of the court, that, during the said term of two years he has behaved as a man of good moral character, attached to the constitution of the United States, and well disposed to the good order and happiness of the same; and where the alien applying for admission to citizenship shall have borne any hereditary title, or been of any of the orders of nobility in the kingdom or state from which he came, on his moreover making in the court an express renunciation of his title or order of nobility, before he shall be entitled to such admission; all of which proceedings required in this proviso to be performed in the court, shall be recorded by the clerk thereof.

Any alien, being a free white person, who was residing within the limits and under the jurisdiction of the United States, at any time between the eighteenth day of June, one thousand seven hundred and ninety-eight, and the fourteenth day of April, one thousand eight hundred and two, and who has continued to reside within the same, may be admitted to become a citizen of the United States, without a compliance with the first condition specified in the first section of the act, entitled "An act to establish a uniform rule of naturalization, and to repeal the acts heretofore passed on that subject."

Nothing in the first section of the act 22nd of March, 1816, shall be construed to exclude from admission to citizenship, any free white person who was residing within the limits and under the jurisdiction of the United States at any time between the eighteenth day of June, one thousand seven hundred and ninety-eight, and the fourteenth day of April, one thousand eight hundred and two, and who, having continued to reside therein without having made any declaration of intention before a court of record as aforesaid, may be entitled to become a citizen of the United States according to act 26th of March, 1804. Whenever any person without a certificate of such declaration of intention, as aforesaid, shall make application to be admitted a citizen of the United States, it shall be proved to the satisfaction of the court that the applicant was residing within the limits and under the jurisdiction of the United States before the fourteenth day of April, one thousand eight hundred and two, and has continued to reside within the same, or he shall not be so admitted. And the residence of the applicant within the limits and under the jurisdiction of the United States for at least five years immediately preceding the time of such application shall be proved by the oath or affirmation of citizens of the United States, which citizens shall be named in the record as witnesses. And such continued residence within the limits and under the jurisdiction of the United States, when satisfactorily proved, and the place or places where the applicant has resided for at least five years, as aforesaid, shall be stated and set forth, together with the names of such citizens, in the record of the court admitting the applicant, otherwise the same shall not entitle him to be considered and deemed a citizen of the United States.

Any alien, being a free white person, who was residing within the limits and under the jurisdiction of the United States between the fourteenth day of April, one thousand eight hundred and two, and the eighteenth day of June, one thousand eight hundred and twelve, and who has continued to reside within the same, may be admitted to become a citizen of the United States, without having made any previous declaration of his intention to become a citizen: Provided, That whenever any person, without a certificate of such declaration of intention, shall make application to be admitted a citizen of the United States, it shall be proved to the satisfaction of the court that the applicant was residing within the limits and under the jurisdiction of the United States before the eighteenth day of June, one thousand eight hundred and twelve, and has continued to reside within the same, or he shall not be so admitted; and the residence of the applicant within the limits and under the jurisdiction of the United States, for at least five years immediately preceding the time of such application, shall be proved by the oath or affirmation of citizens of the United States which citizens shall be named in the record as witnesses; and such continued residence within the limits and under the jurisdiction of the United States, when satisfactorily proved, and the place or places where the applicant has resided for at least five years, as aforesaid, shall be stated and set forth, together with the names of such citizens, in the record of the court admitting the applicant; otherwise the same shall not entitle him to be considered and deemed a citizen of the United States.

Any alien, being a free white person and a minor, under the age of twenty-one years, who shall have resided in the United States three years next preceding his arrival at the age of twenty one years, and who shall have continued to reside therein to the time he may make application to be admitted a citizen thereof, may, after he arrives at the age of twenty-one years, and after he shall have resided five years within the United States, including the three years of his minority, be admitted a citizen of the United States, without having made the declaration required in the first condition of the first section of the act to which this is in addition, three years previous to his admission: Provided, Such alien shall make the declaration required therein at the time of his or her admission; and shall further declare on oath, and prove to the satisfaction of the court that, for three years next preceding, it has been the bonafide intention of such alien to become a citizen of the United States; and shall, in all other respects, comply with the laws in regard to naturalization.

In case the alien applying to be admitted to citizenship shall have borne any hereditary title, or been of any of the orders of nobility in the kingdom or state from which he came, he shall, in addition to the above requisites, make an express renunciation of his title or order of nobility, in the court to which his application shall be made, which renunciation shall be recorded in the said court: Provided, That no alien who shall be a native citizen, denizen, or subject of any country, state, or sovereign, with whom the United States shall be at war at the time of his application, shall be then admitted to be a citizen of the United States.

SECTION III.

And whereas doubts have arisen whether certain courts of record in some of the states are included within the description of district or circuit courts: Be it further enacted that every court of record in any individual state, having common law jurisdiction, and a seal and clerk or prothonotory, shall be considered as a district court within the meaning of this act; and every alien who may have been naturalized in any such court shall enjoy, from and after the passing of this act, the same rights and privileges as if he had been naturalized in a district or circuit court of the United States.

SECTION IV.

The children of persons duly naturalized under any of the laws of the United States, or who, previous to the passing of any law on that subject by the government of the United States, may have become citizens of any one of the said states, under the laws thereof, being under the age of twenty-one years at the time of their parents being so naturalized or admitted to the rights of citizenship, shall, if dwelling in the United States, be considered as citizens of the United States; and the children of persons who now are or have been citizens of the United States shall, though born out of the limits and jurisdiction of the United States, be considered as citizens of the United States. The right of citizenship shall not descend to persons whose fathers have never resided within the United States. And no person heretofore proscribed by any state, or who has been legally convicted of having joined the army of Great Britain during the war of the revolution, shall be admitted a citizen without the consent of the legislature of the state in which such person was proscribed. Children of persons naturalized before the fourteenth of April, 1802, under age at the time of their parents' naturalization, were, if dwelling in the United States on the fourteenth of April, 1802, to be considered as citizens of the United States.

When any alien who shall have complied with the first condition specified in the first section of the said original act (of 14th April, 1802) and who shall have pursued the directions prescribed in the second section of the said act, may die before he is actually naturalized, the widow and the children of such alien shall be considered as citizens of the United States, and shall be entitled to all rights and privileges as such, upon taking the oaths prescribed by law.

No person who shall arrive in the United States after February the seventeenth, 1815, shall be admitted to become a citizen of the United States, who shall not, for the continued term of five years next preceding his admission, have resided within the United States, without being at any time, during the said five years, out of the territory of the United States.

AN ACT TO ESTABLISH

A

TERRITORIAL GOVERNMENT FOR UTAH.

SEC. 1.—Be it enacted by the Senate and House of Representatives of the United States of America in Congress assembled: That all that part of the Territory of the United States included within the following limits, to wit: bounded on the west by the State of California, on the north by the Territory of Oregon, and on the east by the summit of the Rocky Mountains, and on the south by the thirty-seventh parallel of north latitude, be, and the same is hereby created into a temporary government by the name of the Territory of Utah; and, when admitted as a State, the said Territory, or any portion of the same, shall be received into the Union, with or without slavery, as their Constitution may prescribe at the time of their admission: *Provided*, That nothing in this act contained shall be construed to inhibit the Government of the United States from dividing said Territory into two or more Territories, in such manner and at such times as Congress shall deem convenient and proper, or from attaching any portion of said Territory to any other State or Territory of the United States.

SEC. 2.—And be it further enacted: That the Executive power and authority in and over said Territory of Utah shall be vested in a Governor, who shall hold his office for four years, and until his successor shall be appointed and qualified, unless sooner removed by the President of the United States. The Governor shall reside within the said Territory, shall be Commander-in-Chief of the Militia thereof, shall perform the duties and receive the emoluments of Superintendent of Indian Affairs, and shall approve all laws passed by the Legislative Assembly before they shall take effect; he may grant pardons for offences against the laws of said Territory, and reprieves for offences against the laws of the United States until the decision of the President can be made known thereon; he shall commission all officers who shall be appointed to office under the laws of the said Territory, and shall take care that the laws be faithfully executed.

SEC. 3.—And be it further enacted: That there shall be a Secretary of said Territory, who shall reside therein, and hold his office for four years, unless sooner removed by the President of the United States; he shall record and preserve all the laws and proceedings of the Legislative Assembly hereinafter constituted, and all the acts and proceedings of the Governor in his executive department; he shall transmit one copy of the laws and one copy of the executive proceedings, on or before the first day of December in each year, to the President of the United States, and at the same time two copies of the laws to the Speaker of the House of Representatives and the President of the Senate, for the use of Congress. And in case of the death, removal, resignation, or other necessary absence of the Governor from the Territory, the Secretary shall have, and he is hereby authorized and required to execute and perform all the powers and duties of the Governor during such vacancy or necessary absence, or until another Governor shall be duly appointed to fill such vacancy.

SEC. 4.—And be it further enacted: That the legislative power and authority of said Territory shall be vested in the Governor and a Legislative Assembly. The Legislative Assembly shall consist of a Council and House of Representatives. The Council shall consist of thirteen members, having the qualifications of voters as hereinafter prescribed, whose term of service shall continue two years. The House of Representatives shall consist of twenty-six members, possessing the same qualifications as prescribed for members of the Council, and whose term of service shall continue one year. An apportionment shall be made, as nearly equal as practicable, among the several counties or districts, for the election of the Council and House of Representatives, giving to each section of the Territory representation in the ratio of its population, Indians excepted, as nearly as may be. And the members of the Council and of the House of Representatives shall reside in and be inhabitants of the district for which they may be elected respectively. Previous to the first election, the Governor shall cause a census or enumeration of the inhabitants of the several counties and districts of the Territory to be taken, and the first election shall be held at such time and places, and be conducted in such manner as the Governor shall appoint and direct; and he shall, at the same time, declare the number of members of the Council and House of Representatives to which each of the counties or districts shall be entitled under this act. The number of persons authorized to be elected having the highest number of votes in each said Council districts, for members of the Council, shall be declared by the Governor to be duly elected to the Council; and the person or persons authorized to be elected having the highest number of votes for the House of Representatives, equal to the number to which each county or district shall be entitled, shall be declared by the Governor to be duly elected members of the House of Representatives: Provided, that in case of a tie between two or more persons voted for, the Governor shall order a new election to supply the vacancy made by such a tie. And the persons thus elected to the Legislative Assembly shall meet at such place and on such day as the Governor shall appoint; but thereafter, the time, place and manner of holding and conducting all elections by the people, and the apportioning the representation in the several counties or districts to the Council and House of Representatives, according to the population, shall be prescribed by law, as well as the day of the commencement of the regular sessions of the Legislative Assembly: Provided, that no one session shall exceed the term of forty days.

SEC. 5.—And be it further enacted: That every free white male inhabitant above the age of twenty-one years, who shall have been a resident of said Territory at the time of the passage of this act, shall be entitled to vote at the first election, and shall be eligible to any office within the said Territory; but the qualifications of voters and of holding office at all subsequent elections shall be such as shall be prescribed by the Legislative Assembly: Provided, that the right of suffrage and of holding office shall be exercised only by citizens of the United States, including those recognized as citizens by the treaty with the Republic of Mexico, concluded February second, eighteen hundred and forty-eight.

SEC. 6.—And be it further enacted: That the Legislative power of said Territory shall extend to all rightful subjects of legislation, consistent with the Constitution of the United States and the provisions of this act; but no law shall be passed interfering with the primary disposal of the soil; no tax shall be imposed upon the property of the United States; nor shall the lands or other property of non-residents be taxed higher than the lands or other property of residents. All the laws passed by the Legislative Assembly and Governor shall be submitted to the Congress of the United States, and if disapproved shall be null and of no effect.

SEC. 7.—And be it further enacted: That all township, district, and county officers, not herein otherwise provided for, shall be appointed or elected, as the case may be, in such manner as shall be provided by the Governor and Legislative Assembly of the Territory of Utah. The Governor shall nominate, and, by and with the advice and consent of the Legislative Council, appoint all officers not herein otherwise provided for; and in the first instance the Governor alone may appoint all said officers, who shall hold their offices until the end of the first session of the Legislative Assembly, and shall lay off the necessary districts for members of the Council and House of Representatives, and all other offices.

SEC. 8.—And be it further enacted: That no member of the Legislative Assembly shall hold or be appointed to any office which shall have been created, or the salary or emoluments of which shall have been increased while he was a member, during the term for which he was elected, and for one year after the expiration of such term; and no person holding a commission or appointment under the United States, except postmasters, shall be a member of the Legislative Assembly, or shall hold any office under the government of said Territory.

SEC. 9.—And be it further enacted: That the judicial power of said Territory shall be vested in a Supreme Court, District Courts, Probate Courts, and in Justices of the Peace. The Supreme Court shall consist of a Chief Justice and two Associate Justices, any two of whom shall constitute a quorum, and who shall hold a term at the seat of government of said Territory annually, and they shall hold their offices during the period of four years. The said Territory shall be divided into three judicial districts, and a district court shall be held in each of said districts by one of the justices of the supreme court, at such time and place as may be prescribed by law; and the judges shall, after their appointments, respectively reside in the districts which shall be assigned them. The jurisdiction of the several courts herein provided for, both appelate and original, and that of the probate courts, and of justices of the peace, shall be as limited by law: Provided, that justices of the peace shall not have jurisdiction of any matter in controversy when the title or boundaries of land may be in dispute, or where the debt or sum claimed shall exceed one hundred dollars; and the said supreme and district courts respectively shall possess chancery as well as common law jurisdiction. Each district court, or the judge thereof, shall appoint its clerk, who shall also be the registrar in chancery, and shall keep his office at the place where the court may be held. Writs of error, bills of exception, and appeals shall be allowed in all cases from the final decisions of said district courts to the supreme court, under such regulations as may be prescribed by law; but in no case removed to the supreme court shall trial by jury be allowed in said court. The supreme court, or the justices thereof, shall appoint its own clerk, and every clerk shall hold his office at the pleasure of the court for which he shall have been appointed. Writs of error and appeals from the final decision of said supreme court shall be allowed, and may be taken to the Supreme Court of the United States, in the same manner and under the same regulations as from the circuit courts of the United States, where the value of the property or the amount in controversy, to be ascertained by the oath or affirmation of either party, or other competent witness, shall exceed one thousand dollars, except only, that in all cases involving title to slaves, the said writs of error or appeals shall be allowed and decided by the said supreme court, without regard to the value of the matter, property, or title in controversy; and except, also, that a writ of error or appeal, shall also be allowed to the Supreme Court of the United States, from the decisions of the said supreme court created by this act, or of any judge thereof, upon any writ of habeas corpus involving the question of personal freedom; and each of the said district courts shall have and exercise the same jurisdiction in all cases arising under the Constitution and laws of the United States as is vested in the circuit and district courts of the United States: and the said supreme and district courts of the said Territory, and the respective judges thereof, shall and may grant writs of habeas corpus in all cases in which the same are granted by the judges of the United States in the district of Columbia; and the first six days of every term of said courts, or so much thereof as shall be necessary, shall be appropriated to the trial of causes arising under the said Constitution and laws; and writs of error and appeal, in all such cases, shall be made to the supreme court of said Territory, the same as in other cases. The said clerk shall receive in all such cases the same fees which the clerks of the district courts of Oregon Territory now receive for similar services.

SEC. 10.—And be it further enacted: That there shall be appointed an Attorney for said Territory, who shall continue in office for four years, unless sooner removed by the President, and who shall receive the same fees and salary as the attorney of the United States for the present Territory of Oregon. There shall also be a Marshal for the Territory appointed, who shall hold his office for four years, unless sooner removed by the President, and who shall execute all processes issuing from the said courts when exercising their jurisdiction as circuit and district courts of the United States; he shall perform the duties, be subject to the same regulation and penalties, and be entitled to the same fees as the marshal of the district court of the United States for the present Territory of Oregon, and shall, in addition, be paid two hundred dollars annually as a compensation for extra services.

SEC. 11.—And be it further enacted: That the governor, secretary, chief justice and associate justices, attorney, and marshal, shall be nominated, and, by and with the advice and consent of the Senate, appointed by the President of the United States. The governor and secretary to be appointed as aforesaid shall, before they act as such, respectively take an oath or affirmation before the district judge, or some justice of the peace in the limits of said Territory, duly authorized to administer oaths and affirmations by the laws now in force therein, or before the chief justice or some associate justice of the Supreme Court of the United States, to support the Constitution of the United States, and faithfully to discharge the duties of their respective offices; which said oaths, when so taken, shall be certified by the person by whom the same shall have been taken, and such certificates shall be received and recorded by the said secretary among the executive proceedings; and the chief justice and associate justices, and all other civil officers in said Territory, before they act as such, shall take a like oath or affirmation before the said governor or secretary, or some judge or justice of the peace of the Territory who may be duly commissioned or qualified, which said oath or affirmation shall be certified and transmitted by the person taking the same to the secretary, to be by him recorded as aforesaid; and afterwards, the like oath or affirmation shall be taken, certified, and recorded in such manner and form as may be prescribed by law. The Governor shall receive an annual salary of fifteen hundred dollars as governor, and one thousand dollars as Superintendent of Indian Affairs.

The Chief Justice and Associate Justices shall each receive an annual salary of eighteen hundred dollars. The Secretary shall receive an annual salary of eighteen hundred dollars. The said salaries shall be paid quarter-yearly, at the Treasury of the United States. The members of the Legislative Assembly shall be entitled to receive three dollars each per day during their attendance at the sessions thereof, and three dollars each for twenty miles' travel, in going to and returning from the said sessions, estimated according to the nearest usually traveled route. There shall be appropriated annually the sum of one thousand dollars, to be expended by the Governor to defray the contingent expenses of the Territory. There shall also be appropriated annually a sufficient sum to be expended by the Secretary of the Territory, and upon an estimate to be made by the Secretary of the Treasury of the United States, to defray the expenses of the Legislative Assembly, the printing of the laws, and other incidental expenses; and the Secretary of the Territory shall annually account to the Secretary of the Treasury of the United States for the manner in which the aforesaid sum shall have been expended.

SEC. 12.—And be it further enacted: That the Legislative Assembly of the Territory of Utah shall hold its first session at such time and place in said Territory as the Governor thereof shall appoint and direct; and at said first session, or as soon thereafter as they shall deem expedient, the Governor and Legislative Assembly shall proceed to locate and establish the seat of government for said Territory, at such place as they may deem eligible; which place, however, shall thereafter be subject to be changed by the said Governor and Legislative Assembly. And the sum of twenty thousand dollars, out of any money in the Treasury not otherwise appropriated, is hereby appropriated and granted to said Territory of Utah to be applied by the Governor and Legislative Assembly to the erection of suitable public buildings at the seat of government.

SEC. 13.—And be it further enacted: That a Delegate to the House of Representatives of the United States to serve during each Congress of the United States, may be elected by the voters qualified to elect members of the Legislative Assembly, who shall be entitled to the same rights and privileges as are exercised and enjoyed by the delegates from the several other Territories of the United States to the said House of Representatives. The first election shall be held at such time and places, and be conducted in such manner as the Governor shall appoint and direct; and at all subsequent elections, the times, places, and manner of holding the elections shall be prescribed by law. The person having the greatest number of votes shall be declared by the Governor to be duly elected, and a certificate thereof shall be given accordingly: Provided, That said delegate shall receive no higher sum for mileage than is allowed by law to the delegate from Oregon.

SEC. 14.—And be it further enacted: That the sum of five thousand dollars be, and the same is hereby appropriated out of any monies in the treasury not otherwise appropriated, to be expended by and under the direction of the said Governor of the Territory of Utah, in the purchase of a library, to be kept at the seat of government for the use of the Governor, Legislative Assembly, Judges of the Supreme Court, Secretary, Marshal, and Attorney of said Territory, and such other persons and under such regulations as shall be prescribed by law.

SEC. 15.—And be it further enacted: That when the lands in said Territory shall be surveyed under the direction of the Government of the United States, preparatory to bringing the same into market, sections numbered sixteen and thirty-six in each township in said Territory shall be, and the same are hereby reserved for the purpose of being applied to schools in said Territory, and in the States and Territories hereafter to be erected out of the same.

SEC. 16.—And be it further enacted: That temporarily, and until otherwise provided by law, the Governor of said Territory may define the judicial districts of said Territory, and assign the judges who may be appointed for said Territory to the several districts, and also appoint the times and places for holding Courts in the several counties or subdivisions in each of said judicial districts, by proclamation to be issued by him; but the Legislative Assembly, at their first or any subsequent session, may organize, alter, or modify such judicial districts, and assign the judges, and alter the times and places of holding the Courts, as to them shall seem proper and convenient.

SEC. 17.—And be it further enacted: That the Constitution and laws of the United States are hereby extended over and declared to be in force in said Territory of Utah, so far as the same, or any provision thereof, may be applicable.

Approved September 9, 1850.

TERRITORIAL LAWS OF UTAH.

———:o:———

CHAPTER I.

An ACT in Relation to the Judiciary.

SEC. 1.—Be it enacted by the Governor and the Legislative Assembly of the Territory of Utah: That the District Courts shall exercise original jurisdiction, both in civil and criminal cases, when not otherwise provided by law. They shall also have a general supervision over all inferior Courts, to prevent and correct abuses where no other remedy is provided.

SEC. 2.—The Sheriff of the county wherein the Court is held, together with all necessary assistants, must attend upon the sessions of the Court, if required.

SEC. 3.—The clerk of each district or county shall keep a record of the proceedings of the Court, under the direction of the Judge. He shall, from time to time, read over all entries therein in open court, which, when correct, shall be signed by the Judge. Entries made in vacation shall be read and approved at the next term of the Court, and may be amended, or any entries therein expunged at any time during the term of the Court at which it is made, or before it is signed by the Judge as aforesaid; but entries made, approved, and signed by the Judge, cannot be altered only to correct an evident mistake.

SEC. 4.—The Judges of the District Courts, respectively, shall report to the Legislature at each regular session thereof, all omissions, discrepancies, or other evident imperfections of the law which have fallen under their observation.

SEC. 5.—The Judges of the Court may report their own decisions, or they may appoint a reporter who shall hold his office at the pleasure of the Court, and all decisions or opinions, and all questions received on appeal, as well as motions, collateral questions, and points of practice, as they may think of sufficient importance, shall be reduced to writing and filed with the Clerk of the Court.

SEC. 6.—Each of the clerks must keep a complete register of all proceedings of the Court, with an index to the same; and generally they must perform all the other duties ordinarily pertaining to their offices.

SEC. 7.—The said Courts may adopt all such rules as they may deem expedient, consistent with the law, the prime object of which shall be to carry out the purposes of the statutes, and to subserve the ends of justice, dispensing with all needless forms, and disregarding and abridging all technical pleadings with a view to the attainment of justice; all technical forms of actions and pleadings are hereby abolished.

SEC. 8.—Any pleading which possesses the following requisites shall be deemed sufficient: First, when to the common understanding it conveys a reasonable certainty of meaning. Second, when by a fair and natural construction it shows a substantial cause of action or defence. If defective in the first above particulars, the Court shall direct a more specific statement. If in the latter, it is ground for demurrer; demurrers for formal defects are abolished, those for substantial defects must set forth the true ground of objection to the pleading demurred to; upon the determination of any demurrer, the party failing, may amend or plead upon such terms as the Court deems just, or as it may by general rule prescribe.

SEC. 9.—Immaterial variancies, errors, or defects, may be disregarded, or the Court may direct an amendment, with or without costs. No variance, error, or defect shall be deemed material, unless the Court is satisfied that the objecting party will be prejudiced by disregarding it, or by allowing it to be amended. The Court may allow material amendments at any stage of the proceedings upon such terms, and subject to such rules as it may prescribe. If an original pleading or paper be lost, or withheld by any person, the Court may authorize a copy thereof to be filed and used instead of the original.

SEC. 10.—By the consent of the Court and the parties, any person may be selected to act as Judge for the trial of any particular cause or question; and while thus acting he shall possess all the powers of the District Judge in the case.

SEC. 11.—The plaintiff cannot take a non-suit without the consent of the defendant, after the latter has claimed a set-off; but he may dismiss his cause of action, leaving the defendant to proceed on his set off in the capacity of plaintiff; either may withdraw his claim at any time before the jury retire, but not after.

SEC. 12.—Costs may be apportioned to either party, or apportioned between them, as shall be deemed equitable by the Court.

SEC. 13.—When a judgment is set aside or satisfied by execution or otherwise, the Clerk shall enter a memorandum thereof in the column left for that purpose in the judgment docket.

SEC. 14.—Parties to a question in difference, which might be the subject of a civil action, may present an agreed statement of the facts thereof to any Court having jurisdiction of the subject matter.

SEC. 15.—It must be shown by affidavit that the subject matter is real, and that the proceeding is in good faith to determine the rights of the parties thereto.

SEC. 16.—The Court must thereupon hear and determine the case, and the judgment rendered thereon will be the same in all respects as though suit had been brought in the regular manner, and will be followed by the same consequences.

SEC. 17.—All judicial proceedings must be public, unless otherwise specially provided by statute, or otherwise agreed upon by the parties.

SEC. 18.—The Judge or Justice shall not be disqualified in consequence of interest, consanguinity, or otherwise, unless objected to previous to the parties joining issue and introducing testimony.

SEC. 19.—The Court shall have power to punish by fine, or imprisonment, or both, at their discretion, for contempts, or any wilful disturbing calculated to interrupt the due course of its official proceedings, or which may tend to impair the respect due to its authority.

SEC. 20.—Public buildings owned by the Territory, or any county, city, school district, ward, university, or religious society, and burying grounds are exempt from execution.

SEC. 21.—The following property of individuals is also exempt from execution; all wearing apparel kept for actual use and suitable to the condition of the party, and trunks and other receptacles to contain the same; one musket, or rifle, and accoutrements, and amunition required for one hundred charges of loading; the proper tools, instruments, or books of any farmer, mechanic, surveyor, physician, teacher, or professor; the horse or team, and wagon or other vehicle with the proper harness or tackle by the use of which any physician, public officer, farmer, teamster, or other laborer habitually earns his living; all libraries; family books, portraits and paintings; any interest owned by the debtor or his parents in one house of public worship, school house, or burying ground. If the debtor is head of a family, there is a further exempt from execution; one cow and calf for every three persons in the family; one horse; fifty sheep and the wool therefrom; five hogs and all pigs under six months old; the necessary food for all animals for sixty days; all flax raised by the defendant, and the manufactures therefrom; one bedstead and the necessary bed and bedding for every two in the family; all cloth manufactured in the family of the defendant, or by the defendant; household and kitchen furniture not exceeding one hundred dollars in value; all spinning wheels and looms and other instruments of domestic labor kept for actual use; and the necessary provisions and fuel for the use of the family for six months; said term family does not include strangers or boarders. The earnings of such debtor for his personal services or those of his family at any time within ninety days next preceding the levy are also exempt from execution or attachment.

SEC. 22.—None of the exemptions herein made are intended for the benefit of non-residents, but their property is liable to execution, with the exception of the ordinary wearing apparel; but any person coming within the Territory with the intention of remaining is a resident within the meaning of this act; and nothing herein shall be so construed as to exempt the property of any transient person or persons about to depart from the Territory or county, with the intention of removing their effects therefrom.

SEC. 23.—There shall be a Judge of Probate in each county within the Territory, whose juridisction within his court, in all cases, arises within their respective counties under the laws of the Territory; said Judge shall be elected by the joint vote of the Legislative Assembly, and commissioned by the Governor, they shall hold their offices for the term of one year, and until their successors are elected and qualified. They shall be qualified and sworn by any person authorized to administer oaths, and give bonds and security in the sum of not less than ten thousand dollars, to be approved by the Auditor of Public Accounts; and the Auditor shall give the person filing bonds a certificate that such bond has been approved by him and filed in his office.

Sec. 24.—In case of a vacancy occurring in the office of the Judge of Probate, the Governor may appoint and fill such vacancy until the next succeeding Legislative Assembly, or some subsequent one, shall elect one: said Judge of Probate so appointed shall qualify and give bond as above provided.

Sec. 25.—The Probate Court shall be considered in law as always open; but the Judge shall hold regular sessions on the second Mondays of March, June, September and December of each year, and shall continue at each session one week, or until the business ready for trial shall be disposed of.

Sec. 26.—When the District court is to sit in a county on any of the days appointed in the preceding section for the sessions of the Probate court, the latter shall be held on the Monday preceding, and when the Judge is required by law to perform any duty which takes him from the county, on one of the appointed days, the session of the court shall be holden on the following Monday, or such day as the Judge may appoint.

Sec. 27.—The Judge of Probate has jurisdiction of the Probate of Wills, the administration of the estates of deceased persons, and of the guardianship of minors, idiots and insane persons.

Sec. 28.—The Probate records shall be kept in books separate from those of the other business of the court.

Sec. 29.—The several Probate courts in their respective counties have power to exercise original jurisdiction both civil and criminal, and as well in Chancery as at Common law, when not prohibited by legislative enactment; and they shall be governed in all respects by the same general rules and regulations as regards practice as the District courts.

Sec. 30.—Appeals are allowed from all decrees or decisions of the Probate to the District courts, except when otherwise expressed on the merit of any matter affecting the rights or interests of individuals; the appeal shall be taken within thirty days from the day on which the decision was made, and shall be taken by claiming the appeal and filing, in the clerk of the Probate court's office, a bond with one or more sureties and a penal sum to be approved by the Probate Judge or clerk; said bond shall be conditioned that said appellant will prosecute the appeal with effect; that if the appeal be dismissed or the judgment below affirmed, he will comply with the judgment and orders made by the court below, and that he will pay all costs, and sums of money that may be adjudged against him in the court appealed to, and will comply with the orders of that court; the appeal shall be taken to the next term of the District court in the county, or next nearest county, where the same shall be holden, if there be ten days between the day when the judgment was rendered and the day of the sitting of the District court.

Sec. 31.—Within twenty days from the day of the appeal, and within five days in the case mentioned in the last paragraph of the preceding section, the Clerk of the Probate Court is required to file a transcript of the proceedings in the matter in which the appeal is taken, authenticated by the seal of the Probate Court, with the Clerk of the District Court, who shall enter the same among the cases pending in that Court. Transcripts of the records and copies of the papers pertaining to the Probate Court, may be certified and signed by either the Clerk or Judge.

Sec. 32.—The Probate Judges in their respective counties shall appoint a Clerk, who shall keep his office at the county seat, and who shall attend all sessions of the Probate Court, as also sessions of the County Court for the transaction of county business. It shall be the duty of the Clerk of the Probate Court to keep a true and faithful record of all the proceedings in the Probate Court in session, entering distinctly each step in the progress of any proceedings; but such record shall be equally valid if made by the Judge.

Sec. 33.—The Clerks of the District Courts and of the Probate Courts respectively are hereby required to report to the Secretary of the Territory, on or before the first Monday of November of each year, the number of convictions for all crime and misdemeanors in their respective courts for the year preceding such report; shall show the character of the offence and the sentence of punishment, the occupation of the convict, whether he can read or write, and his general habits, and also the expenses of the county for criminal prosecution during the year, including but distinguishing the compensation of the prosecuting attorney. The Clerks aforesaid shall also forward to the Secretary copies of all reports made of decisions and opinions, which shall be reported or filed in his office.

Sec. 34.—The Judges of the District and Probate Courts shall be conservators of the peace in their respective districts and counties throughout the Territory, and it is their duty to use all diligence and influence in their power to prevent litigation.

Sec. 35.—Any matter involving litigation may be referred to arbitrators or referees, who may be chosen by the parties, or selected by the court, as the parties shall elect; all such arbitrators have authority to subpœna witnesses, administer oaths or affirmations, and issue process as the court. And when they shall have made their decision shall report the case, if necessary to enforce the same, to the clerk of the county in which the case has arisen, or when the case has not arisen in any court, to the clerk of the Probate Court; and it shall be the duty of the clerk in whose office any such decision has been filed, to make a record thereof, and proceed in the same manner as if the case had been prosecuted and decided in the usual manner.

Approved Jan. 19, 1855.

———:o:———

CHAPTER II.

An ACT Containing provisions applicable to the Laws of the Territory of Utah.

SEC. 1.—Be it enacted by the Governor and Legislative Assembly of the Territory of Utah: That all questions of law, the meaning of writings other than laws, and the admissibility of testimony, shall be decided by the court; and no laws nor parts of laws shall be read, argued, cited, or adopted in any court, during any trial, except those enacted by the Governor and Legislative Assembly of this Territory, and those passed by the Congress of the United States when applicable; and no report, decision or doings of any court shall be read, argued, cited, or adopted as precedent in any other trial.

SEC. 2.—The repeal of a law does not revive one previously repealed by it, nor affect any rights, duties, or penalties which have arisen under it.

SEC. 3.—Laws, and parts thereof, and words, and phrases, shall be construed in accordance with the customary usage of the language.

SEC. 4.—Words used in one tense may include either; and words used in one gender may include either; the singular may be read plural, and the plural singular; "person" may include a partnership, and a body corporate and politic; "writing" may include printing; "oath" may include affirmation or declaration; "signature" or "subscription" may include a mark, with the person's name written near it, and witnessed by one who can write. "Property" includes everything usually bought and sold, unless restricted. Joint authority given to three or more persons is given to the majority, unless restricted.

Approved Jan. 14, 1854.

———:o:———

CHAPTER III.

An ACT in relation to Justices of the Peace.

SEC. 1.—Be it enacted by the Governor and Legislative Assembly of the Territory of Utah: That each Precinct in this Territory shall elect one Justice of the Peace, and one Constable, and the same may be increased in any Precinct by the County court, whenever they shall deem that the public good requires it.

SEC. 2.—Each Justice of the Peace and Constable shall take an oath of office and give bond, with approved securities, in the sum of one thousand dollars, which bond shall be approved by the County court, and filed in the clerk's office; said Justices and Constable shall hold their offices for the term of two years, and until their successors are elected and qualified, and they shall be commissioned by the Governor.

SEC. 3.—It shall be the duty of every Justice of the Peace to examine strictly and faithfully into the merits and demerits of all civil and criminal cases which may come before him, and execute justice without respect to persons, or favor, or the technicalities of the law; preserve the public peace; sit in judgment in all cases referred to him; and keep a true record of all proceedings laid before him; and, in case of appeal, transmit a copy of the same to the Clerk of the Court to which the appeal is made, within five days from the time the appeal is taken.

SEC. 4.—Justices of the Peace have jurisdiction over all cases where the amount in controversy does not exceed one hundred dollars; and when the amount claimed exceeds that sum, but by fair credits may be reduced to that amount, Justices may decide cases without process; but if it shall become necessary to enforce such decisions, they shall enter such cases so decided upon their dockets, and proceed as in other cases. Justices of the Peace in their respective counties have jurisdiction of and may try, hear, and determine public offences, where the punishment imposed by law does not exceed one hundred dollars fine, or imprisonment does not exceed six months, or when the punishment is by both such fine and imprisonment.

SEC. 5.—Criminal actions for the commission of public offences may be commenced before a Justice of the Peace, by information subscribed and sworn to and filed with the Justice; the Justice must file such information and note the time of filing.

SEC. 6.—Immediately upon the filing of such information, the Justice may in his discretion issue his warrant, directed to any Sheriff, Constable, or peace officer, for the arrest of the defendant, and such warrant may be served in any county or district within the Territory.

SEC. 7.—The officer who receives the warrant must serve the same by arresting the defendant, if in his power, and bring him without unnecessary delay before the Justice who issued the same.

SEC. 8.—If the defendant do not demand a trial by jury, the Magistrate must proceed to try the issue; in case a jury be demanded, the Justice shall cause a jury of six men having the qualifications of jurors, inhabitants of the county, to be empanuelled, who, being duly sworn or affirmed, shall constitute the jury. No challenge to the panel is allowed; but the prosecutor and defendant may each challenge for cause; and the defendant may be allowed the pre-emptory challenge of three jurors; a further number of jurors shall be summoned to fill up, as the jury shall be exhausted by challenges.

SEC. 9.—The verdict of the jury shall be entered upon the Magistrate's docket, and the Magistrate must render judgment thereon of fine, or imprisonment, or both, as the case may require; and when a fine is assessed, the Justice may direct that the defendant be also imprisoned until the fine is satisfied: Provided, that the Magistrate may hire out said defendant to service until the fine is paid. If the defendant be acquitted by either the Justice or jury, he must be immediately discharged.

SEC. 10.—Within twenty days after any such conviction, the Justice shall make out a certificate in which he shall briefly state the offence charged, the conviction and judgment thereon, and, if any fine has been collected, the amount thereof, and file the the same in the Judge of Probate's office. All fines collected either by Justice, Sheriff Constable or other officer, shall be paid into the county treasury within ninety days after the same have been collected.

SEC. 11.—Upon the affidavit being filed, in which the alleged error of the proceedings is stated, and that the affiant verily believes injustice has been done, the Justice shall grant an appeal to the Court of Probate of the county, and shall take a written undertaking from the defendant, with two or more sureties, and shall cause all material witnesses to enter into recognizance to appear at the time and place of trial, and return all such papers, together with a certified copy of entries on his docket, on or before the first term of the Probate Court next to be holden, which return and papers shall be filed in the Clerk's office of the Probate Court.

SEC. 12.—It shall be the duty of the Probate Court to hear and determine the said appeal in the same manner as an issue of fact upon an indictment.

SEC. 13.—The jurisdiction of Justices extends to the limits of their respective counties, and within that limit it extends to all civil cases (except where the question of title to, and boundaries of land may arise) when the amount in controversy does not exceed one hundred dollars, and by the wish and consent of parties may be extended to any amount: Provided, That where the amount in controversy exceeds one hundred dollars, the Justice shall have the same powers as other Courts of arbitration, and shall have power to enforce his decision thereon, which decision shall be an end of controversy; but all suits shall be brought in the precinct where the defendant resides: Provided, if payment is agreed to be made in any particular place, the suit may be brought in that place, if within the county; and, Provided also, if the defendant does not reside in the Territory nor county, suit may be commenced in any place in this Territory, wherever he may be found.

SEC. 14.—The parties in any action before a Justice of the Peace shall combine all their demands, which are of a nature to be consolidated, in one action or defence; and for a failure so to do shall forfeit the right of any remedy at law for their recovery; and the defendant may at any time pay the demand against him, and cost thus far accrued, either to the Justice or officer having the process, whereupon proceedings shall cease.

SEC. 15.—Before any party before a Justice is entitled to a jury, the party demanding the jury shall deposit the fees to which they will be entitled; and the same shall be included in the judgment as part of the costs to be received, if adjudged against the party who did not advance them.

SEC. 16.—All records, dockets, and papers pertaining to the office of any Justice of the Peace, must be transmitted to his successor in office; and such successor may issue execution, and act in any case so transmitted, the same as if the case had been commenced before him; and in case of any disability or necessary absence of the Justice at the time fixed for trial or proceeding, any other Justice of the Precinct may, at his request, attend and transact the business for him without any transfer of the business to another office.

SEC. 17.—The Justice may in writing depute any discreet person to act as Constable, when no Constable is at hand, and the nature of the business shall require immediate attention.

SEC. 18.—Any Justice of the Peace may officiate as Coroner when occasion may require, by holding inquest upon the bodies of such persons as may be found dead, or may have died suddenly, or by violence, or in any manner that may create suspicion of crime; it shall be his duty to take in writing the evidences that may be adduced in such cases, also his own decision thereon, the names of several persons present at the investigation, and file the same in the Clerk of Probate's office; and he shall have authority to summon to his assistance such persons as he may deem necessary to hold such inquest, and dispose of or inter said body as he shall think proper.

SEC. 19.—It shall be the duty of each and every Justice of the Peace to punish by fine not exceeding one hundred dollars, at his discretion, any person or persons who shall bring before him a vexatious lawsuit through malice, or private pique, against the defendant; all fines so collected shall be paid into the country treasury.

Approved Feb. 4, 1852.

——:o:——

CHAPTER IV.

An ACT regulating the mode of procedure in civil cases in the Courts of the Territory of Utah.

SEC. 1.—Be it enacted by the Governor and Legislative Assembly of the Territory of Utah: That all the courts of this Territory shall have law and equity jurisdiction in civil cases, and the mode of procedure shall be uniform in said courts.

SEC. 2.—Any person seeking redress shall make his complaint in writing and under oath, before the justice or judge of the proper court.

SEC. 3.—When a complaint is filed, the court shall issue to the defendant a notice containing a copy of the complaint, and the time and place for the investigation thereof.

SEC. 4.—The notice, or any process required before trial, may be served by the party, or agent, by reading the same to the person to whom directed, or by leaving a certified copy thereof at his usual place of abode; and certification of the time and manner of such service shall be made to the court, on or before the day of trial, under oath and in writing, signed by the party serving.

SEC. 5.—At the time named for trial, if either or both parties be absent, or if present, either party, having used due diligence, is not ready for trial, the court may adjourn the case or proceed, as justice shall require; and no demands of either party that have arisen after the date of the complaint shall be admitted in the trial.

SEC. 6—The defendant shall file his answer in writing and under oath, at the time of trial, unless by order of the justice or judge he has previously so filed it; the plaintiff shall then introduce his evidence, which shall be followed by that of the defendant; and thus alternately until all the evidence is introduced; and either party may then be required to give his testimony in the case. When the evidence is closed, the plaintiff may make such applicable remarks as he deems proper, to be followed by the defendant with the same privilege, whereupon the court shall render judgment as soon as practicable.

SEC. 7.—When judgment is rendered and the party in fault refuses or neglects to comply, upon request or of its own will the court shall issue an order to the proper officer, requiring him to enforce the judgment.

SEC. 8.—The officer shall execute the order without unnecessary delay, and make return of his proceedings at the earliest possible date.

SEC. 9.—Every court shall preserve its papers, and shall keep records of its proceedings, which shall be subject to the inspection of any interested person or court; and upon requirement such party shall be furnished a certified copy of any part thereof, which shall be evidence of the matter set forth therein, provided pay be tendered for so doing.

SEC. 10.—All trials shall be had in the county where the cause of action originated, or where the defendant resides, if a citizen of the Territory; otherwise where the plaintiff may prefer: Provided, it may be tried in any place where the parties may agree.

SEC. 11.—Previous to trial, when the sum in question exceeds twenty dollars, if either party request a jury, the court shall issue an order to the proper officer, requiring him to summon for that purpose, not less than three nor more than twelve qualified persons and residents of the county.

SEC. 12.—Previous to swearing persons drawn or selected to serve as a petit jury, each party may challenge, for cause, to the number that either or both parties may be able to produce what to them seems to be good cause, the validity of said cause to be determined by the court; and each party may, as aforesaid, peremptorily challenge as many as four persons.

SEC. 13.—When the persons for jurors are selected they shall be sworn to give a just verdict, and to have no communication about the case in trial with any but the court or a fellow juror, until they have agreed upon their answer, which must be done with diligence, and may be given when two-thirds of their number concur.

SEC. 14.—Depositions may be taken and used in evidence, when the circumstances require it: Provided, when there is an opposite party, he is seasonably notified of the person, time and place.

SEC. 15.—The Court of its own will, or at the request of either party, may require proper bail for the appearance of person, or for the security or forthcoming of property, and in cases of appeal.

SEC. 16.—When property taken by virtue of an order of a court is to be sold at auction, the officer in charge shall give notice of the time and place of sale, and a summary of the kind of property, allowing the intervention of a reasonable length of time.

SEC. 17.—Every person required to execute the order of a court shall proceed therein with diligence, and make return without delay.

SEC. 18.—All persons over eighteen years of age, (excepting insane persons and idiots) whether male or female, may sue or be sued in the Courts of this Territory.

SEC. 19.—Any Court having jurisdiction of the matter of grievance may appoint a temporary guardian to prosecute or defend for a person under eighteen years of age, an insane person, or idiot.

SEC. 20.—If a defendant has reasonable objection to the Court, he shall make it known without delay, after receiving notification, and if found good, upon agreement of the parties and Court, another person may be substituted with full power to try that case, or the case shall be removed forthwith to another Court.

SEC. 21.—When ordered by a Court, an officer shall take any and every description of property wherever it can be found, and shall search for any and every description of property that is concealed.

SEC. 22.—Every Court is empowered to enforce its orders, and to punish by a reasonable preventive amount of fine, when the circumstances obviously require it, and all such fines shall be paid into the county treasury.

SEC. 23.—An appeal from the decision of a Justice's Court may be taken when the sum in question exceeds twenty dollars; and from the Probate and District Courts for any sum exceeding fifty dollars; and the Court may require the costs paid, and security given that the final judgment shall be complied with and the appeal prosecuted with diligence.

SEC. 24.—Justices of the Peace and Judges of Probate shall issue papers and hear and determine cases when business requires.

SEC. 25.—The plaintiff shall state in his complaint every known item of grievance, and the defendant shall state in his answer every known set off, so that the issue of the trial may be a final settlement: Provided, that any matter accidentally omitted may be included after joining issue.

SEC. 26.—If a person instigate or bring a suit which upon investigation proves to be vexatious, so soon as this fact is known, all proceedings therein shall be stopped; and he shall be compelled to make restitution to the aggrieved party in double the amount of damages sustained, and may be fined at the discretion of the Court.

SEC. 27.—Any deed of conveyance made by a sheriff or collector of taxes, in pursuance of an order of Court, and executed and recorded according to the statutes of the Territory, shall be deemed valid in law; and any deed heretofore made by those officers, or by the Courts themselves, in pursuance of law and by virtue of an order or decree of Court, is hereby legalized.

SEC. 28.—All laws, or parts of laws conflicting with this act are hereby repealed.

Approved Dec. 30, 1852.

———:o:———

CHAPTER V.

An ACT Authorizing the Issuing of Executions against Judgment Debtors, non-residents of the County.

SEC. 1.—Be it enacted by the Governor and Legislative Assembly of the Territory of Utah: That whenever judgment is rendered in any of the Courts of this Territory, and it shall be made to appear to the Court in which such judgment is rendered, by affidavit of the judgment creditor or his attorney, that the judgment debtor is a resident of another county, stating in said affidavit the name of the county in which said judgment debtor resides, the Court rendering such judgment is hereby authorized to issue a writ of execution on such judgment against the non-resident judgment debtor, in the same manner as if such judgment debtor was a resident of the county in which the judgment was rendered, directed to the proper officer of the county in which such judgment debtor resides: Provided, that if such writ be isued by a Justice of the Peace, it shall be duly attested by the Clerk of the Probate Court of the county in which said Justice resides.

SEC. 2.—It shall be the duty of the officer, to whom such writ of execution is directed, to proceed thereon in the same manner as if such writ had issued from a Court in his own county, and make returns thereof to the Court issuing the same, without unnecessary delay.

Approved Jan. 14, 1864.

———:o:———

CHAPTER VI.

An ACT in relation to Abatement in Civil Actions.

Be it enacted by the Governor and Legislative Assembly of the Territory of Utah: That no action shall abate by the death, marriage or other disability of a party, nor by the transfer of any interest therein, if the cause of action survive or continue; and in case of the death, marriage or other disability of a party, the court may, on motion, allow the action to be continued by or against his representative or successor in interest.

Approved, Jan. 16, 1861.

———:o:———

CHAPTER VII.

An ACT Concerning Stay of Executions.

SEC. 1.—Be it enacted by the Governor and Legislative Assembly of the Territory of Utah: That on all judgments rendered by any of the courts in this Territory the stay of execution shall be had by the defendant or defendants giving security for the payment of debt and cost, to the acceptance of the Court, or the plaintiff; the request to stay eexcution shall be made known on the day of trial, and security given within five days from the time judgment is rendered.

SEC. 2.—That all sums of twenty dollars and under may be staid thirty days; all sums over twenty dollars and not to exceed fifty dollars may be staid sixty days; all sums over fifty dollars and not to exceed one hundred dollars may be staid ninety days; all sums over one hundred dollars may be staid six months.

SEC. 3.—That at the expiration of the stay of any execution, if not satisfied, it shall be the duty of the Court to issue an execution for the property of the defendant or defendants; and in all cases the security to stay an execution shall be considered one of the defendants; but in all cases the property of the principal shall first be taken and exposed to pay the debt.

Approved March 3, 1852.

------:o:------

CHAPTER VIII.

An ACT for the Regulation of Attorneys

SEC. 1.—Be it enacted by the Governor and Legislative Assembly of the Territory of Utah: That the right of being heard by self or counsel shall not be denied to any person claiming a trial as plaintiff or defendant, in any court in this Territory; and it shall be the duty of all Judges of Courts in this Territory to grant a hearing as counsel to any person of good moral character, chosen by any person or persons to prosecute or defend a case in which he, she, or they are a party.

SEC. 2.—No person or persons employing counsel, in any of the courts of this Territory, shall be compelled by any process of law to pay the counsel so employed for any services rendered as counsel, before, or after, or during the process of trial in the case.

SEC. 3.—It shall be the duty of the Judges of all Courts in this Territory to forbid and prevent all indecent and exciting language and behavior in their courts; and in case of a rebuke to counsel being disregarded and resented by said counsel, it shall be the duty of the Judge giving such rebuke to nullify the right to plead of such counsel, and to take measures to prohibit him from being heard as counsel in any court in this Territory, until such time as satisfaction has been given for his good conduct in future. And it shall further be his duty to impose a fine, not exceeding one hundred dollars, on such counsel, as he may deem just, and he may commit said counsel to prison during the term of the court then being holden.

SEC. 4.—It shall be the duty of the executive officers of all courts in this Territory to arrest without process and put in safe keeping all persons, whether counsel, or other officers of courts, or persons within the hearing of such courts, who shall in any way behave indecently or riotously, or use indecent, riotous or exciting language, subject to the release or action of the court in which such arrest is made; and such executive officers may call for such assistance as may be necessary in making such arrest, and for the safe keeping of such person or persons so offending.

SEC. 5.—Any attorney or person otherwise assuming to appear before any Court in this Territory, in any cause whatever, shall present all the facts in the case, whether they are calculated to make against his client or not, of which he is in possession, and shall present the best evidence that he can in the case to the intent that the true state of the case in litigation may be presented before the Court, and for a failure to do so, or to comply with all the requirements of this act, shall be liable to all the penalty hereinbefore provided for, and the further penalty of not less than one dollar at the discretion of the court.

Approved Feb. 18, 1852.

CHAPTER IX.

An ACT in relation to Marshals and Attorneys.

SEC. 1.—Be it enacted by the Governor and Legislative Assembly of the Territory of Utah: That a Marshal shall be elected by a joint vote of both Houses of the Legislative Assembly, whose term of office shall be one year, unless sooner removed by the Legislative Assembly, or until his successor is elected and qualified. Said Marshal shall, before entering upon the duties of his office, take an oath of office, and file bonds with securities in the penal sum of not exceeding twenty thousand dollars, conditioned for the faithful discharge of his duties, which bond with securities is to be approved by the Secretary of the Territory, and filed in his office.

SEC. 2—Said Marshal shall have power to appoint one or more Deputy Marshals in each judicial district of the Territory, as the necessity of the case may require, whose term of office shall expire with that of the Marshal; but they may at any time be removed at his discretion.

SEC. 3.—It shall be the duty of the Marshal, or any of his Deputies, to execute all orders or processes of the Supreme or District Court, in all cases arising under the laws of the Territory, and such other duties as the executive may direct, or may be required by law pertaining to the duties of his office.

SEC. 4.—An Attorney General shall be elected by the joint vote of the Legislative Assembly, whose term of office shall be one year, unless sooner removed by the Legislative Assembly, or until his successor is elected and qualified, and shall, before entering on the duties of his office, take an oath of office, and give bonds and security to the people of the Territory, conditioned for the faithful performance of his duty, to be approved by the Secretary ot the Territory, and filed in his office.

SEC. 5.—It shall be the duty of the Attorney General to attend to all legal business on the part of the Territory, before the courts, where the Territory is a party, and prosecute individuals accused of crimes in the judicial district in which he keeps his office, in cases arising under the laws of the Territory, and such other duties as pertain to his office.

SEC. 6.—There shall be elected for each judicial district (except the one in which the Attorney General keeps his office) a District Attorney by the joint vote of both Houses of the Legislative Assembly, who shall hold his office for one year, unless sooner removed by the Legislative Assembly, or until his successor is elected and qualified, and shall, before entering on the duties of his office, take an oath of office, and give bonds to the people of the Territory, conditioned for the faithful performance of his duties, to be approved by the Secretary of the Territory, and filed in his office.

SEC. 7.—It shall be the duty of the District Attorneys to attend to legal business before the courts in their respective districts, where the Territory is a party, prosecute individuals accused of crimes, in cases arising under the laws of the Territory, and do such other duties as pertain to their office.

SEC. 8.—A Prosecuting Attorney shall be appointed by the Probate Judge in each organized county in this Territory, whose term of office shall be four years, unless sooner removed by the Probate Judge, or until his successor is appointed and qualified, whose duty it shall be to attend to all legal business in the county in which the Territory is a party, and prosecute before the Probate Court of his county all individuals accused of crimes. Said Attorneys shall, before entering upon the duties of their respective offices, take an oath of office, and give bonds with securities, conditioned for the faithful performance of their duties, to be approved by the clerk of the Probate court, and filed in his office.

Approved March 3, 1852.

———:o:———

CHAPTER X.

An ACT in relation to Writs of Habeas Corpus.

SEC. 1.—Be it enacted by the Governor and Legislative Assembly of the Territory of Utah: That the petition for a Writ of Habeas Corpus must be in writing, and be sworn to, and signed by the prisoner, or some person on his, her, or their behalf, setting forth the facts concerning his, her, or their imprisonment, and in whose custody he, she, or they are detained, and shall be accompanied by a copy of the warrant or warrants of commitment, or an affidavit that the said copy had been demanded of the person or persons in whose custody the prisoner or prisoners are detained, and by him or them refused, or neglected to be given.

SEC. 2.—Upon the presentation of the foregoing petition to any court having jurisdiction, the Writ of Habeas Corpus shall be awarded, unless it shall appear from the petition itself, or the documents annexed, or the showing of the petitioner, the party so applying would not be entitled to any relief.

SEC. 3.—The Writ of Habeas Corpus may be allowed by the Supreme, District, or Probate Court, or any Judge thereof, and may be served in any part of the Territory.

SEC. 4.—Application for this writ must be made to the court or judge most convenient in point of distance to the applicant, and the more remote court or judge, if applied to for the writ, may refuse the same, unless a sufficient reason be adduced in the petition for not making application to the more convenient court or judge.

SEC. 5.—When the writ shall be awarded, it shall appear under the seal of court issuing the same, or if it be issued by any judge it shall be signed by him, and shall be substantially in the following words, to wit:

Territory of Utah, } To the Marshal, or Sheriff, officer, or to A. B. (as the
County of——— } case may be,)

You are hereby commanded to have the body of C. D., by you detained as alleged, before the court, or before me, E. F., Judge, &c., (as the case may be,) at———,on———, or forthwith, after being served with this writ, to be dealt with according to law, and to abide such order as the court or judge shall make in the premises, and have you then and there this writ, with a return of your doings in the premises.

SEC. 6.—When the writ is disallowed, the court or judge shall cause the reasons of said disallowance to be appended to the petition, and returned to the person applying for the writ.

SEC. 7.—To the intent that no officer, sheriff, jailor, constable, or other person or persons whatsoever, upon whom such writ shall be served, may pretend ignorance thereof, such writ or copy thereof shall be endorsed with the following words: "By the Habeas Corpus Act," and all persons upon whom such writs shall be served, holding said prisoner or prisoners, shall make return of such writ, and shall bring or cause to be brought the body or bodies of such person or persons before the court or judge issuing said writ according to the requirements of the same.

SEC. 8.—Whenever the Court or Judge, authorized to grant this writ, has evidence that any person within the jurisdiction of such court or judge is unjustly imprisoned or restrained of his liberty, it is the duty of each court or judge to issue, or cause to be issued, the writ as aforesaid, though no application be made therefor.

SEC. 9.—The writ may be served by the officer, or by any other person appointed for that purpose by the court or judge by whom it is issued or allowed. If served by any other person than the officer, he possesses the same power and is liable to the same penalty for a non-performance of his duty as though he were the officer.

SEC. 10.—The proper mode of service is by leaving the original writ with the defendant or person holding or detaining such plaintiff or prisoner, and preserving a copy on which to make the return of service.

SEC. 11.—If the defendant cannot be found, or if he have not the plaintiff in custody, the service shall be made upon any person having the plaintiff in custody, in the manner and with the same effect as though he had been made defendant therein.

SEC. 12.—If the defendant conceal himself, or refuse admittance to the person attempting to serve the writ, or if he attempt wrongfully to carry the person out of the county or Territory after the service of the writ as aforesaid, the officer, or the person who is attempting to serve, or who has served the writ, as above contemplated, is authorized to arrest the defendant, or other person so resisting, and bring him or them together with the plaintiff forthwith before the officer or court before whom the writ is made returnable. In order to make such arrest, the officer or other person having the writ possesses the same power to execute the same as is given to a sheriff for the arrest of a person charged with felony.

SEC. 13.—The Writ of Habeas Corpus must not be disobeyed for any defect of form or mis-description of the plaintiff or defendant: Provided, enough is stated to show the meaning and intent of the writ. Service being made in any mode, the defendant must appear at the proper time and place, and answer the petition. He must also bring the body of the plaintiff, or show good cause for not doing so; to get possession of a plaintiff's person, when there is no person appearing to have him in charge or custody, the same power is given to the officer or person having the writ, as is given to the sheriff for the arrest of a person charged with felony.

SEC. 14.—A wilful failure to comply with the requisitions of this act renders the defendant or offending party liable to be attached for a contempt, and to be imprisoned till a compliance is obtained, and also subjects him to a forfeiture of one thousand dollars to the party thereby aggrieved.

SEC. 15.—The defendant in his answer must state plainly and unequivocally whether he then has, or at any time has had the plaintiff under his control and restraint, and, if so, the cause thereof. If he has transferred him, he must state the fact, and to whom, and the time thereof, as well as the reason or authority therefor.

SEC. 16.—Any judge, whether acting individually or as a member of the court, who wrongfully and wilfully refuses to award such writ, whenever proper application for the same is made, shall forfeit and pay the sum of one thousand dollars, which may be recovered by an action of debt for the use of the Territory; and may be imprisoned for a term not exceeding one year.

SEC. 17.—Until the sufficiency of the cause of restraint is determined, the defendant may retain the plaintiff in his custody, and may use all necessary and proper means for that purpose.

SEC. 18.—The plaintiff in writing, or by his attorney, may waive his right to be present at the trial, in which case the proceedings may be had in his absence. The writ in such cases will be modified accordingly. If no sufficient, just, legal cause of detention is shown, the plaintiff must be discharged.

SEC. 19—Upon the return of any Writ of Habeas Corpus, the court or judge shall, after having given sufficient notice, proceed in a summary manner to settle the said facts, by hearing the testimony and arguments, as well of all parties interested civily, if any there be, as of the prisoner or prisoners, and the person or persons who hold him, her, or them in custody; and shall dispose of the prisoner or prisoners, as the case may require, in all cases where the imprisonment is for a criminal offence, and there is not sufficient cause for discharge; and, although the commitment may have been informally made, or without due authority, or the process may have been executed by a person not duly authorized, the court may make a new commitment, or admit the party to bail, if the case be bailable.

SEC. 20.—Disobedience to any order of discharge, or attempt to elude the service of the Writ of Habeas Corpus, or to avoid the effect thereof, subjects the defendant to a fine of one thousand dollars, and imprisonment for the term of one year; and any person knowingly aiding and abetting in any such act shall be subject to the like punishment.

SEC. 21.—Any officer refusing to deliver a copy of any legal process, by which he detains the plaintiff in custody, to any person who demands such copy for the purpose of taking out a Writ of Habeas Corpus, shall forfeit not exceeding two hundred dollars to the person so detained.

SEC. 22.—All persons admitted to bail on Habeas Corpus shall enter recognizance, with sufficient sureties, in such sum as the court shall direct, having regard to the circumstances of the plaintiff, and the nature of the offence, conditioned for his, her, or their appearance at the next term of the court to be holden in the county where the offence was committed, or where the same is to be tried. And all material witnesses shall also be required to enter recognizance to appear at the same time and place, and not depart therefrom, without leave. All such papers must be filed in the clerk's office where the same is made returnable.

SEC. 23.—The recovery of any penalties incurred by reason of the provisons of this act shall be no bar to a civil suit for damages.

Approved Feb. 2, 1852.

———:o:———

CHAPTER XI.

An ACT Governing Writs of Attachments and Garnishments.

SEC. 1.—Be it enacted by the Governor and Legislative Assembly of the Territory of Utah: That if any creditor, his agent or attorney, shall file an affidavit in any of the courts in this Territory, according to their respective jurisdiction, setting forth that any person is indebted to such creditor, stating the nature and amount of such indebtedness as near as may be, and that such debtor has departed or is about to depart from this Territory or the county in which he resides, or wherein the complaint was made, with the intention of having his effects removed from this Territory or county aforesaid, or is about removing his property as aforesaid; to the injury of such creditor, or that such debtor conceals himself or stands in defiance of an officer, so that process cannot be served upon him, or is not a resident of this Territory, it shall be lawful for said courts to issue a writ of attachment directed to the proper officer, commanding him to attach, in whose possession the same may be found, the land claims and improvements thereon, or other property of such debtor, or so much thereof as will be sufficient to satisfy the claim sworn to and the interest, damage and costs of suit.

SEC. 2.—Such officers shall, without delay, execute such writ of attachment upon the land claims and improvements thereon, or other property of the debtor of value sufficient to satisfy the demand sworn to, and interest, damage and costs, as he may have been commanded in said writ, and make return of his doings thereon as on other writs, with an inventory of the property, by him attached, indorsed thereon, or thereunto annexed. If the defendant or any person for him is in the act of removing any personal property, the officer may pursue and take the same in any county of this Territory, and return the same to the county from which such attachment issued. He shall also serve said writ of attachment upon the defendant, if he can be found, by reading the same to him, or delivering a copy thereof, and the return to such writ must state the manner in which it was served.

SEC. 3.—Every court, before granting an attachment, shall take bond and security from the party for whom the same shall be issued, his agent or attorney, payable to the defendant in double the sum sworn to be due, conditioned for satisfying all costs and damages which may be awarded to such defendant, or others interested in the proceedings, by reason of plaintiff wrongfully sueing such attachment.

SEC. 4.—When the Sheriff or other officer having charge of said writ is unable to find property of any defendant sufficient to satisfy any attachment under the provisions of this act, he is hereby required to summon any person or persons the plaintiff shall designate as having any property or things in action in his or their possession or power belonging to the defendant, or who are in any wise indebted to such defendant, to appear before the court to which the writ is returnable on the return day of the attachment, then and there to answer upon oath what amount he is or they are indebted to the defendant in the attachment, or what property or things in action he has or they have in possession or power at the time of serving the attachment. The person or persons so summoned shall be considered a garnishee or garnishees, and the officer shall state in his return the name or names of the person or persons so summoned and the date of service, and the court may render judgment against said garnishee or garnishees for the amount found due: Provided, that a person garnisheed shall not be liable for any costs or damages that may have been awarded to any one interested in the proceedings, beyond the actual amount of his indebtedness to the defendant in the attachment.

SEC. 5.—The officer serving the writ shall take and retain the possession of the property attached, to be subject to a judgment or decree of the court, unless the person in whose possession the same may be found enters into bond and security to the officer, to be approved by him, in at least double the value of the property attached, with condition that the property shall be forthcoming to answer the judgment of the court in said suit.

SEC. 6.—When a person is served with a summons as garnishee, according to the provisions of this act, it shall be lawful for the garnishee to pay to the officer the amount due from him to the defendant: Provided it does not exceed the amount claimed and sworn to in the attachment; and the officer's receipt to him shall be his exonerator from the amount so paid.

SEC. 7.—Whenever judgment is rendered against any garnishee, and it shall appear that the debt from him to the defendant in the attachment is not yet due, execution shall not issue against him until the same shall become due; and property sold by virtue of a writ of attachment shall be governed by the rules governing property taken and sold by execution.

SEC. 8.—If, upon the sale of any property under the provision of this act, there is any surplus left in the hands of the officer after satisfaction of the judgement and all costs, he is hereby required to forthwith pay all such surplus to the defendant, if he is present; and, if he is not present, as soon thereafter as the same shall be legally demanded: Provided, that if the defendant be a non-resident of the county, the officer shall deposit said surplus with the court, who shall notify the defendant, as soon as practicable, of the amount so deposited in his hands.

SEC. 9.—That sections fourteen and fifteen of an act entitled "an act regulating the mode of procedure in civil cases in the courts of the Territory of Utah" approved Dec. 30, 1852, also an act entitled "an act in relation to attachments and garnishments," approved Jan. 16, 1862, are hereby repealed.

Approved Jan. 20, 1865.

CHAPTER XII.

An ACT concerning Writs of Replevin.

SEC. 1.—Be it enacted by the Governor and Legislative Assembly of the Territory of Utah: That when any person or persons shall have any species of property in his, her, or their possession, and such property shall be claimed by some other person or persons, and be demanded by such other person or persons, and if it be not given to the party or persons that have made the demand, the party demanding may file an affidavit, giving good security to the opposite party for costs and damages, before any Justice of the Peace within the county where such property may be situated, or other court having jurisdiction, or such person or party holding such property may be found, (or where he, she, or they may reside) the affidavit shall state that he, she, or they are the rightful owner of such property, describing the same, and in whose possession it may be found, the court of justice shall issue a writ, directed to the sheriff, or constable, or other officer.

SEC. 2.—Such sheriff, or constable, or other officer, shall serve such writ of replevin, and the officer shall execute such writ by taking into his custody all such property that is specified in the writ, and safely keep the same until a decree of the court shall be had thereon; the officer shall deliver all such property to the person or party in whose favor the decree of the court shall have been made.

SEC. 3.—In all cases the defendant shall have the right to give good and sufficient bail to the court issuing a writ of replevin, conditioned for the payment of all damages and costs; and when bail is extended, the defendant may retain the property replevied, until a decision of court shall be had, when it shall be delivered to the person in whose favor the decision of the court shall be given. In case the defendant shall not give bail as herein provided for, the plaintiff may, by giving bonds with securities approved by the court, for all costs and damages that may accrue, take into his possession the property in dispute, and retain the same until a decree of the court shall be had thereon.

SEC. 4.—A justice of the peace may issue a writ for the replevy of property, and try all cases of replevin, where the amount of property in dispute shall not exceed one hundred dollars; where the amount in dispute shall exceed that sum, he shall transmit a copy of his proceedings in issuing said writ to a higher court, who shall try all such cases, the same as if the writ had been issued from that respective court.

Approved March 3, 1852.

———:o:———

CHAPTER XIII.

An ACT declaring certain things to be property, specifying the owner thereof, defining the mode for recovering its possession, and providing for redress of any grievances that may arise from proceedings under this act.

SEC. 1.—Be it enacted by the Governor and Legislative Assembly of the Territory of Utah: That any person who has inclosed, or may hereafter inclose, a portion or portions of unclaimed government land, or caused it to be done at his expense; or has purchased, or may hereafter purchase, such inclosure; or erected, caused to be erected, or purchased any building or other improvement thereon, or may hereafter do so, is hereby declared to be the lawful owner of the claim to the possession of such inclosed land, and the lawful owner of the improvements thereon and thereunto appertaining; and he shall be so deemed and held in all legal proceedings, and in all rights and doings pertaining or relating to the aforesaid property.

SEC. 2.—The owner of any property specified in the foregoing section is hereby authorized, in order to recover possession thereof, to request, without process from any court or officer thereof, any constable, sheriff, or any deputy of either of said officers, to proceed forthwith to remove any person and his effects, who has unlawful or forcible possession of said property; or to remove any tenant thereon or therein, when said tenant fails or refuses to fulfil any of the terms of his contract with its owner, or when the lease of said tenant has expired, or when said tenant is wasting or otherwise damaging the aforesaid property, or when said tenant has underlet said property or any part thereof, contrary to contract or against the express wish of the owner, or when said tenant shall use said property or any part thereof for any unlawful or disorderly purpose, or purpose not specified in the contract; and the aforesaid constable or sheriff, or a deputy of either, is hereby required and empowered to take at least two persons with him, and to at once proceed and use such course and resources as shall be requisite to remove the aforesaid person, and his effects, in unlawful or forcible possession; or to remove any tenant and his effects when in possession as hereinbefore specified, and place the owner in full and peaceable possession of his property. Any sheriff or other officer, refusing to discharge the duties as required in this section, shall, on conviction thereof, be fined not exceeding one hundred dollars.

SEC. 3.—Should any person, in unlawful or violent possession of property as aforesaid, or any tenant, deem himself aggrieved or damaged by the action, under this act, of any owner of property, or of any constable, sheriff, or deputy of either, any court having jurisdiction is hereby required and empowered to hear and adjudicate the complaint of the aforesaid person or tenant.

Approved Jan. 20, 1860.

———:o:———

CHAPTER XIV.

An ACT in relation to the estates of decedents.

SEC. 1.—Be it enacted by the Governor and Legislative Assembly of the Territory of Utah: That any person of full age and sound mind may dispose, by will, of all his property, except what is sufficient to pay his debts, or what is allowed as homestead or otherwise to wife or family; property subsequently acquired may also be devised.

SEC. 2.—Personal property may be bequeathed by verbal will, if witnessed by two competent witnesses; all other wills to be valid must be in writing, witnessed by two competent witnesses, and signed by the testator, or by some person in his presence and by his express direction.

SEC. 3.—Posthumous children, unprovided for by the father's will, shall inherit the same interest as though no will had been made.

SEC. 4.—Wills duly sealed up and endorsed may be deposited with the clerk of the probate court, whose duty it is to file and safely preserve the same until the death of the testator or testators, unless they themselves sooner demand them.

SEC. 5.—Any person having the custody of a will shall, at the first stated term of the court, after being informed of the death of the testator, bring the same into court, where it shall be publicly read.

SEC. 6.—Wills, when proved and allowed, shall have a certificate thereof endorsed or annexed thereto, signed by the clerk, and attested by the seal of the court, all of which shall be recorded in a book to be kept for that purpose; and every will so certified, or record thereof, or a transcript of such record duly authenticated, may be read in evidence in all courts within this Territory, without further proof. Wills must be thus allowed and attested, to be carried into effect.

SEC. 7.—Executors are entitled to a copy of the will; and if there is no executor appointed in the will, or if he, or they shall fail to qualify or act, they may be appointed by the court. The court may also, for good cause, remove executors, as also fill vacancies.

SEC. 8.—In the administration of the estate of any deceased non-resident, an executor may be appointed and qualify himself as required of other executors, unless another executor has previously been appointed in this Territory.

SEC. 9.—Where no executor is appointed by will, administration shall be granted: first, to the wife of the deceased; second, to his next of kin; third, to his creditors; fourth, to any other person whom the court may select; and the court may unite individuals belonging to the same or different classes as executors, whenever it deems such a course expedient. The court must not appoint a person, as executor, who is manifestly unsuitable for the discharge of the trust, nor who is a minor.

SEC. 10.—Every executor, before entering upon the discharge of his duties, must give bonds in such penalty and securities as the judge of the court approves, conditioned for the faithful discharge of his duties, and take and subscribe an oath to the same import, which oath and bond shall be filed in the probate court's office. New bonds, and increased penalties and new securities may be required, whenever the court shall deem it necessary or expedient.

SEC. 11.—The court, when there is necessary delay in granting a commission to any executor to act, may, in its discretion, appoint one or more special executors, to collect and preserve the property of the deceased, who shall qualify as above required. All executors shall make out and file an inventory of all the estate and effects, personal and real, belonging to such estate, in the probate court's office within thirty days from the date of his commission. Upon granting full administration the powers of special executors shall cease, and all the business shall be transferred to the general executor.

SEC. 12.—Nothing herein shall be so construed, when the interests of creditors are not prejudiced thereby, as to hinder the testator or the court prescribing the manner of winding up the affairs of the estate, or continuing his business in which the deceased was engaged at the time of his death, in order to wind up his affairs with greater advantage to the interest of the estate.

SEC. 13.—All personal property of the deceased must be appraised by appraisers appointed by the court; and if any portion of such property be in another county, the same appraisers may serve, or others may be appointed by the court or by a disinterested justice of the peace of such county; and a supplemental inventory and appraisement must be made out whenever the existence of other property is discovered.

SEC. 14.—When the deceased leaves a wife or family, no property exempt by law from execution shall be considered assets, or administered upon, but shall be held for the exclusive benefit of the wife or family, and shall not be liable for any debts against the estate.

SEC. 15.—All persons having any of the property or effects of a deceased person in their hands wrongfully, are required to deliver them up to the executor of the estate. The executor, with the approbation of the court, may compound with any debtor of the estate who may be thought unable to pay his whole indebtedness, or in order to avoid doubtful litigation.

SEC. 16.—The court, on application of the executor, shall, from time to time, direct the sale of such portions of personal effects as are of a perishable nature, or which from any cause would otherwise be likely to depreciate in value, and also such portions as are necessary to pay off the debts and charges upon the estate. If the personal effects are found insufficient to satisfy such charges, a sufficient portion of real estate may be ordered to be sold for that purpose.

SEC. 17.—Property may be sold either at public or private sale, as shall be most conducive to the interest of said estate, and reasonable and general notice of public sale must always previously be given.

SEC. 18—When real estate is sold, conveyance of the interest of the decedent may be made by the executor, under the approval of the court.

SEC. 19.—Property may also be sold upon credit, not exceeding twelve months, whenever the court is satisfied that the interest of the estate will be promoted thereby.

SEC. 20.—As soon as the executors are possessed of sufficient means, over and above the expense of administration, they shall pay off the charges of the last sickness and funeral of the deceased.

SEC. 21.—They shall, in the next place, pay any allowance which may be made by the court for the maintenance of a widow or minor children. Other demands against the estate are next payable; after which, legacies may be paid and distribution made to heirs by descent. A neglect or failure on the part of any creditor to give notice of his claim to the executor or the court, and not proving the same within two years from and after the granting of administration upon said estate, shall prove a bar to the filing of it ever after, unless the said claim is in litigation, or unless unavoidable circumstances entitle the claimant to equitable relief.

SEC. 22.—If there are not likely to be sufficient means in all to pay off the whole of the debts of any one class, the court shall, from time to time, strike a dividend of the means on hand among the creditors of that class, and the executor shall pay the several amounts accordingly.

SEC. 23.—The personal estate of the deceased, not necessary for the payment of debts not otherwise disposed of as herein provided, shall be distributed to the same persons and in the same proportions as though it were real estate. The distribution shares shall be paid over as fast as the executor can properly do so. The property itself shall be distributed in kind, whenever that can be done satisfactorily and equitably; in other cases the court may direct the property to be sold, and the proceeds to be distributed. When the circumstances of the family require it, the court, in addition to what is herein before set apart for their use, may direct impartial distribution of the money or effects on hand at any time after filing the inventory, he being satisfied that said amount, so distributed, will eventually be coming to said family.

SEC. 24.—The homestead occupied by the wife, or any portion of the family of the deceased at the time of his death, shall in all cases be held free to the use of the wife and family of the deceased, and shall not be liable to any claim or claims against said estate; and if there be other property remaining after the liabilities of the estate are liquidated, then it shall, in the absence of other arrangements by will, descend in equal shares to his children or their heirs; one share to such heirs through the mother of such children, if she shall survive him, during her natural life, or during her widowhood; or if he has had more than one wife who either died or survived in lawful wedlock, it shall be equally divided between the living and the heirs of those who are dead, such heirs taken by right of representation.

SEC. 25.—Illegitimate children and their mothers inherit in like manner from the father, whether acknowledged by him or not: Provided it shall be made to appear, to the satisfaction of the court, that he was the father of such illegitimate child or children.

SEC. 26.—The parents or parent, if only one be living, may inherit the estate of their children when they shall die without wife or issue; but in all cases where the deceased leaves a wife, the inheritance shall not pass therefrom, so long as the name of the dead shall be perpetuated thereon.

SEC. 27.—Property given by an intestate by way of advancement to an heir shall be considered part of the estate, so far as regards the division and distribution thereof, and shall be taken by such heir towards his share of the estate at what it would at the time be worth, if in the condition in which it was when given to him; but if such advancement exceeds the amount to which he would be entitled, he cannot be required to refund any portion thereof.

SEC. 28.—The husband shall inherit the estate of a deceased wife in the same manner as the wife the estate of the deceased husband, and the like interest shall in the same manner descend to their respective heirs.

SEC. 29—Executors have power to complete the performance of contracts made by the intestate, either to receive or give conveyances to real estates upon the fulfilment of the terms of any contract previously so made.

SEC. 30.—Executors shall at least once a year, and oftener if required by the court, render his account to the court, showing the condition of the estate, its debts and effects; he must account for all property mentioned; but the appraisement shall be taken only as presumptive evidence of its value, neither shall the executor claim any benefit from the sale of property at a higher price than the appraisement; nor is he chargeable with any loss occasioned without any fault of his own.

SEC. 31.—Upon the final settlement by the executor, an order shall be entered discharging him from further duties and responsibilities.

SEC. 32.—Nothing herein contained shall be so construed as to hinder or delay any proceedings or orders already made by any court having, previous to this act, had jurisdiction in the settlement of estates.

Approved March 3, 1852.

———:o:———

CHAPTER XV.

An ACT Concerning Surplus Stock.

SEC. 1.—Be it enacted by the Governor and Legislative Assembly of the Territory of Utah: That when two thirds of the citizens of any settlement vote to remove the surplus stock from the grass needed for their milch cows and work animals, if any person refuses or neglects to remove his surplus stock, to wit: all stock except milch cows and their sucking calves, animals needed and being used for riding, breaking, packing, or draft, and swine con-tantly kept in pens or yards, any person having the care of the surplus stock of said settlement is hereby authorized and required to remove and take care of the surplus stock of any owner refusing or neglecting to remove his own, and for such services shall be entitled to the same amount others pay for herding the stock of said settlement, and five dollars in addition to that amount, and may retain lawful possession of said animals until said sum is paid, and may proceed for its collection as in action for debt.

Approved January 16, 1865.

———:o:———

CHAPTER XVI.

An ACT Defining what may be Trespass and Damage.

SEC. 1.—Be it enacted by the Governor and Legislative Assembly of the Territory of Utah: That if any person or persons shall cut grass for hay on any land belonging to another person or persons, without his, or their consent, an action of trespass may be had against such offender, and damages recovered by process of law.

SEC. 2.—If any person shall cut or haul off timber from the possession of another person, without his or their consent, an action of trespass and damage may be had against such offender.

SEC. 3.—If any person shall take any species of property belonging to another, publicly, but without the consent of the owner, an action of trespass may be had against such offender, and damages recovered by law.

SEC. 4.—If any person shall ride across, or drive a wagon through a field of grain, or over any enclosed ground, belonging to another person, an action of trespass may be had against such offender, and all damages recovered.

SEC. 5.—If any person shall drive through, or lay down, a fence belonging to another person, and shall fail to put the same up, such offender shall be liable for all damages, to be recovered under an action of trespass.

SEC. 6.—An action for damages may be sustained for goods stored or property in the possession of another person, that may be damaged while in such possession.

SEC. 7.—That if any person or persons, after there shall have been a division of water lawfully made in any county or precinct in this Territory, for irrigation or other purposes, shall in any way infringe upon the rights of any person or persons, they shall be liable in an action of trespass to the parties damaged, and liable to be fined at the discretion of the court having jurisdiction.

SEC. 8.—That all damage done to fruit or shade trees in or around enclosures or lots, by careless driving, or the tying up of cattle and horses, or any needless destruction of any such shade or fruit trees, shall be considered a trespass, and such person or persons shall be liable for damage and fine according to the discretion of the court having jurisdiction.

Approved March 3, 1852.

———:o:———

CHAPTER XVII.

An ACT concerning Masters and Apprentices.

SEC. 1.—Be it enacted by the Governor and Legislative Assembly of the Territory of Utah, That any minor child may be bound to service until the attainment of the age of legal majority; such binding must be by written indenture, specifying the terms of agreement, age of the minor (if known,) and shall moreover be signed by the minor if over twelve years of age. Nothing herein shall be so construed as to prevent the Selectmen or Probate Court from binding out any idle, vicious or vagrant minor child without his or her consent, or the consent of the parent or guardian of uch minor child, if such parent or guardian neglects, refuses, or otherwise fails in roperly controlling the actions and education of such minor, and does not train him or her up in some useful avocation.

SEC. 2.—It is hereby made the duty of Selectmen to look after and take notice of all such cases, and when they shall find the minor child incorrigible, and the parents unable, unwilling, or negligent, as hereinbefore mentioned, bind him or her out to some suitable person, to be trained to some useful vocation.

SEC. 3.—The powers, liabilities and duties of master, and the rights of the apprentice are the same as those of parent and child respectively, except as to inheritance, and except as is otherwise provided by law.

SEC. 4.—The parent, guardian, or officer, by whose act or consent any minor is thus bound, must watch over the interest of the minor so bound, and take measures for his or her relief, whenever circumstances shall justify or the true interest of the minor child shall require it.

SEC. 5.—If the master shall illtreat his apprentice, or in any manner palpably fail in the discharge of his duties in regard to said apprentice, the said apprentice may be discharged from further service, and may moreover recover damages and compensation for services.

SEC. 6.—It shall be the duty of the master to correct and teach such minor child to observe the principles of good order and industry, and train him or her to some useful avocation. And it is hereby made the duty of such minor child to observe obedience to and respect for the requirements of the master. But if the apprentice, bound as aforesaid, shall refuse to serve according to the terms of the indenture, or grossly misbehave, and the master shall be incapable or unable to influence or control such apprentice, he may be discharged from further obligations or liability, at the discretion of the court; and in the event of a dissolution, the apprentice shall receive such allowance for the service previously rendered as may be considered just under the circumstances of the case.

SEC. 7.—The death of the master, or his removal from the Territory, works a dissolution of the indentures, unless otherwise provided therein, or unless the apprentice shall elect to continue in his service.

SEC. 8.—Any person, apprentice or servant, who shall have so elected, or agreed to render service in any other Territory, State, or country, shall come under the same regulations and requirements as herein provided, all such agreements or indentures for services being held as inviolate and binding as if they had been entered into, and executed within this Territory.

SEC. 9.—If from habitual intemperance, and vicious and brutal conduct, or from vicious, brutal and criminal conduct towards said minor child, the parent of the same shall be considered an unsuitable person to retain the guardianship or control the education of said child, the Judge of Probate Court or Selectmen may appoint a suitable person to be the guardian of such child, and may, if deemed expedient, also cause said minor child to be bound as an apprentice to some suitable person, during his or her minority. Nothing herein shall be so construed as to take such minor child, if either the father or mother be a proper guardian.

SEC. 10.—The strict observance of the provisions of the indentures on the part of the master and apprentice must be considered essential to entitle either party to the benefits arising under the provisions of this act, and the Selectmen or the probate court shall inquire into such observance, before either awarding compensation or damages, or otherwise discharging or releasing either party from the requirements of such indentures, or the provisions of law in such cases made and provided. Nothing herein contained shall be so construed as to effect a release of either party from service or obligation, as the case may be, where the agreement or indentures have been entered into in any foreign state or country, or in this Territory for a longer period.

SEC. 11.—The master shall send the said minor child to school betweeen the ages of six and sixteen, three months in each year, if there be a school in the district or vicinity; and at all times, and in all cases the master shall clothe the minor child in a comfortable and becoming manner.

Approved Feb. 7, 1852.

CHAPTER XVIII.

An ACT in Relation to Minors.

SEC. 1.—Be it enacted by the Governor and Legislative Assembly of the Territory of Utah: That the period of minority extends in males to the age of twenty-one years; and in females to that of eighteen years; but all minors obtain their majority by marriage.

SEC. 2.—A minor is bound, not only by contracts for necessaries, but also by his other contracts, unless he disaffirms them within a reasonable time after he attains his majority, and restores to the other party all money or property received by him by virtue of said contract, and remaining within his control at any time after attaining his majority.

SEC. 3.—No contract can be thus disaffirmed in cases where on account of the minor's own misrepresentations as to his majority, or from his having engaged in business as adult, the other party had good reason to believe the minor capable of contracting.

SEC. 4.—When a contract for the personal services of a minor has been made with him alone, and those services are afterwards performed, payment made therefor to such minor in accordance with the terms of the contract, is a full satisfaction for those services, and the parent or guardian cannot recover therefor a second time.

Approved Feb 6, 1852.

———:o:———

CHAPTER XIX.

An ACT in relation to Guardians.

SEC. 1.—Be it enacted by the Governor and Legislative Assembly of the Territory of Utah: That the father is the natural guardian of the person or persons of his minor children. If he dies without appointing any guardian, or is incapable of acting, the mother becomes the guardian.

SEC. 2.—The natural and actual guardian of any minor child may by will appoint another guardian for such minor: Provided, where both parents are dead, or disqualified to act as guardian, the Probate Judge or Selectmen may appoint one.

SEC. 3.—When a divorce is decreed or obtained, such order in relation to the children and property of the parties, and the maintenance of the wife may be made as shall be deemed right and proper; subsequent changes may be made by the probate court or Selectmen, in those respects when circumstances render them expedient.

SEC. 4.—In cases where the minor has property not derived from either parent, a guardian may be appointed by the court or Selectmen to manage such property. The father or mother, if deemed a suitable person for that purpose, may be appointed the guardian to take charge of the property of his or her minor child.

SEC. 5.—If the minor be over the age of fourteen years, and of sound intellect, he may select his own guardian, subject to the appointment of the Probate Court or Selectmen.

SEC. 6.—Guardians must be sworn to the faithful performance of their duties, and give bond and security to be approved by the court or Selectmen, and filed in the office of the court of probate.

SEC. 7.—All property belonging to minors must be inventoried, appraised, and a copy of the appraisement filed in the Probate Court's office, within twenty days after the guardian shall have been qualified. Guardians of the persons of minors have the same power and control over them that parents would have if living.

SEC. 8.—If necessary for the minor's support or education, to dispose of the minor's property, either personal or real, the guardian may do so, by giving general notice ten days previous to said sale; all sales must be under the direction of the Probate Court, who shall cause the bonds of the guardian to be increased, if he shall deem it necessary. The Court or Selectmen may also direct the postponement of such sale for further notice or consideration, if they are of opinion that the interest of the minor would be promoted thereby. The avails of all such sales shall be accounted for, and the inventory filed in the Court of Probate's office, and applied under his direction.

SEC. 9.—Conveyances of property may be made under the direction of the court by the guardian.

SEC. 10.—A failure to comply with any order of the court or requirement of the Selectmen, in relation to guardianship, may involve the dismissal of the guardian, and may be deemed a breach of the condition of his bond, for which he shall be liable, and the court may appoint a new guardian, if it shall deem it necessary. Guardians shall account to the court annually on oath, or oftener if required by the court or select men.

SEC. 11.—Where a new guardian is appointed, the effects of the minor, which are in the hands of his predecessor, are to be delivered up to such new guardian.

SEC. 12.—Guardians shall receive such compensation as the court may from time to time allow. The amount allowed, and the service for which the allowance was made, must be entered upon the records of the court.

Approved Feb. 3, 1852.

———:o:———

CHAPTER XX.

An ACT in relation to Bills of Divorce.

SEC. 1.—Be it enacted by the the Governor and Legislative Assembly of the Territory of Utah: That the court of probate in the county where the plaintiff resides shall have jurisdiction in all cases of divorce and alimony, and of guardianship, and distribution of property connected therewith.

SEC. 2.—The petition for a bill of divorce must be made in writing, upon oath or affirmation, and must state clearly and specifically the causes on account of which the plaintiff seeks relief. If the court is satisfied that the person so applying is a resident of the Territory, or wishes to become one; and that the application is made in sincerity and of her own free will and choice, and for the purpose set forth in the petition; then the court may decree a divorce from the bonds of matrimony against the husband; for any of the following causes, to wit:

Impotence of the defendant at the time of marriage; adultery committed by defendant subsequent to marriage; wilful desertion of his wife by the defendant, or absenting himself without a reasonable cause for more than one year; habitual drunkeness of defendant subsequent to marriage; conviction of defendant for felony subsequent to marriage; inhuman treatment so as to endanger the life of the defendant's wife; when it shall be made to appear to the satisfaction and conviction of the court, that the parties cannot live in peace and union together, and that their welfare requires a separation.

SEC. 3.—The husband may in all cases obtain a divorce from his wife for the like causes, and in the same manner as the wife obtains a divorce from her husband.

SEC. 4.—Nothing herein contained shall be so construed as to prevent courts of probate from deferring their decree of a divorce, when the same is applied for, to any specified time, not exceeding one year, when it appears to him that a compromise might at a future time be made between the parties. During the time of such deferance on the part of the court, the bonds and engagements of matrimony may not be violated by the parties.

SEC. 5.—The defendant, unless in a case of absence heretofore provided for on his or her part, shall have the right to appear, and shall receive a proper and timely warning thereto; should the defendant fail to appear, the court may, if satisfied that the complainant is the injured party, and his or her claims are just and well grounded, decree a dissolution of the marriage contract between the complainant and defendant.

SEC. 6.—When a divorce is decreed, the court shall make such order in relation to the children and property of the parties, and the maintenance of the wife, and such portion of the children as may be awarded to her, as may be just and equitable: Provided, that if the children shall have attained the age of ten years, and possess sound mind, they shall have the privilege to select of their own free will and choice, to which of their parents they will attach themselves: Provided further, that the parties may, with the approval of the court, themselves agree upon the distribution of the property and disposal of the children: Provided further, that when it shall appear to the court at a future time, that it would be for the interest of the parties concerned, that a change should be effected in regard to the former disposal of children or distribution of property, the court shall have power to make such change as will be conducive to the best interests of all parties concerned.

SEC. 7.—When a divorce is decreed, the defendant or guilty party forfeits all rights acquired by marriage.

SEC. 8.—It shall be the duty of the courts of probate in their respective counties, to punish by fine or imprisonment, or both, at their discretion, any person or persons who shall stir up unwarrantable litigation between husband and wife, or seek to bring about a separation between them.

Approved March 6, 1852.

———:o:———

CHAPTER XXI.

An ACT providing for the management of certain property.

SEC. 1.—Be it enacted by the Governor and Legislative Assembly of the Territory of Utah: That the Probate Judge in each county is empowered and required to take possession of all property left by any deceased or abscondent person, when there is no legal claimant known, or sufficiently near to see to it in season; and shall forthwith appraise and make two lists of said property, and keep one on file, and furnish one to the Treasurer of the Perpetual Emigrating Fund.

SEC. 2.—It is hereby made the duty of every person having such property in his possession, or knowing it to be in the possession of any other person, to report the property forthwith, and the name of the person in possession thereof, to the Probate Judge of the county where said possessor is at the time; and said Judge shall take possession of such property as soon as practicable, and proceed therewith as required above.

SEC. 3.—At the earliest practicable date, the Probate Judge shall place said property, or the avails thereof, in the possession of said Fund, the value thereof to remain there until proven away by a legal claimant, when said Judge shall give an order therefor on the Treasurer of the Fund.

SEC. 4.—A failure to comply with the requisitions of this act may be punished by costs, damages, and fine, adjudged by any court having jurisdiction.

Approved Jan 20, 1854.

———:o:———

CHAPTER XXII.

An ACT in relation to Crimes and Punishment.

TITLE I.

Offences against the Territory.

SEC. 1.—Be it enacted by the Governor and Legislative Assembly of the Territory of Utah: That whoever is guilty of treason, by levying war against the Territory, or by adhering to its enemies, giving them aid and comfort, shall be punished with death.

SEC. 2.—If any person have knowledge of the commission of the crime of treason against the Territory, and conceal the same, and not, as soon as may be, disclose such offence to the Governor, or some judge of the Territory, he is guilty of misprision of treason, and shall be fined not exceeding one thousand dollars, or be imprisoned not exceeding ten years, nor less than one year.

SEC. 3.—No person can be convicted of the crime of treason, unless on the evidence of two witnesses to the same overt act, or on open confession in open court.

TITLE II.

Offences against the lives and persons of individuals.

SEC. 4.—Whoever kills any human being, with malice aforethought, either expressed or implied, is guilty of murder.

SEC. 5.—All murder which is perpetrated by means of poison, or lying in wait, or any other kind of wilful, deliberate, and premeditated killing, or which is committed in the perpetration, or attempt to perpetrate any arson, rape, robbery, mayhem, or burglary, is murder of the first degree, and shall be punished with death.

SEC. 6.—Whoever commits murder, otherwise than is set forth in the preceding section, is guilty of murder of the second degree, and shall be punished by imprisonment for life, or for a term not less than ten years.

SEC. 7.—Upon the trial of an indictment for murder, the jury, if they find the defendant guilty, must inquire, and in their verdict declare whether he be guilty of murder in the first or second degree. But if such defendant be convicted upon his own confession in open court, the court must proceed, by the examination of witnesses, to determine the degree of murder, and award sentence accordingly.

SEC. 8.—Whoever fights a duel with deadly weapons, and inflicts a mortal wound on his antagonist, wherefrom death ensues, is guilty of murder of the first degree, and shall be punished accordingly.

SEC. 9.—Any person who fights a duel with deadly weapons, or is present at the fighting of such duel, as aid, second, or surgeon, or advises, encourages, or promotes such duel, although death do not ensue; and any person who challenges another to fight a duel, or sends or delivers any verbal or written message, purporting, or intended to be such challenge, although no duel ensue; and any person who accepts such challenge, or who consents to act as a second, aid, or surgeon, on such acceptance, or who advises, encourages, or promotes the same, although no duel ensue; shall be fined in a sum not exceeding one thousand dollars, nor less than four hundred dollars, and imprisoned not more than three years, nor less than one year.

SEC. 10.—If any person vex another, or in writing or print use any reproachful or contemptuous language to, or concerning another, for not fighting a duel, or for not sending or accepting a challenge, he shall be fined not exceeding three hundred dollars, nor less than one hundred dollars, and imprisoned not more than six months, nor less than two months.

SEC. 11.—Any person guilty of manslaughter shall be punished by imprisonment not more than ten years, nor less than one year, and by fine not more than one thousand dollars, nor less than one hundred dollars.

SEC. 12.—If any person, with intent to maim or disfigure, cut or maim the tongue, put out or destroy an eye, cut, slit, or tear off an ear, cut, slit, or mutilate the nose, or lip, or cut off, or disable a limb, or any member of any other person, he shall be punished by imprisonment not more than five years, and by fine not exceeding one thousand dollars, nor less than one hundred dollars.

SEC. 13.—If any person with force or violence, or by putting in fear, steal and take from the person of another any property that is the subject of larceny, he is guilty of robbery, and shall be punished according to the aggravation of the offence, as is provided in the following two sections.

SEC. 14.—If such offender, at the time of such robbery, is armed with a dangerous weapon, with intent, if resisted, to kill or maim the person robbed; or if, being so armed, he wound or strike the person robbed; or if he have any confederates aiding and abetting him in such robbery present, and so armed; he shall be punished by imprisonment for a term of not exceeding twenty-five years, and not less than ten years.

SEC. 15.—If such offender commit such robbery, otherwise than is mentioned in the preceding section, he shall be punished by imprisonment not exceeding ten years, nor less than two years.

SEC. 16.—If any person ravish and carnally know any female of the age of ten years, or more, by force and against her will, or carnally know and abuse any female child, under the age of ten years, he shall be punished by imprisonment for life, or not less than ten years.

SEC. 17.—If any person take any woman unlawfully and against her will, and by force, menace, or duress, compel her to marry him, or any other person, or to be defiled, he shall be fined not exceeding one thousand dollars, and imprisonment not exceeding ten years.

SEC. 18.—If any person unlawfully have carnal knowledge of any female by administering to her any substance, or by any other means, producing such stupor, or such imbecility of mind or weakness of body as to prevent effectual resistance, he shall, upon conviction, be punished as provided in the sixteenth section of this act relating to ravishment.

SEC. 19.—If any person take or entice away any unmarried female from her father, mother, guardian, or other person having the legal charge of her person, for the purpose of prostitution, he shall, upon conviction, be punished by imprisonment not more than ten years, nor less than one year; or by fine not exceeding one thousand dollars, and not less than one hundred dollars.

SEC. 20.—If any person maliciously, forcibly, or fraudulently lead, take, decoy, or entice away any person with intent to detain, or conceal such person from its parent, guardian, or other person having the lawful charge of such person, he shall be punished by imprisonment not more than ten years, or by fine not exceeding one thousand dollars; or by both such fine and imprisonment.

SEC. 21.—If any person seduce and debauch any unmarried woman of previously chaste character, he shall be punished by imprisonment not more than twenty years, nor less than one year, and fined not more than one thousand dollars, nor less than one hundred dollars. If, before judgment upon an indictment, the defendant marry the woman thus seduced, it is a bar to any further prosecution for the offence. In case the person so offending shall marry such female as herein provided, he shall be liable, if required, to give bonds with approved securities for her maintenance.

SEC. 22.—If any person wilfully and without lawful authority, forcibly or secretly confine or imprison any other person within this Territory, against his will, or forcibly seize and confine, or inveigle, or kidnap any other person with the intent either to cause such person to be secretly confined, or imprisoned in this Territory against his will, or cause such person to be sent out of this Territory against his will, he shall be punished by imprisonment not more that ten years, or by fine not exceeding one thousand dollars; or by both fine and imprisonment at the discretion of the court.

SEC. 23.—If the father or mother of any child under the age of six years, or any person to whom such child has been entrusted or confided, expose such child in any highway, street, field, house or outhouse, or in any other place with intent wholly to abandon it, he or she, upon conviction thereof, shall be punished by imprisonment not exceeding five years, or fined not exceeding five hundred dollars.

SEC. 24.—If any person either verbally, or by any written or printed communication, maliciously threaten to accuse another of crime or offence; or to do any injury to the person or property of another with intent thereby to extort any money, or pecuniary advantage whatever; or to compel the person so threatened to do any act against his will, he shall be punished by imprisonment not more than two years, or by fine not exceeding five hundred dollars.

SEC. 25.—If any person assault another, with intent to commit murder, he shall be punished by imprisonment not exceeding twenty years, nor less than one year, and fined at the discretion of the court.

SEC. 26.—If any person assault a female, with intent to commit a rape, he shall be punished by imprisonment not exceeding twenty years, and fined at the discretion of the court.

SEC. 27.—If any person assault another, with intent to maim, rob, steal, or commit arson, or burglary, he shall be punished by imprisonment not exceeding eight years, or by fine not exceeding one thousand dollars; or by both fine and imprisonment at the discretion of the court.

SEC. 28.—If any person assault another, with intent to inflict a bodily injury, he shall be punished by imprisonment not exceeding six months, or fined not exceeding one hundred dollars.

SEC. 29.—If any person assault another, with intent to commit any felony, or crime punishable by imprisonment, where the punishment is not otherwise prescribed, he shall be punished by imprisonment not more than five years, or by fine not exceeding five hundred dollars, or both at the discretion of the court.

SEC. 30.—If any person mingle any poison with any food, drink, or medicine, with intent to kill or injure any human being; or wilfully poison any spring, well, cistern, or reservoir of water, he shall be punished by imprisonment not exceeding twenty-five years, or by fine not exceeding five thousand dollars, or both at the discretion of the court.

TITLE III.

Offenses against Chastity, Morality, and Decency.

SEC. 31.—Every person who commits the crime of adultry, shall be punished by imprisonment not exceeding twenty years, and not less than three years, or by fine not exceeding one thousand dollars, and not less than three hundred dollars; or by both fine and imprisonment at the discretion of the court. And when the crime is committed between parties, any one of whom is married, both are guilty of adultry, and shall be punished accordingly. No prosecution for adultry can be commenced but on the complaint of the husband or wife.

SEC. 32.—If any man or woman, not being married to each other, lewdly and laciviously associate, and cohabit together; or if any man or woman, married or unmarried, is guilty of open and gross lewdness, and designedly make any open and indecent or obscene exposure of his or her person, or of the person of another, every such person so offending shall be punished by imprisonment not exceeding ten years, and not less than six months, and fined not more than one thousand dollars, and not less than one hundred dollars, or both, at the discretion of the court.

SEC. 33.—If any person keep a house of ill fame, resorted to for the purpose of prostitution or lewdness, he shall be punished by imprisonment not exceeding ten years, and not less than one year, or by fine not exceeding five hundred dollars, or both fine and imprisonment. And any person who, after being once convicted of such offence, is again convicted of the like offence shall be punished not more than double the above specified penalties.

SEC. 34.—If any person inveigle, or entice any female, before reputed virtuous, to a house of ill fame or knowingly conceal, aid, or abet in concealing such female so deluded or enticed, for the purpose of prostitution or lewdness, he shall be punished by imprisonment not more than fifteen years, nor less than five years.

SEC. 35.—If any person, without lawful authority, wilfully dig up, disinter, remove, or carry any human body, or the remains thereof, from its place of interment, or aid or assist in so doing; or wilfully receive, conceal or dispose of any such human body, or the remains thereof; or if any person wilfully and unnecessarily, and in an improper manner, indecently expose those remains, or abandon any human body, of the remains thereof, in any public place, or in any river, stream, pond, or other place, every such offender shall be punished by imprisonment not exceeding one year, or by fine not exceeding one thousand dollars, or by both fine and imprisonment, at the discretion of the court.

SEC. 36.—If any person torture or cruelly beat any horse, ox, or other beast, whether belonging to himself or another, he shall be punished by fine not more than one hundred dollars.

SEC. 37.—If any person import, print, publish, sell or distribute any book, pamphlet, ballad, or any printed paper containing obscene language, or obscene prints, pictures or descriptions manifestly tending to corrupt the morals of youth, or introduce into any family, school or place of education, or buy, procure, receive, or have in his possession any such book, pamphlet, ballad, printed paper, picture, or description, either for the purpose of loan, sale, exhibition, or circulation, or with intent to introduce the same into any family, school, or place of education, he shall be punished by a fine not exceeding four hundred dollars.

SEC. 38.—If any person keep a house, shop, or place resorted to for the purpose of gambling, or permit or suffer any person in any house, shop, or other place, under his control, or care, to play at cards, dice, faro, roulette, or other game for money or other things, such offender shall be fined not more than eight hundred dollars, or imprisoned not exceeding one year, or both, at the discretion of the court. In a prosecution under this section, any person who has the charge of or attends to any such house, shop, or place, may be deemed the keeper thereof.

SEC. 39.—If any person play at any game for any sum of money or other property of any value, or make any bet a wager for money or other property of value, he shall be punished by fine not exceeding three hundred dollars, or by imprisonment not exceeding six months.

SEC. 40.—All promises, agreements, notes, bills, bonds, or other contracts, mortgages, or other securities, when the whole or any part of the consideration thereof is for money or other valuable thing won or lost, laid stakes, or bet at or upon any game of any kind, or on any wager, are absolutely void and of no effect.

TITLE IV.

Offenses against Property.

SEC. 41.—If any person wilfully and maliciously burn the inhabited building, boat or vessel of another; or wilfully and maliciously set fire to any other building, boat or vessel owned by himself, or another, by which meanssuch inhabited building, boat or vessel is burnt; if such offence is perpetrated in the night time, or so caused to be burnt in the night time, such offender shall be punished by imprisonment for life, or any term of years; or if the crime shall have been committed in the day time, such offender shall be punished by imprisonment not exceeding thirty years.

SEC. 42.—If any person wilfully and maliciously so burn any uninhabited dwelling house, boat or vessel, belonging to another; or any court house, or other public building; if in the night time, he shall be punished by imprisonment not exceeding twenty-five years; or if in the day time, not more than twenty years.

SEC. 43.—If any person wilfully and maliciously burn, either in the night or day time, any warehouse, store, manufactory, mill, barn, stable, shop, office, out-house, or any building whatsoever of another, other than is mentioned in the preceding sections: or any bridge, lock, dam, or flume, he shall be punished by imprisonment not exceeding fifteen years, and fined not exceeding one thousand dollars.

SEC. 44.—If any person set fire to any building, boat or vessel, mentioned in the preceding sections, or to any material, with intent to cause any such building to be burnt, he shall be punished by imprisonment not exceeding ten years, or fined not more than five hundred dollars.

SEC. 45.—If any person wilfully and maliciously burn, or otherwise destroy or injure any pile or parcel of wood, boards, timber, or other lumber; or any fence, bars or gate; or any stack of grain, hay, or other vegetable product severed from the soil, and not stacked; or any standing trees, grain, grass, or other standing product of the soil of another, he shall be punished by imprisonment not more than five years, or by fine not more than five hundred dollars, or both fine and imprisonment, at the discretion of the court.

SEC. 46.—The preceding sections under this title severally extend to a married woman who commits either of the offences therein described, though the property burnt or set fire to may belong wholly or in part to her husband.

SEC. 47.—If any person break and enter any dwelling house in the night time, with intent to commit the crime of murder, rape, robbery, larceny, or any other felony; or after having entered with such intent, break any such dwelling house in the night time, any person being then lawfully therein, such offender shall be punished according to the aggravation of the offense, as provided in the following two sections.

SEC. 48.—If such offender, at the time of committing such burglary, is armed with a dangerous weapon, or so arm himself after having entered such dwelling house, or actually assault any person being lawfully therein; or have any confederates present aiding and abetting in such burglary, he shall be punished by imprisonment for life, or any term of years.

SEC. 49.—If such offender commit such burglary otherwise than is mentioned in the preceding section, he shall be punished by imprisonment not exceeding twenty-five years.

SEC. 50.—If any person, with intent to commit a felony in the day time, break and enter, or in the night time enter without breaking any dwelling house, or at any time break and enter any office, shop, store, warehouse, boat or vessel, or any building in which goods are kept for use, sale or deposit, he shall be punished by imprisonment not more than ten years, or by fine not more than five hundred dollars, or both fine and imprisonment.

TITLE V.

Larceny.

SEC. 51.—If any person steal, take, and carry away of the property of another, any money, goods, or chattels, any writ, process, or public record, any bond, bank note, promissory note, bill of exchange, or other bill, order or certificate, or any book of accounts respecting money, goods, or other things, or any deed, or writing containing a conveyance of real estate, or any contract in force, or any receipt, release, or defeasance, or any instrument, or writing whereby any demand, right, or obligation is created, increased, extinguished or diminished, he is guilty of larceny and shall be punished, when the value of the property stolen exceeds the sum of twenty dollars, by imprisonment not more than ten years, or by fine not exceeding five hundred dollars, or both: and when the value of the property stolen does not exceed the sum of twenty dollars, by fine not exceeding one hundred dollars, or imprisonment not exceeding six months.

SEC. 52.—If any person commit the crime of larceny by stealing from any building that is on fire, or stealing any property that is removed in consequence of an alarm caused by fire, or by stealing from the person of another, he shall be punished by imprisonment not exceeding fifteen years, nor less than one year.

SEC. 53.—If any person falsely personate or represent another, and in such assumed character receive any money or property intended to be delivered to the party so personated, with intent to convert the same to his own use, he is guilty of larceny, and shall be punished accordingly.

SEC. 54.—If any person come by finding to the possession of any personal property, of which he knows the owner, and unlawfully appropriate the same, or any part thereof, to his use, he is guilty of larceny, and shall be punished accordingly.

SEC. 55.—If any officer entrusted with the collection, safe keeping, transfer, or disbursement of the public funds, unlawfully convert them, or any part thereof, to his own use, every such act is an embezzlement of so much as is thus taken, converted, used, or unaccounted for, and the person so offending shall be punished by imprisonment not exceeding five years, and fined in a sum equal to the amount embezzled; and, moreover, he is for ever after disqualified from holding any office under the laws of this Territory.

SEC. 56.—If any other person to whom any money, goods, or other property which may be the subject of larceny, has been entrusted as clerk, agent, or carrier, embezzle, or fraudulently convert to his own use, any such money, goods, or other property, he is guilty of larceny, and shall be punished accordingly.

SEC. 57.—If any person buy, receive, or aid in concealing any stolen money, goods, or any property, the stealing of which is declared to be larceny, or property obtained by robbery or burglary, knowing the same was so obtained, he shall be punished by imprisonment, not more than five years, or fine not more than five hundred dollars, or both fine and imprisonment at the discretion of the court.

SEC. 58.—If any person, having been before convicted of larceny, afterwards commit another larceny, and be thereof convicted; or if any person at the same term of court is convicted of as principal, or as accessory after the fact in three distinct larcenies, he is deemed a common and notorious thief, and shall be punished by imprisonment not less than five years. The provision of this section shall apply to the buyer, receiver, or concealer of money, goods, &c., as mentioned in the preceding section; and if any person is convicted three distinct times, at the same term of the court, or as above mentioned in case of a common and notorious thief, he shall be punished in the same manner.

SEC. 59.—In any prosecution for the offense of buying, receiving, or aiding in the concealment of property so obtained, it shall not be necessary to aver, or to prove on the trial thereof, that the person who stole, robbed, or took the property, has been convicted.

SEC. 60.—If the property stolen consist of any bank note, bond, bill, covenant, bill of exchange, draft, order or receipt, or any evidence whatever, or any public security, or any instrument whereby any demand, right or obligation may be assigned, transferred, created, increased, released, extinguished, or diminished, the money due thereon, or secured thereby, and remaining unsatisfied, or which in any event or contingency might be collected thereon, or the value of the property transferred, or effected, as the case may be, shall be adjudged the value of the thing stolen.

TITLE VI.

Of Forgery and Counterfeiting.

SEC. 61.—If any person, with intent to defraud, falsely make, alter, forge, or counterfeit any public record, or any process issued or purporting to be issued by any competent authority, or any pleading or proceeding filed or entered in any court of law or equity, or any attestation or certificate of any public officer or other person, in relation to any matter wherein such attestation or certificate is required by law, or may be received or be taken as legal proof, any charter, deed, will, testament, bond, writing, obligation, power of attorney, letter of credit, policy of insurance, bill of lading, bill of exchange, prommissory note, or any order, acquittance, discharge, or accountable receipt for money or other valuable thing, or any acceptance of any bill of exchange, prommissory note or order, or of any debt or contract, or any other instrument in writing, being or purporting to be the act of another, by which any pecuniary demand, or obligation, or any right or interest in or to any property whatever is or purports to be created, increased, transferred, conveyed, discharged, or diminished, he shall be punished by imprisonment not more than ten years.

SEC. 62.—If any person utter and publish, as true, any record, process, certificate, deed, will or any other instrument of writing mentioned in the preceding sections, knowing the same to be false, altered, forged, or counterfeited, with intent to defraud, he shall be punished by imprisonment not exceeding fifteen years, and fined not more than one thousand dollars.

SEC. 63.—If any person, with intent to defraud, falsely make, alter, forge, or counterfeit any note, certificate, bond, warrant, or other instrument, being public security for money, or other property issued or purporting to be issued by authority of this or any other Territory, or any State of the United States, or any indorsement or other writing, purporting to transfer the right or interest of any holder of such public security, he shall be punished by imprisonment not more than twenty years, nor less than five years.

SEC. 64.—If any person make, alter, forge, or counterfeit any bank bill, promissory note, draft, or other evidence of debt issued or purporting to be issued by any corporation or company duly authorized for that purpose by any State or Territory of the United States, or any other government or country, with intent to injure or defraud, he shall be punished by imprisonment not more than ten years, or by fine not more than one thousand dollars.

SEC. 65.—If any person has in his possession any forged, counterfeited, or altered bank bill, promissory note, draft, or other evidence of debt issued or purporting to be issued, as is mentioned in the preceding section, with intent to defraud, knowing it to be so forged, counterfeited, or altered, he shall be punished by imprisonment not more than five years, or by fine not exceeding five hundred dollars.

SEC. 66.—If any person utter or pass or tender in payment, as true, any false, altered, forged or counterfeit note, certificate, bond, warrant, or other instrument of public security, or any bank bill, promissory note, draft, or other evidence of debt, issued or purporting to be issued, by any corporation or company, duly authorized as heretofore mentioned, knowing the same to be false, altered, forged, or counterfeit, with intent to injure or defraud, he shall be punished by imprisonment not more than ten years, or fine not exceeding one thousand dollars.

SEC. 67.—If any person engrave, make or mend, or begin to engrave, make or mend any plate, block, press, or other tool, instrument, or implement, or make or provide any paper or other materials adapted and designed for the forging or making any false and counterfeit note, certificate, bond, warrant, or other instrument of public security for money or other property of this or any other Territory or State of the United States, or any bank bill, promissory note, draft, or other evidence of debts issued or purporting to be issued by any corporation or company, and every person who has in his possession any such plate or block engraved in any part, or any press or other instrument or implement, paper, or other material adapted and designed as aforesaid, with intent to use the same, or to cause or permit the same to be used in forging, or making any such false and forged certificates, notes, bonds, warrants, public securities, or evidences of debts, shall be punished by imprisonment not more than five years, nor less than one year.

SEC. 68.—If any person forge or counterfeit any gold or silver coin, current by law or usage within this Territory, and if any person have in his possession at the same time to the amount of twenty dollars or more of false money or coin counterfeited in the similitude of any gold or silver coin current as aforesaid, knowing the same to be false and counterfeit, and with intent to utter or pass the same as true, he shall be punished by imprisonment not exceeding ten years, nor less than one year.

SEC. 69.—Any person who has in his possession any amount less than twenty dollars of counterfeit coin or false money, mentioned in the preceding section, knowing the same to be false or counterfeit, and with intent to utter or pass the same as true, and any person who utters or tenders in payment any false and counterfeit coin, knowing the same to be false and counterfeit, shall be punished by imprisonment not more than eight years, or fined not more than one thousand dollars.

SEC. 70.—If any person fraudulently connect together different parts of several given bank bills, notes or other instruments in writing, so as to produce one instrument; or alter any note or instrument in writing in a matter that is material, with intent to defraud, the same shall be declared forgery in like manner as if such bill, or note or other instrument had been forged and counterfeited, and the offender shall be punished accordingly.

SEC. 71.—If any fictitious or pretended signature of any officer or agent of any corporation be fraudulently affixed to any instrument of writing, purporting to be a note, draft, or other evidence of debt issued by such corporation, with intent to utter or pass the same as true, it is forgery, though no such person may ever have been an officer or agent of such corporation, nor such corporation have ever existed; every person guilty of this offence shall be punished by imprisonment not more than five years, or by fine not exceeding one thousand dollars.

SEC. 72.—The total or partial erasure or obliteration of any record, process, certificate, deed, will, or any other instrument in writing mentioned in this division, with intent to defraud, shall be deemed a forgery, and the offender shall be punished by imprisonment not more than five years, or fined not exceeding one thousand dollars.

SEC. 73.—If any person, having been convicted of either of the offences mentioned in sections from 64 to 70 in this division, be afterwards convicted of a like offence, or if any person at the same term of court be convicted of three such distinct offences, he shall be punished by imprisonment not exceeding ten years, nor less than three years

SEC. 74.—If any person cast, stamp, engrave, make or mend, or have in his possession any mould, die, press or other instrument or tool, adapted and designed for forging or counterfeiting of any coin before mentioned, with intent to use the same or permit the same to be used for that purpose, he shall be punished by imprisonment not more than five years, or by fine not more than one thousand dollars.

SEC. 75.—If any person forge or counterfeit any gold or silver coin of any foreign government or country, with the intent to export the same to injure or defraud any such government or the citizens thereof, he shall be punished by imprisonment not exceeding ten years.

SEC. 76.—Any person who is convicted of having forged, counterfeited, or falsely obtained the great seal of the Territory, or the seal of any public office authorized by law, or the seal of any court, corporation, city or county; or who falsely makes, forges, or counterfeits any impression purporting to be the impression of any such seal, with intent to defraud, shall be punished by imprisonment not exceeding ten years.

TITLE VII.

Offences against Public Justice.

SEC. 77.—If any person, on oath or affirmation lawfully administered, willfully and corruptly swear or affirm falsely to any material matter in any proceeding in any court of justice, or before any officer thereof, or before any tribunal or officer created by law, or in any proceeding, or in regard to any matter or thing in or respecting which an oath or affirmation is or may be required or authorized by law, he is guilty of perjury, and shall be punished, if the perjury was committed on the trial of a capital or felonious crime, by imprisonment for life, or any term of years not less than ten; and if committed in any other case, by imprisonment not more than ten years, nor less than two years: Provided, that any person who, by wilful and corrupt perjury or subornation of perjury shall procure the conviction and execution of any innocent person, shall be deemed and adjudged guilty of murder of the first degree and punished accordingly.

SEC. 78.—If any person endeavor to incite or procure another to commit perjury, he is guilty of subornation of perjury, and shall be punished as provided of the preceding section.

SEC. 79.—If any person endeavor to incite another to commit perjury, though no perjury be committed, he shall be punished by imprisonment not more than five years, or by fine not more than five hundred dollars.

SEC. 80.—If any person give, offer, or promise to any executive or judicial officer, or member of the Legislative Assembly, any valuable consideration, gratuity, service or benefit whatever, with intent to influence his act, vote, opinion, or judgment in any matter, question, cause, or proceeding which may be pending, or which may legally come or be brought before him in his official capacity, he shall be punished by imprisonment not more than five years, or by fine not more than one thousand dollars.

SEC. 81.—If any executive or judicial officer or member of the Legislative Assembly accept any valuable consideration, gratuity, service, or benefit whatever, or any promise to make the same, or to do any act beneficial to such officer or member under the agreement or with the understanding that his vote, opinion, decision, or judgment shall be given in any particular manner, or upon any particular side of any question, cause, or other proceeding which is or may by law be brought before him in his official capacity, or that in such capacity he will make any particular nomination or appointment, he shall be imprisoned not more than ten years or be fined not more than two thousand dollars, or fine and imprisonment at the discretion of the court.

SEC. 82.—Any person who is convicted under either of the two preceding sections, shall for ever afterwards be disqualified from holding any office under the laws of this Territory.

SEC. 83.—If any person give, offer, or promise any valuable consideration or gratuity whatever to any one summoned, appointed, or sworn as juror, or appointed or chosen arbitrator, or umpire, or referee, or to any appraiser of real or personal estate, or any public officer, with intent to influence the opinion or decision of any such person in any matter, inquest, or cause which may be pending or can legally come before him, or which he may be called on to decide in either of said capacities, he shall be punished by imprisonment not more than five years, or by fine not exceeding one thousand dollars.

SEC. 84.—If any person, mentioned or referred to in the preceding section, shall take or receive any such valuable consideration or gratuity whatever to give his verdict, award, or report in favor of any particular party in a matter for the hearing or decision of which such person has been summoned, appointed, or chosen as aforesaid, he shall be punished by imprisonment not more than ten years, or by fine not exceeding one thousand dollars, or by both fine and imprisonment at the discretion of the court.

SEC. 85.—If any Marshal, Sheriff, Deputy Sheriff, Constable, or other officer receive from a defendant, or any other person, any money or other valuable thing as a consideration or inducement for omitting or delaying to arrest any defendant, or to carry him before a magistrate or to prison, or for postponing, delaying or neglecting to perform any thing pertaining to the duties of his office, he shall be punished by imprisonment not more than one year, or fine not more than five hundred dollars.

SEC. 86.—If any officer wilfully neglect or refuse to serve any process, or delay or omit to execute such process, whereby any person charged with crime or any criminal escape, he shall be punished by imprisonment not more than one year, or by fine not exceeding one thousand dollars, or both fine and imprisonment at the discretion of the court.

SEC. 87.—If any person, having knowledge of the commission of any offence punishable with death or imprisonment for life, take any money or valuable consideration or gratuity, or any promise therefor, upon an agreement or understanding, expressed or implied, to compound or conceal such offence, or not to prosecute the same, or not to give evidence thereof, he shall be punished by imprisonment not more than one year, or by fine not exceeding four hundred dollars, or both fine and imprisonment at the discretion of the court.

SEC. 88.—If any person, having knowledge of the commission of any offence punishable with imprisonment for a limited term of years, is guilty of the offence described in the preceding section, he shall be punished by imprisonment not more than one year, or by fine not exceeding four hundred dollars, or both fine and imprisonment at the discretion of the court.

SEC. 89.—If any jailor or other officer voluntarily suffer any prisoner in his custody to escape, if upon charge or conviction of capital offence, he shall be punished by imprisonment not more than ten, nor less than one year; or if it be upon charge or conviction of a felony other than a capital offence, he shall be punished by imprisonment not more than eight years, or by fine not more than one thousand dollars.

SEC. 90.—If any jailor or other officer voluntarily suffer any prisoner, upon charge or conviction of any public offense, to escape, he shall be fined not more than five hundred dollars, or imprisoned not exceeding one year, or both fined and imprisoned.

SEC. 91.—If any person by any means whatever aid or assist any prisoner lawfully detained in the custody of any officer or in any place of confinement for any felony or misdemeanor, in an attempt to escape, whether such escape be effected or not; or forcibly rescue any person held in legal custody upon any criminal charge, he shall be punished by imprisonment not more than ten years, or fine not more than one thousand dollars, or both fine and imprisonment.

SEC. 92.—If any prisoner convicted of any crime, and sentenced to imprisonment for a less term than for life, shall break his confinement and escape from custody, he shall be punished by imprisonment not exceeding five years, to commence from and after the expiration of the original term of his imprisonment.

SEC. 93.—If any person shall knowingly and wilfully resist or oppose any officer of this Territory, or any person authorized by law or any court, in serving or attempting to serve or execute any legal writ, will, order or process whatsoever, he shall be punished by imprisonment not exceeding one year, or by fine not more than one thousand dollars nor less than one hundred dollars, or both fine and imprisonment at the discretion of the court.

SEC. 94.—If any person, being lawfully required by any Marshal, Sheriff, Constable or other officer, wilfully neglect or refuse to assist him in the execution of his office in any criminal case, or in any case of escape or rescue, he shall be punished by imprisonment not exceeding six months, or fine not more than one hundred dollars.

SEC. 95.—If any Judge, Justice of the Peace, Clerk of any Court, Sheriff, Constable, Attorney or Counselor at Law encourage, excite or stir up any suit, quarrel or controversy between two or more persons, he shall be punished by fine not exceeding five hundred dollars, and shall be answerable to the party injured in treble damages sustained in consequence thereof.

SEC. 96.—When any duty is or shall be required by law of any public officer, or of any person holding any public trust or employment, every wilful neglect to perform such duty, where no special provision has been made for the punishment of such delinquency, is a misdemeanor.

SEC. 97.—When the performance of any act is prohibited by any statute, and no penalty for the violation of such statute is imposed, the doing of such act is a misdemeanor.

SEC. 98.—Any person, who is convicted of a misdemeanor the punishment of which is not otherwise prescribed by any statute, shall be punished by imprisonment not more than one year, or by fine not more than five hundred dollars, or by both fine and imprisonment.

SEC. 99.—If any public officer fraudulently make or give false returns, entries, certificates or receipts in cases where returns, entries, certificates or receipts are authorized by law, he shall be fined not exceeding five hundred dollars, or imprisoned not more than one year, or both at the discretion of the court.

TITLE VIII.

Malicious Mischief.

SEC. 100.—If any person maliciously kill, maim or disfigure any horse, cattle or other domestic beast of another, or maliciously administer poison to any such animals, or expose any poisonous substances, with intent that the same should be taken by them, he shall be punished by imprisonment not exceeding six months, or fine not exceeding one hundred dollars.

SEC. 101.—If any person maliciously take down, injure or remove any monument erected or any tree marked as a boundary of any tract of land, city or town lot, or destroy, deface or alter the marks of any monument or tree made for the purpose of designating such boundary, he shall be punished by imprisonment not more than one year, or by fine not more than two hundred dollars, or fine and imprisonment at the discretion of the court.

SEC. 102.—If any person maliciously injure, deface or destroy any building or fixture attached thereto, or wilfully and maliciously injure, destroy or secrete any goods, chattels or valuable paper of another, or maliciously, prepare any dead fall, or dig any pit, or set any gun, or arrange any other trap to injure another's person or property, he shall be imprisoned not more than one year, or fined not exceeding five hundred dollars, or both fined and imprisoned at the discretion of the court; and is liable to the party injured in a sum equal to three times the value of the property so destroyed or injured or damage sustained, in a civil action.

TITLE IX.

Offenses against Public Health.

SEC. 103.—If any person knowingly sell any kind of diseased, corrupted or unwholesome provisions, whether for meat or drink, without making the same fully known to the buyer; or if any person adulterate fruadulently, for the purpose of sale, any substance intended for food, or any wine, spirituous or malt liquor or other liquor intended for drinking, he shall be punished by imprisonment not more than one year, or by fine not more than five hundred dollars, or both fine and imprisonment; and the article so adulterated shall be forfeited and destroyed.

SEC. 104.—If any person fradulently adulterate, for the purpose of sale, any drug or medicine in such manner as to lessen its efficiency or change the effect or operation of such drug or medicine or to make it injurious to health, or sell it knowing it is thus adulterated, he shall be punished by imprisonment not more than one year, or fined not more than five hundred dollars, or both at the discretion of the court; and such adulterated drugs and medicines shall be forfeited and destroyed.

SEC. 105.—If any apothecary, druggist or other person sell and deliver any arsenic, corrosive sublimate, prussic acid or any poisonous liquid or substance, without having the word "poison" and the true name thereof written or printed upon a label attached to the vial, box or parcel containing the same, he shall be punished by fine not exceeding five hundred dollars, and imprisoned not more than one year, or both at the discretion of the court.

SEC. 106.—If any doctor, physician, apothecary or any other person shall give, communicate or administer, or by their influence, counsel, advice, persuasion, suggestion or by any means whatsoever give or cause to be given by themselves directly or indirectly, or through the aid or medium of any other person or persons, agency or means whatever, any deadly poison, whether animal, mineral or vegetable, such as quicksilver, arsenic, antimony, or any mercurial, arsenical or antimonial preparations therefrom, or cicuta, deadly nightshade, hen-bane, opium or any of the diversified preparations therefrom, or any drugs, medicines and other preparations, such as chloroform, ether, exhilarating gas, calculated in their nature to destroy sensibility, from any other poisonous minerals or vegetables, to any citizen of the Territory of Utah, whether sick or well, old or young, man, woman or child, under pretence of curing disease, or from any other real or pretended cause, influence, argument, or from any design or purpose whatsover, without first explaining fully, definitely, critically, simply and unequivocally to the patient and surrounding friends and relatives, such as father, mother, husband, wife, children, guardian or others, as the case may be, and in plain, simple English language, the specific nature, operation and design of said poison or poisonous preparation about to be or intended to be given, and procuring the unequivocal approval, approbation and consent of the patient, if of mature years and sound mind, and of the parents, guardians or other friends, to the giving, administering or communicating said poison so intended, said doctor, physician, apothecary, person or persons so administering said poison, without the full and free assent of said patient and friends, shall be adjudged guilty of a high misdemeanor, and be punishable in any sum not less than one thousand dollars, and be imprisoned or confined to hard labor for any time not less than one year; and if the death of the patient or person so receiving the poison, as above specified, shall follow the taking of the same, without being made acquainted with the nature thereof, then the doctor, physician, apothecary, person or persons so giving or causing to be given said poison, shall be adjudged guilty of manslaughter or murder, as the case may be, by any court having jurisdiction, and be punished according to law for such crimes: Provided, that the administration of poisons, as specified in the forepart of this section, and the penalties thereof shall not attach to doctors, physicians and apothecaries, having their own drugs, poisons and medicines, accompanying and administering to companies and individuals traveling through the Territory, the same not being citizens of the Territory; but all such doctors and companies so traveling may administer to and receive of their own drugs, poisons or medicines, with good intent, on their own responsibility.

TITLE X.

Offenses against the Public Peace.

SEC. 107.—If two or more persons voluntarily or by agreement engage in any fight, or use blows or violence toward each other in an angry or quarrelsome manner, in any public place, to the disturbance of the peace, they are guilty of an affray, and shall be punished by imprisonment not more than three months, or fine not more than fifty dollars.

SEC. 108.—When three or more persons together, and in a violent or tumultuous manner, commit an unlawful act, or together do a lawful act in an unlawful, violent or tumultuous manner, to the disturbance of others, they are guilty of riot; and every such offender shall be punished by imprisonment not more than one year, or by fine not more than five hundred dollars.

TITLE XI.

Justifiable Killing and the Prevention of Public Offenses.

SEC. 109.—Lawful resistance to the commission of a public offense may be made by the party about to be injured, or by others. Resistance sufficient to prevent the offense may be made by the party about to be injured, first, to prevent an offense against his person; second, to prevent an offense against his wife, child, father or mother, brother or sister; third, to prevent an illegal attempt by force to take or injure property in his lawful possession.

SEC. 110.—Any other person, in aid or defence of the person about to be injured, may make resistance sufficient to prevent the offense.

SEC. 111.—If any person shall kill another in his own defence, as above provided, or in a sudden heat of pession caused by the attempt of any such offender to commit a rape upon his wife, daughter, sister, mother or other female relation or dependant, or to defile the same, or when the defilement has actually been committed, or in defence of his habitation against any person who attempts to enter in a violent, tumultuous or riotous manner; or offers any personal violence to any inmate thereof, either dwelling or being therein, shall be deemed justifiable homicide.

SEC. 112.—A bare fear of any of these offenses being about to be or having been committed shall not be sufficient to justify the killing. It must appear that the circumstances were sufficient to excite the fears of a reasonable person, and that the party killing really acted under the influence of those fears, and not in a spirit of revenge.

SEC. 113.—If an officer in the execution of his office in a criminal case, having a legal process, be resisted and assailed, he shall be justified if he kill the assailant. If any officer or private person attempt to take a person charged with treason, murder, rape, burglary, robbery, arson, perjury, forgery, counterfeiting or other crime known, denominated felony by the law, and he or they be resisted in the endeavor to take the person accused, and, to prevent the escape of the accused by reason of such resistance, he or she be killed, the officer or private person so killing shall be justified.

SEC. 114.—Justifiable homicide may also consist in unavoidable necessity, without any will or desire, and without any intention or negligence in the party killing.

An officer, who in the execution of public justice puts a person to death in virtue of a judgment of a competent court of justice, shall be justified; the officer must, however, proceed in the performance of his duty according to the direction of the court and the law of the land.

SEC. 115.—Excusable homicide, by misadventure, is when a person, in doing a lawful act without any intention of killing, yet unfortunately kills another, as when a man is at work with an axe, and the axe flies off the handle and kills a bystander, it is only a misadventure; and all other instances which stand upon the same footing of reason and justice as those enumerated, shall be considered justifiable or excusable homicide. The homicide appearing justifiable or excusable, the person indicted shall, upon his trial, be fully acquitted and discharged.

TITLE XII.

General definitions and provisions as to Crimes and Offenses.

SEC. 116.—Public offenses are divided into felony and misdemeanors. A felony is an offense punishable with death, or imprisonment for a term of one year or more; every other offense is a misdemeanor. No person can be punished for a public offense, except upon legal conviction in a court having jurisdiction thereof. All criminal prosecution shall be commenced and carried on in the name of "the people of the United States in the Territory of Utah."

SEC. 117.—No person shall be subject to a second prosecution for a public offense for which he has been once prosecuted, and legally convicted or acquitted.

SEC. 118.—Words importing the singular number only may be extended to several persons or things; and words importing the plural number only may be applied to one person or thing; and words importing the masculine gender only may be extended to females. All words and phrases shall be construed according to the context and the approved usage of the language; but technical words and phrases, and such others as may have acquired a peculiar and appropriate meaning in law, shall be construed according to such peculiar and appropriate meaning.

SEC. 119.—A private person, who has arrested another for the commission of a public offense, must without unnecessary delay take him before a magistrate, or deliver him to a peace officer.

SEC. 120.—There is no distinction between an accessory before the fact and a principal, in the commission of a public offense; whether they directly commit the act constituting the offense, or aid and abet in its commission, though not present, they must be indicted, tried and punished as principals. An accessory after the fact may be indicted, tried and punished, though the principal be neither tried nor convicted.

SEC. 121.—Upon a trial for enticing or taking away an unmarried female of previously chaste character, for the purpose of prostitution, or aiding or assisting therein, or for seducing and debauching any unmarried woman of previously chaste character, or on trial for rape or attempt to commit rape, the testimony of the party injured being corroborated by the attending circumstances, tending to convict the defendant of the commission of the offense shall be deemed sufficient.

SEC. 122.—When a person is convicted of a public offence, the punishment for which is imprisonment, the court may direct that he wear a ball and chain, and that he perform hard labor during the term of his imprisonment.

SEC. 123.—No conviction and consequent punishment of imprisonment and fine shall be any bar to a civil suit for damages.

SEC. 124.—When any person shall be convicted of any crime, the punishment of which is death according to the provisions of this act, and sentenced to die, said person shall suffer death by being shot, hung, or beheaded, as the court may direct; or the person so condemned shall have his option as to the manner of his execution.

Approved March 6, 1852.

ing any land or land claim or improvement thereon, any bond, execution or any other description of property with intent to deceive or defraud, or to delay or defeat the payment of just debts, or who shall sell or exchange any description of property which he at the time knows is adulterated, damaged or diseased, without first truly informing the purchaser concerning the actual condition or quality of said property, shall be deemed guilty of fraud, and shall, on conviction thereof, be fined not exceeding one thousand dollars, or be imprisoned in the county jail not exceeding one year, at daily hard labor, during customary hours, upon the streets, highways and public works and buildings of the county: Provided, such labor shall be performed with a ball and chain attached to a prisoner whenever the jailer deems it necessary; or both fine and imprisonment as aforesaid.

SEC. 2.—Any person, knowingly obtaining any property through any false pretense or representation made by himself or at his instigation, shall be deemed a cheat or swindler, and shall, on conviction thereof, be fined or imprisoned, or both, as provided in the foregoing section for the punishment of fraud.

SEC. 3.—Any person convicted under this act shall also be liable to make full restitution and pay all damages to the party aggrieved.

Approved Jan. 20, 1865.

———:o:———

CHAPTER XXIV.

An ACT in relation to Fires on the Public Domain.

SEC. 1.—Be it enacted by the Governor and Legislative Assembly of the Territory of Utah: That if any person wilfully and maliciously, or through carelessness, set on fire the grass on the public domain or the timber in the cañons or mountains he shall be punished by imprisonment not more than one year, or by fine not less than five nor more than five hundred dollars, at the discretion of the court having jurisdiction; and shall also be liable for all damages done to private property.

SEC. 2.—That if any person shall set fire on his own premises, he shall be liable for all damages that may accrue to others by reason of the fire spreading.

SEC. 3.—Whenever it shall be deemed necessary to burn off the hay ground of any town or settlement in this Territory, a Justice of the Peace of said town or settlement shall cause due notice to be given of the intention, in a public manner, as to time and place; and all necessary precaution shall be taken to prevent the fire from spreading or running beyond the intended limits.

Approved Jan. 20, 1864.

———:o:———

CHAPTER XXV.

An ACT to prohibit the use of certain paper as money.

SEC. 1.—Be it enacted by the Governor and Legislative Assembly of the Territoy of Utah: That any person, private corporation, firm or association issuing or circulating any note, check, memorandum, token or other obligation for the use as money in lieu of lawful money or other lawful medium of exchange, shall be deemed guilty of a misdemeanor, and shall, on conviction thereof in any court having jurisdiction, be punished for each offence by fine not exceeding one thousand dollars, to be paid into the Territorial Treasury, or by imprisonment not exceeding six months, or by both fine and imprisonment.

SEC. 2.—This act shall not be construed to in any manner apply to Territorial, County, or City paper, nor to prevent any person from returning the class of paper prohibited in this act, but issued or in circulation previous to the time this act takes effect, to the person, corporation, firm or association purporting to have issued it; and if said person, corporation, firm, or association refuses or neglects to pay or redeem the aforesaid paper when it is presented for payment, or to make satisfactory arrangements for paying or redeeming it, he shall, in addition to the amount claimed on the paper so returned, be liable for all loss that may accrue through such neglect or refusal; and the interest on the aforesaid amount shall be calculated and paid at the rate of six per cent. per month during the time of such neglect or refusal.

Approved Jan. 22, 1868.

———:o———

CHAPTER XXVI.

An ORDINANCE prohibiting the sale of Arms, Ammunition, or Spirituous Liquors to the Indians.

SEC. 1.—Be it ordained by the General Assembly of the State of Deseret: That if any person shall hereafter trade or give any guns, rifles, pistols or any other deadly weapons, ammunition or spirituous liquors to any Indian, without having a license, he shall, on conviction thereof before any Justice of the Peace, be fined in a sum not exceeding one hundred dollars for each offense, and also forfeit all the property received from the Indian, which shall be sold and the proceeds thereof paid into the public treasury.

Approved March 28th, 1850.

———:o:———

CHAPTER XXVII.

An ORDINANCE in reference to Vagrants.

SEC. 1.—Be it ordained by the General Assembly of the State of Deseret: That any person residing within the limits of this State, who has no visible means of support, shall be deemed a vagrant.

SEC. 2.—Be it further ordained that, upon complaint on oath being made and filed with any Justice of the Peace that there is, within the county wherein such Justice resides, any person who is engaged in no useful employment, and has apparently no manner of support, it shall be the duty of such Justice forthwith to issue a warrant to bring such delinquent before him.

SEC. 3.—Be it further ordained that, upon the return of such warrant, with the defendant therein named, in Court, said complaint shall be distinctly read to such defendant, when he shall be required to answer the same on oath; and the justice shall inquire into the truth of such complaint in a summary manner.

SEC. 4.—Be it further ordained that, if the justice find on such investigation that such complaint be true, he shall record the same in his docket, and thereupon enter judgment, declaring such delinquent a vagrant.

SEC. 5.—Be it further ordained that any person convicted as aforesaid, shall be compelled to labor on the public works a sufficient length of time to pay the cost of prosecution: Provided, the same be not less than twenty days.

SEC. 6—And be it further ordained that it shall be the duty of every officer of State, in this State, to report to the magistrate of their respective precincts any person whom they may have good reason to suspect as being a vagrant under this ordinance.

SEC. 7.—The foregoing ordinance shall apply to all loafers who hang about the corners of streets, court houses, or any other public place, who have no business, whether they have property or not.

Approved Feb. 12, 1851.

———:o:———

CHAPTER XXVIII.

An ACT to provide against disturbing Religious Meetings of Lawful Assemblies of the People.

SEC. 1.—Be it enacted by the Governor and Legislative Assembly of the Territory of Utah: That any person or persons who shall wilfully disturb any religious meeting or lawful assembly of the people, by noisy or riotous actions, menaces, ludicrous language, or threats, shall be liable to arrest by any officer of the peace, and fined in any sum not less than five nor over one hundred dollars, or imprisonment not over six months, or both.

Approved March 3, 1852.

———:o:———

CHAPTER XXIX.

An ACT in relation to Profanity and Drunkenness.

SEC. 1.—Be it enacted by the Governor and Legislative Assembly of the Territory of Utah: That it shall be unlawful to use, with disrespect, the name of the Deity; and any person profaning the name of God shall be subject to fine not less than two nor more than ten dollars, or from one to five days hard labor on the public highway, at the discretion of the court.

SEC. 2.—Any person who shall become publicly intoxicated, so as to endanger the peace and quiet of the community, shall be liable to arrest by any officer of the peace, and fined in any sum not less than one nor more than ten dollars, at the discretion of the court.

Approved March 3, 1852.

———:o:———

CHAPTER XXX.

An ACT regulating the mode of procedure in Criminal Cases.

SEC. 1.—Be it enacted by the Governor and Legislative Assembly of the Territory of Utah: That when a Justice or Judge knows, or has information under oath, that a person has threatened to commit an offense, he shall issue an order requiring an officer to bring such person before him, when he shall examine the matter, and may require bonds for good behavior for not less than three months nor longer than his stay in this Territory, or retain him a discretionary length of time.

SEC. 2.—Any person being present at the commission of an offense, shall forthwith take the offender before the nearest Justice or Probate Judge for examination.

SEC. 3.—When a complaint is made, under oath, that an offense has been committed, the Justice or Judge shall issue an order, requiring an officer to take all requisite steps to bring the offender before him.

SEC. 4.—When a person accused of committing an offense is brought before a Justice or Judge, he shall determine whether such person shall be put upon trial or released.

SEC. 5.—If it be determined that the accused be put upon trial, and the Justice or Judge has jurisdiction of the case, he shall appoint a time therefor; and if not, he shall order an officer to take him and the necessary papers to a court having jurisdiction.

SEC. 6.—The Justice or Judge shall issue an order to an officer to summon all the witnesses required, but neither party shall have more than three witnesses to prove the same fact.

SEC. 7.—At the time of trial if the accused or an important witness be absent, the Court shall issue a compulsory order for his appearance, and may adjourn until it can be had.

SEC. 8.—When the accusation is read, if the accused confess he is guilty, the Court may inquire into the amount of guilt and decide accordingly; and if not, the evidence on the part of the accusation shall be heard, and then that of the accused; after which, if either party can satisfy the Court that important evidence, which he can procure, is still wanting, his demand may be complied with; when all the evidence is heard, the accuser may make such applicable remarks as he deems proper, and also the accused, and the Court shall render judgment as soon as practicable.

SEC. 9.—In jury cases, before the introduction of any evidence, the Court shall issue an order, requiring an officer to summon for that purpose a reasonable number of judicious men residents of the county, out of which twelve, or a less number if agreed upon, shall be selected; and if the number first summoned is not sufficient, the officer shall continue to summon till the number is complete.

SEC. 10.—Previous to swearing persons drawn or selected to serve as a petit jury, each party may challenge for cause to the number that either or both parties may be able to produce what to them seems to be good cause, the validity of said cause to be determined by the Court, and each party may, as aforesaid, peremptorily challenge as many as six persons.

SEC. 11.—The persons selected shall be sworn to try the case faithfully and give a just verdict, and have no communication concerning the case, until they are discharged, with any but a fellow juror, or with the Court personally, or through the officer in whose charge they may be placed.

SEC. 12.—The Court shall instruct the jury on the law and equity in the case, and give them such other instructions as may be necessary.

SEC. 13.—If the jury have to retire to agree upon their verdict, the Court shall direct an officer to keep them separate from all others, and to prevent their communicating with any but the Court, until they are discharged.

SEC. 14.—The verdict of the jury shall be made by their unanimous agreement, and in writing, and be presented to the Court and read in the presence of the accused; and in capital cases shall read "guilty" or "not guilty;" and in other cases, if against the accused, shall state the amount of damages and the nature and extent of the punishment.

SEC. 15.—After being furnished all necessary information, if the jury satisfy the Court that they cannot agree, they shall be discharged, and the Court shall cause another jury to be arranged and proceed again to try the case.

SEC. 16.—The Court shall award the costs, and authorize and require a proper officer to execute the judgment.

SEC. 17.—When necessary, the Court shall issue an order requiring an officer to summon fifteen judicious men, residents of the county, for a grand jury, who shall be sworn to inquire faithfully into offences, and present indictments by the agreement of at least twelve of their number against offenders who should be prosecuted; and the Foreman shall have power to swear witnesses and compel their attendance.

SEC. 18.—The indictments must be made in the name of the people, and must state the name of the offender, the offense, the manner of committing it, and, as near as may be, the time and place of its occurrence; be signed by the Foreman, with the names of the required witnesses written thereon, and be presented to the Court, who may correct mistakes that do not prejudice the trial. When the name of an offender is not known, he may be proceeded against with any name.

SEC. 19.—In answer to the accusation the accused may state "guilty," or "not guilty;" may object to the jurisdiction of the Court, or urge a former acquittal in the same case; and during the trial either party may object, in writing, to any decision of the Court which he considers unjust.

SEC. 20.—When the Court has not jurisdiction, or the accused give other satisfactory evidence for removal, an officer shall be required to take the accused, the indictment and all necessary papers to the nearest Court having jurisdiction.

SEC. 21—In all cases bail may be required of witnesses, and in all but capital offenses may be taken of the accused for appearance at time and place of trial.

SEC. 22.—When it is not reasonable that the witness be present at the trial, his deposition may be taken in the presence of the parties, or without that presence if it be waived.

SEC. 23.—If a juror by any cause be incapacitated for attendance through the trial, it may proceed, and the verdict shall be valid.

SEC. 24.—The property of a person accused of an offense shall be held depending the execution of the judgment.

SEC. 25.—Immediately after judgment appeals may be taken by either party, on written objections to illegal or unjust proceedings on the part of the Court or jury, and the objections must be certified up by the Court, upon which a Superior Court may confirm, reverse or modify the judgment, or order a new trial.

SEC. 26.—Prosecution for offense must be commenced as soon after the offense has been committed, or the offender is known, as the circumstances will warrant.

SEC. 27.—The officer entrusted shall execute the order or judgment of the Court; and is hereby authorized and empowered to break any and every description of fastenings that may obstruct his search for such persons or property as he presumes to be concealed; and shall make return thereof with diligence.

SEC. 28.—The Court shall have power to punish for contempt and disobedience to orders, by a reasonable preventive amount of fine; and all fines shall be paid into the county treasury.

Approved Jan. 21, 1853.

———:o:———

CHAPTER XXXI.

Providing for Appeals to the Supreme Court.

SEC. 1.—Be it enacted by the Governor and Legislative Assembly of the Territory of Utah: That hereafter whenever any final order, judgment or decree is made or rendered in the District Court of the Territory, the party aggrieved may have the same reviewed in the Supreme Court on appeal, by obtaining, from the Clerk of the Court making or rendering such order, judgment or decree, a complete transcript of the record of the case, which shall be filed with the Clerk of the Supreme Court.

SEC. 2.—On application for such record and tender of the legal fees therefor, if the Clerk shall refuse or neglect to make out and deliver or transmit the same, he shall be punished for contempt and be disqualified to act as Clerk.

SEC. 3.—In case the order, judgment or decree in the District Court is for the payment of money, the appeal to the Supreme Court shall not operate as a stay of execution, unless the party appealing shall enter into a supersedeas bond in double the amount of the money adjudged to be paid, with sureties to be approved by the Clerk or Court, and conditioned to pay the amount awarded against the appelant in the Supreme Court, and all costs that may accrue by reason of such appeal.

SEC. 4.—From judgments in criminal cases less than capital, the defendant may appeal by entering into bonds, with sureties to be approved in like manner, in such sum as the District Court or Judge may determine, conditioned to abide the judgment of the Supreme Court; and in capital cases, the defendant may also appeal, as provided in the first section for civil cases, but must remain committed, unless the judgment is reversed and a discharge ordered by the Supreme Court.

SEC. 5.—In all cases of appeal, as herein provided, the party appealing in civil cases shall serve a written notice upon the adverse party, or the attorneys of record in the case, sixty days before the sitting of the Supreme Court, (unless such notice be waived), that an appeal has been taken; and, in criminal cases, a similar notice shall be served upon the attorney who prosecuted the defendant in the District Court.

SEC. 6.—No appeal shall be taken to the Supreme Court, unless within two years after the rendition of the judgment in civil cases; or, in case the person, entitled to such appeal be an infant or of unsound mind, or imprisoned, then within three years after such disability ceases, except the party appealing be a non-resident, and, if so, within four years; and, in criminal cases; the appeal must be taken to the next Supreme Court after the judgment, provided there is sufficient time after the rendition of judgment; if not, then to the next Supreme Court succeeding.

SEC. 7.—The hearing of the Supreme Court shall be upon the record and argument of counsel; and the District Court is hereby required to sign all bills of exceptions taken to its rulings, decisions or charge to the jury, which shall be incorporated into and constitute part of the record of the cause; and, upon refusal to sign such bills of exceptions, the same may be signed by two spectators, under, oath, or two disinterested attorneys; and when so signed shall be of equal validity as if signed by the Judge.

SEC. 8.—When the judgment, final order or decree shall be reversed, either in whole or in part, the Supreme Court may render such judgment as the Court below should have rendered, or remand the cause to the Court below to proceed according to the decision of the Supreme Court; and execution may issue from the Supreme Court, or a special mandate to the Clerk of the Court below to proceed upon the judgment as the Supreme Court may direct.

SEC. 9.—When a judgment, order or decree is reversed, the appelant shall recover his cost; and when reversed in part and affirmed in part, the cost shall be equally divided between the parties.

SEC. 10.—In case the Supreme Court at any regular session adjourn the term of said Court, all cases tried and determined in the District Court may be removed to such adjourned term in the same manner as provided in this act for taking cases to the regular term, and may be heard and determined at such adjourned term of said Court.

Approved January 18, 1861.

———:o:———

CHAPTER XXXII.

In relation to Commitment and Bail.

SEC. 1.—Be it enacted by the Governor and Legislative Assembly of the Territory of Utah: That, if it shall appear to any Magistrate, to whom complaint is made or before whom any prisoner is brought, that an offense has been committed, and that there is probable cause to believe the prisoner guilty, and if the offense be bailable and the prisoner offer sufficient bail, or the amount of money in lieu thereof, it shall be taken and the prisoner discharged; but if no sufficient bail be offered, or the offense be not bailable, the prisoner shall be committed for trial.

SEC. 2.—When a Magistrate admits a prisoner to bail, or commits him, he shall also bind by recognizance such witnesses against the prisoner as he shall deem material, to appear and testify at the next Court having recognizance of the offense, and in which the prisoner shall be held to answer.

SEC. 3.—The testimony of the witnesses examined shall be reduced to writing by the Magistrate, or under his direction, when he shall think it necessary, and shall be signed by the witnesses, if required by the Magistrate.

SEC. 4.—All examinations and recognizance taken by any Magistrate shall be certified and returned by him to the Prosecuting Attorney, or to the Clerk of the Court, before which the party charged is bound to appear, on or before the first day of the sitting thereof; and if such Magistrate shall neglect or refuse to return the same he may be compelled forthwith, by rule of Court; and in case of disobedience may be proceeded against by attachment as for contempt.

Approved January 16, 1861.

CHAPTER XXXIII.

Concerning Arrests.

Be it enacted by the Governor and Legislative Assembly of the Territory of Utah: That if a person, against whom a warrant has been issued for an alleged offense committed in any county, shall, either before or after the issuing of such warrant, escape from or be out of said county, the Sheriff or other officer to whom such warrant is directed may pursue and apprehend said person in any county in this Territory; and for that purpose may command aid and exercise the same authority as in his own county; and if an arrested person escapes or is rescued, the officer from whose custody he has escaped or been rescued may, without a warrant, pursue and retake him in any place in the Territory.

Approved January 18, 1861.

——:o:——

CHAPTER XXXIV.

An ACT prescribing certain Qualifications necessary to enable a Person to be eligible to hold office, vote or serve as a Juror.

SEC. 1.—Be it enacted by the Governor and Legislative Assembly of the Territory of Utah: That no person shall be elected a Delegate to the Congress of the United States from this Territory, who has not been a resident therein during one year next preceeding the day of election.

SEC. 2.—No person shall be eligible to a seat in either branch of the Legislative Assembly, unless he has been a resident in the county or district to be represented, during at least one year next preceding the day of election.

SEC. 3.—No person shall be elected or appointed to any Territorial, district, county or precinct office, unless he shall have been a constant resident therein during at least one year next preceding such election or appointment; neither shall any person be entitled to hold any office of trust or profit in the Territory or vote at any election unless he is a free, white male citizen of the United States, over twenty one years of age, and has been a constant resident in the Territory during the six months next preceding said election or appointment.

SEC. 4.—A person is not eligible to serve and therefore shall not serve on any grand or petit jury in any court in this Territory unless he is a free, white male citizen of the United States, is over twenty one years of age, is of reputed sound mind and discretion, is not so disabled in body as to be unable to serve, has not been convicted of any capital or infamous crime, owns taxable property and pays taxes in this Territory, and has been a constant resident therein during the year last preceding his being selected to serve as a juror.

SEC. 5.—And be it further enacted that no officer or soldier of the United States army or other person subject to their military authority is eligible to hold any office or serve on any jury or vote at any election in this Territory, unless his home and place of residence was therein at the time of engaging in such service.

SEC. 6.—No person shall be deemed a resident within the meaning of this act, unless he is a tax payer in this Territory.

Approved Jan. 21, 1859.

CHAPTER XXXV.

An ACT defining who are exempt from serving on Juries, and prescribing the mode of procuring Grand and Petit Jurors and Juries for District Courts, and for other Purposes.

SEC. 1.—Be it enacted by the Governor and Legislative Assembly of the Territory of Utah: That members and officers of the Legislative Assembly, Judges of Probate Courts, Selectmen, County Treasurers, Clerks of the Supreme, District, Probate and County Courts, the Territorial Marshal, Deputy Marshalls, Sheriffs, Deputy Sheriffs, Constables, Attorneys and Counselors at law, persons at the time engaged in teaching school, Ferrymen, Millers, Physicians, Surgeons and Editors of newspapers and other periodical publications are exempt from serving either as grand or petit jurors.

SEC. 2.—The County Court in each county shall, at its first session in each year, and at such subsequent session, or other time as a neglect so to do at said first session or as other circumstances may require, make, from the assessment roll of the county, a list containing the names of at least fifty men, residents of the county, eligible to serve as jurors.

SEC. 3.—Said list shall contain only the names of such persons as are known or believed to possess the requisite qualifications for jurors, and not entitled to exemption from jury service; and the names thereon shall be apportioned among the different sections of the county, as nearly as may be, according to the names on the assessment roll; and the selections of persons to serve as jurors shall, from time to time be made in such manner, so far as the County Court can judge, as to cause the eligible persons to perform jury duty as nearly as may be in rotation.

SEC. 4.—Said list shall contain the christian and surname at length, and the place of residence and occupation of each person named therein, and shall be filed with the Clerk of the County Court, who shall keep in his office a box or other safe place of deposit in which he shall deposit the names on the list, having previously written each name on a separate ticket and so folded said ticket that the name thereon does not appear.

SEC. 5.—When a District Court is to be held, whether for a district or for a county, the Clerk of said Court shall, at least thirty days previous to the time of holding said Court, issue a writ to a Marshal or any of his Deputies, if said Court is to be holden for a district, or to the Sheriff or any of his Deputies of the county in which said Court is to be held, if it is to be held for a county, specifying the time and place of holding said Court, and requiring him to summon, if for a grand jury, twenty-four eligible men to serve as grand jurors, and, if for petit jurors, twenty-four eligible men to serve as petit jurors; and said twenty-four men shall constitute a grand jury: and said twenty-four men shall constitute two full petit juries.

SEC. 6.—Upon the reception of said writ, a Marshal or a Sheriff, as the case may be, or either of their Deputies, shall proceed to the Clerk of the County Court of the county in which jurors are to be summoned, and said Clerk shall forthwith repair, with said officer having said writ, to the office of said Clerk, who shall if a grand jury is required, in the presence of said officer, thoroughly shake the tickets previously deposited in a box or other safe place of deposit, and draw therefrom promiscuously twenty-four tickets, and the persons whose names are on those twenty-four tickets shall be summoned to serve as a grand jury, a minute of which drawing shall be kept by said Clerk, with the names entered thereon in the order they are drawn; when, if petit jurors are also required, said Clerk shall proceed in like manner to draw and minute twenty-four tickets, and the twenty-four persons named on said tickets shall be summoned to serve as petit jurors; said Clerk and attending officer shall then sign the minutes of the drawing, which minutes shall be filled by said Clerk in the office of the County Court of the country in which said drawing was had.

SEC. 7.—Upon the conclusion of the drawing, and previous to the filing as aforesaid, said Clerk shall forthwith make a list of the names of the persons drawn, if any, to serve as grand jurors, and a list of the names of the persons drawn, if any, to serve as petit jurors, and certify to said list, or lists, and deliver it, or them, to the officer having the writ from the Clerk of a District Court to summon jurors.

SEC. 8.—The officer having the writ and jury list, or lists, in charge, as hereinbefore provided, shall, immediately upon his reception of said list, or lists, proceed to summon the persons named on said list, or lists, to attend said Court, specifying the time and place of its sitting; which summons shall be served by giving each person a written notice, or by leaving a copy of the summons at his residence in care of some person of suitable age and discretion.

SEC. 9.—If, in summoning the persons named on said list or lists, said officer becomes aware that, from any cause beyond his control, there will be a failure by one or more of said persons to appear as required, he shall forthwith repair to the aforesaid Clerk of the County Court, who shall with said officer proceed to draw, as hereinbefore provided, until the required number of jurors can be procured; and said officer shall return said list or lists, and writ to said District Court at the time specified, and shall specify the persons summoned and the manner in which each was summoned.

SEC. 10.—When a District Court is to be held for a district, and the Judge thereof is reliably advised that the ends of justice will be materially promoted by so doing, said Judge may apportion the twenty-four grand jurors among two or more counties in his district.

SEC. 11.—After a grand jury is empanelled, sworn or affirmed and charged by the Court, said Court shall appoint one of their number to be their Foreman; and said Foreman shall have power to swear or affirm all witnesses to testify before said grand jury; and shall, when the grand jury or any twelve of them have, upon to them good and sufficient evidence, found a bill of indictment, endorse thereon the words, to wit —"A True Bill," and officially sign his name to said endorsement, and also note or cause to be noted on the bill of indictment the name or names of the witnesses upon whose evidence it was found.

SEC. 12.—The Clerk of the District Court shall write upon separate tickets the names of the persons returned to serve as petit jurors, shall so fold said tickets that their names thereon do not appear, shall deposit them in a box or other safe place of deposit, and, when ordered by the Court, draw from said box or place twelve names; and the persons whose names are drawn shall constitute a petit jury, except such as are legally rejected; and, in case of such rejection, said Clerk shall continue to draw until said petit jury is complete; and if the number of the petit jurors returned to said Court shall be exhausted, then the proper officer shall, upon the order of the Judge, summon talismen from the body of the county to complete said panel.

SEC. 13.—If during any term of a District Court, the number of jurors provided proves insufficient, the Clerk of said Court shall immediately issue a writ, directed to one of the officers before named as the persons to serve such writs, for the requisite number; and said officer shall at once proceed to procure them in the manner hereinbefore provided; and in case said writ exhausts the names already selected, the Clerk of the County Court of the proper county shall forthwith call a meeting of said Court, which shall immediately select, in the manner already specified, at least as many names as may at that time be deemed sufficient.

SEC. 14.—A District Court is hereby empowered to sit at the county seat of any county within its district, to try cases arising in such county, whenever the County Court of said county shall make provision to defray the expenses of said District Court.

SEC. 15.—If any person fails to appear as a grand or petit juror when lawfully summoned, or if a Marshal, or his Deputy, or any Clerk of the District or County Court, or any Sheriff, or his Deputy fails to fulfil the duties enjoined upon him in this act, without having a reasonable excuse, he shall be considered guilty of contempt, and may be fined for each offense, for the use of the county in which the defendant resides, in any sum not exceeding fifty dollars, unless, at or before the next term of said District Court, good cause be shown for such failure: Provided, that the oath or affirmation of any such delinquent shall at all times be received as competent evidence in his favour.

SEC. 16.—It shall be the duty of the Clerk of a District Court, at the close of each term of said Court, to make out and give to each juror a certificate, certifying the number of days attendance of and amount of compensation due to said juror, which certificate, upon being presented to the County Court of the county from which said juror was summoned, shall entitle said juror to be allowed and paid by said county, the sum specified in said certificate, as other demands against the county are paid: Provided, that no juror shall be paid out of the county treasury for any jury service for which he may have received or be entitled to receive pay for sitting as a juror upon United States business.

Approved January 21, 1859.

CHAPTER XXXVI.

An ACT concerning Costs and Fees of Courts, and for other purposes.

SEC. 1—Be it enacted by the Governor and Legislative Assembly of the Territory of Utah: That the fees and compensation in District Courts, of officers and other persons herein named, shall be as follows:—

The Clerk's fees shall be, for issuing and sealing a writ	50
Docketing a case 15c. Each subsequent docketing	10
Entering judgment on a suit, without process,	25
Entering cause on judgment docket	20
Entering each order of Court	20
Filing each case in a suit, except appeals	10
Entering special bail	20
Swearing and empanelling each jury	20
Administering oath to each witness on trial	5
Entering verdict of jury and judgment	25
Entering satisfaction of judgment	5
Issuing writ of execution	25
Taxing cost	15
Entering exonerator	10
Entering surrender	10
A commission to take depositions	30
All motions in one suit	15
All the rules in one suit	20
If there be but one	10
A venire for a jury	15
Making a complete record in each cause, when ordered by the Court, for every hundred words	15
Copy of record, when required, per 100 words	10
Every certificate, when required with seal of Court,	25
A subpœna, to include all the witnesses called for at the time of issuing	25
Filing record of appeal, writ of error, supercedeas, certiorari, or habeas corpus	5
Recording assessment of damages	15
Copy of paper not herein provided, for every hundred words	10
For administering oath in naturalizatin cases	10
Filing the same	10
For certficate of application	20
Certificate of naturalization	50
Taking a recognizance	15
Each bond required by law	50
Certificate of admission to the bar	50

No fees shall be demanded from grand or petit juries, or witnesses, for issuing a certificate entitling them to fees as such.

A County Court may allow the Clerk of a District Court any sum not exceeding $50 per annum for services in criminal cases where the defendants are acquitted; and in all civil and criminal cases the fees of a Clerk of a Probate Court shall be the same as hereinbefore provided for a Clerk of a District Court.

SEC. 2.—And be it further enacted that the fees of the Clerk of the Supreme Court shall be,

For issuing and sealing each writ	75
Docketing cause each time	15
Entering cause on judgment docket	25
Entering each order, motion, or rule	20
Filing each paper	10
Entering judgment	25
Entering nonsuit, discontinuance, dismissal, or nolle prosequi	15
Entering satisfaction of judgment	15
Entering return of execution	15
Taxing costs	25
Copy of paper or record, per 100 words	10
Certificate	40
Taking bond	50
Assessment of damage	25
Entering cause on court calendar	15
Entering appearance of parties	10
Signing final record	20
Making complete record, per 100 words	15
Certificate of admission to the bar	2 00
For all services not specified he shall receive such compensation as shall be allowed a Clerk of a District Court for like services,	

SEC. 3.—And be it further enacted that the fees of the Territorial Marshal, or a Sheriff, or either of their Deputies shall be,

For serving any Writ and returning the same (subpœnas excepted) for one defendant	50
For each additional defendant	25
Commitment to prison	25
Discharge from prison	25
Attending with a person before a Judge or Court, when required at any time not a regular term	1 50
Mileage going with such person before said Judge and returning, per mile,	5

Serving a writ of possession or restitution	50
Copy of a paper required by law for each 100 words,	15
Serving and returning a subpœna, for each person therein named,	20
Calling a jury in each cause	20
Summoning a grand and petit jury	5 00
Traveling fees going and returning, per mile,	5
Selling land or other property on execution, per day,	1 50
Making and executing a deed for property sold on execution	1 00
Serving one person with an order of court, besides mileage,	15
Summoning a jury in cases of forcible entry and detainer	1 00
Serving an execution or order for partition of real estate, or assigning dower, besides mileage,	50
Each bond	25
For collecting and paying over all sums under $200	5 per cent.
All sums over $200 and less than $500	3 per cent.
All sums over $500 and under $1,000	2 per cent.
And all over $1,000	1 per cent.
Returning a writ not served	10
Receiving a prisoner on surrender by bail	25
Taking new bail	25
Dieting a prisoner, (to be paid out of the County Treasury when the prisoner is insolvent), per day,	35

The Territorial Marshal, or a Sheriff may be allowed by the proper County Court a sum not exceeding $50 for services rendered the county in delivering notices and other duties actually performed, for which no specified sum is provided by law.

SEC. 4.—Be it further enacted that the fees of the Clerks of County Courts shall be,

For recording proceedings in term time, per day,	2 00
For entering other records and accounts kept in his office, for each folio of 100 words,	10
For making calculation and carrying out the amount of taxes on the assessment roll, per day,	2 00
For making out abstracts of assessment roll, for each 100 words (4 figures counting one word)	10
For each bond for an officer, to be paid by such officer	50
Filing all returns of an election	50
For each certificate	25
Copy of any paper or record, per 100 words,	10
For each advertisement of an election	15

SEC. 5.—Be it further enacted that the fees of Justices of the Peace in civil cases shall be,

For docketing each suit	10
For summons or warrant	25
Precept for jury	15
Every subpœna including all witnesses asked for at the time	20
Swearing a jury	15
Entering a verdict	15
Entering judgment	25
Taking and certifying any acknowledgment	25
Administering oath	25
Every rule of reference	10
Every continuance or adjournment	15
Taking depositions, per 100 words,	15
Certifying a deposition	20
Taking bail, recognizances, or security,	25
For every discontinuance or satisfaction	15
Entering amicable judgment	25
Transfer of judgment	25
Filing each paper	5
Opening judgment, after default,	15
Taxing cost	10
Issuing writ of attachment	25
Taking bond for the same	25
For holding inquiry in cases of forcible entry and detainer, in addition to other fees, per day,	1 00
Writ of restitution, including execution for costs,	25
Rule to take deposition, when the witness is out of the Territory,	25
For every execution	25
Transcript of judgment, per 100 words,	15
For hearing any matter wherein a jury is called	25
For administering an oath out of Court	15
When Justices are called from their offices, mileage, per mile,	5
Copy of the proceedings in any case	10
Certificate thereof	15

Affidavit for attachment	15
For renewing execution	10

SEC. 6.—And be it further enacted that the fees of Justices of the Peace in criminal cases shall be,

For warrant or search warrant	25
Commitment to jail	15
For affidavit	15
Taking recognizance	25
Entering judgment for fine or punishment	25
Order of discharge to Jailor	25
For other services, fees as in civil cases.	

SEC. 7.—And be it further enacted that the fees of a Justice of the Peace, when acting as Coroner, to be paid by the estate of the deceased when solvent, shall be,

For summoning and swearing a jury	50
For issuing subpœna or warrant	25
For viewing each body, taking and returning inquest to Probate Court	5 00
For other services and expenses an allowance may be made by the County Courts, not exceeding	12 00

SEC. 8.—And be it further enacted that fees of Constables in civil and criminal cases shall be,

For serving summons, for each person therein named,	25
For serving warrant	25
Copy of every summons or warrant	15
Traveling to and from place of service, per mile	5
Summoning a jury	50
Attending the same on trial	50
For serving execution	25
Advertising and selling property	75
Advertising without selling	25
For notifying plaintiff of service	20
Return of execution, when no levy is made	10
Each notice of attachment being issued,	15
Bond for the same	25
For serving attachment	50
On all sums collected and paid over on executions	7 per cent.
Serving subpœna	15
Commitment to prison	25

SEC. 9.—And be it further enacted that witnesses' fees shall be,

Each witness for a day's attendance before a District or Probate Court	50
Attendance before a Justice of the Peace, per day	50
Mileage, per mile	5

Provided that no witness shall be compelled to attend any Court in civil cases, unless he shall receive in advance, from the party subpœning him, his mileage going and returning, and his fee for one day's attendance, and shall not be required to remain in court longer than one day, unless he is paid in advance for each day's attendance.

SEC. 10.—Be it further enacted that jurors' fees shall be,

For grand jurors, per day, to be paid by the proper county	75
Petit jurors, per day	75
Mileage, per mile	5
Jurors each day before a Justice of the Peace	50

SEC. 11.—And be it further enacted that fees of Judges of Probate shall be,

For granting letters of administrators or probate of wills	1 00
When the same are contested	1 00
Hearing a complaint against spendthrift or lunatic	1 00
Appointing a guardian for minor or lunatic	50
Decree for probate of will	75
When contested	1 00
Decree for settlement of estate	50
Order for distribution	50
Examining and allowing inventory, for the first page	25
Every succeding page	10
Any writ or process issued under seal	25
Examining and allowing accounts, not exceeding one page	25
Every additional page	10
Warrant to appraise or divide estate	25
Isssuing commission to receive and examine claims of creditors, when an estate is represented insolvent	25
Allowing an appeal	25
Approving securities of executor or administrator	25
Assigning personal estate to widow	25
Assignment of dower in real estate	25
Disallowance of application for letters of administration or probate of will, to be paid by the losing party	75
For every continuance	15
Order for sale of personal estate	25
Certificate of necessity for sale of real estate	25
Extending letters of administration	50
For bonds upon letters of administration or appointment of guardian	50
Probate of will and letters testamentary thereon	50
Drawing a decree respecting the probate of will or codicil	50

Bond for the execution	25
Drawing order of distribution	25
A quietus	25
Filing each paper	5
Administering an oath	5
Recording all papers required by law to be recorded, for every one hundred words	15
Appeal or other bonds	25
A warrant to divide an intestate estate among the heirs, a warrant to set off the widow's dower, or a warrant to receive and examine the claims of an insolvent estate	25
A citation or summons for the first person named therein	25
Each other person named therein	10
Entering and filing a caveat	15
To apportion an insolvent estate among the creditors	75
Seal to an exemplification	15
When a translation of any will, deed or other writing is required, he shall be entitled to receive for every one hundred words	25
When sitting on civil or criminal cases, per day	3 00
Hearing each divorce case	5 00

SEC. 12.—Be it further enacted that the fees of Notaries Public shall be,

For every protest with seal	1 00
Attesting letters of attorney and seal	50
Drawing and taking proof and acknowledgment of any legal instrument not exceeding two pages	1 00
Certifying power of attorney	25
Affidavit with seal	25
Registering protest of bill of exchange	50
For non-acceptance or non-payment	50
Drawing and certifying affidavit	25
Each oath or affirmation	10
Every certificate	25
Being present at demand, tender or deposit	50

Other fees the same as are allowed other officers in similar cases.

SEC. 13.—In all cases of criminal prosecution, where the complainant is not an eye witness of the crime alleged, and the defendant is not found guilty on trial, the complainant shall pay the costs, unless probable cause shall have been shown in said trial; and all persons found guilty of crime, upon trial, shall pay the costs, except where the party is insolvent, in which case a County Court may authorize the payment of said costs, or such part thereof as their discretion shall dictate, out of the county treasury: Provided, that a County Court shall not appropriate more than one-third of the county revenue to defray the expenses of Courts for any one year; and that, in all appropriations of a County Court for Court expenses, that of dieting prisoners shall have the precedence.

SEC. 14.—The Territorial Marshal, or a Sheriff, or either of their Deputies shall be allowed one dollar and fifty cents a day for every day he shall attend upon the Supreme Court, which compensation may be paid from the Territorial treasury.

SEC. 15.—A Sheriff shall be allowed one dollar for every day he is required to attend and does so attend a District Court, which may be paid out of the county treasury of the proper county: Provided that, if a District Court shall deem it expedient, said Court may make an order to command any number of Constables to attend said Court, not exceeding three, to be entitled to one dollar per day each for every day such constables shall actually attend; and said order shall be entered on the record.

SEC. 16.—Fees of Prosecuting Attorneys in the District and Probate Courts shall be

For drawing an indictment	75
For attendance on the grand jury, for each indictment	50
For prosecuting each criminal	3 00
For entering nolle prosequi	1 00
For replying to motion to quash	25
Replying to demurrer	25
Attendance on District Court, per day,	1 00
Attendance on Probate Court, per day,	75

That in all cases where fees shall not be collected from complainant or defendant, the County Court is authorized to pay not exceeding fifty per cent. of the above costs of Attorneys from the county treasury; and the Attorney General may also receive from the territorial treasurer a sum not exceeding $50 annually, for services rendered in suits to which the Territory is a party.

SEC. 17.—When two or more persons are served, mileage shall be computed by the officer only from the most remote place, unless the places are in opposite directions; and a successful party in any suit shall in no case recover the costs of more than two witnesses to one fact.

SEC. 18.—If any officer shall wilfully or corruptly take greater fees than are herein before expressed and limited, for any service, to be done by him in his office, such officer, for every such offense, shall, on conviction thereof before any Justice of the Peace of the proper county, forfeit and pay into the county treasury a sum not exceeding ninety dollars.

Approved January 21, 1859.

CHAPTER XXXVII.

RESOLUTION in relation to Recorder of Marks and Brands.

Resolved by the Governor and Legislative Assembly of the Territory of Utah: That the sum of two hundred and fifty-eight dollars and sixty-four cents be appropriated, out of any moneys in the Treasury not otherwise appropriated, to pay the Recorder of Marks and Brands for the expense incurred for the publication of the books containing the marks and brands; and that the said books; brand sheets and characters and property pertaining to said office become the property of the Territory.

Approved Jan. 14, 1857.

CHAPTER XXXVIII.

An ACT to provide for the appointment of a Territorial Treasurer and Auditor of Public Accounts.

SEC. 1.—Be it enacted by the Governor and Legislative Assembly of the Territory of Utah: That a treasurer and auditor of public accounts shall be elected, by the joint vote of both houses of the Legislative Assembly, whose term of office shall be one year, and until their successors are elected and qualified.

SEC. 2.—The Treasurer, previous to entering upon the duties of his office, shall give bonds to the people of the Territory of Utah, in the penal sum of twenty thousand dollars; which sum shall be increased at the discretion of the Legislative Assembly, or during its recess, by the Governor, with sufficient securities, to be approved by the Governor; which bonds shall be filed in the office of the Secretary of the Territory of Utah; and shall also take an oath or affirmation to support the Constitution of the United States, and faithfully discharge the duties of his office.

SEC. 3.—The Treasurer shall receive all moneys or other property belonging to the Territory that may be raised by taxation or otherwise; and shall procure suitable books in which he shall enter an account of his receipts and disbursements, to whom made, and on what account.

SEC. 4.—The Treasurer shall pay all moneys that may come into his hands, by virtue of his office, upon drafts or orders countersigned by the auditor of public accounts; and shall annually report to the Governor, on or before the first day of November, or oftener, if required by the Governor, a true account of his receipts and disbursements, with the necessary vouchers for the same; and shall deliver to his successor in office, all books, moneys, accounts, or other property belonging to the Territory, so soon as his successor shall become qualified.

SEC. 5.—The auditor of public accounts, previous to entering upon the duties of his office, shall give bonds to the people of the Territory of Utah, in the penal sum of five thousand dollars, which sum may be increased at the discretion of the Legislature, or during its recess, by the Governor, with sufficient securities to be approved by the Governor; and shall also take an oath or affirmation, to support the Constitution of the United States, and faithfully discharge the duties of his office.

SEC. 6.—The auditor of public accounts shall examine and audit all public accounts connected with the pecuniary affairs of the Territory, and shall report the same to the Governor, on or before the first day of November in each year, and oftener if required by the Governor, and shall deliver to his successor in office, all books, moneys, accounts, or other property, belonging to the Territory, so soon as his successor shall become qualified.

SEC. 7.—It shall be the duty of all Territorial officers having the handling of the public funds, in either collecting or disbursing the same, (when not otherwise provided for by law) to make a report to the auditor of public accounts, on or before the first day of October in each year.

SEC. 8.—Vacancies may be filled by executive appointment in the foregoing, or any offices, when the mode of supplying vacancies is not prescribed by law.

Approved January 20, 1852.

———:o:———

CHAPTER XXXIX.

An ACT authorizing and empowering the Secretary of the Territory to receive and collect fees in certain cases.

SEC. 1—Be it enacted by the Governor and Legislative Assembly of the Territory of Utah: That the Secretary of the Territory is hereby authorized to receive and empowered to collect a fee not exceeding one dollar, to be paid to him, in every case, by the party or parties at whose instance he shall certify, under his official seal, to the official acts and authority of any Judge of the Probate Courts, Justice of the Peace, Notary Public, or other public officer of the said Territory: Provided, that the said certificate be not connected with the public business, but designed to promote the private interest of the said party or parties.

SEC. 2.—That the Secretary of the Territory is hereby authorized to receive of any person who may be hereafter appointed a Commissioner of Deeds for the Territory of Utah, in any other State or Territory, a fee not exceeding five dollars for issuing to the said appointee his commission as said commissioner.

SEC. 3.—That nothing in the preceding sections shall be construed to authorize the Secretary of the Territory to demand any fee for issuing any commission in the case of any officer elected or appointed under the laws of said Territory, save in the case covered by section second.

Approved January 18, 1861.

———:o:———

CHAPTER XL.

An ORDINANCE providing for State and County Road Commissioners.

SEC. 1.—Be it ordained by the General Assembly of the State of Deseret: That a State Road Commissioner shall be elected by the General Assembly, whose term of office shall be one year, and until his successor is elected and qualified; who shall take an oath and give bond with security for the faithful performance of the duties of his office; which bond shall be approved by the Auditor of Public Accounts, and filed in his office.

SEC. 2.—Whenever the General Assembly shall grant a State road, from one given point to another, it shall be the duty of the State Road Commissioner to institute a speedy survey for said road, on the most feasible and practicable route, having special reference to public convenience, utility and durability; showing distances, altitude of hill, soils, rivers, ravines and all such like information relating to convenience and expense, and report the same with all reasonable dispatch to the Governor, who with the Commissioner, shall decide on the location of said road, and all such, and other maps and reports; and maps, and reports of all surveys made by the State Road Commissioner, shall be filed in the office of the Secretary of State, within a reasonable time.

SEC. 3.—If it shall appear evident that there is but one feasible route for any road granted by the General Assembly, or if the Governor shall instruct the Commissioner to locate any given road on any particular route, previous to a survey; then it shall be the duty of the Commissioner to locate said road without delay, and file a report of each and every location of a State road, in the Secretary's office, as in the second section.

SEC. 4.—It shall be the duty of State Road Commissioners to make all contracts for building bridges, acqueducts culverts, turnpikes and all other fixtures necessary for the completion of any public road, located by himself or predecessors in office, yet remaining uncompleted, and draw upon the public Treasury for such money as shall from time to time be granted by the General Assembly for the payment of said contracts; keep an accurate account of all sums of money by him received, and how expended, and make a true report of the same, on or before the first of December of each year to the Auditor of Public Accounts.

SEC. 5.—The County Court in each county, shall have power to appoint one or more Road Commissioners whenever they shall deem it necessary, to locate all county roads within the limits of said county, whose term of office shall be two years, and until their successors are appointed and qualified. They shall also give bond and security for the faithful performance of the duties of their office, to be approved by the Clerk of said court, and filed in his office.

SEC. 6.—It shall be the duty of all County Road Commissioners so appointed to make all contracts for improvements upon all such roads, locating the same upon the most judicious routes, and keep and make a true and full report of all their proceedings, and lay the same before the county court at each regular session of the same; and before they shall cease to officiate in said office file all such reports in the office of the Clerk of the county court.

SEC. 7.—The Commissioners herein provided for shall locate all roads herein contemplated, upon such ground as shall be most conducive to the public benefit, and have power to open the same through enclosures, farming lands, &c., where necessary.

SEC. 8.—Any person feeling him or herself damaged by the opening of any such road, through or across their premises, may have the same appraised by three judicious men, who shall in calculating such damages, also consider the benefit accruing to said premises in consideration of said road, and if it shall appear that the premises, through which said road shall pass, are damaged more than benefited by the same, the owners thereof may recover the same by an appeal to the county courts, all such amounts to be paid out of the public treasury.

Approved Jan. 15, 1850.

SEC. 3.—The Surveyor General shall keep a record of all surveys made by himself or reported to him by other surveyors in a book suitable for the purpose. He shall also have a general superintendant and supervison of all surveys of land made within the State.

SEC. 4.—It shall be the duty of the Surveyor General, and all County Surveyors, to supervise all surveys made in their respective jurisdiction, that the same may be accurate, and no report shall be filed for record until the same shall be certified to by the Surveyor General or County Surveyor, as being correct.

SEC. 5.—All surveys made in this State shall be made to correspond with the original survey of Great Salt Lake City, and in all new surveys certificates approved by authorized surveyors shall be considered title of possession to the holding of the same for the amount of land therein described.

Approved March 2, 1850.

———:o:———

CHAPTER XLII.

An ACT in relation to Quarantine.

SEC. 1.—Be it enacted by the Governor and Legislative Assembly of the Territory of Utah: That the county courts of the several counties be, and are hereby anthorized to locate quarantine grounds, and to make such quarantine regulations as they may deem proper, to prevent the introduction of contagious diseases and the spread of the same within their jurisdiction.

SEC. 2.—Any person refusing to comply with the requirements of the county courts, or who shall wilfully or knowingly introduce any contagious disease into any settlement, shall be liable to pay a fine of not less than fifty, nor more than one thousand dollars, before any court having jurisdiction.

Approved Jan. 14, 1857.

———:o:———

CHAPTER XLIII.

An ACT creating the office of Sealer of Weights and Measures for the Territory of Utah.

SEC. 1.—Be it enacted by the Governor and Legislative Assembly of the Territory of Utah: That there shall be elected annually by the joint vote of the Legislative Assembly, a Sealer of Weights and Measures, who shall, immediately after receiving official notice of his election, give bonds to be approved by and filed with the Territorial Treasurer, and be commissioned by the Governor as other Territorial officers.

SEC. 2.—It shall be the duty of the person so elected, to procure, so soon as practicible after his election, a full set of weights and measures, which shall be according to the seal and standard of the United States: who shall appoint a deputy in each organized county, on application of the County Court, except the county in which he resides, and shall furnish said deputy with a set of weights and measures at the expense of the county making application.

SEC. 3.—All weights and measures used by millers, merchants or any other dealers in dry or wine measures or other merchandise, shall be guaged and sealed according to said standard by the Territorial Sealer of Weights and Measures or his deputy, who is hereby authorized to demand and collect from any person obtaining from him his official seal, to any weight or measure, a reasonable compensation for the same.

SEC. 4.—Any person dealing in any article of produce or merchandise who shall use weights or measures, other than the standard herein specified, shall be liable to pay a fine of not less than one, nor more than five hundred dollars for each offense, and all damages accruing therefrom to the party injured, by an action before any court having jurisdiction thereof.

Approved Jan. 14, 1857.

——:o:——

CHAPTER XLIV.

RESOLUTION Creating the office of Superintendent of Meteorological Observations, and appropriating money therefor.

Be it resolved by the Governor and Legislative Assembly of the Territory of Utah: That there shall be appointed a Superintendent of Meteorological Observations, whose duty it shall be to take charge of the instruments and apparatus appertaining thereto; to keep a journal of such daily readings and observations as may be required, and furnish monthly reports therefrom for publication; for which service he shall receive a yearly compensation of two hundred dollars, payable quarterly upon the Auditor's warrant drawn upon the Treasurer.

Resolved: That the said Superintendent shall be appointed and removed at pleasure by the Governor; shall be under the direction and control of the Governor, and of the Chancellor of the University of the State of Deseret, and shall keep his office and take his observations in Great Salt Lake City.

Approved Jan. 15, 1857.

——:o:——

CHAPTER XLV.

An ACT in relation to Utah Library.

SEC. 1.—Be it enacted by the Governor and Legislative Assembly of the Territory of Utah: That a Librarian shall be elected by a joint vote of the Legislative Assembly of the Territory of Utah, whose duty it shall be to take charge of the library, (known in law as the Utah Library), as hereinafter prescribed.

SEC. 2.—Said Librarian shall hold his office during the term of one year, or until his successor is appointed, and shall give bonds for the faithful discharge of his duties in the sum of six thousand dollars, and file the same in the office of Secretary of the Territory before entering upon his duties, who may also appoint a deputy as occasion requires to act in his stead under the same restrictions as the principal Librarian.

SEC. 3.—It shall be the duty of the Librarian to cause to be printed at as early a date as practicable, a full and accurate catalogue of all books, maps, globes, charts, papers, apparatus and valuable specimens in any way belonging to said library; also to use dilligent efforts to preserve from waste, loss or damage, any portion of said library.

SEC. 4.—It shall be the duty of the Librarian, for and in behalf of the Territory of Utah, to plant suits, collect fines, prosecute or defend the interests of said library, or otherwise act as a legal plaintiff or defendant in behalf of the Territory, where the interests of the library are concerned.

SEC. 5.—The location of the library shall be at the seat of government of the Territory of Utah; and it shall be the duty of the Librarian to have all the books of the library orderly and properly arranged within the library room, for the use of such officers and persons as are named in the fourteenth section of the Organic Act for Utah Territory, during each session of the Legislative Assembly of Utah: Provided, however, that nothing herein contained shall debar the Librarian, in vacation of the Legislative Assembly, from permitting books, maps and papers being drawn from said library, for professional and scientific purposes by officers of the United States and of Utah Territory, and other citizens of Utah, where the Librarian shall judge the public good may justify.

SEC. 6.—It shall be the duty of the Librarian to let out books for a specified time, and call in the same when due, inflict fines for damage or loss of books, and collect the same, and keep an accurate account of all his official doings in a book kept for that purpose, and make an annual report of the same to the Legislative Assembly of Utah: Provided, that no fine shall be excessive, or more than four times the purchase price of the book or books, for the loss or damage of which the fine may be inflicted.

Approved March 6, 1852.

———:o:———

CHAPTER XLVI.

An ORDINANCE in relation to County Recorders.

SEC. 1.—Be it ordained by the General Assembly of the State of Deseret: That a County Recorder shall be elected at the usual place of holding elections in each organized county of this State, whose term of office shall be four years, and until his successor is qualified.

SEC. 2.—The Recorders in their respective counties shall take an oath of office, and give bond and security to be approved by the County Court, and filed in the County Clerk's office.

SEC. 3.—It shall be the duty of Recorders in their respective counties to provide themselves with good and well bound books suitable for the purpose, and record therein all transfers or conveyances of land or tenements, and all other instruments of writing and documents suitable, necessary and proper to be recorded in a fair and legible manner.

SEC. 4.—The Recorders in their respective counties shall also procure and keep a suitable book for the purpose of recording town and city plats, and plats of all surveys of lands, roads and surveys of public works, whenever the same shall be permanently located, and being within their respective counties.

SEC. 5.—The books of record shall be indexed in alphabetical order, and free to the examination of all persons, and, upon the filing of any paper for record, the Recorder shall endorse upon the back thereof the time of receiving it.

Approved March 2, 1850.

———:o:———

CHAPTER XLVII.

An ACT in relation to County Recorders, and the Acknowledgment of Instruments of Writing.

SEC. 1.—Be it enacted by the Governor and Legislative Assembly of the Territory of Utah: That the County Recorders in their respective counties, shall keep books in which they shall record deeds and all other instruments of writing, necessary and proper to be recorded by letter, line and figure, precisely as they occur therein, and in a fair legible manner; city plats and plats of surveys shall be recorded in the same manner; which books he shall duly transmit to his successor in office.

SEC. 2.—The Judges of the Supreme and Probate Courts, their Clerks, the Clerks of the District Courts, Notaries Public, the Mayors and Aldermen of the several incorporated cities, the County and City Recorders, and Justices of the Peace, in their respective jurisdiction are authorized to take the acknowledgment of deeds, transfers and other instruments of writing.

SEC. 3.—Whenever the acknowledgment of any instruments of writing is made, the officer before whom the acknowledgment is taken shall affix his official signature thereto. The Recorder shall certify on each instrument of writing recorded by him, the book, page and date of the record.

SEC. 4.—The County Recorder shall not record any land to any person on application or by transfer, until a certificate of the survey has been produced that such land has been surveyed, and such certificate of survey has been approved and countersigned by one or more of the Selectmen of the county.

SEC. 5.—One year shall be allowed to persons having land surveyed to enclose and fence said land; and, on their failing to enclose said land within one year, their title to said land shall be nullified; and such land is common, and may be surveyed to any person applying for the same.

SEC. 6.—The Recorder shall be entitled to fifty cents for the first one hundred words, and twenty cents for each subsequent one hundred words, for each instrument of writing recorded by him, including the acknowledgment; and fifteen cents a lot for each plot recorded including the letters and figures thereon, and the certificate of record.

Approved, Jan. 19, 1855.

———:o:———

CHAPTER XLVIII.

An ACT to regulate Surveyors and Surveying.

SEC. 1.—Be it enacted by the Governor and Legislative Assembly of the Territory of Utah; That the office of County Surveyor, be and hereby is created; and that there shall be a County Surveyor to be elected in each county by the qualified voters at the next general election, whose term of office shall be two years, and until his successor in office shall be qualified.

SEC. 2.—The County Surveyor shall, before entering upon the duties of his office, take an oath of office, and give bonds and security, to be approved by the Probate Judge, and to be filed in the office of the Clerk of the Probate Court.

SEC. 3.—The County Surveyor shall, within thirty days after completing any survey, make true copies or diagrams of the same, and transmit one to the Surveyor General, and one to the County Recorder; and give a certificate of such survey to the person for whom it was made, describing the tract, block or lot, and number of acres contained; and such certificate shall be title of possession to the person or persons holding the same.

SEC. 4.—Where any survey has been made within this Territory, and the bounds cannot be identified, and disputes arise between rightful claimants, respecting said lines and bounds, the parties so in dispute, or either of them, may, by notifying the other party, of his, her, or their intention, have a re-survey of said lines so in dispute, to be re-surveyed by either the Surveyor General, or the County Surveyor, at the option of the party, or parties so requiring such re-survey. Should the parties or either of them be dissatisfied with such re-survey, they, or either of them, may, at his, her, or their expense, have another re-survey by both the Surveyor General and County Surveyor, whose duty it shall be to make the re-survey as near like the former survey as they can, and such re-survey shall be final, and establish such bounds.

SEC. 5.—Where any transfer shall be made of any surveyed lands, or part or parts thereof, it shall be the duty of the transferer to certify in writing such transfer to the person to whom the transfer is made, with a full description of what part or parts, how much or length of line or lines, and number of acres, and the person or persons to whom transferred; to legalize a claim to such land, shall within thirty days thereafter cause such transfer to be recorded in the County Recorder's office.

SEC. 6.—If any surveyor shall survey land or lands for the purpose of cultivation, where to irrigate it would rob the previously cultivated lands of their needful portion of water, such last survey shall be void for cultivating purposes.

SEC. 7.—Whenever a surveyor shall survey a piece of land for a joint enclosure, he shall plot, and number the fence around the survey, noting the length of each person's portion of fence.

SEC. 8.—All books, records, plots and papers of surveys made within the Territory, kept by and in the possession of the Surveyor General appertaining to his office, are hereby made the property of the said Territory, and it shall be his duty to transmit the same to his successor in office.

SEC. 9.—Surveyor's fees shall be regulated as follows:

For surveying twenty acres,..$2,00
" thirty acres,... 2,50
" forty acres,... 3,00
" sixty acres,.. 3,50
" eighty acres,.. 4,00
" one hundred acres,.. 4,50
" one hundred and twenty acres,... 4,75
" one hundred and sixty acres,... 5,00
" three hundred and twenty acres,..................................... 6,75
" six hundred and forty acres,.. 8,50

And for traveling to and from, ten cents per mile: Provided, that if more than one piece is surveyed at the same time, in the same place and journey, the traveling fees for mileage shall be apportioned according to equity: Provided, that the route to survey through shall be bad and rough; in such case, the surveyor shall be allowed to charge in proportion, to make it equal to a good route.

Approved March 3, 1852.

———:o:———

CHAPTER XLIX.

An ACT Pertaining to the Duties of County Surveyors.

SEC. 1.—Be it enacted by the Governor and Legislative Assembly of the Territory of Utah: That each County Surveyor shall keep a book, in which shall be recorded all the blocks and lots of each survey by him made; also a record of all certificates by him given, which certificates shall certify the number of block and lot, with the number of acres or square rods in each lot, and to whom given which, when countersigned by one or more of the Selectmen, shall be filed in the County Recorder's Office within thirty days from the date thereof. No certificate shall be valid, unless filed in the Recorder's Office, as provided for in this act. The book thus kept is hereby made the property of the county, and shall be delivered to his successor in office; said record shall be open to the inspection of any person having an interest therein.

SEC. 2.—It shall be the duty of each surveyor to make a sufficient corner (of stone or wood) at the southeast corner of each survey by him made, and make a record of said corner on his return diagrams.

Approved January 19, 1855.

———:o:———

CHAPTER L.

An ACT Concerning County Surveyors.

SEC. 1.—Be it enacted by the Governor and Legislative Assembly of the Territory of Utah: That the County Surveyors, in their respective counties, may appoint one or more deputies, who, before entering upon the duties of their office shall take the oath of office and give bonds and security in like sum and in like manner as their principals, and any survey or surveys made by such deputy or deputies, when certified to by the County Surveyor, shall be valid, the same as if made by the County Surveyor himself in person.

Approved, Jan. 18, 1861.

———:o:———

CHAPTER LI.

An ACT to create the office of a County Treasurer in each county of the Territory of Utah, and to define the duties thereof.

SEC. 1.—Be it enacted by the Governor and Legislative Assembly of the Territory of Utah: That there shall be, and hereby is created the office of County Treasurer in each county of the Territory of Utah.

SEC. 2.—The Treasurer shall be elected by the qualified electors of their respective counties at the time of the general election of the Territory; whose term of office shall be four years, and until his successor shall be elected and qualified; and said Treasurer, before entering upon the duties of his office, shall take an oath or affirmation, before the Clerk of the County Court, to support the Constitution of the United States, and the laws of this Territory; and faithfully discharge the duties of his office, and shall give bonds to the people of their respective counties; the amount of bonds to be prescribed by the County Court, with security, to be approved by said court, for the faithful discharge of the duties of his office, which bonds shall be filed in the office of the Clerk of the County Court.

SEC. 3.—The County Treasurer shall keep an accurate account of all moneys or other property received or disbursed, and shall pay over all demands that shall be legally presented, and shall render a true account, with necessary vouchers for the same, semi-annually to the County Court, or whenever it shall be called for by said court, and his office shall be kept at the county seat.

SEC. 4.—The County Courts are hereby authorized to appoint a County Treasurer in their respective counties, who shall be qualified as provided by this act, to serve until the first general election, and until his successor shall be elected and qualified.

Approved, February 3, 1852.

———:o:———

CHAPTER LII.

An ACT relating to Sheriffs and Constables.

SEC. 1.—Be it enacted by the Governor and Legislative Assembly of the Territory of Utah: That at the next general election, and every two years thereafter, a Sheriff shall be elected in each county, whose term of office shall be two years, and until his successor is qualified.

SEC. 2.—Before entering upon the duties of his office, the Sheriff shall give bonds in at least five thousand dollars, with approved security, and take and subscribe an oath for the faithful performance of his duties; said bonds and oath to be approved by the Probate Judge, and filed in the office of the Country Clerk.

SEC. 3.—The Sheriff may appoint a deputy or deputies, for whose acts he shall be responsible; and who shall qualify in the same manner as the Sheriff, except that the bonds may be in the sum of two thousand dollars each.

SEC. 4.—When a reasonable compensation is tendered or satisfaction given that the costs of service will be seasonably paid, it is the duty of Sheriffs and Constables to faithfully and diligently execute all orders, processes, and requirements of a court, under penalty of whatsoever costs, damages and fine may be adjudged.

Approved Jan. 17, 1854.

———:o:———

CHAPTER LIII.

An ACT prescribing the manner of assessing and collecting Territorial and County Taxes, and for other purposes.

SEC. 1.—Be it enacted by the Governor and Legislative Assembly of the Territory of Utah: That annually at its session in December, each County Court shall appoint an Assessor, who shall also be the Collector, to assess and collect Territorial and County Taxes, and who shall give bonds before entering upon the duties of his office, with approved security, payable to the Territory and County, in at least twice the amount of the taxes to be collected, conditioned for the faithful performance of his duties; and he shall take and subscribe an oath to the like effect; said bond shall be filed with the Probate Judge, and may be increased whenever the County Court shall deem it necessary: Provided, that for the current year Assessors and Collectors may be appointed at any regular or special term of the County Court, and until they are so appointed and qualified, existing Assessors and Collectors are continued in office.

SEC. 2.—An annual assessment shall be made on all taxable property in the several counties of the Territory, between the first day of January and the first Monday in June; property shall be assessed at a fair cash value; and such assessment when so made shall constitute a lien on the property assessed, until such tax is paid, or remitted by the County Court: Provided, that the Assessor and Collector shall assess and collect a tax upon all taxable property brought into this Territory and offered for sale, after the assessment list is completed, at the rates of the regular assessment for the current year. And further provided: That where money may have been assessed and afterwards sent outside of the Territory for the purchase of merchandise or any articles whatever, then the assessment on the cash value of such merchandise or articles shall be decreased by the amount of such purchase money.

SEC. 3.—A Territorial tax of one half of one per cent. on the assessed value of all taxable property in the Territory shall be collected annually, and a county tax, at a rate prescribed by the County Court, not to exceed one half of one per cent. on the assessed value of all taxable property in the County, may be collected annually in each county.

SEC. 4.—As soon as the Assessor and Collector shall have filed his bonds, the County Clerk in each County shall furnish the Assessor and Collector with a suitable book conveniently ruled throughout, and headed as follows:

Names of owners or possessors.	Residence.	Value of land claims and improvements.	Number of Cattle.	Value.	Number of Horses.	Value.	Number of Asses.	Value.	Number of Mules.	Value.	Number of Sheep and Goats.	Value.	Number of Swine.	Value.	Number of Vehicles.	Value.	Number of Clocks and Watches.	Value.	Value of Merchandize.	Value of Stock in Trading and Manufacturing Companies.	Value of Gold Dust and Bullion.	Value of Gold and Silver Ornaments.	Money loaned and on hand.	Value of Taxable Property, not enumerated.	Total value.	Amount of Territorial Tax.	Amount of County Tax.	Amount paid.	Name of payers.	REMARKS.

SEC. 5.—The Assessor and Collector must make his tax list in alphabetical order, and shall pursue that course in his official duties which, in his judgment, will en-

able him to complete the assessment in the most uniform manner and in the shortest time; and to aid him therein may, when necessary, leave with any person, at the residence of the person to be assessed, a copy of the aforesaid heading, with the name of the person required to fill it and a reasonable date on or before which it must be returned written on the back thereof; and any person furnished with said list must comply with its requirements.

SEC. 6.—The Assessor and Collector shall annually present the tax list to the County Court at its June session; and all complaints or error in the assessment may be presented to the Court during said session, when they shall be examined and adjudicated: Provided, that any person desirous of moving his property out of the county, before the proper time for adjudication of such cases, may give notice to the Probate Judge of said county, who may immediately cause a special term, if required, of the Court to be held, and shall adjudicate all such cases as may be presented.

SEC. 7. Immediately after the adjournment of the June session, the Clerk of the Court shall write upon the head of the tax list the Territorial and County rate per cent. for that year, and set each person's amount of the Territorial and County tax in the proper columns opposite his name, and furnish it to the Assessor and Collector, and inform the Territorial Treasurer and the Auditor of Public Accounts of the total amount of the Territorial tax, the name of the Assessor and Collector and the amount allowed for his services, which must be paid by the Territory and County, in proportion to their share of taxes; and safely file the original list with the office records.

SEC. 8.—When the Assessor and Collector receives the tax list, he shall immediately proceed to collect the same, by requiring of each tax-payer his amount of tax, and shall pay the part collected for the County to the County Treasurer once a month, or oftener if required by the County Court; and the part collected for the Territory to the Territorial Treasurer, quarter yearly or oftener if required by said Treasurer; and take receipts for all payments. It shall be the duty of and the Territorial Treasurer may instruct the County Court to audit the Assessor's and Collector's books, and compare the same with the Auditor's receipts which he may have received; and in all cases of neglect or refusal on the part of the Assessor and Collector to pay over to the Treasurers the taxes collected as provided in this section, the County Court is hereby authorized and required to proceed against him in a civil suit on his bonds, and he shall be liable to endictment for embezzlement and, upon conviction thereof, shall be punished by fine in any sum not exceeding twice the amount of the sum so embezzled, or be imprisoned not exceeding five years at daily hard labor, (provided such labor shall be performed by ball and chain attached, whenever the jailor deems it necessary, or both at the discretion of the court having jurisdiction.) The proceeds of such fines to be equally divided between the Territorial and County Treasuries.

SEC. 9.—It shall be the duty of the Auditor of Public Accounts and the Clerks of the County Courts to keep an account with the Assessors and Colllectors, debiting each Collector with the amount of tax, and crediting him with amounts paid in, the amount remitted by the Courts and the compensation allowed for his services.

SEC. 10.—In case any person neglect or refuse to pay his tax when required, the Assessor and Collector is hereby required and empowered to take and sell enough taxable property belonging to the delinquent to pay his tax and the costs of collection. Said property shall be sold to the highest bidder at public sale, after at least six days' public notice shall have been given of the time, place of sale and kind of property to be sold: Provided, proceedings may be staid at any time by the delinquent paying his tax and the amount of costs already accrued. Auditors' warrants shall be received on Territorial taxes, and County orders on County taxes in the respective counties.

SEC. 11.—If necessary, the Assessor and Collector may appoint a Deputy or Deputies to assist him in the discharge of his duties, for whose official acts and compensations he shall be responsible; and the Assessors and Collectors and their Deputies are hereby empowered to administer oaths, when necessary in the assessment of property, and may require any person to give a statement of his property under oath.

SEC. 12.—If at any time after an assessment has been made, it shall appear that any person has undervalued or has not given in a correct statement of his taxable property, the Assessor and Collector is hereby authorized to assess and collect a tax on said property at double the rates per cent. on the current year, fifty per cent. of the penalty to be retained for the benefit of the Assessor and Collector, the balance to be paid over as other taxes to the Territorial and County Treasurer: Provided, that if any Collector, by undue means, shall seek to obtain the fifty per cent. herein provided for, he shall be liable to a suit on his bonds for double the amount of the damage done to any individual thereby.

SEC. 13.—When the public good of any county or any portion thereof requires an expenditure exceeding its revenue, the County Court may, at any general or special election, after at least twenty days' public notice has been given, submit to the tax-payers of the County or portion thereof, for their approval or disapproval, the object of such expenditure, the amount required, and the rate per cent. necessary to raise the amount; and if, upon counting the votes, it shall appear that two-thirds of the votes polled shall be in the affirmative, the County Court may proceed to assess and collect the same in the manner heretofore provided for Territorial and County taxes. Said election shall be held and conducted and returns made in the manner prescribed in an act regulating elections, approved Jan. 3, 1853.

SEC. 14.—The County Court shall during its June session examine the tax list and hear complaints for errors in assessment; and if, in their judgment, all or part of any person's taxes ought to be remitted, the Clerk of the County Court shall write the word remitted against such person's name, with the amount of the remittance, all or in part; and when the examination of the list is completed, the Clerk of the Court shall forthwith report to the Territorial Treasurer and the Auditor of Public Accounts the amount of the Territorial taxes remitted; and said Court at its September session shall again examine said tax list and hear petitions for remittances, and proceed as at the June session in regard to remittances, and, on or before the thirtieth day of November, in each year, the Assessor and Collector shall settle with the Auditor of Public Accounts, and shall pay over to the Territorial Treasurer all delinquent taxes due to the Territory; and the Assessor and Collector is hereby empowered to collect such delinquent taxes for his own benefit: Provided, that the Treasurer may extend to the Assessor and Collector, the time for payment of such delinquencies, at his discretion.

SEC. 15.—The Assessors and Collectors in their respective counties shall establish an office at the county seat, and shall give public notice of the time and place that they will be in attendance to receive taxes; and it shall be the duty of every person owing taxes to pay the same at the office of the Assessor and Collector, on or before the thirtieth day of November.

SEC. 16.—Property belonging to the United States, this Territory, or any county, city, or town thereof, to literary, scientific and benevolent institutions, when used for those purposes, buildings for worship and the grounds and materials and appurtenances thereto belonging, to insane or idiotic persons to the value of one thousand dollars, private libraries, burial grounds and monuments for the dead are exempt from taxation.

SEC. 17.—If any tax-payer or Assessor and Collector shall wilfully neglect or refuse to comply with any requisition of this act he shall, upon conviction, for each offense be liable to a fine not exceeding one hundred dollars, at the discretion of the Court having jurisdiction.

SEC. 18.—Be it further enacted that an act prescribing the manner of assessing and collecting Territorial and County Taxes, approved Jan. 7, 1854, and the amendments to the same in the second section of an Act in relation to the compilation and revision of the laws and resolutions in force in Utah Territory, and embodying certain amendments, approved Jan. 16, 1862, and an act in relation to Territorial, County, City and School taxes, approved Jan. 22, 1864, are hereby repealed.

Approved January 20, 1865.

———:o:———

CHAPTER LIV.

An ACT regulating the passing and meeting of teams on the public highways.

SEC. 1.—Be it enacted by the Governor and Legislative Assembly of the Territory of Utah: That whenever it is necessary for a fast traveling team to pass a slower one, it shall be the duty of the teamster of the slow team to give the other a convenient opportunity to do so, if it can be done without endangering his own.

SEC. 2.—Whenever teams of any kind meet, each shall turn to the right, so as to give the other half of the traveled part of the road, whenever it can be done with safety.

SEC. 3.—Any person neglecting to conform to the provisions of this act shall be liable to pay all damage accruing therefrom, and be fined not exceeding one hundred dollars.

Approved March 3, 1852.

CHAPTER LV.

A PREAMBLE and An ACT for the further relief of Indian Slaves and Prisoners.

Whereas, By reason of the acquisition of Upper California and New Mexico, and the subsequent organization of the Territorial Governments of New Mexico and Utah by the acts of the Congress of the United States, these Territories have organized Governments within and upon what would otherwise be considered Indian territory, and which really is Indian territory so far as the right of soil is involved, thereby presenting the novel feature of a white legalized government on Indian lands: and

Whereas, The laws of the United States in relation to intercourse with Indians are designed for and only applicable to territories and countries under the sole and exclusive jurisdiction ef the United States; and

Whereas, From time immemorial, the practice of purchasing Indian women and children of the Utah tribe of Indians by Mexican traders has been indulged in and carried on by those respective people, until the Indians consider it an allowable traffic, and frequently offer their prisoners or children for sale; and

Whereas, It is a common practice among these Indians to gamble away their own children and women; and it is a well established fact that women and children thus obtained, or obtained by war, or theft, or in any other manner, are by them frequently carried from place to place packed upon horses or mules; lariatted out to subsist upon grass, roots or starve; and are frequently bound with thongs made of raw hide, until their hands and feet become swollen, mutilated, inflamed with pain and wounded, and, when with suffering, cold, hunger and abuse they fall sick so as to become troublesome, are frequently slain by their masters to get rid of them; and

Whereas, They do frequently kill their women and children taken prisoners, either in revenge, or for amusement, or through the influence of tradition, unless they are tempted to exchange them for trade, which they usually do if they have an opportunity; and

Whereas, One family frequently steals the children and women of another family, and such robberies and murders are continually committed, in times of their greatest peace and amity, thus dragging free Indian women and children into Mexican servitude and slavery, or death, to the almost entire extirpation of the whole Indian race; and

Whereas, These inhuman practices are being daily enacted before our eyes in the midst of the white settlements and within the organized counties of the Territory; and when the inhabitants do not purchase or trade for those so offered for sale, they are generally doomed to the most miserable existence, suffering the tortures of every species of cruelty, until death kindly relieves them and closes the revolting scenery:

Wherefore, When all these facts are taken into consideration, it becomes the duty of all humane and christian people to extend unto this degraded and downtrodden race such relief as can be awarded to them, according to their situation and circumstances; it therefore becomes necessary to consider;

First, The circumstances of our location among these savage tribes under the authority of Congress, while yet the Indian title to the soil is left unextinguished not even a treaty having been held by which a partition of territory or country has been made, thereby bringing them into our door-yards, our houses and in contact with our every avocation;

Second, Their situation and our duty towards them, upon the common principles of humanity;

Third, The remedy, or what will be the most conducive to ameliorate their condition, preserve their lives and their liberties, and redeem them from a worse than African bondage. It suggests itself to your committee that to memorialize Congress to provide by some act of national legislation for the new and unparalleled situation of the inhabitants of this Territory, in relation to their intercourse with these Indians, would be one resource prolific in its results for our mutual benefit; and further, that we ask their concurrence in the following enactment, passed by the Legislature of the Territory of Utah, January 31, A. D., 1852, entitled

An ACT for the relief of Indian Slaves and Prisoners.

SEC. 1.—Be it enacted by the Governor and Legislative Assembly of the Territory of Utah: That whenever any white person within any organized county of this Territory shall have any Indian prisoner, child, or woman in his possession, whether by purchase or otherwise, such person shall immediately go, together with such Indian prisoner, child, or woman, before the Selectmen or Probate Judge of the county. If in the opinion of the Selectmen or Probate Judge the person having such Indian prisoner, child, or woman, is a suitable person, and properly qualified to raise or retain and educate said Indian prisoner, child, or woman, it shall be his or their duty to bind out the same by indenture for the term of not exceeding twenty years, at the discretion of the Judge or Selectmen.

SEC. 2.—The Probate Judge or Selectmen shall cause to be written in the indenture the name and age, place where born, name of parents, if known, tribe to which said Indian person belonged, name of the person having him in possession, name of Indian from whom said person was obtained and date of the indenture, a copy of which shall be filed in the Probate Clerk's office.

SEC. 3.—The Selectmen in their respective counties are hereby authorized to obtain such Indian prisoners, children or women, and bind them to some useful avocation.

SEC. 4.—The master to whom the indenture is made is hereby required to send said apprentice to school, if there be a school in the district or vicinity, for the term of three months in each year, at a time when said Indian child shall be between the ages of seven years and sixteen. The master shall clothe his apprentice in a comfortable and becoming manner, according to his, said master's condition in life.

Approved March 7, 1852.

———:0:———

CHAPTER LVI.

An ACT in relation to the assembling of Indians.

SEC. 1.—Be it enacted by the Governor and Legislative Assembly of the Territory of Utah: That if any Indian trader or traders shall, by any notice or previous arrangement, assemble or cause to be assembled any number of Indians within the neighbourhood or immediate vicinity of any white settlement in this Territory, for the purpose of trading with them, to the annoyance of the citizens or any neighbourhood in this Territory he shall be considered as breaking the peace, and may be proceeded against by any citizen of this Territory in a suit at law, and may be fined in any sum not less than twenty-five dollars nor exceeding one thousand dollars, at the discretion of the Court having jurisdiction.

Approved March 3, 1852.

———:0:———

CHAPTER LVII.

An ACT providing for the bridging of Ditches or Sects leading across the Highways.

SEC. 1.—Be it enacted by the Governor and Legislative Assembly of the Territory of Utah: That if any person or persons shall have taken or may hereafter take water out of the natural stream or sect where it is wont to flow, and conduct the same or any part thereof across any public highway or road by means of a ditch or sect, any person or persons so conducting water shall be required to make or cause to be made a good and sufficient culvert, or gravel ford, or bridge over such ditch or sect, and kept the same in repair where the same crosses any such public road or highway, to the acceptance of the Supervisor of the district where the ditch or sect shall have been made.

SEC. 2.—If any person or persons so conducting water shall neglect or refuse to make the necessary bridge, culvert, or ford, agreeably to the provisions of this act, then it shall be the duty of the Supervisor to make or cause to be made a suitable bridge, culvert, or ford across the ditch or sect at the expense of the person or persons so offending, and may recover the same by a suit at law before any court having jurisdiction in the matter.

Approved March 3, 1852.

———:o:———

CHAPTER LVIII.

An ACT in relation to the inspection of Spirituous Liquors.

SEC. 1.—Be it enacted by the Governor and Legislative Assembly of the Territory of Utah: That there shall be and hereby is created the office of a Territorial Inspector of spirituous liquors.

SEC. 2.—The Territorial Inspector of liquors shall be appointed by the Governor, and may be removed at pleasure.

SEC. 3.—All spirituous liquors manufactured or imported into this Territory, before being offered for sale, shall be inspected by the Territorial Inspector of liquors, or his Deputy.

SEC. 4.—It shall be the duty of the Inspector of liquors, or Deputy, to inspect and prove all liquors that he may be called to prove or gague, &c., and attach his mark or seal on the vessels containing the same.

SEC. 5.—Be it further enacted: That Sykes Hydrometer and Scale adopted by the British Board of Excise, July 2nd, 1816, be and is hereby adopted as the standard for the proving spirits in the Territory of Utah.

SEC. 6.—All spirits shall be deemed of the strength which Sykes Hydrometer denotes them.

SEC. 7.—Any person selling spirituous liquors that have not been inspected and approved by the Inspector, or Deputy, according to the provisions of this act, shall forfeit and pay any sum not exceeding five hundred dollars for every such offense, at the discretion of the Court having jurisdiction, to be paid into the Territorial treasury.

Approved Feb. 5, 1852.

———:o:———

CHAPTER LIX.

An ACT regulating Elections.

SEC. 1.—Be it enacted by the Governor and Legislative Assembly of the Territory of Utah: That annually on the first Monday of August there shall be a general election held in each precinct in the several counties, for choosing all officers not otherwise provided for.

SEC. 2.—The County Clerk shall cause a notice of the time and place, and the number and kind of officers to be chosen, to be put up in two public places in each precinct, at least six days before the time of election.

SEC. 3.—The senior Justice of the Peace shall be the Judge of elections in his precinct, and shall appoint one clerk, and furnish the necessary stationery and a ballot box; and, in the absence of a Justice of the Peace, the electors first assembled on the day of election, to the number of six, may appoint some suitable person to act as Judge of that election.

SEC. 4.—The election shall be held from one hour after sunrise until sunset; and no elector shall vote in any precinct excepting where he resides.

SEC. 5.—Each elector shall provide himself with a vote containing the names of the persons he wishes elected and the offices he would have them to fill, and present it neatly folded to the Judge of the election, who shall number and deposit it in the ballot box; the Clerk shall then write the name of the elector, and opposite it the number of his vote.

SEC. 6.—At the close of the election the Judge shall seal up the ballot box and the list of the names of the electors, and transmit the same without delay to the County Clerk.

SEC. 7.—Immediately upon receiving the electoral returns of any precinct, the County Clerk and Probate Judge, or, in his absence, one of the Selectmen shall unseal the list and ballot box, and count and compare the votes with the names on the list, and make a brief abstract of the offices and names voted for, and the number of votes each person received; the ballot box shall then be returned, and the votes and list preserved for reference in case the election of any person shall be contested.

SEC. 8.—When all the returns and abstracts are made the Clerk shall forthwith make a general abstract and post it up in his office, and forward to the Secretary of the Territory a certified copy of the names of the persons voted for, and the number of votes each has received for Territorial offices and furnish each person having the highest number of votes for county and precinct offices a certificate of his election.

SEC. 9.—So soon as all the returns are received, the Secretary, in the presence of the Governor, shall unseal and examine them, and furnish to each person having the highest number of votes for any Territorial office a certificate of his election.

SEC. 10.—If the returns are not made within a reasonable time, the Secretary or County Clerk, as the case may be, shall institute inquiry, which must be promptly responded to, and a new abstract furnished if necessary.

SEC. 11.—Any person designing to contest an election shall make his intentions specifically known in writing to the County Clerk within ten days after the result of the election is known; in which case the Clerk shall retain the votes and lists until the contest is decided; otherwise he shall destroy them.

SEC. 12.—When ties occur, if for a Territorial officer, the Secretary shall determine the election by lot in the presence of the Governor; and if for a county or precinct officer it shall in like manner be determined by the County Clerk in the presence of the Probate Judge.

SEC. 13.—Any person contesting the election of a county or precinct officer shall proceed therein before the County Court, who shall determine the question; all of which shall be done without delay.

SEC. 14.—When a vacancy occurs in Territorial elective offices, the Governor shall order a special election to fill such vacancy; and should a vacancy occur in a county or precinct office, necessary to be filled previous to the general election, the County Court shall fill such vacancy by appointment.

SEC. 15.—All officers acting in elections shall be allowed a reasonable compensation for their services, and shall be punished with a reasonable preventive amount of fine for fraud or negligence, by any court having jurisdiction.

Approved Jan. 3, 1853.

———:0:———

CHAPTER LX.

An ACT concerning certain Animals running at large.

SEC. 1.—Be it enacted by the Governor and Legislative Assembly of the Territory of Utah: That after the first day of March next, any stud horse, jack, or ridgil over the age of eighteen months, found running at large, may be forfeited, and the proceeds paid into the Emigrating Poor Fund.

SEC. 2.—Any ram over three months old, found running at large within any settlement from the first day of June to the first day of October in each year, may be forfeited, and the proceeds paid as in section 1.

SEC. 3.—If any person allow his sheep to run at large in any agricultural settlement, he may be compelled to pay for all damages they may do, by any Court having jurisdiction.

———:o:———

CHAPTER LXI.

An ACT pertaining to Damage done by Animals.

SEC. 1.—Be it enacted by the Governor and Legislative Assembly of the Territory of Utah: That owners of horses, mules, cattle, hogs, sheep and all other domestic animals shall be held liable to pay all damage done by said animals upon the premises of other persons, whether said premises are protected by fence or not.

SEC. 2.—Upon petition stating that a specified region in any county is better adapted to grazing than to other agricultural purposes, if the County Court of said county so decide, then the first section of this act shall be inoperative within said specified region during such time as said Court in their judgment may determine.

SEC. 3.—Any county in this Territory declaring, by a vote of two-thirds majority of its legal voters, in favor of fencing their farms and of allowing their stock to run at large, may do so, by the County Court's calling a special election for that purpose. In such case, the foregoing sections of this act shall be inoperative and void, provided the stock owned in any such county shall be liable for all damage they may do to any crops growing in an adjoining county that may not have declared by vote its exemption from the provisions of the foregoing sections of this act.

SEC. 4.—All laws or parts of laws conflicting with this act are hereby repealed.

Approved January 19, 1865.

———:o:———

CHAPTER LXII.

An ACT regulating herdsmen, herding, herd grounds, and the driving of animals.

SEC. 1.—Be it enacted by the Governor and Legislative Assembly of the Territory of Utah: That every person, before engaging in the business of herding, shall give bonds with security, and take and subscribe an oath, conditioned for the faithful performance of his duty and for the indemnifying for all loss of time or animals through his neglect; said bonds and security to be given to the acceptance of the Probate Judge of the county where the herd ground is to be located, and with the oath to be filed in his office, and may be altered or others given on the requirement of said Judge; and when said bonds and oath are accepted and filed, the Probate Judge shall grant the applicant a license to herd for a period not exceeding one year next ensuing after the date of the location of the herd ground.

SEC. 2.—When a license to herd is presented to a County Court, said Court shall give a certificate granting the holder of the license the right to employ a Surveyor to designate the boundaries of the desired herd ground, and specifying the locality and, as near as may be, the size of said herd ground, a plot of which must be made by the Surveyor, and a copy thereof filed in the office of the County Clerk as soon as practicable.

SEC. 3.—No herd ground shall be so located as to interfere with any previous rights, nor with the range necessary for the animals of any settler or settlement.

SEC. 4.—All herdsmen shall be responsible for the safe keeping and return of animals placed in their care; and if any such animal dies or is missing by neglect, the owner thereof has claim on the herdsmen for its value, and for any damage that may have accrued from its loss.

SEC. 5.—Improvements on herd grounds are all pertaining to them which can be sold or transferred, and no improvements shall be construed to imply any claim for herding purposes after the expiration of the time specified in the license.

SEC. 6.—Any person driving animals shall use due diligence to prevent driving those not in his care; and if he cannot prevent such animals from mingling, he shall leave them in the first estray pound or yard or inclosure for animals that he can obtain, and notify the owner, if known, and if not, some resident, of the number, kind and brief description of the animals which have mingled with his, and where he has left them.

SEC. 7.—Any person driving animals into this Territory shall, on arrival in the settlements, have them marked or branded, if they are not, and forthwith report his mark or brand and the number of his animals, specifying the number of each hind; and as soon as possible report, over his signature, said number and mark or brand to the Clerk of the County Court of the first organized county which he reaches.

SEC. 8.—In case that any herd shall be found upon the range in the neighborhood or vicinity of any settlement in this Territory, encroaching or intruding upon the range necessary for the animals of such settlement, and the owner of such herd shall refuse or neglect to remove the same, when required so to do by a Selectman of the proper county, the County Court of such county is hereby authorized, at the expense of the owner of such herd, to cause the same to be removed to some more distant locality beyond the limits of the summer and winter range or hay grounds necessary for the support of the stock of that or any other settlement.

SEC. 9.—Any person failing to comply with the requirements contained in this act is liable for all cost and damage arising from his neglect, and to be fined at the discretion of any court having jurisdiction.

Approved Jan. 18, 1854.

———:o:———

CHAPTER LXIII.

An ACT specifying the time when Acts and Resolutions begin to be in force and making them equally valid.

Be it enacted by the Governor and Legislative Assembly of the Territory of Utah: That each act and resolution is in force from the date of its publication in any public manner, unless a certain time is specified; and resolutions are equally valid with acts.

Approved January 19, 1854.

———:o:———

CHAPTER LXIV.

An ACT concerning transfer of land claims and other property.

SEC. 1.—Be it enacted by the Governor and Legislative Assembly of the Territory of Utah: That the transfer of a land claim with the improvements thereon must be

substantially in form as follows:...Be it known by these presents that......................
..................of.......................................the rightful claimant and owner of [here describe the property and its location, and, if required, any peculiar rights and appurtenances] do for the sum of...............................dollars paid by.......................
......................of.......................................; or in consideration of.........................
good will to..........................., (as the case may be) transfer all my claim to and ownership of the aforesaid property to the said.. heirs and assigns. Dated this.........................day of..............................in the year...............

SEC. 2.—To be valid, a transfer must be witnessed by two or more competent persons, be acknowledged before some person authorized to take acknowledgments; be recorded; and the record, page and book be certified thereon by the recorder in the county where the property is located.

SEC. 3.—Other property than land claims and the improvements thereon, when disposed of by gift, must be transferred substantially in the same manner, and by specification of kind and number or amount, but, unless required, the details may be omitted.

SEC. 4.—Any person or body corporate, legally authorized to purchase and dispose of property, may transfer to any other person or body corporate all rightful claim and ownership of property by gift, and such transfer is and shall be deemed valid and a bar to all claims whatever, except just liabilities incurred previous to the time of transfer.

Approved Jan. 18, 1855.

———:o:———

CHAPTER LXV.

An ACT concerning Partnership.

SEC. 1.—Be it enacted by the Governor and Legislative Assembly of the Territory of Utah: That the private property of persons engaged in co-partnerships shall be held liable for the debts of the firm, when the partnership property shall prove insufficient to pay them.

SEC. 2.—The assignment of any partner in trade, made to secure or satisfy a creditor of such firm, shall be deemed valid in law.

SEC. 3.—This act shall not be so construed as to authorize the assignment of any of the effects of such copartnership to satisfy the individual claim of any of the parties, or other than such debts as are incurred for the effects or proceeds thereof thus assigned.

Approved Jan. 14, 1857.

———:o:———

CHAPTER LXVI.

An ACT to provide for the selection and location of a quantity of Land, [illegible] two townships, for the establishment of a University.

SEC. 1.—Be it enacted by the Governor and Legislative Assembly [illegible] of Utah: That there shall be elected by the [illegible] tion to be held on the first [illegible] subsequent said general election, a [illegible] to select and [illegible] quantity of land equal [illegible] third section of an Act of Congress entitled "An Act to establish the office of Surveyor General of Utah, and to grant land for School and University purposes," approved Feb. 21, 1855.

SEC. 2.—Said Commissioners, after being duly sworn faithfully to discharge their duties, shall proceed, as soon as practicable after the land shall have been surveyed, to select and locate such lands in such manner as they shall deem proper, or as the Legislative Assembly may direct; and they shall, from time to time, inform the Surveyor General of the precise tract or tracts so selected or located, or, should the Surveyor General's office be closed, they shall in like manner inform the Register of the land office in the district where said tract or tracts are selected or located by them; and shall annually report and present a schedule of the sections or tracts of lands selected by them and approved by the Surveyor General, or by a Register or Registers of public lands, as the case may be, to the Legislative Assembly.

SEC. 3.—Said Commissioners shall receive, out of the Territorial Treasury, out of any money not otherwise appropriated, such compensation as may be allowed by the Legislative Assembly, and shall keep a suitable book, in which they shall enter and record the numbers of the sections, or the part or parts thereof, so located by them; and shall transmit to their successors in office all books and papers appertaining to the location of said lands.

Approved Jan. 21, 1859.

———:o:———

CHAPTER LXVII.

An ACT in relation to the entering of Public Lands.

SEC. 1.—Be it enacted by the Governor and Legislative Assembly of the Territory of Utah: That, so soon as a land office shall be established in this Territory, it shall be the duty of the County Courts, respectively, to select and enter a quarter section of land for county purposes, as contemplated in an act of Congress entitled an "Act granting to the counties or parishes of each State and Territory of the United States, in which the public lands are situated, the right of pre-emption to quarter sections of land for seats of justice within the same." Approved May 26, 1824.

SEC. 2.—And be it further enacted that, on petition of the residents of any unincorporated town to the County Court, it shall be the duty of said Court to select and enter, at the proper land office, not exceeding one half section of the land so occupied, for the several use and benefit of the rightful claimants thereof, according to their respective interests, as contemplated in an act of Congress entitled "An Act for the relief of citizens of towns upon the public lands of the United States under certain circumstances." "Approved May 23, 1844:" Provided the requisite amount of means or money necessary for the purchase of said lands and the incidental expenses accruing therefrom be furnished and delivered to the Court by the rightful claimants to said lands.

SEC. 3.—The County Courts, respectively, acting as trustees under the provisions of this act, are hereby authorized and required, on application of the rightful claimants, to execute transfers of said lands held by them in trust, which transfers shall be valid in law; and are further empowered to adopt such rules and regulations as may be necessary to carry into effect the provisions of this act: Provided such rules and regulations do not conflict with the Constitution and laws of the United States and the laws of this Territory.

SEC. 4.—Be it further enacted that the provisions of this act, so far as applicable, shall apply to the corporate authorities of incorporated towns and cities.

Approved Jan. 21, 1859.

CHAPTER LXVIII.

Resolution in relation to notifying persons elected to office by joint vote of the Assembly.

Be it resolved by the Governor and Legislative Assembly of the Territory of Utah: That it shall be the duty of the Secretary of the Council and the Chief Clerk of the House to issue a certificate to each person elected by the joint vote of the Legislative Assembly, notifying them of the office to which they have been elected.

Approved Feb. 21, 1859.

———:0:———

CHAPTER LXIX.

An ACT Regulating the Manufacture, Sale or Other Disposal of Intoxicating Liquors.

SEC. 1.—Be it enacted by the Governor and Legislative Assembly of the Territory of Utah: That, on and after the first Monday of March, eighteen hundred and sixty, no person shall be permitted to manufacture, sell, barter or otherwise dispose of any spirituous, vinous or malt liquors, without first obtaining license therefor, as hereinafter provided.

SEC. 2.—The County Courts in their respective counties are hereby authorized to grant licenses, as contemplated in the first section of this act: Provided, always, that said courts shall be fully satisfied that the applicant or applicants are of good moral character, safe and proper persons to be intrusted with the aforesaid business, and that it is expedient for the public good to grant such licenses.

SEC. 3.—Said County Courts shall fix the price of any and every such license by them granted, and shall require payment for the same invariably in advance; upon the applicants presenting the County Treasurer's receipt for the sum required by the Court for such license, the said Court may issue or cause to be issued the desired license, for any term not exceeding one year.

SEC. 4.—The place where any liquors named in the first section of this act are intended to be manufactured, sold, bartered or otherwise disposed of, shall be named or described in the license; which license shall also state the kind or kinds of liquors to be manufactured, sold, bartered or disposed of; and said County Courts may annul any such license at pleasure for a violation of this act, or the terms of the license, or whenever they shall deem the public good requires it.

SEC. 5.—No such license shall be transferable, unless sanctioned by the County Court; and the said Courts shall cause to be endorsed on the back of every such license granted by them these words, "not transferable, unless sanctioned by the county court," which shall be officially signed by the Clerk.

SEC. 6.—If any person shall violate the provisions of any of the preceding sections of this act, he shall forfeit and pay, for the use of the county wherein such violation shall have been committed, upon complaint of any citizen of the county before any Justice of the Peace having jurisdiction, any sum not exceeding one hundred dollars for each and every such violation, to be recovered as an action of debt.

SEC. 7.—If any person shall barter, sell or dispose of any intoxicating liquors on the day of the week commonly called Sunday, he shall forfeit and pay, for the use of the county wherein such offense shall have been committed, any sum not exceeding twenty dollars for each offence, upon complaint of any citizen thereof, to be recovered as provided for in the sixth section of this act.

SEC. 8.—No provision of this act shall be so construed as to interfere in any way with the rights of the municipal authorities of incorporated towns and cities.

Approved January 20, 1860.

CHAPTER LXX.

An ACT in Relation to the Penitentiary.

Sec. 1.—Be it enacted by the Governor and Legislative Assembly of the Territory of Utah: That the office termed "Inspectors of the Penitentiary," created by "an act in relation to the Penitentiary," approved Jan. 16, 1855, shall hereafter be styled, "Board of Directors of the Utah Penitentiary."

Sec. 2.—The Penitentiary shall be under the control of a board of three Directors, who shall be elected by the joint vote of the Legislative Assembly, and whose term of office shall be one year, and until their successors are elected and qualified. Said Directors shall, before entering upon the duties of their office, qualify by giving bonds with security to the people of the Territory of Utah, in the penal sum of one thousand dollars each, conditioned for the faithful performance of the duties of their office, to be approved by and filed with the Auditor of Public Accounts; and the same may be increased, when in the Auditor's judgment the public good requires it.

Sec. 3.—There shall be elected annually, by the joint vote of the Legislative Assembly, a Warden whose term of office shall be one year, and until his successor shall be elected and qualified; said Warden shall qualify by taking and subscribing an oath to faithfully perform the duties of his office according to law, and give bonds in the penal sum of ten thousand dollars, in the same manner as prescribed for the Directors in section second to this act.

Sec. 4.—The Directors shall appoint one of their number President of the Board, a majority of whom shall form a quorum for business; they shall appoint a Clerk, Overseers, Guards and all other necessary officers for the Penitentiary, not otherwise provided for; and all persons so appointed may be required by the Directors to give bonds, with security, to the people of the Territory of Utah, which bonds shall be approved by and filed with the Auditor of public accounts.

Sec. 5.—It shall be the duty of the Directors to visit the Penitentiary as often as they may deem it necessary, to examine and inquire into all matters connected with the government and discipline thereof; and to give necessary directions to the Warden relative to all matters pertaining thereto; and may require the convicts, who may hereafter be convicted, to labor outside the wall on any public or private works; and when thus employed cause that they be well secured and properly guarded.

Sec. 6.—The Directors shall at all times have free access to all parts of the Penitentiary, and may inspect all books, papers, documents, communications and correspondence pertaining thereto.

Sec. 7.—The Directors shall annually report to the Legislative Assembly, during the first week of its session, the condition of the Penitentiary, the number of convicts, their condition; also for what and how long they were sentenced, specifying how many are Territorial; the fiscal affairs, and all the avails arising from the labor of convicts, and an approximate estimate of the means necessary to defray expenses for the ensuing year.

Sec. 8.—The Warden shall receive and keep all persons duly committed, and not allow them to hold conversation with any person, except in his or the presence of some other officer in charge, and see that the sentence of each prisoner is properly executed, and that they be diligently employed at the labor assigned them.

Sec. 9.—In case any convict or convicts shall offer any violence or resistance to any officer in charge, or do violence to any other convict, attempt to do injury to the buildings or appurtenances thereunto belonging, attempt to escape, resist or disobey any lawful commands, the officers shall defend themselves, enforce the observance of dicipline necessary to secure the persons of offenders and prevent any such aggression or escape of any prisoner; and may punish them at discretion for their misconduct in such manner as shall be prescribed by the Board of Directors.

Sec. 10.—Whenever any convict shall be legally discharged, the Warden may, by the consent of the Directors, furnish for said convict clothing not exceeding in value fifty dollars, and money not exceeding thirty dollars, as may by the Directors be deemed proper and consistent with the emergency of the case.

Sec. 11.—No person shall communicate or deliver to any prisoner any writing, message or package, without the inspection and approval of the Warden: and any person so offending, upon conviction thereof, shall be punished by imprisonment not exceeding six months, or by fine not exceeding one hundred dollars, recoverable before any Court having jurisdiction.

Sec. 12.—Male and female prisoners shall not be kept in the same room, and females shall be under the supervision of a suitable Matron.

Sec. 13.—Whenever any prisoner escapes from custody, the Warden shall use all due diligence for his apprehension, and for this purpose may, under the instruction of the Directors, offer a reward for his arrest and delivery to the Warden of the Penitentiary.

Sec. 14.—In case any contagious disease break out among the convicts, or in case of fire or other casualty from which danger may be apprehended, the Warden may remove the convicts to some safe and convenient place, there to remain in his charge until said danger is past.

Sec. 15.—No spiritous or fermented liquors shall be brought into the Penitentiary for the use of any prisoner, unless prescribed for his health by a physician, in which case he shall specify in writing to the Warden, the quantity and quality of the liquor to be furnished.

Sec. 16.—The Warden shall have power to sue and be sued, defend and be defended in his official capacity, in all Courts of law and equity; to direct all persons employed as Overseers, Guards, Assistants and all minor officers, and, by the consent of the Directors, to appoint a deputy, for whose official acts he is responsible.

Sec. 17.—The Clerk shall be Clerk for the Warden and Directors, and shall record all precepts by which persons are committed, and keep a register of each convict, his name, age, place of birth, particularly describing his person and former occupation, and shall record the time for which he was sentenced, and all contracts and business matters deemed essential by the Directors.

Sec. 18.—Whenever an attempt is made or about to be made to release any convict belonging to the Penitentiary, or to commit any unlawful act upon any person or premises thereunto appertaining, any officer thereof is authorized to summons a sufficient posse in the most summary manner, to repair forthwith to the place where such danger is apprehended, for the purpose of repelling such contemplated invasion. Any person refusing or neglecting to obey said summons or any lawful commands of the officer in charge shall, on conviction thereof, be imprisoned not exceeding six months, nor fined not exceeding one hundred dollars, by any Court having jurisdiction.

Sec. 19.—The Auditor of public accounts, is hereby authorized to issue warrants on the Territorial treasury for the relief of the Warden, his Deputy, or other persons employed in Penitentiary service; also for tools, clothing, furniture and all other necessary supplies to the amount which may be ordered by the Directors, payable out of any money in the treasury appropriated for Penitentiary purposes: Provided, That nothing herein shall be so construed as to justify issuing warrants for official services of the Directors.

Approved January 20, 1869.

———:o:———

CHAPTER LXXI.

An ACT further defining the duties of the Officers of the Penitentiary, and for other purposes.

Sec. 1.—Be it enacted by the Governor and Legislative Assembly of the Territory of Utah: That the Warden of the Penitentiary is hereby authorized and required to advertise, in the consecutive numbers of some newspaper published in Great Salt Lake county for sealed proposals for leasing the Penitentiary for not less than one nor more than three years.

The said advertisement shall set forth the place, day and hour that the proposals shall be opened, and that the Penitentiary, Warden house and other buildings connected therewith or belonging to the Penitentiary will be let, in consideration of which the lessor will for a certain sum take the care and custody of all convicts that are now or may be committed to said Penitentiary during the term of contract, and that the lessee may appoint the Guards, Overseers and other officers that may be necessary to keep safely and securely and to carry out the sentence of the convicts, pay the Guards, Overseers and other officers and assistants by him employed. He shall direct and control the labor of the convicts, and have the avails thereof in addition to the sum set forth in the proposition or article of agreement.

All proposals shall be made under seal, and endorsed proposals for leasing the Penitentiary, addressed to the Warden on or before the day set forth in the advertisement, on which day, and not before, they shall be opened by the Warden in the presence of the Directors and all the bidders who may choose to be present; and the Warden, after reading all the proposals in the presence of the Directors and the bidders, shall submit the several bids to the Directors; the said Directors may thereupon determine which is the best responsible bidder, provided the bidder is a resident citizen of the Territory and of a reputed good, moral character, and will file sufficient bonds with them for the faithful performance of the conditions of the contract; then they shall direct the Warden to accept such bid and file papers accordingly: Provided, it may be at the discretion of the Directors to accept or decline any or all of the bids, if in their judgment the bids are for a greater amount than is reasonable to give, in which case they may proceed as though the first section of this act had not been passed, or they may at any other time thereafter let the Penitentiary as provided in this act.

Sec. 2.—The person whose bid may be accepted and files bonds and takes possession of the premises and tenements, as contemplated in this act, is hereby constituted an Assistant Warden, and, as such, shall file sufficient bonds with security with the Directors, payable to the people of the Territory of Utah, for the faithful performance of his duties as Assistent Warden: Provided he shall not have any claims for services as such Assistant Warden.

Sec. 3.—In the event that the Penitentiary and convicts are not rented as contemplated in this act, the Warden may hire out any or all the convicts under such regulations as may be prescribed by the Directors: Provided such regulations do not conflict with the laws of this Territory.

Sec. 4.—All convicts hereafter sentenced, excepting such as may be sentenced to solitary confinement, may be put to hard labor not exceeding ten hours each day, Sundays excepted, under the regulations that are or may be hereafter prescribed by the Directors.

Approved Jan. 18, 1861.

———:o:———

CHAPTER LXXII.

An ACT concerning the construction and protection of Electric Telegraph Lines in the Territory of Utah.

Sec. 1.—Be it enacted by the Governor and Legislative Assembly of the Territory of Utah: That Hiram Sibley, Isaac Butts, Jeptha H. Wade, Isaac R. Elwood, Charles M. Stebbins, Thomas R. Walker, John H. Beneyhill, Edward Creighton, Samuel L. Selden, John H. Harmon, Albert W. Bee, James S. Graham and Joseph Medeary are hereby granted the privilege of constructing a line or lines of electric telegraph upon and along any of the highways and public roads within the limits of this Territory, by the erection of the necessary fixtures, including posts, piers or abutments for sustaining the wire or wires of such line or lines: Provided the same shall be so constructed as not to discommode, endanger, or interrupt the free, legitimate use of said highways, or of any waters within this Territory.

Sec. 2.—The persons named and designated, as aforesaid, are also authorized to construct their line or lines, and to erect all necessary fixtures therefor, upon any lands in this Territory, subject, however, to the right of the owners or claimants to full compensation for the same; and if said persons or their agents cannot agree with any owner or claimants of the land so taken or used for the compensation to be paid therefor, either of said persons or agents, or such owner or claimant may apply to any Judge of any Court of record within the Territory, by petition, stating the facts and circumstances bearing upon the subject, a copy of which petition shall be served upon the said persons or agents, or upon such owner or claimant, as the case may be, with notice of the time when the same will be presented, at least ten days before the time so fixed; and upon the presentation of the petition, pursuant to such notice, or at any time within twenty days afterwards, such Judge may appoint three disinterested persons to make a just and equitable assessment and appraisal of the loss or damage, if any, which may have been or is likely to be sustained by the owner or claimant in consequence of the use of such lands as hereby authorized; duplicates of which appraisal shall be reduced to writing and signed by the said appraisers, or a majority of them, one copy of which shall be delivered to the owner or claimant of the land, and the other to either or any one of the persons above named or their agents, upon demand; such appraisal to determine either the annual cost or compensation to be paid by the persons named in this act, or by their agents, for the use of the land, or, in lieu thereof, a sum in gross, as the compensation for allowing the fixtures belonging to such persons permanently to continue, and to be repaired and improved from time to time as said persons or their agents may legitimately require; and in case any damage shall be adjudged to such owner or claimant, the persons herein named or their agents shall pay the amount thereof with costs of such appraisal, said costs to be ascertained and determined by the appraisers in their written award: the appraisers to be entitled to two dollars per day, besides expenses, for their services, to be paid by the aforesaid persons or their agents.

Sec. 3.—Every person who shall wilfully injure, molest or destroy any of the lines, wires, posts, piers or abutments belonging to the persons aforesaid, or any other materials or property appertaining to said electric telegraph line or lines within this Territory, or shall wilfully or maliciously interfere with or obstruct in any way the use of such line or lines, or the transmission of messages or communications of any sort upon, along or over the same, or who shall aid, abet, procure or advise any such interference, obstruction or injury, shall upon conviction, be punished for the first offense by imprisonment and sentence to hard labor for a term of one year, or by fine not exceeding five hundred dollars, and for the second offense, by like imprisonment and sentence not exceeding five years, or a fine not exceeding two thousand dollars. Nothing herein contained shall be so construed as to inhibit the Legislature of this Territory from altering, changing or repealing this act.

Approved Jan. 18, 1861.

——:0:——

CHAPTER LXXIII.

An ACT to provide for the organization of Telegraphic Companies.

Sec. 1.—Be it enacted by the Governor and Legislative Assembly of the Territory of Utah: That any number of persons, not less than three, two-thirds of whom must be residents of this Territory, may associate and form a company for the purpose of constructing, owning, holding and working a line or lines of telegraph in this Territory, upon the terms and conditions and subject to the liabilities prescribed in this act.

Sec. 2.—Such persons under their hands shall make a certificate which shall specify:

1st.—The corporate name of the company.

2d.—The general route of the principal line or lines of telegraph, designating the principal points to be connected thereby.

3d.—The amount of the capital stock of the company and the number of shares into which the same shall be divided.

4th.—The names and places of residence of the principal shareholders, and the number of shares subscribed for by each.

5th.—The period of the existence of said company, not to exceed fifty years. Which certificate shall be proved or acknowledged, and filed in the office of the County Clerk of the county in which one of the principal offices of said company shall be established, and a copy or duplicate thereof filed in the office of the Secretary of State.

Sec. 3.—Upon complying with the provisions of the preceding section, such company shall become a body corporate by the name designated in said certificate, and shall be entitled to all the rights and privileges, and subject to the liabilities common to corporations; and a copy of said certificate, certified by the Clerk where the same is filed, or by the Secretary of State, may be used as evidence in all Courts and places.

Sec. 4.—Such company shall have power to purchase, take, receive, hold use and vend to others to be used any patent or patents for telegraphing, and any and all rights thereunder; to purchase, take, receive, hold and maintain any and all rights, privileges and franchises relating to the business of telegraphing; to make, receive by assignment, or ratify by contract or agreement for the building, maintaining, controlling or working of any line or lines of tèlegraph; to construct, purchase, lease, take, receive, hold, control and work any lines for telegraphing within the Territory of Utah; and to purchase, take, lease, hold, own, use and occupy any personal or real estate, rights, property, telegraph lines, grants, franchises and privileges that may be proper or convenient for the complete transaction of its business, or for effectually and conveniently carrying out the objects and purposes of said company. It shall also have power to appoint such directors, officers and agents, and to make such rules, regulations and by-laws as may be necessary or proper in the transaction of its business, and not inconsistent with the laws of this Territory or of the United States.

Sec. 5.—Such company is authorized to construct lines of telegraph along and upon any road or highway, or across any of the waters or over any lands within the limits of this Territory, by the erection of the necessary fixtures, including posts, piers, or abutments, and the appropriation of any standing trees, except fruit and ornamental trees and trees within enclosures, for sustaining the wires of said lines: Provided the same shall not be so constructed as to incommode the public use of said road or highway or injuriously interrupt the navigation of said waters.

Sec. 6.—If any person over whose lands said lines shall pass, upon which posts, piers, or abutments shall be placed, or standing trees appropriated, shall consider himself aggrieved or damaged thereby, it shall be the duty of the Probate Court of the county within which such lands are, on the application of such person and on notice of such appplication being served on the President or any director of such company, to appoint three discreet and disinterested persons as Commissioners, who shall severally take an oath before any person authorized to administer oaths, faithfully and impartially to perform the duties required of them by this act, and it shall be the duty of said Commissioners or a majority of them to make a just and equitable appraisal of all the loss or damage sustained by said applicant by reason of said lines, posts, piers, or abutments, or appropriation of standing trees, duplicates of which said appraisement shall be reduced to writing and signed by said Commissioners or a majority of them; one copy shall be delivered to the applicant and the other to the President or any director or officer of said company or corporation, on demand; and in case any damage shall be adjudged to said applicant, the company or corporation shall pay the amount thereof, with the costs of said appraisal, said costs to be set forth and liquidated with the damages appraised; and said Commissioners shall receive for their services such compensation as the Probate Judge may award, to be paid in like manner as the costs and damages appraised. But in no case shall the person feeling himself aggrieved or injured be entitled to any damage, when application is not made to the Probate Court within six months after the erection of said telegraph lines across the lands of such persons.

Sec. 7.—Any telegraph company may at any time, with the consent of the persons holding two-thirds of the issued stock of said company, sell, lease, assign, transfer and convey any rights, privileges, franchises and property of said company.

Sec. 8.—This act shall not be construed to limit or impair any rights of the California State Telegraph Company.

Approved January 14, 1864.

———:o:———

CHAPTER LXXIV.

An ACT for the Regulation of the Telegraph, and to secure Secrecy and Fidelity in the transmission of Telegraphic Messages.

Sec. 1.—Be it enacted by the Governor and Legislative Assembly of the Territory of Utah: That if any officer, agent, operator, clerk or employee of any telegraph company or any other person, shall wilfully divulge to any other person than the party from whom the same was received, or to whom the same is addressed, or his agent or attorney, any message received or sent or intended to be sent over any telegraph line, or the contents, substance, purport, effect or meaning of such message or any part thereof, or shall wilfully alter any such message by adding thereto or omitting therefrom any word or words, figure or figures, so as to materially change the sense, purport or meaning of such message to the injury of the person sending or desiring to send the same, or to whom the same was directed, the person so offending shall be deemed guilty of a misdemeanor, and shall be punished by fine not to exceed one thousand dollars, or imprisonment not to exceed one year, or by both such fine and imprisonment, in the discretion of the court: Provided, that when numerals or words of number occur in any message, the operator or clerk sending or receiving may express the same in words or in both words and figures, and such fact shall not be deemed an alteration of the message, nor in any manner affect its genuineness, force or validity.

Sec. 2.—If any agent, operator or employee in any telegraph office, or any other person, shall, knowingly and wilfully, send by telegraph to any person or persons any false or forged message purporting to be from such telegraph office, or from any other person, or shall wilfully deliver or cause to be delivered to any person any such message falsely purporting to have been received by telegraph, or if any person or persons shall furnish or conspire to furnish or cause to be furnished to any such agent, operator or employee, to be so sent by telegraph or to be so delivered, any such message, knowing the same to be false or forged, with the intent to deceive, injure or defraud any individual, partnership or corporation or the public, the person or persons so offending shall be deemed guilty of a misdemeanor, and shall be punished by fine not to exceed one thousand dollars, or imprisonment not to exceed one year, or by both such fine and imprisonment, in the discretion of the court.

Sec. 3.—If any agent, operator or employee in any telegraph office shall in any way use or appropriate any information derived by him from any private message or messages passing through his hands, and addressed to any other person or persons, or in any other manner acquired by him by reason of his trust as such agent, operator or employee, or shall trade or speculate upon any such information so obtained, or in any manner turn or attempt to turn the same to his own account, profit or advantage, the person so offending shall be deemed guilty of a misdemeanor, and shall be punished by fine not to exceed one thousand dollars, or imprisonment not to exceed one year, or by both such fine and imprisonment, in the discretion of the Court, and shall also be liable in treble damages to the party aggrieved for all loss or injury sustained by reason of such wrongful act.

Sec. 4.—If any agent, operator or employee in any telegraph office shall unreasonably and wilfully refuse or neglect to send any message received at such office for transmission, or shall unreasonably and wilfully postpone the same out of its order, or shall unreasonably and wilfully refuse or neglect to deliver any message received by telegraph, the person so offending shall be deemed guilty of a misdemeanor, and may be punished by fine not to exceed five hundred dollars, or imprisonment not to exceed six months, or by both such fine and imprisonment, in the discretion of the Court: Provided, that nothing herein contained shall be construed to require any message to be received, transmitted or delivered, unless the charges thereon shall have been paid or tendered, nor to require the sending, receiving or delivery of any message counselling, aiding, abetting or encouraging treason against the Government of the United States or other resistance to lawful authority, or any message calculated to instigate or further any fraudulent plan or purpose, or to instigate or encourage the perpetration of any unlawful act, or to facilitate the escape of any criminal or person accused of crime.

Sec. 5.—If any person not connected with any telegraph office shall, without the authority or consent of the person or persons to whom the same may be directed, wilfully or unlawfully open any sealed envelope inclosing a telegraphic message and addressed to any other person or persons, with the purpose of learning the contents of such message, or shall fraudulently represent any other person or persons, and thereby procure to be delivered to himself any telegraphic message addressed to such other person or persons, with the intent to use, destroy or detain the same from the person or persons entitled to receive such message, the person so offending shall be deemed guilty of a misdemeanor, and shall be punished by fine not to exceed one thousand dollars, or imprisonment not to exceed one year, or by both such fine and imprisonment, in the discretion of the Court, and shall moreover be liable in treble damages to the party injured for all loss and damage sustained by reason of such wrongful act.

Sec 6.—If any person not connected with any telegraphic company shall, by means of any machine, instrument or contrivance, or in any other manner, wilfully and fraudulently read or attempt to read any message, or to learn the contents thereof, whilst the same is being sent over any telegraph line; or shall wilfully and fraudulently or clandestinely learn or attempt to learn the contents or meaning of any message while the same is in any telegraph office, or is being received thereat or sent therefrom; or shall use or attempt to use or communicate to others any information so obtained by any person, the person so offending shall be deemed guilty of a misdemeanor, and shall be punished by fine not to exceed one thousand dollars, or imprisonment not to exceed one year, or by both such fine and imprisonment, in the discretion of the Court.

Sec. 7.—If any person shall, by the payment or promise of any bribe, inducement or reward, procure, or attempt to procure any telegraphic agent, operator or employee to disclose any private message or the contents, purport, substance or meaning thereof; or shall offer to any such agent, operator or employee any bribe, compensation or reward for the disclosure of any private information received by him, by reason of his trust as such agent, operator or employee; or shall use or attempt to use any such information so obtained, the person so offending shall be deemed guilty of a misdemeanor, and shall be punished by fine not to exceed one thousand dollars, or imprisonment not to exceed one year, or by both such fine and imprisonment, in the discretion of the Court.

Sec. 8.—If any person shall wilfully or maliciously cut, break or throw down any telegraph pole or any tree or other material used in any line of telegraph; or shall wilfully or maliciously break, displace or injure any insulator in use in any telegraph line; or shall wilfully or maliciously cut, break or remove from its insulator any wire used as a telegraph line; or shall, by the attachment of a ground wire or by any other contrivance, wilfully destroy the insulation of such telegraph line, or interrupt the transmission of the electric current through the same; or shall in any other manner wilfully injure, molest or destroy any property or materials appertaining to any telegraph line; or shall wilfully interfere with the use of any telegraph line; or obstruct or postpone the transmission of any message over the same; or procure or advise any such injury, interference or obstruction, the person so offending shall be deemed guilty of a misdemeanor, and shall be punished by fine not to exceed five hundred dollars, or imprisonment not to exceed six months, or by both such fine and imprisonment, in the discretion of the Court.

Sec. 9.—Any person offending against the provisions of any section of this Act shall, in addition to the penalties therein prescribed, be liable to the party damaged in a civil suit for all damages occasioned thereby.

Sec. 10.—All operators, clerks and persons in the employ of any telegraph company, whilst employed in the offices of said company or along the route of its telegraph lines, shall be exempt from militia duty and from serving on juries.

Sec. 11.—Contracts made by telegraph shall be deemed to be contracts in writing; and all communications sent by telegraph and signed by the person or persons sending the same, or by his or their authority, shall be held and deemed to be communications in writing.

Sec. 12.—Whenever any notice, information or intelligence, written or otherwise, is required to be given, the same may be given by telegraph: Provided, that the dispatch containing the same be delivered to the person entitled thereto, or to his agent or attorney. Notice by telegraph shall be deemed actual notice.

Sec. 13.—Any power of attorney or other instrument in writing duly proved, or acknowledged and certified so as to be entitled to record, may, together with the certificate of its proof or acknowledgment, be sent by telegraph; and the telegraphic copy or duplicate thereof shall, prima facie, have the same force and effect, in all respects, and may be admitted to record and recorded in the same manner and with like effect as the original.

Sec. 14.—Checks, due bills, promissory notes, bills of exchange and all orders or agreements for the payment or delivery of money or other thing of value, may be made or drawn by telegraph; and when so made or drawn shall have the same force and effect to charge the maker, drawer, indorser or acceptor thereof, and shall create the same rights and equities in favor of the payee, drawer, indorsee, acceptor, holder or bearer thereof, and shall be entitled to the same days of grace, as if duly made or drawn and delivered in writing; but it shall not be lawful for any person, other than the maker or drawer thereof, to cause any such instrument to be sent by telegraph so as to charge any person thereby, except as hereinafter in the next section otherwise provided. Whenever the genuineness or execution of any such instrument received by telegraph shall be denied on oath by or on behalf of the person sought to be charged thereby, it shall be incumbent upon the party claiming under or alleging the same to prove the existence an execution of the original writing from which the telegraphic copy or duplicate was transmitted. The original message shall in all cases be preserved in the telegraph office from which the same is sent.

Sec. 15.—Except as hereinbefore otherwise provided, any instrument in writing, duly certified under his hand and official seal by a Notary Public, Commissioner of Deeds or a Clerk of a Court of record, to be genuine within the personal knowledge of such officer, may, together with such certificate, be sent by telegraph; and the telegraphic copy thereof shall, prima facie only, have the same force, effect and validity, in all respects whatsoever, as the original; and the burden of proof shall rest with the party denying the genuineness or due execution of the original.

Sec. 16.—Whenever any person or persons shall have been indicted or accused on oath of any public offense, or thereof convicted, and a warrant of arrest shall have been issued, the Magistrate issuing such warrant, or any Judge of the Supreme Court, or of any District, County or Probate Court may indorse thereon an order signed by him and authorizing the service thereof by telegraph, and thereupon such warrant and order may be sent by telegraph to any Marshal, Sheriff, Constable or Policeman; and on the receipt of the telegraphic copy thereof by any such officer, he shall have the same authority and be under the same obligation to arrest, take into custody and detain the said person or persons, as if the said original warrant of arrest with the proper direction for the service duly indorsed thereon had been placed in his hands; and the said telegraphic copy shall be entitled to full faith and credit and have the same force and effect in all Courts and places as the original. But prior to indictment or conviction, no such order shall be made by any officer unless in his judgment there is probable cause to believe the said accused person or persons guilty of the offense charged: Provided, the making of such order by any officer, as aforesaid, shall be prima facie evidence of the regularity thereof, and of all proceedings prior thereto. The original warrant and order, or a copy thereof certified by the officer making the order, shall be preserved in the telegraph office from which the same is sent; and in telegraphing the same the original or the said certified copy may be used.

Sec. 17.—Any writ or order in any civil suit or proceeding and all other papers requiring service may be transmitted by telegraph for service in any place, and the telegraphic copy of such writ or order or paper so transmitted may be served or executed by the officer or person to whom it is sent for that purpose and returned by him, if any return be requisite, in the same manner and with the same force and effect in all respects as the originial thereof might be if delivered to him; and the officer or person serving or executing the same shall have the same authority and be subject to the same liabilities as if the said copy were the original. The original, when a writ or order shall also be filed in the Court from which it was issued, and a certified copy thereof shall be preserved in the telegraph office from which it was sent. In sending it, either the original or the certified copy may be used by the operator for that purpose.

Sec. 18.—Whenever any document to be sent by telegraph bears a seal, either private or official, it shall not be necessary for the operator, in sending the same, to telegraph a description of the seal, or any words or device thereon, but the same may be expressed in the telegraphic copy by the letters "L.S.," or by the word "Seal."

Sec. 19.—The President or Secretary of any telegraph company doing business in this Territory may file in the office of the County Clerk of the county in which the prnicipal office of said company within this Territory is situated, a copy of any printed blank or envelope, picture or device, used or intended so to be, by said company, with his certificate that the same is commonly used, or is intended so to be, in the business of said company as a distinguishing mark, notice or index of said business, and thereupon such blank, envelope, picture or device shall become the property of said company; and it shall not be lawful for any person, unless by the employment or permission of said company, to print, publish, distribute or use, or cause to be printed, published, distributed or used, either of them, or any copy, counterfeit, similitude or imitation thereof. Any person willfully offending against the provisions of this section may be punished by fine not to exceed five hundred dollars, or imprisonment not to exceed six months.

Sec. 20.—It shall be the duty of any telegraph company doing business in this Territory to transmit all dispatches in the order in which they are received, under the penalty of one hundred dollars, to be recovered with costs of suit by the person or persons whose dispatch is postponed out of its order: Provided, that communications to and from public officers on official business may have precedence over all other communications: And, provided also, that intelligence of general and public interest may be transmitted for publication out of its order.

Sec. 21.—The term "telegraphic copy" or "telegraphic duplicate," wherever used in this Act, shall be construed to mean any copy of a message made or prepared for delivery at the office to which said message may have been sent by telegraph.

Sec. 22.—The California State Telegraph Company, a company formed within the State of California, and having its principal office in the city of San Francisco and doing business within the Territory of Utah, is hereby declared to be duly incorporated under its present corporate name, style and organization; and the right is hereby granted to said company to acquire, own and enjoy, and to dispose of any and all property real and personal, franchises and privileges as may be proper or convenient for the transaction of its business and for effectually carrying out the objects and purposes of said company, as fully and completely as if said company had been originally formed and duly incorporated under the laws of this Territory, hereby conferring upon said company as ample power to do and transact business and maintain its rights in all Courts and places as is or may be possessed by domestic corporations or natural persons.

Approved Jan. 16, 1863.

---:o:---

CHAPTER LXXV.

An ACT providing for a Poll Tax for Road Purposes.

Sec. 1.—Be it enacted by the Governor and Legislative Assembly of the Territory of Utah: That each County Court shall, at its next December term, district its respective county into as many portions as may, in its judgment, render it convenient to carry out the provisions of this act most effectively for the general good, and appoint a Supervisor for each district. It shall require annually a poll tax, not to exceed two day's labor, or one and a half dollars per day in lieu thereof, of every able-bodied male inhabitant over sixteen and under fifty years of age; said labor to be performed upon any Territorial or county road within the limits of the county, under the direction of their respective Supervisors; and all means, other than labor, accruing from said tax, shall be paid over to the Supervisor of the district, to be by him expended to the best advantage upon the roads aforesaid, after reserving therefrom an amount sufficient to remunerate himself for his servisces, as hereinafter provided.

Sec. 2.—Each Supervisor shall give bonds, with security, to be approved by the Probate Judge or Clerk of the County Court, payable to the people of their respective counties, for a sum not exceeding five hundred dollars, for the faithful performance of his duties according to the requirements of this act, which bond shall be filed in the office of the Clerk of the County Court, and shall receive the sum of two dollars for each day's faithful service in the duties of his office, to be paid out of the poll tax of his district.

Sec. 3.—It shall be the duty of the County Court to furnish each Supervisor with a suitable book for his official accounts, containing a list of poll tax payers within his district, so near as may be, together with a statement of the amount of poll tax required of each person liable under the first section of this act, to which the Supervisor is authorized and required to add the names of all persons within his district thus liable, whose names may have been omitted.

Sec. 4.—Each Supervisor shall, at his discretion, notify so many persons, whose names are on his list, as he may deem practicable, to appear at such time and place as their services may be required, with appropriate tools for the kind of work to be performed, giving the parties at least three days' notice of such requirement. When teams may be required, the Supervisor shall negotiate for the same at an equitable rate.

Sec. 5.—Any person notified, as provided by section four, desirous of making other pay than labor, may give the supervisor notice accordingly; and if he pay the amount of his tax for the current year before the day he has been required to perform the labor, he shall be justified in non-appearance; but, otherwise, the Supervisor may, as such, sue and collect the same as an action of debt, and no property shall be exempt from execution on judgment so recovered.

Sec. 6.—Each Supervisor shall, at the December term of the County Court, annually make a full report to said Court of the amount of labor performed, the amount collected in other means, and in what manner expended, with the amount and kind of means on hand.

Approved Jan. 16, 1862.

CHAPTER LXXVI.

An ACT to Regulate Fisheries, and to Prohibit Fish Traps and other Contrivances for Catching Fish in the River Jordan.

Sec. 1.—Be it enacted by the Governor and Legislative Assembly of the Territory of Utah: That the County Courts of the several counties are hereby authorized to control all fisheries in their respective counties, to permit, regulate, license, restrain or cause to be removed any and all fish traps or other contrivances for catching fish in any and all the rivers and streams of this Territory, excepting only the river Jordan, which shall, from and after the passage of this act, be kept open and free from all traps and other contrivances for catching fish, which would block up or turn the main current of the stream into any other channel for the purpose of preventing the free migration of fish down said river Jordan.

Sec. 2.—It shall be the duty of any person or persons wishing to erect a fish trap or other contrivance for catching fish, which would tend to hinder the free migration of fish in any of the rivers or streams of this Territory, to petition the County Court of the county in which such fish trap or other contrivance for catching fish is designed to be erected or placed, giving at least thirty days' notice of their intention to make such application, by posting up notices in three public places in said county, or by advertising for three consecutive weeks in some newspaper printed in this Territory. On such application being made, the County Court may grant license to the party or parties so applying: Provided, that such grant does not interfere with the rights and privileges of any other citizen, or tend to the needless destruction of fish: And, provided further, that the river Jordan shall be exempt from the control of all the County Courts.

Sec. 3.—All persons now owning fish traps or other contrivances for catching fish, which have been heretofore placed in any of the rivers or streams in this Territory, shall remove the same within thirty days after the passage of this act, under penalty of fine not exceeding one thousand dollars, excepting said person or persons owning such fish trap or other contrivance for catching fish shall obtain, from the County Court of the county in which the same is located, the right to continue the same.

Sec. 4.—Any person or persons violating the provisions of this act shall be liable to a fine not less than five nor more than one hundred dollars for each offense, to be collected before any Court having jurisdiction; and all such fines, when collected, shall be paid into the County treasury.

Sec. 5.—That an act entitled "An act to prevent the needless destruction of fish," approved January 13, 1853, is hereby repealed.

Approved Jan. 17, 1862.

———:o:———

CHAPTER LXXVII.

RESOLUTION in relation to Grants of Lands.

Resolved by the Governor and Legislative Assembly of the Territory of Utah: That whereas, by Act of Congress, approved July 2, 1862, and an Act amendatory of the same, approved April 14, 1864, grants of land were proffered the several States and Territories, for the benefit of agriculture and the mechanic arts and for the establishment of Agricultural Colleges in the several States and Territories, under certain conditions and restrictions.

Resolved that, in behalf of the Territory of Utah, this Assembly accept the said grant of land proffered by Acts referred to, and agree to the conditions therein contained.

Approved January 13, 1865.

CHAPTER LXXVIII.

JOINT RESOLUTION authorizing the Territorial Treasurer to collect Delinquent Taxes.

Be it resolved by the Governor and Legislative Assembly of the Territory of Utah: That the Territorial Treasurer is hereby authorized and empowered to collect the delinquent Territorial tax due in the several counties from the Collectors.

Approved January 20, 1865.

———:o:———

CHAPTER LXXIX.

RESOLUTION changing the Seat of Government of Utah Territory, and the place of holding the Supreme Court therein.

Be it resolved by the Governor and Legislative Assembly of the Territory of Utah: That the Seat of Government is removed from Fillmore City to Great Salt Lake City, until otherwise provided by law. And be it further resolved: That the Supreme Court hold its annual sessions in Great Salt Lake City, so long as the Seat of Government remains at that place.

Approved Dec. 15, 1856.

———:o:———

CHAPTER LXXX.

RESOLUTION exempting the members of the Legislative Assembly of the Territory of Utah, from arrest and summons during the sitting of the Legislature, and while going to and from the same.

Be it resolved by the Governor and Legislative Assembly of the Territory of Utah: That the members of the Council and House of Representatives shall be privileged from arrest and summons during the sessions of the Legislative Assembly, or during the time of their going to and returning from said sessions, except for treason or murder; and no suit at law against any member shall be prosecuted during said sessions.

Approved Jan. 14, 1857.

———:o:———

CHAPTER LXXXI.

An ACT apportioning the Representation of Utah Territory.

Sec. 1.—Be it enacted by the Governor and Legislative Assembly of the Territory of Utah: That, at the general election for eighteen hundred and sixty-two, and yearly thereafter, Washington and Kane Counties shall elect one Representative to the Legislative Assembly; Iron County one; Beaver and Piute Counties one; Millard County one; Juab County one; Sanpete and Sevier Counties two; Utah County three; Wasatch County one; Summit and Green River Counties one; Great Salt Lake County six; Tooele County one; Davis and Morgan Counties two; Weber County two; Box Elder County one; and Cache and Richland Counties two.

Sec. 2.—At the general election in eighteen hundred and sixty-three, and bienially thereafter, Washington and Kane Counties shall elect one Councilor to the Legislative Assembly; Iron, Beaver and Piute Counties one; Millard and Juab Counties one; Sanpete and Sevier Counties one; Utah and Wasatch Counties two; Great Salt Lake, Tooele, Summit and Green River Counties four; Davis and Morgan Counties one; Weber and Box Elder Counties one; and Cache and Richland Counties one.

Approved Jan 17, 1862.

———:o:———

CHAPTER LXXXII.

RESOLUTION giving authority to the Hon. John F. Kinney to collect a certain amount due the Territory.

Resolved that the Hon. John F. Kinney be instructed and empowered to present the claim of the Territorial Treasury to the Treasury Department at Washington, D. C., for collection, said claim of seven hundred and fifty-two dollars and twenty-five cents, ($752 25), being for boarding, clothing and guarding a United States convict, in the year 1860; and that all necessary authority for the collection of said claim be forwarded by the Territorial Treasurer, at an early day.

Approved Jan. 21, 1864.

———:o:———

CHAPTER LXXXIII.

An ACT in relation to Butchering and Meat Markets outside the limits of Incorporated Cities that are acting under their Charters.

Sec. 1.—Be it enacted by the Governor and Legislative Assembly of the Territory of Utah: That no person shall be allowed to erect a slaughter-house or yard, or to commence the business of butchering or keeping a meat market, without first obtaining a license therefor from the County Court of the county in which such business is designed to be carried on.

Sec. 2.—All persons so licensed as butchers shall keep a book in which they shall record a faithful description of the age, size and colors of all cattle by them killed, with the brands and ear marks thereon, together with the name of the person from whom received and the time when killed, which book shall be open to the inspection of the public.

Sec. 3.—All persons who receive license from the County Court for establishing a butchery or meat market, shall pay quarterly in advance into the County Treasury such sum as may be deemed necessary or sufficient by the County Court of the proper county.

Sec. 4.—Any person violating this act shall upon conviction thereof, pay a fine not to exceed one hundred dollars for each offense.

Sec. 5.—Nothing in this act shall be so construed as to interfere with any incorporated city.

Approved Jan. 11, 1865.

CHAPTER LXXXIV.

A JOINT RESOLUTION legalizing the laws of the Provisional Government of the State of Deseret.

Resolved by the Legislative Assembly of the Territory of Utah: That the laws heretofore passed by the Provisional Government of the State of Deseret, and which do not conflict with the "Organic Act," of said Territory, be, and the same are hereby declared to be legal, and in full force and virtue, and shall so remain until superseded by the action of the Legislative Assembly of the Territory of Utah.

Approved Oct. 4, 1851.

———:o:———

CHAPTER LXXXV.

An ORDINANCE incorporating the Church of Jesus Christ of Latter-day Saints.

Sec. 1.—Be it ordained by the General Assembly of the State of Deseret: That all that portion of the inhabitants of said State which now are or hereafter may become residents therein, and which are known and distinguished as "The Church of Jesus Christ of Latter-day Saints," are hereby incorporated, constituted, made and declared a Body Corporate, with perpetual succession, under the original name and style of "The Church of Jesus Christ of Latter-day Saints," as now organized, with full power and authority to sue and be sued, defend and be defended in all Courts of law or equity in this State; to establish order and regulate worship; and hold and occupy real and personal estate; and have and use a seal, which they may alter at pleasure.

Sec. 2.—And be it further ordained that said Body or Church, as a religious society, may, at a general or special Conference, elect one "Trustee in Trust" and not to exceed twelve Assistant Trustees, to receive, hold, buy, sell, manage, use and control the real and personal property of said Church, which said property shall be free from taxation; which Trustee and Assistant Trustees, when elected or appointed, shall give bonds with approved security, in whatever sum the said Conference may deem sufficient, for the faithful performance of their several duties; which said bonds, when approved, shall be filed in the General Church Recorder's office, at the seat of general church business, when said bonds are approved by said conference; and said Trustee and Assistant Trustees shall continue in office during the pleasure of said Church; and there shall also be made, by the Clerk of the Conference of said Church, a certificate of such election or appointment of said Trustee and Assistant Trustees, which shall be recorded in the General Church Recorder's office, at the seat of general church business; and when said bonds are filed and said certificates recorded, said Trustee or Assistant Trustees may receive property, real or personal, by gift, donation, bequest, or in any manner not incompatible with the principles of righteousnes or the rules of justice, inasmuch as the same shall be used, managed, or disposed of for the benefit, improvement, erection of houses for public worship and instruction, and the well being of said Church.

Sec. 3.—And be it further ordained that as said Church holds the constitutional and original right, in common with all civil and religious communities, "to worship God according to the dictates of conscience;" to reverence communion agreeably to the principles of truth, and to solemnize marriage compatible with the revelations of Jesus Christ, for the security and full enjoyment of all blessings and privileges embodied in the religion of Jesus Christ free to all, it is also declared that said Church does and shall possess and enjoy continually the power and authority, in and of itself, to originate, make, pass and establish rules, regulations, ordinances, laws, customs and criterions for the good order, safety, government, conveniences, comfort and control of said Church, and for the punishment or forgiveness of all offences relative to fellowship, according to Church covenants; that the pursuit of bliss and the enjoyment of life in every capacity of public association and domestic happiness, temporal expansion or spiritual increase upon the earth may not legally be questioned: Provided however, that each and every act or practice so established or adopted for law or custom, shall relate to solemnities, sacraments, ceremonies, consecrations, endowments, tithings, marriages, fellowship, or the religious duties of man to his Maker; inasmuch as the doctrines, principles, practices or performances support virtue and increase morality, and are not inconsistent with or repugnant to the Constitution of the United States or of this State, and are founded in the revelations of the Lord.

Sec. 4.—And be it further ordained that said Church shall keep, at every full organized Branch or Stake, a registry of marriages, births and deaths, free for the inspection of all members and for their benefit.

Sec. 5.—And be it further ordained that the Presidency of said Church shall fill all vacancies of the Assistant Trustees, necessary to be filled, until superceded by the Conference of said Church.

Sec. 6.—Be it further ordained that no Assistant Trustee or Trustees, shall transact business in relation to buying, selling or otherwise disposing of Church property, without the consent or approval of the Trustee in Trust of said Church.

Approved Feb. 8, 1851.

———:o:———

CHAPTER LXXXVI.

An ORDINANCE incorporating the University of the State of Deseret.

Sec. 1.—Be it ordained by the General Assembly of the State of Deseret: That a University is hereby instituted and incorporated, located at Great Salt Lake City, by the name and title of the University of the State of Deseret.

Sec. 2.—The powers of the University shall be vested in a Chancellor and twelve Regents, the number of which Regents may be increased when necessary, who shall be chosen by the joint vote of both Houses of the General Assembly, and shall hold their office for the term of one year, and until their successors are qualified.

Sec. 3.—The Chancellor shall be the chief executive officer of the University, and chairman of the Board of Regents.

Sec. 4.—The Chancellor and Board of Regents are a body corporate, to sue and be sued; to act as Trustees of the University; to transact or cause to be transacted all business needful to the prosperity of the University in advancing all useful and fine arts and sciences; to select and procure lands; erect and purchase buildings; solicit donations; send agents abroad; receive subscriptions; purchase books, maps, charts and all apparatus necessary for the most liberal endowment of any library and scientific institution; employ professors and teachers; make by-laws; establish branches of the University throughout the State; and do all other things that fathers and guardians of the Institution ought to do.

Sec. 5.—The Chancellor and Regents may appoint a Secretary, and define his duties.

Sec. 6.—The Chancellor, Regents and Secretary, before entering upon the duties of their respective offices, shall each take an oath of office, and file a bond in the office of the Auditor of Public Accounts, with approved securities, in a sum not less than ten thousand dollars, conditioned for the faithful performance of their several duties; which sum may be increased at the discretion of the Executive of the State.

Sec. 7.—There shall be a Treasurer of the University elected in the same manner and for the same time as the Chancellors and Regents, whose duty it shall be to receive and safely keep the funds of the University or dispose of the same as he shall be directed by the Board of Regents; and keep accurate records of all funds that may come into his possession; and keep his books open at all times for the inspection of the Chancellor and Regents, or any of them, and of the Executive and Secretary of State.

Sec. 8.—The Treasurer, before entering upon the duties of his office, shall take an oath of office and file a bond, with approved security, in the office of the Auditor of Public Accounts, in the sum of one hundred thousand dollars, conditioned for the faithful performance of his duties, which sum may be increased at the discretion of the Executive of the State.

Sec. 9.—Should a vacancy occur in the Board of Regents or any office in the Institution, during the recess of the General Assembly, the Executive of the State may fill such vacancy.

Sec. 10.—It shall be the duty of the officers of the University to prepare and open books, and be ready to receive subscriptions, donations and appropriations, on or before the sixth day of April next; and shall legibly enter upon their books all subscriptions and donations to the University, with the names of the donors, time and place, and preserve the same.

Sec. 11.—The Board of Regents shall have a seal known as the seal of the University, which may accompany all their official correspondence, and all other legal documents given under the hands of the Regency of the University.

Sec. 12.—It shall be the duty of the Chancellor and Board of Regents, as soon as the funds arising from donations or otherwise may justify, to establish a free school institution for the benefit of orphans and other indigent worthy persons.

Sec. 13.—The Secretary and Treasurer shall each present a full and explicit report in writing of the situation, funds and doings of the University in their several departments, by the fifteenth of October in each year, to the Auditor of Public Accounts.

Approved Feb. 28, 1850.

———:o:———

CHAPTER LXXXVII.

An ACT granting and confirming unto the University of the State of Deseret certain land claims therein mentioned.

Sec. 1—Be it enacted by the Governor and Legislative Assembly of the Territory of Utah: That all that portion of land described as follows, to wit: Beginning at a point one half mile due east from the northeast corner of plot B, in Great Salt Lake City, and extending due south two hundred and eighty rods; thence east one mile; thence north two hundred and eighty rods; thence west to the place of beginning; or as it is now bounded and commonly known as the University ground, granted to the University of the State of Deseret by the Legislative Assembly of the Provisional Government, is granted and confirmed unto the said University of the State of Deseret, together with all the privileges, products, appurtenances and benefits appertaining thereto or arising therefrom.

Approved Dec. 28, 1855.

———:o:———

CHAPTER LXXXVIII.

An ACT appropriating Money for Educational Purposes and defining certain Duties of the Chancellor and Board of Regents of the University of the State of Deseret.

Sec. 1.—Be it enacted by the Governor and Legislative Assembly of the Territory of Utah: That the sum of two thousand five hundred dollars is appropriated, out of any money in the treasury not otherwise appropriated, to be drawn by the Chancellor, and expended under the direction and control of the Chancellor and Board of Regents in procuring fonts of Deseret alphabet type, in paying for printing books with said type, and for other purposes.

Sec. 2.—The Chancellor and Board of Regents are authorized and required to furnish, or cause to be furnished, copy for all publications they may order, to control the sale thereof, and to apply the profits arising therefrom to the most advantageous promotion of education, including such payments to the Superintendent of common schools for services rendered under their direction, as they may from time to time deem proper.

Approved Dec. 28, 1855.

——:0:——

CHAPTER LXXXIX.

An ACT incorporating "The Deseret Agricultural and Manufacturing Society."

Sec. 1.—With a view of promoting the arts of domestic industry, and to encourage the production of acticles from the native elements in this Territory: Be it enacted by the Governor and Legislative Assembly of the Territory of Utah: That the "Deseret Agricultural and Manufacturing Society" be formed and chartered as follows:—

Sec. 2.—There shall be a President and eleven directors who shall, in the first instance, be elected by the joint vote of the Legislative Assembly, and may elect a Treasurer and Secretary, and such other officers as they may deem necessary.

Sec. 3.—Said Board of President and Directors are hereby constituted a body corporate, with perpetual succession; and shall be known by the name and style of "The Deseret Agricultural and Manufacturing Society," and shall have power to sue and be sued, defend and be defended in all Courts of law or equity; and may have a seal which they may use and alter at pleasure.

Sec. 4.—Said Society have power to make, establish and carry out all needful bye-laws, not conflicting with the Constitution of the United States and the laws of this Territory; and to do and perform all acts necessary for the proper exercise of the powers herein conferred, and for promoting the objects contemplated in this act.

Sec. 5.—They shall hold an annual exhibition at Great Salt Lake City, or at such other place or places as they shall deem proper, of all such agricultural products, stock and domestic manufactured articles as, in their opinion, will be best calculated to stimulate the people of this Territory in industrial pursuits, and best subserve the cause of domestic industry; and shall award premiums for the best specimens of all such articles and animals as they will permit to be entered in the lists for competition; and shall annually publish a list of what they will consider entitled to premiums and fix the rate and award premiums as they shall deem proper: Provided, that ther articles than those included in the list shall be admitted and arranged for by the Board, and be exhibited under their direction.

Sec. 6.—A majority of said Board shall form a quorum to do business, may fill vacancies in the Board, and fix the manner and rate of the admission of members to said Society.

Sec. 7.—For the purpose of starting this enterprise and aiding the President and Directors in carrying out the objects contemplated in this act, the sum of fifteen hundred dollars is hereby appropriated, to be drawn by the Treasurer of said Society, and expended by the Board in awarding premiums for the best specimens of native productions on exhibition for premiums under their direction.

Sec. 8.—No person can become a member of this society, or be entitled to receive any premium, without complying with such rules and terms of admission as shall be established by said Board.

Approved January 17, 1856.

pany," passed by the Provisional Government of the State of Deseret, approved Sept. 14, 1850, is hereby amended, confirmed and legalized as follows:—

Be it ordained by the General Assembly of the State of Deseret: That a general Conference of the Church of Jesus Christ of Latter-day Saints, or a special Conference of said Church, to be called at such time and place as the First Presidency of said Church shall appoint, is hereby authorized to elect, by a majority, a company of not less than thirteen men, one of whom shall be designated as their President, and the others as Assistants.

Sec. 2.—This company is hereby made and constituted a body corporate, under the name and style of "The Perpetual Emigrating Fund Company;" and shall have perpetual succession, and may have and use a common seal which they may alter at pleasure.

Sec. 3.—Said company, under the name and style aforesaid, shall have power to sue and be sued, plead and be impleaded, defend and be defended in all courts of law or equity, and in all actions whatsoever; to purchase, receive and hold, either by donation, or deposit, or otherwise, money and every kind of property real and personal; to emit bills of credit and exchange; to sell, lease, convey or dispose of property real and personal; and, finally, to do and perform any and all such acts as shall be necessary and proper for the interest, protection, convenience or benefit of said company.

Sec. 4.—A majority or such members of said company as may at any time be in the immediate neighborhood of their President, shall form a quorum to do business, and shall elect a Secretary and Treasurer, and shall have power to select and appoint all other officers and agents necessary to transact the business of said company.

Sec. 5.—The President and Assistants shall individually give bond and security in a sum not less than ten thousand dollars, to be approved by the First President of said Church, and filed in the General Church Recorder's office.

Sec. 6.—The Secretary and Treasurer, and all other officers or agents appointed by the company, shall give bonds and security, to be approved by the President of the company, and filed in the company Secretary's office.

Sec. 7.—There shall be a general settlement of all business transactions of the company, so far as returns received from abroad will permit, as often as once in each year; and it shall be the duty of all the officers and agents to make out correct returns of all their transactions, and deliver or transmit them to the Secretary of said company on or before the first day of December in each year; and, as soon as practicable thereafter, it shall be the duty of the President of the company to produce or exhibit a manifest thereof, and file it in the Secretary's office and file a copy of said manifest in the General Church Recorder's office.

Sec. 8.—It shall be the duty of the Treasurer to keep an accurate account of all money or property received and disbursed by him, and make returns as hereinbefore directed.

Sec. 9.—The company shall have the power of appointing and removing their officers and agents at pleasure; and it shall be the duty of said persons when removed to pay and pass into the hands of their respective successors, or of the company, all monies, property, books, papers and accounts, of every name and nature, belonging or in any way pertaining to the business of said company.

Sec. 10.—The entire proceeds of the business of this company shall inure to the Perpetual Emigrating Fund for the poor, whether arising from donations, insurance, deposits, exchange, increased value of property, or in any other way or manner whatsoever; and the general business of the company shall be devoted, under the direction and supervision of the First Presidency of said Church, to promote, facilitate and accomplish the emigration of the poor.

Sec. 11.—The members of this company shall hold their offices at the pleasure of the Conferences hereinbefore mentioned; but the First Presidency of said Church shall have power to fill all vacancies that may occur by death, removal, or otherwise; and all persons so appointed shall qualify and serve as hereinbefore directed, and hold their offices until superseded by an election.

Sec. 12.—No officer, agent or member of the company shall be permitted to retain in his hands any portion of the funds of the company as compensation, but may receive such remuneration as shall be awarded upon settlement with the Board of President and Assistants.

Sec. 13.—All persons receiving assistance from the Perpetual Emigrating Fund Company shall be held responsible therefor until paid.

Sec. 14.—The islands in Great Salt Lake known as Stansbury's Island and Antelope Island are hereby reserved and appropriated for the use and benefit of said company, and said islands shall be under the exclusive control of President Brigham Young.

Approved Jan. 12, 1856.

CHAPTER XCI.

An ACT incorporating Great Salt Lake City.

Sec. 1.—Be it enacted by the Governor and Legislative Assembly of the Territory of Utah: That all that district of country embraced in the following boundaries, to wit:—Beginning at a point one hundred and thirty-six rods north of the Hot Spring, thence west to the west bank of the Jordan river, thence up the west bank thereof to a point directly west from the southwest corner of the five acre lots according to the present survey, thence east along the south line of said lots to the southeast corner thereof, thence east nine hundred rods, thence north to a point directly east of the beginning, thence west to the aforsaid place of beginning shall be known and designated by the name and style of Great Salt Lake City; and the inhabitants thereof are hereby constituted a body corporate and politic, by the name and style aforesaid, with perpetual succession; and shall have and use a common seal, which they may change and alter at their pleasure.

Sec. 2.—The inhabitants of said City, by the name and style aforesaid, shall have power to sue and be sued, to plead and be impleaded, defend and be defended in all Courts of law and equity and in all actions whatsoever; to purchase, receive, hold, sell, lease, convey and dispose of property real and personal for the benefit of said City, both within and without its corporate boundaries; to improve and protect such property, and do all other things in relation thereto as natural persons.

Sec. 3.—Said City shall be divided into five Municipal Wards, whose boundaries shall be as prescribed by the city ordinance.

Sec. 4.—The Municipal Government of said city is hereby vested in a City Council, to be composed of a Mayor, five Aldermen, one from each Ward, and nine Councillors, who shall have the qualifications of electors in said city, and shall be chosen by the qualified voters thereof, and shall hold their offices for two years, and until their successors are elected and qualified.

Sec. 5.—An election shall be held on the second Monday of February next, and every two years thereafter on said day, at which there shall be elected one Mayor, five Aldermen, nine Councillors, one Marshal, one Treasurer and one Recorder; and the persons respectively receiving the highest number of votes cast in the city for said offices shall be declared elected. When two or more candidates for an elective office shall have an equal number of votes for the same office, the election shall be determined by the City Council.

Sec. 6.—The first election under this act shall be conducted in the following manner, to wit:—The County Clerk of Great Salt Lake County shall cause notice of the time and place, and the number and kind of officers to be chosen, to be advertised in some newspaper of said city, or posted up in five public places therein, at least ten days previous to said election. Three Judges shall be selected by the Probate Judge of Great Salt Lake County, at least one week previous to the day of election; said Judges shall choose two Clerks; and the Judges and clerks, before entering upon their duties, shall take and subscribe an oath or affirmation for the faithful discharge thereof. At the first election so held, the polls shall be opened at eight o'clock a.m., and shall close at six o'clock p.m. At the close of the election the Judges shall seal up the ballot box and the list of the names of the electors, and transmit the same, within two days, to the County Clerk of Great Salt Lake County. As soon as the returns are received, the County Clerk, in the presence of the Probate Judge, shall unseal and examine them, and furnish, within five days, to each person having the highest number of votes, a certificate of his election.

Sec. 7.—The manner of conducting and voting at all subsequent elections to be held under this act, and contesting the same; the keeping of the poll lists; canvassing the votes; and certifying the returns, and all other things relating thereto, shall be as provided by city ordinance.

Sec. 8.—There shall be appointed an Assessor and Collector, an Auditor of Public Accounts, a Supervisor of Streets, a Surveyor, an Attorney, a Board of School Inspectors, a Sealer of Weights and Measures, a Sexton or keeper of burial grounds, a Chief of Police, Inspectors, Measurers and Weighers, and such other officers and agents as the City Council may from time to time direct and appoint.

Sec. 9.—Every person elected or appointed to any office under the provisions of this act may be removed from such office by a vote of two-thirds of the City Council; and no officer shall be removed except for cause, nor unless furnished with the charges and have an opportunity of being heard in his defence; and the Council shall have power to compel the attendance of witnesses; and the production of papers when necessary for the purpose of such trial, and shall proceed, within ten days, to hear and determine upon the merits of the case; and if such officer shall neglect to appear

K

and answer to such charges, then the Council may declare the office vacant. All officers appointed by the Council may be removed at any time by vote, at discretion of two-thirds of said Council; and any officer may be suspended until the disposition of charges preferred against him.

Sec. 10.—Whenever any vacancy shall happen by the death, resignation, or removal of any officer, such vacancy may be filled by the City Council; and every person elected or appointed to an elective, judicial or administrative office, shall, before he enters upon the duties thereof, take and subscribe an oath or affirmation that he will support the Constitution of the United States, the laws of this Territory and the Ordinances of this city, and that he will well and truly perform all the duties of his office to the best of his knowledge and ability, and file the same, duly certified by the officer before whom it was taken, with the city Recorder.

Sec. 11.—Any person or persons illegally voting at any election under this act, shall be punishable according to law regulating general elections.

Sec. 12.—The Mayor shall, before he enters upon the duties of his office, in addition to the usual oath, swear or affirm that he will devote so much of his time to the duties of his office as an efficient and faithful discharge thereof may require; and shall from time to time give the Council such information and recommend such measurers as he may deem advantageous to the city.

Sec. 13.—The Mayor and Aldermen shall be conservators of the peace within the limits of the city, and shall give bonds and qualify as other Justices of the Peace; and, when so qualified, shall possess the same power and jurisdiction, both in civil and criminal cases arising under the laws of the Territory, and may be commissioned as Justices of the Peace in and for said city by the Governor; they shall account for and pay over to the city Treasurer, with three months, all fines and forfeitures received by them in their judicial capacity; and they shall each keep a docket, subject at all times to the inspection of the City Council and all other parties interested.

Sec. 14.—The Mayor and Aldermen shall have exclusive jurisdiction in all cases arising under the ordinances of the city, and issue such process as may be necessary to carry such ordinances into execution and effect.

Sec. 15.—It shall be the duty of the Recorder to make and keep accurate records of all ordinances made by the City Council and all their proceedings in a corporate capacity; which record shall at all times be open to the inspection of the electors of the city and all other parties interested. He shall have and keep a plat of all surveys within the city, and record all deeds, transfers or other instruments of writing that may be presented to him for that purpose; and he is hereby authorized to take the acknowledgement of deeds, transfers and other instruments of writing, and shall perform such other duties as may be required of him by city ordinance.

Sec. 16.—The Marshal shall perform such duties as shall be prescribed by the City Council for the preservation of the public peace. All process issued by the Mayor or an Alderman shall be directed to the Marshal or his deputy; and in the execution thereof he shall be governed by such rules and regulations as may be provided by city ordinance, and shall be the principal ministerial officer.

Sec. 17.—The Treasurer shall receive all moneys belonging to the city, and shall keep an accurate account of all receipts and expenditures in such manner as the City Council shall direct. He shall pay all moneys that may come to his hand, by virtue of his office, upon orders signed by the Auditor of Public Accounts, and shall report to the City Council a true account of his receipts and disbursements, as they may require.

Sec. 18.—The City Council, a majority of whom shall form a quorum to transact business, shall meet at such times and places as they may direct; and the Mayor, when present, shall preside at said meetings and have a casting vote. In the absence of the Mayor, any Alderman present may be appointed to preside, in such manner as shall be provided by the City Council.

Sec. 19.—The City Council shall hold stated meetings; and the Mayor or any two Aldermen may call special meetings, by notice to each of the members of said Council, served personally or left at their usual place of abode. Said Council shall determine the rules of its own proceedings, and be the judge of the election and qualification of its own members.

Sec. 20.—The City Council shall have the management and control of the finances and property, real, personal and mixed, belonging to the corporation.

Sec. 21.—The City Council is hereby empowered within the jurisdiction of the city, by ordinance and the enforcement thereof, to prevent, punish or prohibit every kind of fraudulent device and practice; all descriptions of gaming, playing at dice, cards or other games of chance, with or without betting.

Sec. 22.—To license, tax, regulate, suppress or prohibit billiard tables, pin alleys, nine or ten pin alleys, or tables and ball alleys; to suppress or restrain bawdy and other disorderly houses and groceries; to authorize the destruction and demolition of all instruments and devices used for the purpose of gaming; to prevent any riot, noise, disturbance or disorderly assemblage; and to restrain and punish vagrants, mendicants, street beggars and prostitutes.

Sec. 23.—To regulate the selling or giving away of any ardent spirits or other intoxicating liquors by any storekeeper, grocer or trader, to be drank in any shop, store, grocery, outhouse, yard, garden or other place within the city, except by persons or at places duly licensed; to forbid the selling or giving away of ardent spirits or other intoxicating liquors to any child, apprentice or servant, without the consent of his or her parent, guardian, master or mistress, or to any Indian.

Sec. 24.—To license, regulate or restrain the manufacturers, sellers or venders of spirituous and fermented liquors, tavern keepers, dram or tippling shop keepers, grocers and keepers of ordinaries, boarding, victualing or coffee hou es, restaurants, saloons or other houses or places for the selling or giving away of wines or other liquors, whether ardent, vinous or fermented.

Sec. 25.—To regulate, license, suppress or prohibit all exhibitions of common showmen, shows of every kind, concerts or other musical entertainments, exhibitions of natural or artificial curiosities, caravans, circuses, theatrical performances and all other exhibitions and amusements.

Sec. 26.—To prevent or regulate the rolling of hoops, playing at ball, flying of kites or any other amusement or practice having a tendency to annoy persons passing in the streets or on the sidewalks, or to frighten teams or horses.

Sec. 27.—To prevent horse-racing, immoderate riding or driving in the streets, and to authorize their being stopped by any person; to punish or prohibit the abuse of animals; to compel persons to put up posts in front of their lots to fasten their horses or other animals; to compel the fastening of horses, mules, oxen or other animals attached to vehicles, while standing or remaining in the street.

Sec. 28.—To prevent the encumbering of the streets or side-walks, lanes, alleys and public grounds with carriages, tents, wagons, carts, sleighs, horses or other animals, sleds, wheelbarrows, boxes, lumber, timber, firewood, posts, awnings, signs, adobies or any material or substance whatever.

Sec. 29.—To restrain, regulate or prohibit the running at large of cattle, horses, mules, sheep, swine, goats and all kinds of poultry; and to authorize the distraining, impounding or sale of the same, for the penalty and costs incurred thereby; and to impose penalties for any violation of city ordinance in relation thereto; and to tax, prevent or regulate the keeping of dogs, and to authorize the destruction of the same, when at large, contrary to city ordinance.

Sec. 30.—To compel the owner or occupant of any grocery, cellar, tallow-chandler shop, soap-factory, tannery, stable, barn, privy, sewer, or any unwholesome place, to cleanse, remove or abate the same from time to time, as often as may be necessary for the health, comfort and convenience of the inhabitants of said city.

Sec. 31.—To direct the location and management of and regulate breweries and tanneries; and to direct the location, management and construction of and restrain or prohibit within the city distilleries, slaughtering establishments and establishments for steaming and rendering lard, oil, tallow, offal and such other substances as can or may be rendered; and all establishments or places where nauseous, offensive or unwholesome business may be carried on.

Sec. 32.—To direct or prohibit the location and management of houses for the storing of gunpowder, tar, pitch rosin or other combustible and dangerous materials within the city, and to regulate the keeping and conveying of gunpowder, and the use of candles and lights in barns, stables or outhouses.

Sec. 33.—To compel persons to keep the snow and ice from the sidewalks in front of the premises owned or occupied by them on East Temple Street, from the Temple Block South to the intersection with Second South Street.

Sec. 34.—To abate or remove nuisances, and punish the authors thereof, by penalties of fine and imprisonment; and to define and declare what are nuisances, and authorize and direct the summary abatement thereof; and to abate all nuisances which are or may be injurious to the public health, peace or good order.

Sec. 35.—To prevent any person from bringing, depositing or having within the limits of the city any dead carcass or any unwholesome substance, and to require the removal or destruction of the same by any person who shall have placed or caused to be placed upon or near his premises or near any of the streams of this city any such substances, or any putrid or unsound beef, pork, or fish, hides or skins of any kind; and, on his default, to authorize the removal or destruction by any officer of said city.

Sec. 36.—To exclusively control, regulate, repair, amend and clear the streets, alleys, bridges, side-walks or cross-walks; and open, widen, straighten or vacate streets and alleys, and put drains or ditches and sewers therein; and prevent the encumbering of the streets in any manner, and protect the same from any encroachment and injury.

Sec. 37.—To lay out, improve and regulate the public grounds belonging to the city; to direct and regulate the planting and preserving trees in the streets and public grounds; and to regulate the fencing of lots within the bounds of the city.

Sec. 38.—To prevent the ringing of bells, blowing of horns and bugles, crying of goods and all other noises, performances and devices tending to the collection of persons on the streets or side-walks by auctioneers and others, for the purpose of business, amusement or otherwise.

Sec. 39.—To regulate and determine the times and places of bathing and swimming in the river or other waters in and adjoining said city, and to prevent any obscene or indecent exhibition, exposure or conduct.

Sec. 40.—To make regulations to prevent the introduction of contageous diseases into the city; to make quarantine laws and enforce the same within the city and around it, not exceeding twelve miles next beyond the bounds thereof.

Sec. 41.—To grant and issue licenses, and direct the manner of issuing and registering thereof, and the fees to be paid therefor. Bonds may be taken, on the granting of licenses, for the due observance of the ordinances or regulations of the City Council.

Sec. 42.—To license, tax and regulate merchants and retailers, auctioneers, distillers, brewers, brokers, pawnbrokers and money changers, and to impose duties upon the sale of goods at auction.

Sec. 43.—To license, tax, regulate or suppress hawkers and pedlers.

Sec. 44.—To regulate and license or prohibit butchers, and to revoke their licenses for malconduct in the course of trade; and to regulate, license and restrain the sale of fresh meat and vegetables in the city; and restrain and punish the forestalling of poultry, fruit and eggs.

Sec. 45.—To establish and regulate markets and other public buildings, and provide for their erection, determine their location, and authorize their erection in the streets, avenues or any other public place or places in the city, and not exceeding four miles beyond the bounds thereof.

Sec. 46.—To provide for taking the enumeration of the inhabitants of the city; to regulate the burial of the dead, and registration of births and deaths; to direct the returning and keeping of bills of mortality; and to impose penalties on physicians, sextons and others for any default in the premises.

Sec. 47.—To appoint watchmen and policemen, and prescribe their duties and powers.

Sec. 48.—To regulate the measuring and inspection of lumber, shingles, timber, posts, staves and heading, and all building materials and all kinds of mechanical work; and appoint one or more inspectors therefor.

Sec. 49.—To regulate the weighing and place and manner of selling hay.

Sec. 50.—To regulate the inspection of tobacco, also of flour, meal, pork, beef and other provisions, and salt to be sold in barrels, hogsheads and other packages.

Sec. 51.—To regulate the measuring of wood and the weighing of coal, and the place and manner of selling the same.

Sec. 52.—To regulate the inspection of whisky and other liquors to be sold in barrels, hogsheads or other vessels.

Sec. 53.—To appoint inspectors, weighers and guagers, and regulate their duties and prescribe their fees.

Sec. 54.—To require every merchant, retailer, trader and dealer in merchandize or property of any discription, which is sold by measure or weight, to cause their weights and measures to be sealed by the city Sealer and to be subject to his inspection; the standard of which weights and measures shall be conformable to those established by law.

Sec. 55.—To establish, make and regulate public pumps, wells, cisterns, hydrants and reservoirs; to distribute, control and so regulate the waters flowing into the city throughout such channels as may be most advantageous, and to prevent the unnecessary waste of water.

Sec. 56.—To erect street lamps and regulate the lighting thereof; and from time to time create, alter and extend lamp districts.

Sec. 57.—To establish and regulate public pounds.

Sec. 58.—To regulate and license ferries.

Sec. 59.—To authorize the taking up and providing for the safe keeping and education, for such periods of time as may be expedient, of all children who are destitute of all proper parental care, wandering about the streets, committing mischief and growing up in mendicancy, ignorance, idleness and vice.

Sec. 60.—To borrow money on the credit of the city: Provided, That the interest on the aggregate of all the sums borrowed and outstanding, shall notdxceed one-foruth of the city revenue arising from taxes assessed within the corporation during the preceding year.

Sec. 61.—The City Council shall have power to make, publish, ordain, amend and repeal all such ordinances, bye laws, or police regulations, not contrary to the Constitution of the United States and the laws of this Territory, for the good government and order of the city, as may be necessary and expedient to carry into effect the powers vested in the City Council or any officer of said city by this act; and enforce observance of all rules, ordinances, resolutions, bye laws and police and other regulations, made in pursuance of this act, by penalties not exceeding one hundred dollars for any offence against the same.

Sec. 62.—The City Council shall have power within the city, by ordinance, to annually levy and collect taxes on the assessed value of all real and personal estate or property in the city; made taxable by the laws of the Territory, for the following named purposes, to wit:—Not to exceed five mills on the dollar to defray the contingent expenses of the city. Not to exceed five mills on the dollar to open, improve and keep in repair the streets of the city. Not to exceed one and a quarter mills on the dollar to control the waters of said city; and they shall annually apportion and apply said taxes as shall in their judgment be deemed most expedient.

Sec. 63.—When the City Council shall deem it expedient for any especial purpose to borrow money, the interest on which shall not exceed one fourth of the city revenue arising from taxes of the preceding year, the amount of taxes shall not be increased.

Sec. 64.—To require, and it is hereby made the duty of every male resident of the city, over the age of eighteen and under the age of fifty years, to labor one day in each year upon the streets; but every person may at his option pay one dollar and fifty cents for the day he shall be so bound to labor: Provided, it be paid within five days from the time he shall be notified by the Street Supervisor. In default of payment as aforesaid, the same may be collected as other taxes.

Sec. 65.—The City Council shall have power by ordinance to regulate the form of assessment rolls, and prescribe the duties and define the powers of Assessors and Collectors. The annual assessment rolls shall be returned by the Assessor on or before the first Monday of April in each year; but the time may be extended or additions made therto by order of the City Council. On the return thereof the City Council shall fix a day for hearing objections thereto, and any person feeling aggrieved by the assessment of his property may appear at the time specified and make his objections, which shall be heard and determined upon by the City Council; and they shall have power to alter, add to, take from and otherwise correct and revise said assessment roll.

Sec. 66.—The Collector shall be furnished, within thirty days after the assessment rolls are corrected, with a list of the taxes to be collected; and if not paid, the Collector shall have power to collect said taxes with interest and cost by suit in the Corporate name, or by distress and sale of any property belonging to persons so indebted. The Assessor's roll shall in all cases be evidence on the part of the Corporation.

Sec. 67.—All taxes and assessments, general and special, shall be collected by the Collector or Collectors in the same manner and with the same power and authority as are given by the law to Collectors of County and Territorial taxes: Provided, the Council shall have power to prescribe by city ordinance the powers, duties and liabilities of Assessors and Collectors.

Sec. 68.—The City Council shall have power to make, ordain and establish all such general regulations for the prevention and extinguishment of fires, fixing of chimneys, flues and stove pipes, as they may deem expedient; to procure fire engines and other apparatus used for the extinguishment of the same, and have the charge and control of and provide, fit up and secure engine houses and other places for the keeping and preserving the same; to organize fire, hose and ladder companies, appoint foremen therefor and prescribe their duties, and make rules and regulations for their government, and to impose reasonable fines and forfeitures for a violation of the same.

Sec. 69.—The City Council shall have power to provide for the election of trustees; to appoint a Board of School Inspectors and to prescribe the powers and duties of the same, and to enact such ordinances as may be necessary to carry their duties and powers into effect.

Sec. 70.—The City Council shall have exclusive authority and power to establish and regulate the Police of the city; to impose fines, forfeitures and penalties for the breach of any ordinance; to provide for the recovery of such fines and forfeitures and the enforcement of such penalties, and to pass, make, ordain, establish and execute all such ordinances, not repugnant to the Constitution of the United States or the laws of this Territory, as they may deem necessary for carrying into effect and execution the powers specified in this act, and for the peace, good order, regulation, convenience and cleanliness of the city, for the protection of property therein from destruction by fire or otherwise, and for the health, safety and happiness of the inhabitants thereof.

Sec. 71.—All ordinances passed by the City Council shall, within one month after they shall have been passed, be published in some newspaper printed in said city, or certified copies thereof be posted up in three of the most public places in the city.

Sec. 72.—All ordinances of the city may be proven by the seal of the Corporation, and, when printed or published in book form, purporting to be printed or published by the authority of the City Council, the same shall be received in evidence in all Courts or places without further proof.

Sec. 73.—The City Council shall have power, from time to time, to require further and other duties of all officers whose duties are herein provided; and prescribe the duties and powers of all officers appointed or elected under this act, whose duties herein are not specifically mentioned, and arrange the fees and fix the compensation of all officers, jurors, witnesses and others. They may also require bonds to be given to Great Salt Lake City by all officers, for the faithful performance of their duties.

Sec. 74.—All persons appointed under this act to the office of Recorder, Marshal, Attorney, Treasurer, Collector, Assessor, Auditor of Public Accounts, Surveyor or Street Commissioner, shall be commissioned by warrant under the Corporate seal, signed by the Mayor or presiding officer of the City Council and Recorder.

Sec. 75.—If any person, having been an officer in Great Salt Lake City, shall not, within ten days after notification and request, deliver to his successor in office all the property, papers and effects of every description in his possession belonging to said city or appertaining to the office he held, he shall forfeit and pay for the use of the city not exceeding one hundred dollars, besides all damages caused by his neglect or refusal so to deliver.

Sec. 76.—When it shall be necessary to take private property for opening, widening or altering any public street, lane, avenue or alley, the Corporation shall make a just compensation therefor to the person whose property is so taken; and if the amount of such compensation cannot be agreed upon, the Mayor shall cause the same to be ascertained by a jury of six disinterested men, who shall be inhabitants of the city.

Sec. 77.—All jurors empannelled to inquire into the amounts of benefit or damages that shall happen to the owners of property so proposed to be taken, shall first be sworn to that effect, and shall return to the Mayor or presiding officer of the City Council their inquest in writing, signed by each juror.

Sec. 78.—The cemetery lots which have or may hereafter be laid out and sold by said city for private places of burial shall, with their appurtenances, forever be exempt from execution or attachment.

Sec. 79.—All ordinances, resolutions and regulations now in force in Great Salt Lake City, and not inconsistent with this act, shall remain in force until altered, modified or repealed by the City Council after this act shall take effect.

Sec. 80.—All actions, rights, fines, penalties and forfeitures, in suit or otherwise, which have accrued under the ordinance incorporating Great Salt Lake City, shall be vested in and prosecuted by the Corporation hereby created.

Sec. 81.—All plots and surveys of lands, lots or other places within said city, heretofore surveyed by the Surveyor, and all plots and surveys of lands, lots or other places that may be hereafter surveyed, and all certificates of surveys given by him shall be deemed valid by this act.

Sec. 82.—All property, real personal or mixed, now belonging to Great Salt Lake City, is hereby vested in the Corporation created by this act; and the officers of said Corporation now in office shall respectively continue in the same, until superseded in conformity to the provisions hereof, but shall be governed by this act, which shall be in force from and after its passage.

Sec. 83.—This act shall be deemed a public act, and may be read in evidence without proof, and judicial notice shall be taken thereof in all Courts and places.

Sec. 84.—This act shall not invalidate any act done by the present City Council of Great Salt Lake City, or by its officers, nor divest their successors under this act of any rights, property or otherwise, or liability which may have accrued to or been created by said Council prior to the passage of this act.

Sec. 85.—All officers of the city, created conservators of the peace by this act, shall have power to arrest or cause to be arrested, with or without process, all persons who shall break the peace; commit for examination, and, if necessary, detain such persons in custody forty-eight hours in the city prison or other safe place; and shall have and exercise such other powers, as conservators of the peace, as the City Council may prescribe.

Sec. 86.—Nothing in this act shall be so construed as to deprive the present City

Council of Great Salt Lake City of any power or authority conferred upon them by the ordinance incorporating said city, and the act amendatory thereto; but said City Council shall possess, exercise and enjoy all the powers and authority heretofore conferred upon them, except so far as such powers and authority have been expressly modified or repealed by this act, until said City Council are superseded by the election and qualification of their successors under this act.

Sec. 87.—That "An ordinance to incorporate Great Salt Lake City," approved Jan. 19, 1851, be and is hereby repealed; and "An act in relation to the assessment, collection and expenditure of a tax for road and other purposes, within incorporated cities," approved June 4, 1853, so far as the same applies to Great Salt Lake City, be and is hereby repealed.

Sec. 88.—The City Council shall publish, in at least one newspaper published in Great Salt Lake City, a quarterly statement of the amount of city revenue, specifying in said statement from whence derived and for what disbursed.

Approved Jan. 20, 1860.

——:o:——

CHAPTER XCII.

An ACT amending the Charter of Great Salt Lake City.

Sec. 1.—Be it enacted by the Governor and Legislative Assembly of the Territory of Utah:

First.—That the City Council of Great Salt Lake City shall have power and authority to license, tax and regulate livery stables.

Second.—To license, tax and suppress hackmen, draymen, carters, porters, omnibus drivers, cabmen, packers, carmen and all others who may pursue like occupations, with or without vehicles, and prescribe their compensation.

Third.—To establish, erect and control hospitals, infirmaries and medical colleges: to purchase grounds for their erection and improve and adorn the same; and license, control and regulate physicians and surgeons.

Fourth.—To purchase and improve suitable grounds for a house of correction; to erect buildings thereon and adopt such rules and regulations for the government and punishment of offenders therein, as said Council may from time to time deem expedient.

Fifth.—To direct and control the location of railroad tracks and depot grounds within the city and regulate or prohibit the use of locomotive engines thereon, and may require the cars to be used within the inhabited portions thereof to be drawn or propelled by other power than that of steam.

Sixth.—To regulate and control the location of gas works, canals, telegraph poles and all improvements of similar nature.

Sec. 2. The City Council shall have power to levy and collect on real estate (or land claims and improvements thereon) in any district or division benefitted, within the limits of said city, a sufficient tax to defray the expense of leveling, paving, macademizing or planking and opening and keeping in repair the streets and sidewalks, of constructing sewers and drains and keeping the same in repair, and of erecting lamps and lighting the streets in such respective districts or divisions: Provided, the money thus raised shall be exclusively expended for such purpose in the district where such taxes are assessed, and by such person or persons as the City Council may appoint. The amount to be assessed for any such improvement shall be determined by the City Council, who shall appoint three Commissioners, reputable citizens, to make such assessment, who shall be sworn to faithfully and impartially execute their duties.

Before entering on their duties the Commissioners shall give six day's notice of the time and place of meeting, to all persons interested. The Commissioners shall assess the amount directed by the City Council on the real estate (or land claims and improvements) by them deemed benefitted by any such improvement, in proportion to the benefit resulting thereto.

When the Commissioners shall have completed their assessment and made a correct copy thereof, they shall deliver the same to the City Recorder within thirty days after their appointment, signed by all the Commissioners.

The City Recorder shall cause a notice to be published to all persons interested, of the completion of the assessment, and the time and place shall be designated therein when the City Council shall hear appeals and objections and correct or confirm said assessment.

When the said assessment shall have been completed, the City Recorder shall, within ten days thereafter, make a correct tax-list, which shall be delivered to the Collector or any authorized agent appointed by the City Council, who shall collect said taxes within such time as may be prescribed by said Council.

If any assessment is set aside by order of any Court, the City Council may cause a new one to be made in like manner for the same purpose, for the collection of the amount so assessed.

If the first assessment prove insufficient, another may be made in the same manner, or, if too large a sum shall at any time be raised, the excess shall be refunded, rateably, to those by whom it was paid.

Approved Jan. 14, 1865.

———:o:———

CHAPTER XCIII.

An ACT to Incorporate Provo City.

Sec. 1.—Be it enacted by the Governor and Legislative Assembly of the Territory of Utah: That all that district of country embraced in the following boundaries, in Utah county, to wit: Commencing two miles south from the present survey of the city of Provo, at the edge of Utah Lake, thence east to the mountain, thence northerly with the mountain to the north bank of Provo river, thence west to the said Lake, thence southerly along the edge of the Lake to the place of beginning shall be known and designated under the name and style of Provo City; and the inhabitants thereof are hereby constituted a body corporate and politic, by the name aforesaid; and shall have perpetual succession, and may have and use a common seal, which they may change and alter at pleasure.

Sec. 2.—The inhabitants of said city, by the name and style aforesaid, shall have power to sue and be sued, to plead and be impleaded, defend and be defended in all Courts of law and equity; and in all actions whatsoever; to purchase, receive, hold, sell, lease, convey and dispose of property real and personal for the benefit of said city, both within and without its corporate boundaries; to improve and protect such property, and to do all other things in relation thereto as natural persons.

Sec. 3.—The municipal government of said city is hereby vested in a City Council, to be composed of a Mayor, three Aldermen, one from each ward, and five Councilors, who shall have the qualifications of electors in said city, and shall be chosen by the qualified voters thereof, and shall hold their office for two years, and until their successors are elected and qualified.

Sec. 4.—An election shall be held on the second Monday in February next, and every two years thereafter, on said day, at which there shall be elected, one Mayor, three Aldermen and five Councilors; and the persons respectively receiving the highest number of votes cast in the city, for said officers, shall be declared elected. When two or more candidates shall have an equal number of votes for the same office, the election shall be determined by the City Council.

Sec. 5.—The first election under this act shall be conducted in the following manner, to wit: The County Clerk of Utah county shall cause notice of the time and place, and the number and kind of officers to be chosen, to be posted up in four public places in said city, at least ten days previous to said election. Two Judges shall be selected by the Probate Judge of Utah county, at least one week previous to the day of election, said Judges shall choose two Clerks, and the Judges and Clerks, before entering upon their duties, shall take and subscribe an oath or affirmation for the faithful discharge thereof. The poll shall be open at 8 o'clock a.m., and shall close at 6 o'clock p.m. At the close of the election the Judges shall seal up the ballot box and the list of names of the electors and transmit the same, within two days, to the County Clerk of Utah county. As soon as the returns are received, the County Clerk, in the presence of the Probate Judge, shall unseal and examine them, and furnish within five days, to each person having the highest number of votes, a certificate of his election. In case of a tie, it shall be decided by lot drawn by the County Clerk in presence of the Probate Judge.

Sec. 6.—All subsequent elections held under this act shall be held, conducted and returns thereof made as may be provided for by ordinance of the City Council.

Sec. 7.—The City Council shall be judge of the qualifications, elections and returns of their own members; and a majority of them shall form a quorum to do business, shall determine the rules of their own proceedings and shall meet at such time and place as they may direct; the Mayor shall preside when present and have a casting vote; and in the absence of the Mayor any Aldermen present may be appointed to preside over said meeting.

Sec. 8.—The City Council may hold stated meetings; and special meetings may be called by the Mayor or any two Aldermen, by notice to each of the members of said council, served personally, or left at their usual places of abode.

Sec. 9.—The City Council shall have power to appoint a Marshal, Recorder, (who shall be the Auditor of Public Accounts) Treasurer, Assessor, and Collector, Supervisor of Streets, Surveyor, an Attorney, a Sexton, a Sealer of Weights and Measures and all such other officers as may be necessary; define their duties, remove them from office at pleasure and fix and establish the fees of all officers, jurors and witnesses.

Sec. 10.—All officers elected in accordance with the fourth section of this act may be removed for cause from such office by a vote of two-thirds of the City Council, and shall be furnished with the charges and have an opportunity to be heard in his defence; and the Council shall have power to compel the attendance of witnesses and the production of papers when necessary.

Sec. 11.—When a vacancy shall happen by the death, resignation or removal of any officer, such vacancy may be filled by the City Council; and every person elected or appointed to any office under this act shall, before he enters upon the duties thereof, take and subscribe an oath or affirmation that he will support the Constitution of the United States, the laws of this Territory and the ordinances of the city, and that he will well and truly perform all the duties of his office to the best of his knowledge and ability, and he may be required to give bonds as shall be prescribed by City Ordinances, which oath and bond shall be filed with the City Recorder.

Sec. 12.—The City Council shall have power to divide the city into Wards and specify the boundaries thereof; and when necessary create additional Wards and add to the number of Aldermen and Councilors, and proportion them among the several Wards as may be just and most conducive to the welfare of said city.

Sec. 13.—The Mayor and Aldermen shall be Conservators of the Peace within the limits of the city, and shall give bonds and qualify as other Justices of the Peace; and when so qualified shall possess the same powers and jurisdiction, both in civil and criminal cases arising under the laws of the Territory, and may be commissioned, as Justices of the Peace in and for said city, by the Governor. They shall acconnt for and pay over all fines and forfeitures arising under the ordinances of the city into the City Treasury, and all fines and forfeitures arising under the laws of the Territory into the County Treasury, and shall issue such process as may be necessary to carry into effect all ordinances of said city. Appeals may be had from any decision or judgment of a Mayor's or Alderman's Court in the same manner as or may be provided by statute for appeals from Justice's Courts; and they shall account for and pay over to the City Treasurer, within three months, all fines and forfeitures received by them by virtue of their office; and they shall each keep a docket, subject at all times to the inspection of the City Council and all other parties interested.

Sec. 14.—All process issued by the Mayor or an Alderman shall be directed to the Marshal or other legal officer, and in execution thereof, he shall be governed by such rules and regulations as may be provided by city ordinance.

Sec. 15.—It shall be the duty of the Recorder to make and keep accurate records of all ordinances made by the City Council and all their proceedings in a corporate capacity, which record shall at all times be open to the inspection of the electors of the city and all other parties interested, and audit all accounts of said incorporation. He shall have and keep a plat of all surveys within the city; and he is hereby authorized to take the acknowledgment of deeds, transfers and other instruments of writing, and shall perform such other duties as may be required of him by city ordinance.

Sec. 16.—The Treasurer shall receive all money or funds belonging to the city, and shall keep an accurate account of all receipts and expenditures in such manner as the City Council shall direct. He shall pay all funds that may come to his hand, by virtue of his office, upon orders signed by the Auditor of Public Accounts; and shall report to the City Council a true account of his receipts and disbursements, as they may require.

Sec. 17.—The City Council shall have power, within the city, by ordinance to annually levy and collect taxes on the assessed value of all property in the city made taxable by the laws of the Territory, for the following named purposes, to wit: not to exceed five mills on the dollar for contingent expenses, nor to exceed five mills on the dollar to open, improve and keep in repair the streets of the city. The City

Council is further empowered to divide the city into School Districts, provide for the election of Trustees, appoint a Board of School Inspectors, annually assess and collect and expend the necessary tax for school purposes and for furnishing the city with water for irrigating and other purposes, and regulate and control the same; and furthermore, so far as may be necessary, control the water courses leading thereto in the immediate vicinity thereof.

Sec. 18.—The City Council shall have the management and control of the finances and property of said city.

Sec. 19.—To require and it is hereby made the duty of every male resident of the city, over the age of eighteen and under the age of fifty years, to labor not to exceed two days in each year upon the streets; but every person may, at his option, pay one dollar and fifty cents for the day he shall be so bound to labor: Provided it be paid within five days from the time he shall be notified by the Street Supervisor. In default of payment as aforesaid, the same may be collected as other taxes.

Sec. 20.—The Council shall have power to borrow money for city purposes, the interest of which shall not exceed one-fourth of the city revenue, arising from taxes of the previous year.

Sec. 21.—The City Council shall have power by ordinance to regulate the form of the assessment rolls. The annual assessment roll shall be returned by the Assessor on or before the first Monday of April in each year, but the time may be extended or additions made thereto by order of the City Council. On the return thereof, the City Council shall fix a day for hearing objections thereto; and any person feeling aggrieved by the assessment of his property may appear at the time specified and make his objections, which shall be heard and determined upon by the City Council, and they shall have power to alter, add to, take from and otherwise correct and revise said assessment roll.

Sec. 22.—The Collector shall be furnished, within thirty days after the assessment rolls are corrected, with a list of taxes to be collected; and if not paid when demanded, the Collector shall have power to collect said taxes with interest and cost by suit in the corporate name, as may be provided by ordinance. The assessment roll shall in all cases be evidence on the part of the corporation.

Sec. 23.—To appropriate and provide for the payment of the expenses and debts of the city.

Sec. 24.—To make regulations to prevent the introduction of contagious diseases into the city; to make quarantine laws and enforce the same within the city and around it, not exceeding twelve miles next beyond the boundaries thereof.

Sec. 25.—To establish hospitals and make regulations for the government of the same; to make regulations to secure the general health of the inhabitants; to declare what shall be nuisances and prevent and remove the same.

Sec. 26.—To provide the city with water, to dig wells, lay pump logs and pipes, and erect pumps in the street for the extinguishment of fires and the convenience of the inhabitants.

Sec. 27.—To direct or prohibit the location and management of houses for the storing of gunpowder, tar, pitch, rosin or other combustible and dangerous materials within the city, and to regulate the conveying of gunpowder.

Sec. 28.—To exclusively control, regulate, repair, amend and clear the streets, alleys, bridges, sidewalks or crosswalks, and open, widen, straighten or vacate streets and alleys and put drains or ditches and sewers therein, and prevent the incumbering of the streets in any manner and protect the same from any encroachment and injury.

Sec. 29.—To provide for the lighting of the streets and erecting lamp posts; to erect market houses and establish markets and market places, and provide for the government and regulation thereof.

Sec. 30.—To provide for the erection of all needful buildings for the use of the city, and for inclosing, improving and regulating all public grounds belonging to the city.

Sec. 31.—To license, regulate, prohibit or restrain the manufacturers, sellers or venders of spirituous or fermented liquors, tavern keepers, dram or tippling shop keepers, boarding, victualling or coffee houses, restaurants, saloons or other houses or places for the selling or giving away of wines or other liquors, whether ardent, vinous or fermented.

Sec. 32.—To license, tax and regulate auctioneers, merchants, retailers, grocers, ordinaries, hawkers, pedlars, brokers, pawnbrokers and money changers.

Sec. 33.—To regulate the selling or giving away of any ardent spirits or other intoxicating liquors by any shopkeeper, grocer or trader, to be drank in any shop, store, grocery, outhouse, yard, garden or other place within the city, except by persons or at places duly licensed; to forbid the selling or giving away of ardent spirits or other intoxicating liquors to any child, apprentice or servant, without the consent of his or her parent, guardian, master or mistress, or to any Indian.

Sec. 34.—To regulate and license or prohibit butchers, and to revoke their license for malconduct in the course of trade; and to regulate, license and restrain the sale of fresh meat and vegetables in the city.

Sec. 35.—To license, tax, regulate, suppress or prohibit billiard tables, pin alleys, nine or ten pin alleys or table and ball alleys; to suppress or restrain all disorderly houses and groceries; to authorize the destruction and demolition of all instruments and devices used for the purpose of gaming, and all kinds of gambling; to prevent any riot, noise, disturbance or disorderly assemblage; and to restrain and punish vagrants, mendicants, street beggars and prostitutes.

Sec. 36.—To regulate, license, suppress or prohibit all exhibitions of common showmen, shows of every kind, concerts or other musical entertainments, exhibitions of natural or artificial curiosities, caravans, circuses, theatrical performances, ball rooms and all other exhibitions and amusements.

Sec. 37.—To license, tax and regulate hacking, carriages, wagons, carts and drays, and fix the rates to be charged for the carrying of persons and for wagonage, cartage and drayage of property, as also to license and regulate porters and fix the rate of porterage.

Sec. 38.—To provide for the prevention and extinguishment of fires; to regulate the fixing of chimneys and the flues thereof and stove pipes; and to organize and establish fire companies.

Sec. 39.—To regulate and order parapet walls and other partition fences.

Sec. 40.—To establish standard weights and measures and to regulate the weights and measures to be used in the city in all cases not provided by law.

Sec. 41.—To provide for the inspecting and measuring of lumber and other building materials, and for the measurement of all kinds of mechanical work.

Sec. 42.—To provide for the inspection and weighing of hay, lime and stone coal, and the measuring of charcoal, firewood and other fuel to be sold or used within the city.

Sec. 43.—To provide for and regulate the inspection of tobacco, beef, pork, flour and meal; also beer, whisky and brandy and all other spirituous or fermented liquors.

Sec. 44.—To regulate the weight and quality and price of bread sold and used in the city.

Sec. 45.—The City Council shall have exclusive power within the city, by ordinance, to license, regulate or restrain the keeping of ferries and toll bridges.

Sec. 46.—To provide for the taking the enumeration of the inhabitants of the city; to regulate the burial of the dead and registration of births and deaths; to direct the returning and keeping of bills of mortality; and to impose penalties on physicians, sextons and others for any default in the premises.

Sec. 47.—To prevent horse-racing, immoderate riding or driving in the streets, and to authorize their being stopped by any person; to punish or prohibit the abuse of animals, to compel persons to put up posts in front of their lots to fasten their horses and other animals; to compel the fastening of horses, mules, oxen or other animals attached to vehicles, whilst standing or remaing in the streets.

Sec. 48.—To prevent the incumbering of the streets or sidewalks, lanes, alleys and public grounds with carriages, tents, wagons, carts, sleighs, horses or other animals, sleds, wheelbarrows, boxes, lumber, timber, firewood, posts, awnings, signs, adobies or any material or substance whatever.

Sec. 49.—To restrain, regulate or prohibit the running at large of cattle, horses, mules, sheep, swine, goats and all kinds of poultry; and to tax, prevent or regulate the keeping of dogs, and to authorize the destruction of the same, when at large contrary to city ordinance.

Sec. 50.—To compel the owner or occupant of any grocery, cellar, tallow chandler shop, soap factory, tannery, stable, barn, privy, sewer or any unwholesome place to cleanse, remove or abate the same from time to time, as oft as may be necessary for the health, comfort and convenience of the inhabitants of said city.

Sec. 51.—To direct the location and management of and regulate breweries and tanneries; and to direct the location, management and construction of and restrain or prohibit within the city distilleries, slaughtering establishments and all establishments or places where nauseous, offensive or unwholesome business may be carried on.

Sec. 52.—To prevent any person from bringing, depositing or having within the limits of the city any dead carcass or any unwholesome substance, and to require the removal or destruction of the same by any person who shall have placed or caused to be placed upon or near his premises or near any of the streams of this city any such substance or any putrid or unsound beef, pork or fish, hides or skins of any kind; and, on his default, to authorize the removal or destruction of the same by any officer of said city.

Sec. 53.—To direct and regulate the planting and preserving trees in the streets and public grounds, and regulate the fencing of lots within the boundaries of the city.

Sec. 54.—To prevent the ringing of bells, the blowing of horns and bugles, the crying of goods and all other noises, performances and devices tending to disturb the peace and quiet of the said city.

Sec. 55.—To grant and issue licenses and direct the manner of issuing and registering thereof. Bonds may be taken on the granting of licenses, for the due observance of the ordinances of the City Council.

Sec. 56.—To require every merchant, retailer, trader and dealer in merchandise or property of every description, which is sold by measure or weight, to cause their weights and measures to be sealed by the City Sealer and to be subject to his inspection, the standard of which weights and measures shall be conformable to those established by law.

Sec. 57.—The City Council shall have power to make such ordinances and resolutions, not contrary to the Constitution and laws of the United States and the laws of the Territory, as may be necessary and expedient to carry into effect the powers vested in the City Council or any officer of said city by this act, and enforce observance of all ordinances and resolutions made in pursuance of this act by penalties not exceeding one hundred dollars or imprisonment not to exceed six months, or both.

Sec. 58.—The City Council shall have exclusive authority and power to establish and regulate the Police of the city; to impose fines, forfeitures and penalties for the breach of any ordinance; to provide for the recovery of such fines and forfeitures and the enforcement of such penalties; and to pass, make, ordain, establish and execute all such ordinances, not repugnant to the Constitution and laws of the United States or the laws of this Territory, as they may deem necessary for carrying into effect and execution the powers specified in this act, and for the peace, good order, regulation, convenience and cleanliness of the city, for the protection of property therein from destruction by fire or otherwise, and for the health, safety and happiness of the inhabitants thereof.

Sec. 59.—To provide for the punishment of offenders and vagrants by imprisonment in the county or city jail, or by compelling them to labor on the streets or other public works until the same shall be fully paid, in all cases where such offenders or vagrants shall fail or refuse to pay the fines and forfeitures which may be awarded against them.

Sec. 60.—All ordinances passed by the City Council shall, within one month after they shall have been passed, be published in some newspaper printed in said city, or certified copies thereof be posted up in three of the most public places in the city.

Sec. 61.—All ordinances of the city may be proven by the seal of the Corporation; and when printed or published in book form, purporting to be printed or published by the authority of the City Council, the same shall be received in evidence in all Courts or places without further proof.

Sec. 62.—When it shall be necessary to take private property for opening, widening or altering any public street, lane, avenue or alley, the Corporation shall make a just compensation thereof to the person whose property is so taken; and if the amount of such compensation cannot be agreed upon, the Mayor shall cause the same to be ascertained by a jury of six disinterested men who shall be inhabitants of the city.

Sec. 63.—All jurors empannelled to inquire into the amounts of benefit or damages that shall happen to be owners of property so proposed to be taken, shall first be sworn to that effect, and shall return to the Mayor or presiding officer of the City Council their inquest in writing, signed by each juror.

Sec. 64.—All ordinances, resolutions and regulations now in force in Provo City, and not inconsistent with this act, shall remain in force until altered, modified or repealed by the City Council after this act shall take effect.

Sec. 65.—All actions, rights, fines, penalties and forfeitures in suit or otherwise, which have accrued under the ordinance incorporating Provo City, shall be vested in and prosecuted by the Corporation hereby created.

Sec. 66.—All plots and surveys of lands, lots or other places within said city heretofore surveyed by the surveyor; and all plots and surveys of land, lots or other places that may be hereafter surveyed and all certificates of surveys given by him shall be deemed valid by this act.

Sec. 67.—All property now belonging to Provo City is hereby vested in the Corporation created by this act; and the officers of said Corporation now in office shall respectively continue in the same, until superceded in conformity to the provisions thereof, but shall be governed by this act.

Sec. 68.—This act shall not invalidate any act done by the present City Council of Provo City or by its officers, nor divest their successors under this act of any right, property or otherwise, or liability which may have accrued to or been created by said Council prior to the passage of this act.

Sec. 69.—All officers of the city, created Conservators of the Peace by this act, shall have power to arrest or cause to be arrested, with or without process, all persons who shall break the peace, commit for examination and, if necessary, detain such persons in custody forty-eight hours in the city prison or other safe place; and shall have and exercise such other powers as Conservators of the Peace as the City Council may prescribe.

Sec. 70.—Nothing in this act shall be so construed as to deprive the present City Council of Provo City of any power or authority conferred upon them by the ordinance incorporating said city and the act amendatory thereto, but said City Council shall possess, exercise and enjoy all the powers and authority heretofore conferred upon them, except so far as such powers and authority have been expressly modified or repealed by this act, until said City Council are superceded by the election and qualification of their successors under this act.

Sec. 71.—That an ordinance to incorporate Provo City, approved February 6, 1851, be and is hereby repealed, and an act in relation to the assessment, collection and expenditure of a tax for road and other purposes within incorporated cities, approved June 4, 1853, so far as the same applies to Provo City, be and is hereby repealed.

Sec. 72.—The City Council shall cause to be published in some newspaper published in Provo City, or posted up in three public places, on or before the first day of December in each year, a statement of the amount of city revenue, specifying in said statement whence derived and for what disbursed.

Sec. 73.—This act shall be in force from and after the 24th day of January, 1864.

Approved January 21, 1864.

———:o:———

CHAPTER XCIV.

An ORDINANCE to incorporate the City of Manti.

Sec. 1.—Be it ordained by the General Assembly of the State of Deseret: That all that portion of the county of Sanpete which lies in the following boundaries, to wit: Beginning at the warm spring (about two miles) south of the present city plat in said county, thence west to the west bank of Sanpete creek, thence north and northeast along the west bank of said creek to a point due west of the mouth of Willow Creek Cañon, thence east to the mouth of Willow Creek Cañon, thence due south to a parallel line due east of the aforesaid warm spring, thence west on said line to the place of beginning, including the survey of said plat, shall be known and designated as the city of Manti; and the inhabitants thereof are hereby constituted a body corporate and politic, by the name aforesaid, and shall have perpetual succession, and may have and use a common seal, which they may change and alter at pleasure.

Sec. 2.—The inhabitants of said city, by the name and style aforesaid, shall have power to sue and be sued, to plead and be impleaded, defend and be defended, in all Courts of law and equity, and in all actions whatsoever; to purchase, receive and hold property, real and personal, in said city; to purchase, receive and hold real property beyond the city for burying grounds or other public purposes for the use of the inhabitants of said city; to sell, lease, convey or dispose of property, real and personal, for the benefit of said city; to improve and protect such property, and to do all other things in relation thereto, as natural persons.

Sec. 3.—There shall be a City Council, to consist of a Mayor, two Aldermen, and three Councilors, who shall have the qualifications of electors of said city, and shall be chosen by the qualified voters hereof, and shall hold their offices for two years, and until their successors be elected and qualified. The City Council shall judge of the qualifications, elections and returns of their own members, and a majority of them shall form a quorum to do business; but a smaller number may adjourn from day to day and compel the attendance of absent members, under such penalties as may be prescribed by ordinance.

Sec. 4.—The Mayor, Aldermen and Councilors, before entering upon the duties of their offices, shall take and subscribe an oath or affirmation that they will support the Constitution of the United States and of this State, and that they will well and truly perform the duties of their offices to the best of their skill and ability.

Sec. 5.—An election, for the election of one Mayor, two Aldermen and three Councilors, shall be held on the second Monday of February, 1863, and every two years thereafter, and shall be held, conducted and the returns thereof made in such manner as shall be provided for by the ordinances of the City Council.

Sec. 6.—All free white male inhabitants of the age of eighteen years, who are entitled to vote for State officers, and who shall have been actual residents of said city sixty days next preceding said election, shall be entitled to vote for city officers.

Sec. 7.—The City Council shall have authority to levy and collect taxes for city purposes upon all taxable property, real and personal, within the limits of the city, not exceeding one half per cent. per annum, upon the assessed value thereof, and may enforce the payment of the same in any manner to be provided by ordinance, not repugnant to the Constitution of the United States, or of this State.

Sec. 8.—The City Council shall have power to appoint a Recorder, Treasurer, Assessor and Collector, Marshal and Supervisor of Streets. They shall also have the power to appoint all such other officers, by ordinance, as may be necessary, define the duties of all city officers, and remove them from office at pleasure.

Sec. 9.—The City Council shall have power to require of all officers, appointed in pursuance of this ordinance, bonds with penalty and security, for the faithful performance of their respective duties, such as may be deemed expedient, and also to require all officers, appointed as aforesaid, to take an oath for the faithful performance of the duties of their respective offices.

Sec. 10.—The City Council shall have power and authority to make, ordain, establish and execute all such ordinances, not repugnant to the Constitution of the United States or of this State, as they may deem necessary for the peace, benefit, good order, regulation, convenience and cleanliness of said city, for the protection of property therein, from destruction by fire or otherwise, and for the health and happiness thereof. They shall have power to fill all vacancies that may happen, by death, resignation or removal, in any of the offices herein made elective; to fix and establish all the fees of the officers of said corporation, not herein established; to impose such fines, not exceeding one hundred dollars for each offence, as they may deem just, for refusing to accept of any office in or under the Corporation, or for misconduct therein; to divide the city into Wards and specify the boundaries thereof.

Sec. 11.—To establish, support and regulate common schools; to borrow money on the credit of the city: Provided that no sum or sums of money be borrowed on a greater interest than six per cent. per annum, nor shall the interest on the aggregate of all the sums borrowed and outstanding ever exceed one half of the city revenue arising from taxes assessed on real estate within this corporation.

Sec. 12.—To make regulations to prevent the introduction of contagious diseases into the city; to make quarantine laws for that purpose and enforce the same.

Sec. 13.—To appropriate and provide for the payment and expenses and debts of the city.

Sec. 14.—To establish hospitals and make regulations for the government of the same; to make regulations to secure the general health of the inhabitants; to declare what shall be nuisances and to prevent and remove the same.

Sec. 15.—To provide the city with water; to dig wells, lay pump logs and pipes and erect pumps in the streets for the extinguishment of fires and convenience of the inhabitants.

Sec. 16.—To open, alter, widen, extend, establish, grade, pave or otherwise improve and keep in repair, streets, avenues, lanes and alleys; and to establish, erect and keep in repair aqueducts and bridges.

Sec. 17.—To provide for the lighting of the streets and erecting lamp posts; and establish, support and regulate night watches, to erect market houses, establish markets and market places and provide for the government and regulation thereof.

Sec. 18.—To provide for erecting all needful buildings for the use of the city, and for enclosing, improving and regulating all public grounds belonging to the city.

Sec. 19.—To license, tax and regulate auctioneers, merchants and retailers, grocers and taverns, ordinaries, hawkers, peddlers, brokers, pawn-brokers and money changers.

Sec. 20.—To license, tax and regulate hacking, carriages; wagons, carts and drays, and fix the rates to be charged for the carriage of persons and for wagonage, cartage and drayage of property; as also to license and regulate porters and fix the rates of porterage.

Sec. 21.—To license, tax and regulate theatricals and other exhibitions, shows and amusements.

Sec. 22.—To tax, restrain, prohibit and suppress tippling houses, dram shops, gaming houses, bawdy and other disorderly houses.

Sec. 23.—To provide for the prevention and extinguishment of fires; to regulate the fixing of chimneys and the flues thereof and stove pipes, and to organize and establish fire companies.

Sec. 24.—To regulate the storage of gunpowder, tar, pitch, rosin and other combustible materials.

Sec. 25.—To regulate and order parapet walls and other partition fences; to restrain, regulate or prohibit the running at large of cattle, horses, mules, sheep, swine, goats and all kind of poultry; and to tax and regulate the keeping of dogs and to authorize the destruction of the same, when at large contrary to city ordinances.

Sec. 26.—To establish standard weights and measures and regulate the weights and measures to be used in the city, in all cases not provided for by law.

Sec. 27.—To provide for the inspection and measuring of lumber and other building materials, and for the measurement of all kinds of mechanical work.

Sec. 28.—To provide for the inspection and weighing of hay, lime and stone coal, and measuring of charcoal, firewood and other fuel to be sold or used within the city.

Sec. 29.—To license, regulate, prohibit or restrain the manufacturing, selling or giving away of spirituous vinous or fermented liquors, tavern keepers, dram or tippling shop keepers, boarding, victualing or coffee houses, restaurants, saloons or other houses or places for the selling or giving away of ardent, vinous or fermented liquors; to provide for and regulate the inspection of tobacco, beef, pork, flour and meal; also beer, whiskey, brandy and all other spirituous or fermented liquors.

Sec. 30.—To regulate the weight, quality and price of bread sold and used in the city.

Sec. 31.—To provide for taking the numeration of the inhabitants of the city.

Sec. 32.—To fix the compensation of all city officers, and regulate the fees of jurors, witnesses and others for services rendered under this or any city ordinance.

Sec. 33.—The City Council shall have exclusive power within the city, by ordinance, to license, regulate, suppress or restrain billiard tables, and from one to twenty pin alleys and every other description of gaming or gambling.

Sec. 34.—The City Council shall have exclusive power within the city, by ordinance, to license, regulate or restrain the keeping of ferries and toll bridges; to regulate the police of the city; to impose fines, forfeitures and penalties for the breach of any ordinance, and provide for the recovery of such fines and forfeitures, and the enforcement of such penalties; and to pass such ordinances as may be necessary and proper for carrying into effect and execution the powers specified in this ordinance: Provided such ordinances are not repugnant to the Constitution of the United States or of this State.

Sec. 35.—All ordinances passed by the City Council shall, within one month after they shall have been passed, be published in some newspaper, printed in said city, or certified copies thereof be posted up in three of the most public places in the city.

Sec. 36.—All ordinances of the city may be proven by the seal of the Corporation; and when printed or published in book or pamphlet form, purporting to be printed or published by the authority of the Corporation, the same shall be received in evidence in all Courts or places without further proof.

Sec. 37.—The Mayor and Aldermen shall be Conservators of the Peace within the limits of the city, and shall have all the powers of Justices of the Peace therein, both in civil and criminal cases arising under the laws of the State. They shall, as Justices of the Peace, within the limits of said city perform the same duties, be governed by the same laws, give the same bonds and securities as other justices of the peace, and be commissioned, as Justices of the Peace in and for said city, by the Governor.

Sec. 38.—The Mayor and Aldermen shall have exclusive jurisdiction in all cases arising under the ordinances of the Corporation, and shall issue such process as may be necessary to carry said ordinances into execution and effect. Appeals may be had from any decision or judgment of said Mayor or Aldermen, arising under the ordinances of said city, to the Municipal Court, under such regulations as may be prescribed by ordinance; which court shall be composed of the Mayor as Chief Justice and the Aldermen as Associate Justices; and from the final judgment of the Municipal Court to the Probate Court of Sanpete county, in the same manner as appeals are taken from Justices of the Peace: Provided the parties litigant shall have a right to a trial by jury of twelve men, in all cases before the Municipal Court. The Municipal Court shall have power to grant writs of *habeas corpus* and try the same, in all cases arising under the ordinances of the City Council.

Sec. 39.—The Municipal Court may sit on the first Monday of every month, and the City Council at such times and places as may be prescribed by city ordinance;

special meetings of which may at any time be called by the Mayor or any two Aldermen.

Sec. 40.—All process issued by the Mayor, Aldermen or Municipal Court shall be directed to the Marshal, and in the execution thereof, he shall be governed by the same laws as are or may be prescribed for the direction and compensation of Constables in similar cases. The Marshal shall also perform such other duties as may be required of him under the ordinances of said city, and shall be the principal ministerial officer.

Sec. 41.—It shall be the duty of the Recorder to make and keep accurate records of all ordinances made by the City Council and of all their proceedings in their Corporate capacity, which record shall at all times be open to the inspection of the electors of said city, and shall perform all other duties as may be required of him by the ordinances of the City Council, and shall serve as Clerk of the Municipal Court.

Sec. 42.—When it shall be necessary to take private property for opening, widening or altering any public street, lane, avenue or alley, the Corporation shall make a just compensation therefor to the person whose property is so tak en; and if the amount of such compensation cannot be agreed upon, the Mayor shall cause the same to be ascertained by a jury of six disinterested men, who shall be inhabitants of the city.

Sec. 43.—All jurors, empannelled to inquire into the amount of benefits or damages that shall happen to the owners of property so proposed to be taken, shall first be sworn to thateffect, and shall return to the Mayor their inquest in writing, signed by each juror.

Sec. 44.—In case the Mayor shall, at any time, be guilty of a palpable omission of duty, or shall wilfully and corruptly be guilty of oppression, malconduct or partiality in the discharge of the duties of his office, he shall be liable to indictment in the Probate Court of Sanpete County; and, on conviction, he shall be liable to fine and imprisonment, and the Court shall have power on the recommend of the jury, to add to the judgment of the Court that he be removed from office.

Sec. 45.—The City Council shall have power to provide for the punishment of offenders and vagrants by imprisonment in the county or city jail, or by compelling them to labor upon the streets or other public works until the same shall be fully paid, in all cases when such offenders or vagrants shall fail or refuse to pay the fine and forfeitures which may be awarded against them.

Sec. 46.—The inhabitants of Manti City shall, from and after the next ensuing two years from the first Monday of April next, be exempt from working on any road or roads beyond the limits of said city. But all taxes devoted to road purposes shall, from and after said term of two years, be collected and expended, by and under the direction of the Supevisor of Streets, within the limits of said city.

Approved Feb. 6, 1851.

——:o:——

CHAPTER XCV.

An Ordinance to incorporate Parowam City.

Sec. 1.—Be it ordained by the General Assembly of the State of Deseret: That all that district of country in Iron county in this State, beginning at the dam above the saw-mill in the mouth of the cañon on Centre creek and running from thence northeast along the base of the mountain two miles, thence north three miles, thence west six miles, thence south to the base of the mountain, thence along the base of the mountain in a northeasterly direction to the place of beginning, including the present location, shall be known and designated as Parowan City; and the inhabitants thereof are hereby constituted a body corporate and politic by the name aforesaid, and shall have perpetual succession, and may have and use a common seal which they may change and alter at pleasure.

Sec. 2.—The inhabitants of said city, by the name and style aforesaid, shall have power to sue and be sued, to plead and be impleaded, defend and be defended, in all Courts of law and equity and in all actions whatsoever; to purchase, receive and hold property, real and personal, in said city; to purchase, receive and hold real property beyond the city for burying grounds or public purposes for the use of the inhabitants of said city; to sell, lease, convey or dispose of property, real and personal, for the benefit of said city; to improve and protect such property, and to do all other things in relation thereto as natural persons.

Sec. 3.—There shall be a City Council, to consist of a Mayor, two Aldermen and three Councilors, who shall have the qualifications of electors of said city, and shall be chosen by the qualified voters thereof, and shall hold their offices for two years and until their successors shall be elected and qualified. The City Council shall judge of the qualifications, elections and returns of their own members; and a majority of them shall form a quorum to do business, but a smaller number may adjourn from day to day and compel the attendance of absent members, under such penalties as may be prescribed by ordinance.

Sec. 4.—The Mayor, Aldermen and Councilors, before entering upon the duties of their offices, shall take and subscribe an oath or affirmation that they will support the Constitution of the United States and of this State, and that they will well and truly perform the duties of their offices to the best of their skill and ability.

Sec. 5.—An election, for the election of one Mayor, two Aldermen and three Councilors, shall be held on the second Monday of February, 1863, and every two years thereafter; and shall be held, conducted and the returns thereof made in such manner as shall be provided for by the ordinances of the City Council.

Sec. 6.—All free white male inhabitants of the age of eighteen years, who are entitled to vote for State officers, and who shall have been actual residents of said city sixty days next preceding said election, shall be entitled to vote for city officers.

Sec. 7.—The City Council shall have authority to levy and collect taxes for city purposes upon all taxable property, real and personal, within the limits of the city, not exceeding one half per cent. per annum upon the assessed value thereof, and may enforce the payment of the same in any manner to be provided by ordinance, not repugnant to the Constitution of the United States or of this State.

Sec. 8.—The City Council shall have power to appoint a Recorder, Treasurer, Assessor and Collector, Marshal and Supervisor of Streets. They shall also have the power to appoint all such other officers, by ordinance, as may be necessary, define the duties of all city officers and remove them from office at pleasure.

Sec. 9.—The City Council shall have power to require of all officers appointed in pursuance of this ordinance, bonds with penalty and security, for the faithful performance of their respective duties, such as may be deemed expedient; and also to require all officers appointed as aforesaid to take an oath for the faithful performance of the duties of their respective offices.

Sec. 10.—The City Council shall have power and authority to make, ordain, establish and execute all such ordinances, not repugnant to the Constitution of the United States or of this State, as they may deem necessary for the peace, benefit, good order, regulation, convenience and cleanliness of said city, for the protection of property therein from destruction by fire or otherwise, and for the health and happiness thereof. They shall have power to fill all vacancies, that may happen by death, resignation or removal, in any of the offices herein made elective; to fix and establish all the fees of the officers of said corporation, not herein established; to impose such fines, not exceeding one hundred dollars for each offense, as they may deem just, for refusing to accept of any office in or under the corporation or for misconduct therein; to divide the city into wards, and specify the boundaries thereof.

Sec. 11.—To establish, support and regulate common schools; to borrow money on the credit of the city: Provided, that no sum or sums of money be borrowed on a greater interest than six per cent. per annum, nor shall the interest on the aggregate of all the sums borrowed and outstanding ever exceed one half of the city revenue arising from taxes assessed on real estate within this corporation.

Sec. 12.—To make regulations to prevent the introduction of contagious diseases into the city; to make quarantine laws for that purpose and enforce the same.

Sec. 13.—To appropriate and provide for the payment of the expenses and debts of the city.

Sec. 14.—To establish hospitals and make regulations for the government of the same; to make rgulations to secure the general health of the inhabitants; to declare what shall be nuisances and to prevent and remove the same.

Sec. 15.—To provide the city with water; to dig wells, lay pump logs and pipes and erect pumps in the streets for the extinguishment of fires and convenience of the inhabitants.

Sec. 16.—To open, alter, widen, extend, establish, grade, pave or otherwise improve and keep in repair streets, avenues, lanes and alleys; and to establish, erect and keep in repair aqueducts and bridges.

Sec. 17.—To provide for the lighting of the streets and erecting lamp posts; and to establish, support and regulate night watches; to erect market houses, establish markets and market places and provide for the government and regulation thereof.

Sec. 18.—To provide for erecting all needful buildings for the use of the city;

and for inclosing, improving and regulating all public grounds belonging to the city.

Sec. 19.—To license, tax and regulate auctioneers, merchants and retailers, grocers and taverns, ordinaries, hawkers, peddlers, brokers, pawnbrokers, and money changers.

Sec. 20.—To license, tax and regulate hacking, carriages, wagons, carts and drays and fix the rates to be charged for the carriage of persons and for wagonage, cartage and drayage of property; as also to license and regulate porters and fix the rates of porterage.

Sec. 21.—To license tax and regulate theatricals and other exhibitions, shows and amusements.

Sec. 22.—To tax, restrain, prohibit and suppress tippling houses, dram shops, gaming houses, bawdy and other disorderly houses.

Sec. 23.—To provide for the prevention and extinguishment of fires; to regulate the fixing of chimneys and flues thereof and stove pipes, and to organize and establish fire companies.

Sec. 24.—To regulate the storage of gunpowder, tar, pitch, rosin and other combustible materials.

Sec. 25.—To regulate and order parapet walls and other partition fences; to restrain, regulate or prohibit the running at large of cattle, horses, mules, sheep, swine, goats and all kinds of poultry; and to tax and regulate the keeping of dogs and authorize the destruction of the same when at large contrary to city ordinance.

Sec. 26.—To establish standard weights and measures and regulate the weights and measures to be used in the city, in all cases not provided for by law.

Sec. 27.—To provide for the inspecting and measuring of lumber and other building materials, and for the measurement of all kinds of mechanical work.

Sec. 28.—To provide for the inspection and weighing of hay, lime and stone coal, and the measuring of charcoal, firewood and other fuel to be sold or used within the city.

Sec. 29.—To license, regulate, prohibit or restrain the manufacturing, selling or giving away of spirituous, vinous or fermented liquors, tavern keepers, dram or tippling shop keepers, boarding, victualing or coffee houses, restaurants, saloons or other houses or places for the selling or giving away of ardent, vinous or fermented liquors; to provide for and regulate the inspection of tobacco, beef, pork, flour and meal; also beer, whisky, brandy and all other spirituous or fermented liquors.

Sec. 30.—To regulate the weight, quality and price of bread sold and used in the city.

Sec. 31.—To provide for taking the enumeration of the inhabitants of the city.

Sec. 32.—To fix the compensation of all city officers and regulate the fees of jurors, witnesses and others for services rendered under this or any city ordinance.

Sec. 33.—The City Council shall have exclusive power within the city, by ordinance, to license, regulate, suppress or restrain billiard tables, and from one to twenty pin alleys and every other description of gaming or gambling.

Sec. 34.—The City Council shall have exclusive power within the city, by ordinance, to license, regulate or restrain the keeping of ferries and toll bridges; to regulate the Police of the city; to impose fines, forfeitures and penalties for the breach of any ordinance, and provide for the recovery of such fines and forfeitures and the enforcement of such penalties; and to pass such ordinances as may be nessesary and proper for carrying into effect and execution the powers specified in this ordinance: Provided such ordinances are not repugnant to the Constitution of the United States or of this State.

Sec. 35.—All ordinances passed by the City Council shall, within one month after they shall have been passed, be published in some newspaper printed in said city, or certified copies thereof, be posted up in three of the most public places in the city.

Sec. 36.—All ordinances of the city may be proven by the seal of the Corporation; and when printed or published in book or pamphlet form, purporting to be printed or published by the authority of the Corporation, the same shall be received in evidence in all Courts or places, without further proof.

Sec. 37.—The Mayor and Aldermen shall be conservators of the peace within the limits of the city, and shall have all the powers of justices of the Peace therein, both in civil and criminal cases arising under the laws of the State. They shall, as Justices of the Peace, within the limits of said city, perform the same duties, be governed by the same laws, give the same bonds and securities as other Justices of the Peace and be commissioned as Justices of the Peace in and for said city, by the Governor.

Sec. 38.—The Mayor and Aldermen shall have exclusive jurisdiction in all cases arising under the ordinances of the Corporation, and shall issue such process as may be necessary to carry said ordinances into execution and effect. Appeals may be had from any decision or judgment of said Mayor or Aldermen, arising under the ordinances of said city, to the Municipal Court, under such regulations as may be prescribed by ordinance, which court shall be composed of the Mayor as Chief Justice and the Aldermen as Associate Justices; and from the final judgment of the Municipal Court to the Probate Court of Iron County in the same manner as appeals are taken from Justices of the Peace: Provided the parties litigant shall have a right to a trial by jury of twelve men, in all cases before the Municipal Court. The Municipal Court shall have power to grant writs of *habeas corpus* and try the same, in all cases arising under the ordinances of the City Council.

Sec. 39.—The Municipal Court may sit on the first Monday of every month, and the City Council at such times and places as may be prescribed by city ordinance; special meetings of which may at any time be called by the Mayor or any two Aldermen.

Sec. 40.—All process issued by the Mayor, Aldermen or Municipal Court shall be directed to the Marshal; and in the execution thereof he shall be governed by the same laws as are or may be prescribed for the direction and compensation of Constables in similar cases. The Marshal shall also perform such other duties as may be required of him under the ordinances of said city, and shall be the principal ministerial officer.

Sec. 41.—It shall be the duty of the Recorder to make and keep accurate records of all ordinances made by the City Council, and of all their proceedings in their corporate capacity, which record shall at all times be open to the inspection of the electors of said city; and shall perform all other duties as may be required of him by the ordinances of the City Council and shall serve as Clerk of the Municipal Court.

Sec. 42.—When it shall be necessary to take private property for opening, widening or altering any public street, lane, avenue or alley, the Corporation shall make a just compensation therefor to the person whose property is so taken; and if the amount of such compensation cannot be agreed upon, the Mayor shall cause the same to be ascertained by a jury of six disinterested men, who shall be inhabitants of the city.

Sec. 43.—All jurors empannelled to inquire into the amount of benefits or damages that shall happen to the owners of property so proposed to be taken, shall first be sworn to that effect, and shall return to the Mayor their inquest in writing, signed by each juror.

Sec. 44.—In case the Mayor shall, at any time, be guilty of a palpable omission of duty, or shall wilfully and corruptly be guilty of oppression, malconduct, or partiality in the discharge of the duties of his office, he shall be liable to indictment in the Probate Court of Iron County; and, on conviction he shall be liable to a fine and imprisonment; and the Court shall have power, on the recommend of the jury, to add to the judgment of the Court, that he be removed from office.

Sec. 45.—The City Council shall have power to provide for the punishment of offenders and vagrants by imprisonment in the county or city jail, or by compelling them to labor on the streets or other public works until the same shall be fully paid, in all cases when such offenders or vagrants shall fail or refuse to pay the fine and forfeitures which may be awarded against them.

Sec. 46.—The inhabitants of the city of Parowan shall, from and after the next ensuing two years from the first Monday of April next, be exempt from working on any road or roads beyond the limits of said city. But all taxes devoted to road purposes shall, from and after said term of two years, be collected and expended, by and under the direction of the Supervisor of Streets, within the limits of said city.

Approved Feb. 6, 1851.

———:o:———

CHAPTER XCVI.

An ACT to incorporate Cedar City, in Iron County, Utah Territory.

Sec. 1.—Be it enacted by the Governor and Legislative Assembly of the Territory of Utah: That all that district of Iron county embraced in the following boundaries, to wit: beginning at the mouth of Coal Creek cañon, thence north three miles, thence west six miles, thence south six miles, thence east six miles, thence north three miles to place of beginning shall be known and designated under the name and style of Cedar City; and the inhabitants thereof are hereby constituted a body corporate and politic by the name aforesaid, and shall have perpetual succession, and may have and use a common seal, which they may change and alter at pleasure.

Sec. 2—The inhabitants of said city, by the name and style aforesaid, shall have power to sue and be sued, to plead and be impleaded, defend and be defended in all Courts of law and equity and in all actions whatsoever; to purchase, receive and hold property, real and personal, in said city; to purchase, receive and hold real property, beyond the city, for burying grounds or other public purposes for the inhabitants of said city; to sell, lease or dispose of property real and personal, for the benefit of said city; to improve and protect such property, and to do all other things in relation thereto, as natural persons.

Sec. 3.—There shall be a City Council, to consist of a Mayor, two Aldermen and three Councilors, who shall have the qualifications of electors of said city, and shall be chosen by the qualified voters thereof, and shall hold their offices for two years, and until their successors shall be elected and qualified. The City Council shall judge of the qualifications, elections and returns of their members; and a majority of them shall form a quorum to do business, but a smaller number may adjourn from day to day and compel the attendance of absent members, under such penalties as may be prescribed by ordinance.

Sec. 4.—The Mayor, Aldermen and Councilors, before entering on the duties of their offices, shall take and subscribe an oath or affirmation that they will support the Constitution of the United States and the laws of this Territory, and that they will well and truly perform all the duties of their offices to the best of their skill and abilities.

Sec. 5.—An election, for the election of one Mayor, two Aldermen and three Councilors, shall be held on the second Monday of February, 1868, and every two years thereafter, and shall be held, conducted and returns thereof made in such manner as shall be provided for by the ordinances of the City Council.

Sec. 6.—All free white male inhabitants who are of the age of twenty-one years, who are entitled to vote for Territorial officers, and who shall have been actual residents of said city sixty days next preceding said election shall be entitled to vote for city officers.

Sec. 7.—The City Council shall have authority to levy and collect taxes, for city purposes, upon all taxable property, real and personal, within the limits of the city, not exceeding one half per cent. per annum upon the assessed value thereof; and may enforce the payment of the same in any manner to be provided by ordinance, not repugnant to the Constitution of the United States and the laws of this Territory.

Sec. 8.—The City Council shall have power to appoint a Recorder, Treasurer, Assessor and Collector, Marshal and Supervisors of Streets. They shall also have the power to appoint all such officers, by ordinance, as may be necessary, define the duties of all city officers and remove them from office at pleasure.

Sec. 9.—The City Council shall have power to require of all officers, appointed in pursuance of this act, bonds with penalty and security, for the faithful performance of their respective duties, such as may be deemed expedient; and also to require of all officers, appointed as aforesaid, to take an oath for the faithful performance of the duties of their respective offices.

Sec. 10.—The City Council shall have power and authority to make, ordain, establish and execute all such ordinances, not repugnant to the Constitution of the United States or the laws of this Territory, as they may deem necessary for the peace, benefit, good order, regulation, convenience and cleanliness of said city; for the protection of property therein from destruction by fire or otherwise, and for the health and happiness thereof. They shall have power to fill all vacancies, that may happen by death, resignation or removal, in any of the offices herein made elective; to fix and establish all the fees of the officers of said Corporation not herein established; to impose such fines, not exceeding one hundred dollars for each offense, as they may deem just, for refusing to accept of any office in or under the Corporation, or for misconduct therein; to divide the city into Wards, and specify the boundaries thereof.

Sec. 11.—To establish, support and regulate common schools; to borrow money on the credit of the city: Provided, that no sum or sums of money be borrowed on a greater interest than six per cent. per annum; nor shall the interest on the aggregate of all the sums borrowed and outstanding ever exceed one half of the city revenue arising from taxes assessed on real estate within this corporation.

Sec. 12.—To make regulations to prevent the introduction of contagious diseases into the city; to make quarantine laws for that purpose, and enforce the same.

Sec. 13.—To appropriate and provide for the payment of the expenses and debts of the city.

Sec. 14.—To establish hospitals and make regulations for the government of the same; to make regulations to secure the general health of the inhabitants; to declare what shall be nuisances and to prevent and remove the same.

Sec. 15.—To provide the city with water; to dig wells, lay pump logs and pipes and erect pumps in the streets, for the extinguishment of fires and convenience of the inhabitants.

Sec. 16.—To open, alter, widen, extend, establish, grade, pave or otherwise improve and keep in repair streets, avenues, lanes and alleys; and to establish, erect and keep in repair aqueducts and bridges.

Sec. 17.—To provide for the lighting of the streets and erecting lamp posts; and establish, support and regulate night watches; to erect market houses, establish markets and market places and provide for the government and regulation thereof.

Sec. 18.—To provide for erecting all needful buildings for the use of the city, and for inclosing, improving and regulating all public grounds belonging to the city.

Sec. 19.—To license, tax and regulate auctioneers, merchants, retailers, grocers and taverns, ordinaries, hawkers, peddlers, brokers, pawn-brokers and money changers.

Sec. 20.—To license, tax and regulate hacking, carriages, wagons, carts and drays; and fix the rates to be charged for the carriage of persons and for wagonage, cartage and draying of property; as also to license and regulate porters and fix the rates of porterage.

Sec. 21.—To license, tax and regulate theatricals and other exhibitions, shows and amusements.

Sec. 22.—To tax, restrain, prohibit and suppress tippling houses, dram shops, gaming houses, bawdy and other disorderly houses.

Sec. 23.—To provide for the prevention and extinguishment of fires: to regulate the fixing of chimneys and the flues thereof and stove pipes, and to organize and establish fire companies.

Sec. 24.—To regulate the storage of gunpowder, tar, pitch, resin and other combustible materials.

Sec. 25.—To regulate and order parapet walls and other partition fences; to restrain, regulate or prohibit the running at large of cattle, horses, mules, sheep, swine. goats and all kinds of poultry; and to tax and regulate the keeping of dogs, and to authorize the destruction of the same when at large contrary to city ordinances.

Sec. 26.—To establish standard weights and measures and regulate the weights and measures to be used in the city, in all cases not provided for by law.

Sec. 27.—To provide for the inspection and measuring of lumber and other building materials, and for the measurement of all kinds of mechanical work.

Sec. 28.—To provide for the inspection and weighing of hay, lime and stone coal, and the measuring of charcoal, fire wood and other fuel to be sold or used within the city.

Sec. 29.—To license, regulate, prohibit or restrain the manufacturing, selling or giving away of spirituous, vinous or fermented liquors, tavern keepers, dram or tippling shop keepers, boarding. victualing or coffee houses, restaurants, saloons or other houses or places for the selling or giving away of ardent. vinous or fermented liquors: to provide for and regulate the inspection of tobacco, beef, pork. flour and meal; also beer, whisky, brandy and all other spirituous and fermented liquors.

Sec. 30.—To regulate the weight, quality and price of bread sold and used in the city.

Sec. 31.—To provide for taking the enumeration of the inhabitants of the city.

Sec. 32.—To fix the compensation of all city officers, and regulate the fees of jurors, witnesses and others for services rendered under this or any city ordinance.

Sec. 33.—The City Council shall have exclusive power within the city, by ordinance, to license, regulate, suppress or restrain billiard tables and from one to twenty pin alleys and every other description of gaming or gambling.

Sec. 34.—The City Council shall have exclusive power within the city, by ordinance, to regulate the police of the city; to impose fines, forfeitures and penalties for the breach of any ordinance, and provide for the recovery of such fines and forfeitures and the enforcement of such penalties; and to pass such ordinances as may be necessary and proper to carry into effect and execution the powers specified in this act: Provided, that such ordinances are not repugnant to the Constitution of the United States or the laws of this Territory.

Sec. 35.—All ordinances passed by the City Council shall, within one month after they shall have been passed, be published in some newspaper printed in said city, or certified copies thereof be posted up in three of the most public places in the city.

Sec. 36.—All ordinances of the city may be proven by seal of the corporation; and when published in book or pamphlet form, purporting to be printed or published by the authority of the corporation, the same shall be received in evidence in all Courts or places, without further proof.

SEC. 37.—The Mayor and Aldermen shall be Conservators of the Peace within the limits of the city, and shall have all the powers of Justices of the Peace therein, both in civil and criminal cases arising under the laws of the Territory. They shall, as Justices of the Peace within the limits of said city, perform the same duties, be governed by the same laws, and give the same bonds and securities as other Justices of the Peace, and be commissioned, as Justices of the Peace in and for said city, by the Governor.

SEC. 38.—The Mayor and Aldermen shall have jurisdiction in all cases arising under the ordinances of the Corporation, and shall issue such process as may be necessary to carry said ordinances into execution and effect. Appeals may be had from any decision or judgment of said Mayor or Aldermen, arising under the ordinances of said city, to the Municipal Court under such regulations as may be prescribed by ordinance, which Court shall be composed of the Mayor as Chief Justice, and the Aldermen as Associate Justices; and from the final judgment of the Mubicipal Court to the Probate Court of Iron county, in the same manner as appeals are taken from Justices of the Peace: Provided the parties litigant shall have a right to a trial by a jury of twelve men, in all cases before the Municipal Court. The Municipal Court shall have power to grant writs of *habeas corpus* and try the same in all cases arising under the ordinances of the City Council.

SEC. 39.—The Municipal Court may sit on the first Monday of every month, and the City Council at such times and places as may be prescribed by city ordinance, special meetings of which may at any time be called by the Mayor or any two Aldermen.

SEC. 40.—All process issued by the Mayor, Aldermen or Municipal Court shall be directed to the Marshal; and in the execution thereof he shall be governed by the same laws as are or may be prescribed for the direction and compensation of Constables in similar cases. The Marshal shall also perform such other duties as may be required of him under the ordinances of said city, and shall be the principal ministerial officer.

SEC. 41.—It shall be the duty of the Recorder to make and keep accurate records of all ordinances made by the City Council and of all their proceedings in their Corporate capacity, which record shall at all times be open to the inspection of the electors of said city, and shall perform all other duties as may be required of him by the ordinances of the City Council, and shall serve as Clerk of the Municipal Court.

SEC. 42.—When it shall be necessary to take private property for opening, widening or altering any public street, lane, avenue or alleys, the Corporation shall make a just compensation therefor, to the person whose property is so taken; and if the amount of such compensation cannot be agreed upon, the Mayor shall cause the same to be ascertained by a jury of six disinterested men, who shall be inhabitants of the city.

SEC. 43.—All jurors, empannelled to inquire into the amount of benefits or damages that shall happen to the owners of property so proposed to be taken, shall first be sworn to that effect, and shall return to the Mayor their inquest in writing, signed by each juror.

SEC. 44.—In case the Mayor shall, at any time, be guilty of any palpable omission of duty, or shall wilfully or corruptly be guilty of oppression, malconduct, or partiality in the discharge of the duties of his office, he shall be liable to indictment in the Probate Court of Iron county; and, on conviction, he shall be liable to fine and imprisonment; and the Court shall have power, on the recommend of the jury, to add to the judgment of the Court that he be removed from office.

SEC. 45.—The City Council shall have power to provide for the punishment of offenders and vagrants by imprisonment in the county or city jail, or by compelling them to labor on the streets or other public works until the same shall be fully paid, in all cases where such offender or vagrants shall fail or refuse to pay the fines and forfeitures which may be recovered against them.

SEC. 46.—The inhabitants of Cedar City shall, from and after the next ensuing two years from the first Monday in March next, be exempt from working on any road or roads beyond the limits of said city. But all taxes devoted to road purposes shall, from and after said term of two years, be collected and expended, by and under the direction of the Supervisor of Streets within the limits of the city.

Approved Feb. 10, 1852.

CHAPTER XCVII.

An ACT to incorporate the City of Lehi.

Sec. 1.—Be it enacted by the Governor and Legislative Assembly of the Territory of Utah: That all that portion of the country lying on Dry Creek, in Utah county, bounded as follows, to wit: commencing at the Utah Lake direct south of the south-east corner of the plat of Evansville and running direct to said corner, from thence north three miles, from thence west to the river Jordan, from thence up the river Jordan to the outlet of the Lake, from thence up the Lake to the place of beginning is hereby incorporated into a city which shall be called "the city of Lehi;" and the inhabitants thereof are hereby constituted a body corporate and politic by the name aforesaid; and shall have perpetual succession, and may have and use a common seal, which they may change and alter at pleasure.

Sec. 2.—The inhabitants of said city, by the name and style aforesaid, shall have power to sue and be sued, to plead and be impleaded, defend and be defended in all Courts of law and equity and in all actions whatsoever; to purchase, receive and hold property, real and personal, in said city to purchase, receive and hold real property beyond the city for burying grounds or other public purposes for the use of the inhabitants of said city; to sell, lease, convey or dispose of property, real and personal, for the benefit of said city; to improve and protect such property, and to do all other things in relation thereto, as natural persons.

Sec. 3.—There shall be a City Council to consist of a Mayor, two Aldermen and three Councilors, who shall have the qualifications of electors of said city, and shall be chosen by the qualified voters thereof, and shall hold their offices for two years, and until their successors shall be elected and qualified. The City Council shall judge of the qualifications, elections and returns of their own members, and a majority of them shall form a quorum to do business; but a smaller number may adjourn from day to day and compel the attendance of absent members, under such penalties as may be prescribed by ordinance.

Sec. 4.—The Mayor, Aldermen and Councilors, before entering upon the duties of their offices, shall take and subscribe an oath or affirmation that they will support the Constitution of the United States and the laws of this Territory, and that they will well and truly perform all the duties of their offices to the best of their skill and abilities.

Sec. 5.—An election, for the election of one Mayor, two Aldermen and three Councilors, shall be held on the second Monday of February, 1863, and every two years thereafter; and shall be held, conducted and returns thereof made in such manner as shall be provided for by the ordinances of the City Council.

Sec. 6.—All free white male inhabitants who are of the age of twenty-one years, who are entitled to vote for Territorial officers and who shall have been actual residents of said city sixty days next preceding said election, shall be entitled to vote for city officers.

Sec. 7.—The City Council shall have authority to levy and collect taxes, for city purposes, upon all taxable property, real and personal, within the limits of the city, not exceeding one half per cent. per annum upon the assessed value thereof; and may enforce the payment of the same in any manner to be provided by ordinance, not repugnant to the Constitution of the United States or the laws of this Territory.

Sec. 8.—The City Council shall have power to appoint a Recorder, Treasurer, Assessor and Collector, Marshal and Supervisors of Streets. They shall also have power to appoint all such officers, by ordinance, as may be necessary, define the duties of all city officers and remove them from office at pleasure.

Sec. 9.—The City Council shall have power to require of all officers, appointed in pursuance of this act, bonds with penalty and security for the faithful performance of their respective duties, such as may be deemed expedient; and also to require of all officers, appointed as aforesaid, to take an oath for the faithful performance of the duties of their respective offices.

Sec. 10.—The City Council shall have power and authority to make, ordain, establish and execute all such ordinances, not repugnant to the Constitution of the United States or the laws of this Territory, as they may deem necessary for the peace, benefit, good order, regulation, convenience and cleanliness of said city; for the protection of property therein from destruction by fire or otherwise, and for the health and hapiness thereof. They shall have power to fill all vacancies, that may happen by death, resignation or removal, in any of the offices herein made elective; to fix and establish all the fees of the officers of said Corporation, not herein established; to impose such fines, not exceeding one hundred dollars for each offence, as they may deem just, for refusing to accept of any office in or under the Corporation, or from misconduct therein; to divide the city into Wards and specify the boundaries thereof.

Sec. 11.—To establish, support and regulate common schools; to borrow money on the credit of the city: Provided, that no sum or sums of money be borrowed on a greater interest than six per cent. per annum; nor shall the interest on the aggregate of all the sums borrowed and outstanding ever exceed one half of the city revenue arising from taxes assessed on real estate within this Corporation.

Sec. 12.—To make regulations to prevent the introduction of contagious diseases into the city; to make quarantine laws for that purpose and enforce the same.

Sec. 13.—To appropriate and provide for the payment of the expenses and debts of the city.

Sec. 14.—To establish hospitals and make regulations for the government of the same; to make regulations to secure the general health of the inhabitants; to declare what shall be nuisances and to prevent and remove the same.

Sec. 15.—To provide the city with water; to dig wells, lay pump logs and pipes and erect pumps in the streets for the extinguishment of fires and convenience of the inhabitants.

Sec. 16.—To open, alter, widen, extend, establish, grade, pave or otherwise improve and keep in repair streets, avenues, lanes and alleys; and to establish, erect and keep in repair aqueducts and bridges.

Sec. 17.—To provide for the lighting of the streets and erecting lamp posts; and establish, support and regulate night watches; to erect market houses; establish market and market places and to provide for the government and regulation thereof.

Sec. 18.—To provide for erecting all needful buildings for the use of the city, and for inclosing, improving and regulating all public grounds belonging to the city.

Sec. 19.—To license, tax and regulate auctioneers, merchants and retailers, grocers and taverns, ordinaries, hawkers, peddlers, brokers, pawnbrokers and money changers.

Sec. 20.—To license, tax and regulate hacking, carriages, wagons, carts and drays; and fix the rates to be charged for the carriage of persons and for wagonage, cartage and drayage of property; as also to license and regulate porters and fix the rate of porterage.

Sec. 21.—To license, tax, and regulate theatricals and other exhibitions, shows and amusements.

Sec. 22.—To tax, restrain, prohibit and suppress tippling houses, dram shops, gaming houses, bawdy and other disorderly houses.

Sec. 23.—To provide for the prevention and extinguishment of fires; to regulate the fixing of chimneys and the flues thereof and stove pipes, and to organize and establish fire companies.

Sec. 24.—To regulate the storage of gunpowder, tar, pitch, rosin and other combustible materials.

Sec. 25.—To regulate and order parapet walls and other partition fences; to restrain, regulate and prohibit the running at large of cattle, horses, mules, sheep, swine, goats and all kinds of poultry; and to tax and regulate the keeping of dogs, and to authorize the destruction of the same when at large contrary to city ordinances.

Sec. 26.—To establish standard weights and measures, and regulate the weights and measures to be used in the city, in all cases not provided for by law.

Sec. 27.—To provide for the inspection and measuring of lumber and other building materials; and for the measurement of all kinds of mechanical work.

Sec. 28.—To provide for the inspection and weighing of hay, lime and stone coal, and the measuring of charcoal, firewood and other fuel to be sold or used within the city.

Sec. 29.—To license, regulate, prohibit or restrain the manufacturing, selling or giving away of spirituous, vinous or fermented liquors, tavern keepers, dram or tippling shop keepers, boarding, victualing or coffee houses, restaurants, saloons or other houses or places for the selling or giving away of ardent, vinous or fermented liquors; to provide for and regulate the inspection of tobacco, beef, pork, flour and meal; also beer, whisky, brandy and other spirituous or fermented liquors.

Sec. 30.—To regulate the weight, quality and price of bread sold and used in the city.

Sec. 31.—To provide for taking the enumeration of the inhabitants of the city.

Sec. 32.—To fix the compensation of all city officers, and regulate the fees of jurors, witnesses and others for services rendered under this or any city ordinance.

Sec. 33.—The City Council shall have exclusive power within the city, by ordinance, to license, regulate, suppress or restrain billiard tables and from one to twenty pin alleys and every other description of gaming or gambling.

Sec. 34.—The City Council shall have exclusive power within the city, by ordinance, to license, regulate or restrain the keeping of ferries and toll bridges; to regulate the Police of the city; to impose fines, forfeitures and penalties for the breach of any ordinance, and provide for the recovery of such fines and forfeitures and the enforcement of such penalties; and to pass such ordinances as may be necessary and proper for carrying into effect and execution the powers specified in this act: Provided, such ordinances are not repugnant to the Constitution of the United States or the laws of this Territory.

Sec. 35.—All ordinances passed by the City Council shall, within one month after they shall have been passed, be published in some newspaper printed in said city, or certified copies thereof be posted up in three of the most public places in the city.

Sec. 36.—All ordinances of the city may be proven by the seal of the Corporation; and when printed or published in book or pamphlet form, purporting to be printed or published by the authority of the Corporation, the same shall be received in evidence in all Courts and places, without further proof.

Sec. 37.—The Mayor and Aldermen shall be Conservators of the Peace within the limits of the city, and shall have all the powers of Justices of the Peace therein, both in civil and criminal cases arising under the laws of the Territory. They shall, as Justices of the Peace, within the limits of said city, perform the same duties, be governed by the same laws, and give the same bonds and securities as other Justices of the Peace, and be commissioned, as other Justices of the Peace in and for said city, by the Governor.

Sec. 38.—The Mayor and Aldermen shall have exclusive jurisdiction in all cases arising under the ordinances of the corporatron, and shall issue such process as may be necessary to carry said ordinances into execution and effect. Appeals may be had from any decision or judgment of said Mayor or Aldermen, arising under the ordinances of said city, to the Municipal Court, under such regulations as may be prescribed by ordinance, which court shall be composed of the Mayor as Chief Justice and the Aldermen as Associate Justices; and from the final judgment of the Municipal Court to the Probate Court of Utah county, in the same manner as appeals are taken from Justices of the Peace: Provided, the parties litigant shall have a right to a trial by a jury of twelve men, in all cases before the Municipal Court. The Municipal Court shall have power to grant writs of *habeas corpus*, and try the same in all cases arising under the ordinances of the City Council.

Sec. 39.—The Municipal Court may sit on the first Monday of every month, and the City Council at such times and places as may be prescribed by city ordinance; special meetings of which may at any time be called by the Mayor or any two Aldermen.

Sec. 40.—All process issued by the Mayor, Aldermen or Municipal Court shall be directed to the Marshal, and in the execution thereof he shall be governed by the same laws as are or may be prescribed for the direction and compensation of Constables in similar cases. The Marshal shall also perform such other duties as may be required of him under the ordinances of said city, and shall be the principal ministerial officer.

Sec. 41.—It shall be the duty of the Recorder, to make and keep accurate records of all ordinances made by the City Council and of all their proceedings in their corporate capacity, which record shall at all times be open to the inspection of the electors of said city, and shall perform all other duties as may be required of him by the ordinances of the City Council, and shall serve as Clerk of the Municipal Court.

Sec. 42.—When it shall be necessary to take private property for opening, widening, or altering any public street, lane, avenue or alley, the Corporation shall make a just compensation therefor to the person whose property is so taken; and if the amount of such compensation cannot be agreed upon, the Mayor shall cause the same to be ascertained by a jury of six disinterested men, who shall be inhabitants of the city.

Sec. 43.—All jurors, empannelled to inquire into the amount of benefits, or damages that shall happen to the owners of property so proposed to be taken, shall first be sworn to that effect, and shall return to the Mayor their inquest in writing, signed by each juror.

Sec. 44.—In case the Mayor shall, at any time, be guilty of a palpable omission of duty, or shall wilfully and corruptly be guilty of oppression, malconduct or partiality in the discharge of the duties of his office, he shall be liable to indictment in the Probate Court of Utah county, and, on conviction, he shall be liable to fine and imprisonment; and the Court shall have power, on the recommend of the jury, to add to the judgment of the Court that he be removed from office.

Sec. 45.—The City Council shall have power to provide for the punishment of offenders and vagrants by imprisonment in the county or city jail, or by compelling them to labor upon the streets or other public works until the same shall be fully paid, in all cases where such offenders or vagrants shall fail or refuse to pay the fines and forfeitures which may be recovered against them.

Sec. 46.—The inhabitants of Lehi city shall, from and after the next ensuing two years from the first Monday of April next, be exempt from working on any road or roads beyond the limits of said city. But all taxes devoted to road purposes shall, from and after said term of two years, be collected and expended, by and under the direction of the Supervisor of Streets, within the limits of said city.

Approved Feb. 5, 1852.

CHAPTER XCVIII.

An ACT to incorporate Fillmore city, Millard county.

Sec. 1.—Be it enacted by the Governor and Legislative Assembly of the Territory of Utah: That all that district of Millard county embraced in the following boundaries, to wit: beginning at a point due east of the southeast corner of the public square, now surveyed, three miles, thence south three miles, thence west six miles, thence north six miles, thence east six miles, and thence south three miles to the place of beginning shall be known and designated under the name and style of Fillmore City; and the inhabitants thereof are hereby constituted a body corporate and politic by the name aforesaid, and shall have perpetual succession, and may have and use a common seal which they may change and alter at pleasure.

Sec. 2.—The inhabitants of said city, by the name and style aforesaid, shall have power to sue and be sued, to plead and be impleaded, defend and be defended in all Courts of law and equity in all actions whatsoever; to purchase, receive and hold property, real and personal, in said city; to purchase, receive and hold real property beyond the city for burying grounds or other public purposes for the inhabitants of said city; to sell, lease, convey or dispose of property, real and personal, for the benefit of said city; to improve and protect such property, and to do all other things in relation thereto, as natural persons.

Sec. 3.—There shall be a City Council to consist of a Mayor, two Aldermen and three Councilors, who shall have the qualifications of electors of said city and shall be chosen by the qualified voters thereof, and shall hold their offices for two years and until their successors shall be elected and qualified. The City Council shall judge of the qualifications, elections and returns of their own members, and a majority of them shall form a quorum to do business, but a smaller number may adjourn from day to day and compel the attendance of absent members, under such penalties as may be prescribed by ordinance.

Sec. 4.—The Mayor, Aldermen and Councilors, before entering on the duties of their offices, shall take and subscribe an oath or affirmation that they will support the Constitution of the United States and the laws of this Territory, and that they will well and truly perform the duties of their offices to the best of their skill and abilities.

Sec. 5.—An election, for the election of one Mayor, two Aldermen and three Councilors shall be held on the second Monday of February, 1863, and every two years thereafter, and shall be held, conducted and returns thereof made in such manner as shall be provided for by the ordinance of the City Council.

Sec. 6.—All free white male inhabitants who are of the age of twenty-one years, who are entitled to vote for Territorial officers and who shall be actual residents of said city sixty days next preceding said election, shall be entitled to vote for city officers.

Sec. 7.—The City Council shall have authority to levy and collect taxes, for city purposes, upon all taxable property, real and personal, within the limits of the city, not exceeding one half per cent. per annum upon the assessed value thereof; and may enforce the payment of the same in any manner to be provided by ordinance, not repugnant to the Constitution of the United States and the laws of this Territory.

Sec. 8.—The City Council shall have power to appoint a Recorder, Treasurer, Assessor and Collector, Marshal and Supervisors of Streets. They shall also have the power to appoint all such other officers, by ordinance, as may be necessary, define the duties of all city officers and remove them from office at pleasure.

Sec. 9.—The City Council shall have power to require of all officers, appointed in pursuance of this act, bonds with penalty and security for the faithful performance of their respective duties, such as may be deemed expedient, and also to require of all officers, appointed as aforesaid, to take an oath for the faithful performance of the duties of their respective offices.

Sec. 10.—The City Council shall have power and authority to make, ordain, establish and execute all such ordinances, not repugnant to the Constitution of the United States or the laws of this Territory, as they may deem necessary for the peace, benefit, good order, regulation, convenience and cleanliness of said city; for the protection of property therein from destruction by fire or otherwise, and for the health and happiness thereof. They shall have power to fill all vacancies, that may happen by death, resignation or removal, in any of the offices herein made elective; to fix and establish all the fees of the officers of said Corporation, not herein established; to impose such fines, not exceeding one hundred dollars for each offence, as they may deem just, for refusing to accept of any office in or under the Corporation, or for misconduct therein, to divide the city into Wards and specify the boundaries thereof.

Sec. 11.—To establish, support and regulate common schools; to borrow money on the credit of the city: Provided that no sum or sums of money be borrowed on a greater interest than six per cent. per annum; nor shall the interest on the aggregate of all the sums borrowed and outstanding ever exceed one half of the city revenue arising from taxes assessed on real estate within this corporation.

Sec. 12.—To make regulations to prevent the introduction of contagious diseases into the city; to make quarantine laws for that purpose and enforce the same.

Sec. 13.—To appropriate and provide for the payment of the expenses and debts of tho city.

Sec. 14.—To establish hospitals and make regulations for the government of the same; to make regulations to secure the general health of the inhabitants; to declare what shall be nuisances and to prevent and remove the same.

Sec. 15.—To provide the city with water; to dig wells, lay pump logs and pipes and erect pumps in the streets for the extinguishment of fires and convenience of the inhabitants.

Sec. 16.—To open alter, widen, extend, establish, grade, pave or otherwise improve and keep in repair streets, avenues, lanes and alleys; and to establish, erect and keep in repair aqueducts and bridges.

Sec. 17.—To provide for the lighting of the streets and erecting lamp posts; and establish, support and regulate night watches; to erect market houses, establish markets and market places and provide for the government and regulation thereof.

Sec. 18.—To provide for erecting all needful buildings for the use of the city, and for inclosing improving and regulating all public grounds belonging to the city.

Sec. 19.—To licence, tax and regulate auctioneers, merchants, retailers, grocers and taverns, ordinaries hawkers, peddlers, brokers, pawn-brokers and money changers.

Sec. 20.—To licence, tax and regulate hacking, carriages, wagons, carts, and drays, and fix the rates to be charged for the carriage of persons and for wagonage, cartage and draying of property as also to licence and regulate porters and fix the rates of porterage.

Sec. 21.—To licence, tax and regulate theatricals and other exhibitions, shows and amusements.

Sec. 22.—To tax, restrain, prohibit and suppress tippling houses, dram shops, gaming houses, bawdy and other disorderly houses.

Sec. 23.—To provide for the prevention and extinguishment of fires; to regulate the fixing of chimneys and the flues thereof and stove pipes; and to organize and establish fire companies.

Sec. 24.—To regulate the storage of gunpowder, tar, pitch, resin and other combustable materials.

Sec. 25.—To regulate and order parapet walls and other partition fences; to restrain, regulate or prohibit the running at large of cattle, horses, mules, sheep, swine, goats and all kinds of poultry; and to tax and regulate the keeping of dogs, and to authorize the destruction of the same when at large contrary to city ordinances.

Sec. 26—To establish standard weights and measures and regulate the weights and measures to be used in the city, in all cases provided for by law.

Sec. 27.—To provide for the inspection and measuring of lumber and other building materials, and for the measurement of all kinds of mechanical work.

Sec. 28. To provide for the inspection and weighing of hay, lime and stone coal, and the measuring of charcoal, firewood and other fuel to be sold or used within the city.

Sec. 29. To licence, regulate, prohibit or restrain the manufacturing, selling or giving away of spirituous, vinous or fermented liquors, tavern keepers, dram or tippling shop keepers, boarding, victualing or coffee houses, restaurants, saloons or other houses or places for the selling or giving away of ardent, vinous or fermented liquors; to provide for and regulate the inspection of tobacco, beef, pork, flour and meal; also beer, whisky, brandy and all other spirituous and fermented liquors.

Sec. 30.—To regulate the weight and quality and price of bread sold and used in the city.

Sec. 31.—To provide for the taking the enumeration of the inhabitants of the city.

Sec. 32.—To fix the compensation of all city officers, and regulate the fees of jurors, witnesses and others for services rendered under this or any other city ordinance.

Sec. 33.—The City Council shall have exclusive power within the city, by ordinance, to license, regulate, suppress or restrain billiard tables and from one to twenty pin alleys and every other description of gaming or gambling.

Sec. 34.—The City Council shall have exclusive power within the city, by ordinance, to regulate the police of the city; to impose fines, forfeitures and penalties for the breach of any ordinance, and provide for the recovery of such fines and forfeitures and the enforcement of such penalties; and to pass such ordinances as may be necessary and proper to carry into effect and execution the powers specified in this act: Provided, that such ordinances are not repugnant to the Constitution of the United States or the laws of this Territory.

Sec. 35.—All ordinances passed by the City Council shall, within one month after they shall have been passed, be published in some newspaper published in said city, or certified copies thereof be posted up in three of the most public places in the city.

Sec. 36 —All ordinances of the city may be proven by the seal of the Corporation; and when published in book or pamphlet form, purporting to be printed or published by the authority of the Corporation, the same shall be received in evidence in all Courts or places, without further proof.

Sec. 37.—The Mayor and Aldermen shall be Conservators of the Peace within the limits of the city, and shall have all the powers of Justices of the Peace therein, both in civil and criminal cases arising under the laws of the Territory. They shall, as Justices of the Peace within the limits of said city, perform the same duties, be governed by the same laws and give the same bonds and securities as other Justices of the Peace, and be commissioned, as Justices of the Peace in and for said city, by the Governor.

Sec. 38.—The Mayor and Aldermen shall have jurisdiction in all cases arising under the ordinances of the Corporation, and shall issue such process as may be necessary to carry said ordinances into execution and effect. Appeals may be had from any decision or judgment of said Mayor or Aldermen, arising under the ordinances of said city, to the Municipal Court, under such regulations as may be prescribed by ordinance, which Court shall be composed of the Mayor as Chief Justice and the Aldermen as Associate Justices; and from the final judgment of the Municipal Court to the Probate Court of Millard county, in the same manner as appeals are taken from Justices of the Peace: Provided, the parties litigant shall have a right to a trial by a jury of twelve men in all cases before a Municipal Court. The Municipal Court shall have power to grant writs of *habeas corpus* and try the same in all cases arising under the ordinances of the City Council.

Sec. 39. The Municipal Court may sit on the first Monday of every month; and the City Council at such times and places as may be prescribed by the city ordinance; special meetings of which may at any time be called by the Mayor or any two Aldermen.

Sec. 40.—All process issued by the Mayor, Aldermen or Municipal Court shall be directed by the Marshal, and in the execution thereof he shall be governed by the same laws as are or may be prescribed for the direction and compensation of Constables in similar cases. The Marshal shall also perform such other duties as may be required of him under the ordinances of said city, and shall be the principal ministerial officer.

Sec. 41.—It shall be the duty of the Recorder to make and keep accurate records of all ordinances made by the City Council and of all their proceedings in their corporate capacity, which record shall at all times be open to the inspection of the electors of said city, and shall perform all other duties as may be required of him by the ordinances of the City Council, and shall serve as Clerk of the municipal Court.

Sec. 42.—When it shall be necessary to take private property for opening, widening or altering any public street, lane avenue or alley, the Corporation shall make a just compensation therefor to the person whose property is so taken; and if the amount of such compensation cannot be agreed upon, the Mayor shall cause the same to be ascertained by a jury of six disinterested men, who shall be inhabitants of the city.

Sec. 43.—All jurors, empanelled to inquire into the amount of benefits or damages that shall happen to the owners of property so proposed to be taken, shall first be sworn to that effect, and shall return to the Mayor their inquest in writing, signed by each juror.

Sec. 44.—In case the Mayor shall, at any time, be guilty of any palpable omission of duty, or shall wilfully or corruptly be guilty of oppression, malconduct or partiality in the discharge of the duties of his office, he shall be liable to indictment in the Probate Court of Millard county, and, on conviction, he shall be liable to fine and imprisonment; and the Court shall have power, on the recommend of the jury, to add to the judgment of the Court that he be removed from office.

Sec. 45.—The City Council shall have power to provide for the punishment of offenders and vagrants by imprisonment in the county or city jail, or by compelling them to labor on the streets or other public works until the same shall be fully paid, in all cases where such offenders or vagrants shall fail or refuse to pay the fines and forfeitures which may be recovered against them.

Sec. 46.—The inhabitants of Fillmore City shall, from and after the next ensuing two years from the first Monday in March next, be exempt from working on any road or roads beyond the limits of said city. But all taxes devoted to road purposes shall, from and after said term of two years, be collected and expended, by and under the direction of the Supervisor of Streets, within the limits of the city.

Approved Feb. 13, 1852.

———:o:———

CHAPTER XCIX.

An ACT incorporating Nephi City.

Sec. 1.—Be it enacted by the Governor and Legislative Assembly of the Territory of Utah: That all that portion of country situated within the following boundaries, to wit: commencing at the south east corner of the plot of Nephi city, in the county of Juab, in said Territory, and running thence west two miles, thence north four miles, thence east to the base of the mountain, thence southerly along the mouth of the cañon and base of the mountain to a point opposite to the place of beginning shall be known and designated as Nephi city, and is hereby incorporated under the name and style aforesaid; and the inhabitants thereof are hereby constituted a body corporate and politic by the name aforesaid; and shall have perpetual succession, and may have and use a common seal, which they may change and alter at pleasure.

Sec. 2.—The inhabitants of said city, by the name and style aforesaid, shall have power to sue and be sued, to plead and be impleaded, defend and be defended in all Courts of law and equity and in all actions whatsoever; to purchase, receive and hold property, real and personal, in said city; to purchase, receive and hold real property beyond the city for burying grounds or other public purposes for the use of the inhabitants of said city; to sell, lease, convey or dispose of property, real and personal, for the benefit of said city; to improve and protect such property, and to do all other things in relation thereto, as natural persons.

Sec. 3.—There shall be a City Council to consist of a Mayor, two Aldermen and three Councilors, who shall have the qualifications of electors of said city, and shall be chosen by the qualified voters thereof, and shall hold their offices for two years, and until their successors shall be elected and qualified. The City Council shall Judge of the qualifications, elections and returns of their own members, and a majority of them shall form a quorum to do business; but a smaller number may adjourn from day to day and compel the attendance of absent members, under such penalties as may be prescribed by ordinance.

Sec. 4.—The Mayor, Alderman and Councilors, before entering upon the duties of their offices, shall take and subscribe an oath or affirmation that they will support the Constitution of the United States and the laws of this Territory, and that they will well and truly perform all the duties of their office to the best of their skill and abilities.

Sec. 5.—An election, for the election of one Mayor, two Aldermen and three Councilors, shall be held on the second Monday of February, 1863, and every two years thereafter, and shall be held, conducted, and returns thereof made in such manner as shall be provided for by the ordinances of the City Council.

Sec. 6.—All free white male inhabitants who are of the age of twenty-one years, who are entitled to vote for Territorial officers, and who shall have been actual residents of said city sixty days next preceding said election, shall be entitled to vote for city officers.

Sec. 7.—The City Council shall have authority to levy and collect taxes, for city purposes, upon all taxable property, real and personal, within the limits of the city, not exceeding one half per cent. per annum upon the assessed value thereof; and may enforce the payment of the same in any manner to be provided by ordinance, not repugnant to the Constitution of the United States or the laws of this Territory.

Sec. 8.—The City Council shall have power to appoint all such officers as may be necessary to carry into effect their legal enactments, define their duties and remove them at pleasure.

Sec. 9.—The City Council shall have power to require bonds, as they shall deem necessary, of all officers appointed by them, and require an oath or affirmation for the faithful discharge of the duties assigned them.

Sec. 10.—The City Council shall have power and authority to make, ordain, establish and execute all such ordinances and grant such licenses, not repugnant to the Constitution of the United States or the laws of this Territory, as they may deem necessary for the welfare of the inhabitants of said city and for the protection of their property. They shall have power to fill all vacancies that may occur by death or otherwise; to fix and establish all the fees of the officers of said corporation, not herein established; regulate the fees of witnesses and jurors and all other services; to divide the city into wards and specify the boundaries thereof.

Sec. 11.—All ordinances passed by the City Council shall, within one month after they shall have been passed, be published in some newspaper printed in said city, or certified copies thereof be posted up in eight of the most public places in the city.

Sec. 12.—The Mayor and Aldermen shall be Conservators of the Peace within the limits of the city, and shall have all the powers of Justices of the Peace, perform the same duties, be governed by the same laws and be commissioned in the same manner as other Justices of the Peace within this Territory.

Sec. 13.—The Mayor and Aldermen shall have exclusive jurisdiction in all cases arising under the ordinances of the corporation; and shall issue such process as may be necessary to carry said ordinances into execution and effect. Appeals may b had from any decision or judgment of said Mayor or Aldermen, arising under the ordinances of said city, to the Probate Court in the county of Juab, in the same manner as appeals are taken from Justices of the Peace.

Sec. 14.—It shall be the duty of the Recorder to make and keep accurate records of all ordinances made by the City Council and of all their proceedings in their corporate capacity, which record shall at all times be open to the inspection of the electors of said city, and shall perform all other duties as may be required of him by the ordinances of the City Council.

Sec. 15.—The City Council shall have power to restrain, regulate or prohibit the running at large of cattle, horses, mules, sheep, swine, goats and all kinds of poultry; and to tax and regulate the keeping of dogs, and to authorize the destruction of the same when at large contrary to city ordinances.

Sec. 16.—To license, regulate, prohibit or restrain the manufacturing, selling or giving away of spirituous, vinous or fermented liquors, tavern keepers, dram or tippling shop keepers, boarding, victualing or coffee houses, restaurants, saloons or other houses or places for the selling or giving away of ardent, vinous or fermented liquors.

Approved March 6, 1852.

———:o:———

CHAPTER C.

An ACT to incorporate the City of Springville.

Sec. 1.—Be it enacted by the Governor and Legislative Assembly of the Territory of Utah: That all that district of country embraced in the following boundaries, to wit: beginning at the southeast corner of Provo City Incorporation, thence easterly and southerly along the base of the mountain to the southeast corner of Springville survey, thence west to Utah Lake, thence northerly along the Lake shore to the southwest corner of Provo City Incorporation, thence east in line of Provo City Incorporation to the place of beginning shall be known and designated under the name and style of Springville; and the inhabitants thereof are hereby constituted a body corporate and politic, by the name aforesaid, and shall have perpetual succession, and may have and use a common seal, which they may change and alter at pleasure.

Sec. 2.—The inhabitants or said city, by the name and style aforesaid, shall have power to sue and be sued, to plead and be impleaded, defend and be defended in all Courts of law and equity and in all actions whatsoever; to purchase, receive and hold property, real and personal, in said city; to purchase, receive and hold real property beyond the city for burying grounds or other public purposes for the inhabitants of said city; to sell, lease, convey or dispose of property, real and personal, for the benefit of said city; to improve and protect such property, and to do all other things in relation thereto, as natural persons.

Sec. 3.—There shall be a City Council to consist of a Mayor, two Aldermen and three Councilors, who shall have the qualifications of electors of said city, and shall be chosen by the qualified voters thereof, and shall hold their offices for two years, and until their successors shall be elected and qualified. The City Council shall judge of the qualifications, elections and returns of their own members, and a majority of them shall form a quorum to do business, but a smaller number may adjourn from day to day, and compel the attendance of absent members, under such penalties as may be prescribed by ordinance.

Sec. 4.—The Mayor, Aldermen and Councilors, before entering on the duties of their offices, shall take and subscribe an oath or affirmation that they will support the Constitution of the United States and the laws of this Territory, and that they will well and truly perform the duties of their offices, to the best of their skill and abilities.

Sec. 5.—An election, for the election of one Mayor, two Aldermen and three Councilors, shall be held on the second Monday of February, 1863, and every two years thereafter, and shall be held, conducted and returns thereof made in such manner as shall be provided for by the ordinances of the City Council.

Sec. 6.—All free white male inhabitants who are of the age of eighteen years, who are entitled to vote for Territorial officers, and who shall have been actual residents of said city sixty days next preceding said election, shall be entitled to vote for city officers.

Sec. 7.—The City Council shall have authority to levy and collect taxes, for city purposes, upon all taxable property, real and personal, within the limits of the city, not exceeding one per cent. per annum upon the assessed value thereof; and may enforce the payment of the same in any manner to be provided by ordinance, not repugnant to the Constitution of the United States and the laws of the Territory.

Sec. 8.—The City Council shall have power to appoint a Recorder, Treasurer, Assessor and Collector, Marshal and Supervisor of Streets. They shall also have the power to appoint all such other officers, by ordinance, as may be necessary, define the duties of all city officers and remove them from office at pleasure.

Sec. 9.—The City Council shall have power to require of all officers, appointed in pursuance of this act, bonds with penalty and secrecy, for the faithful performance of their respective duties, such as may be deemed expedient; and also to require of all officers, appointed as aforesaid, to take an oath for the faithful performance of the duties of their respective offices.

Sec. 10.—The City Council shall have power and authority to make, ordain, establish and excute all such ordinances, not repugnant to the Constitution of the United States or the laws of this Territory, as they may deem necessary for the peace, benefit, good order, regulation, convenience and cleanliness of said city; for the protection of property therein from destruction by fire or otherwise, and for the health and happiness thereof. They shall have power to fill all vacancies, that may happen by death, resignation or removal, in any of the offices herein made elective; to fix and establish all the fees of the officers of said corporation not herein established; to impose such fines, not exceeding one hundred dollars for each offense, as they may deem just, for refusing to accept of any office in or under the Corporation, or for misconduct therein; to divide the city into Wards and specify the boundaries thereof.

Sec. 11.—To establish, support and regulate common schools; to borrow money on the credit of the city: Provided, that no sum or sums of money be borrowed on a greater interest than six per cent. per annum; nor shall the interest on the aggregate of all the sums borrowed and outstaiding ever exceed one half of the city revenue arising from taxes assessed on real estate within this corporation.

Sec. 12.—To make regulations to prevent the introduction of contagious diseases into the city; to make quarantine laws for that purpose and enforce the same.

Sec. 13.—To appropriate and provide for the payment of the expenses and debts of the city.

Sec. 14.—To establish hospitals and make regulations for the government of the same; to make regulations to secure the general health of the inhabitants; to declare what shall be nuisances and to prevent and remove the same.

Sec. 15.—To provide the city with water, to dig wells, lay pump logs and pipes and erect pumps in the streets for the extinguishment of fires and convenience of the inhabitants.

Sec. 16.—To open, alter, widen, extend, establish, grade, pave or otherwise improve and keep in repair streets, avenues, lanes and alleys; and to establish, erect and keep in repair aqueducts and bridges.

Sec. 17.—To provide for the lighting of the streets and erecting lamp posts, and to establish, support and regulate night watches; to erect market houses, establish markets and market places and provide for the government and regulation thereof.

Sec. 18.—To provide for erecting all needful buildings for the use of the city, and for inclosing, improving and regulating all public grounds belonging to the city.

Sec. 19.—To license, tax and regulate auctioneers, merchants, retailers, grocers and taverns, ordinaries, hawkers, peddlers, brokers, pawn-brokers and money changers.

Sec. 20.—To license, tax and regulate hacking, carriages, wagons, carts and drays; and fix the rates to be charged for the carriage of persons and for wagonage, cartage and draying of property; as also to license and regulate porters and fix the rate of porterage.

Sec. 21.—To license, tax and regulate theatricals and other exhibitions, shows and amusements.

Sec. 22.—To tax, restrain, prohibit and suppress tippling houses, dram shops, gaming houses, bawdy and other disorderly houses.

Sec. 23.—To provide for the prevention and extinguishment of fires; to regulate the fixing of chimneys and the flues thereof and stove pipes; and to organize and establish fire companies.

Sec. 24.—To regulate the storage of gunpowder, tar, pitch, resin and other combustible materials.

Sec. 25.—To regulate and order parapet walls and other partition fences; to restrain, regulate or prohibit the running at large of cattle, horses, mules, sheep, swine, goats and all kinds of poultry; and to tax and regulate the keeping of dogs, and to authorize the destruction of the same when at large contrary to city ordinances.

Sec. 26.—To establish standard weights and measures and regulate the weights and measures to be used in the city, in all cases not provided for by law.

Sec. 27.—To provide for the inspection and measuring of lumber and other building materials, and for the measurement of all kinds of mechanical work.

Sec. 28.—To provide for the inspection and weighing of hay, lime and stone coal, and the measuring of charcoal, fire wood and other fuel to be sold or used within the city.

Sec. 29.—To license, regulate, prohibit or restrain the manufacturing, selling, or giving away of spirituous, vinous, or fermented liquors, tavern keepers, dram or tippling shop keepers, boarding, victualing or coffee houses, restaurants, saloons or other houses or places for the selling or giving away of ardent, vinous or fermented liquors; to provide for and regulate the inspection of tobacco, beef, pork, flour and meal; also beer, whisky, brandy and all other spirituous and fermented liquors.

Sec. 30.—To regulate the weight, quality and price of bread sold and used in the city.

Sec. 31.—To provide for taking the enumeration of the inhabitants of the city.

Sec. 32.—To fix the compensation of all city officers and regulate the fees of jurors, witnesses and others for services rendered under this or any city ordinance.

Sec. 33.—The City Council shall have exclusive power within the city, by ordinance, to license, regulate, suppress or restrain billiard tables and from one to twenty pin alleys and every other description of gaming or gambling.

Sec. 34.—The City Council shall have exclusive power within the city, by ordinance, to regulate the Police of the City; to impose fines, forfeitures and penalties for the breach of any ordinance, and provide for the recovery of such fines and forfeitures and the enforcement of such penalties; and to pass such ordinances as may be necessary and proper to carry into effect and execution the powers specified in this act: Provided, that such ordinances are not repugnant to the Constitution of the United States or the laws of this Territory.

Sec. 35.—All ordinances passed by the City Council shall, within one month after they shall have been passed, be published in some newspaper published in said city, or certified copies thereof be posted up in three of the most public places in the city.

Sec. 36.—All ordinances of the city may be proven by the seal of the corporation;

and when published in book or pamphlet form, purporting to be printed or published by the authority of the corporation, the same shall be received in evidence in all Courts or places, without further proof.

Sec. 37.—The Mayor and Aldermen shall be Conservators of the Peace within the limits of the city, and shall have all the powers of Justices of the Peace therein, both in civil and criminal cases arising under the laws of the Territory. They shall, as Justices of the Peace within the limits of said city, perform the same duties, be governed by the same laws, give the same bonds and securities as other Justices of the Peace, and be commissioned, as Justices of the Peace in and for said city, by the Governor.

Sec. 38.—The Mayor and Aldermen shall have jurisdiction in all cases arising under the ordinances of the corporation, and shall issue such process as may be necessary to carry said ordinances into execution and effect. Appeals may be had from any decision or judgment of said Mayor or Aldermen, arising under the ordinances of said city, to the Municipal Court, under such regulations as may be prescribed by ordinance, which Court shall be composed of the Mayor as Chief Justice and the Aldermen as Associate Justices; and from the final judgment of the Municipal Court to the Probate Court of Utah county, in the same manner as appeals are taken from Justices of the Peace: Provided, the parties litigant shall have a right to a trial by a jury of twelve men in all cases before the Municipal Court. The Municipal Court shall have power to grant writs of *habeas corpus* and try the same, in all cases arising under the ordinances of the City Council.

Sec. 39.—The Municipal Court may sit on the first Monday of every month, and the City Council at such times and places as may be prescribed by city ordinance; special meetings of which may at any time be called by the Mayor or any two Aldermen.

Sec. 40.—All process issued by the Mayor, Aldermen or Municipal Court shall be directed to the Marshal, and, in the execution thereof, he shall be governed by the same laws as are or may be prescribed for the direction and compensation of Constables in similar cases. The Marshal shall also perform such other duties as may be reqired of him under the ordinances of said city, and shall be the principal ministerial officer.

Sec 41.—It shall be the duty of the Recorder to make and keep accurate records of all ordinances made by the City Council and of all their proceedings in their corporate capacity, which record shall at all times be open to the inspection of the electors of said city, and shall perform all other duties as may be required of him by the ordinances of the City Council, and shall serve as Clerk of the Municipal Court.

Sec. 42.—When it shall be necessary to take private property for opening, widening or altering any public street, lane, avenue or alley, the Corporation shall make a just compensation therefor to the person whose property is so taken; and if the amount of such compensation cannot be agreed upon, the Mayor shall cause the same to be ascertained by a jury of six disinterested men, who shall be inhabitants of the city.

Sec. 43.—All jurors, empanelled to inquire into the amount of benefits or damages that shall happen to the owners of property so proposed to be taken, shall first be sworn to that effect, and shall return to the Mayor their inquest in writing, signed by each juror.

Sec. 44.—In case the Mayor shall, at any time, be guilty of a palpable omission of duty, or shall wilfully and corruptly be guilty of oppression, malconduct or partiality in the discharge of the duties of his office, he shall be liable to indictment in the Probate Court of Utah county, and, on conviction, he shall be liable to fine and imprisonment; and the Court shall have power, on the recommend of the jury, to add to the judgment of the Court, that he be removed from office.

Sec. 45.—The City Council shall have power to provide for the punishment of offenders and vagrants by imprisonment in the county or city jail, or by compelling them to labor upon the streets or other public works, until the same shall be fully paid, in all cases where such offenders or vagrants shall fail or refuse to pay the fines and forfeitures which may be recovered against them

Sec. 46.—The inhabitants of Springville shall, from and after the next ensuing two years from the first Monday of April next, be exempt from working on any road or roads beyond the limits of said city. But all taxes devoted to road purposes shall, from and after said term of two years, be collected and expended, by and under the direction of the Supervisor of Streets, within the limits of said city.

Approved Feb. 13, 1852.

CHAPTER CI.

An ACT to incorporate American Fork City, Utah County.

Sec. 1.—Be it enacted by the Governor and Legislative Assembly of the Territory of Utah: That all that district of Utah County embraced in the following boundaries, to wit: beginning at a point one mile east of the southeast corner of the public square of the present town plot on the American Fork, thence north to the southeast bank of American Fork creek, thence northeasterly along the bank of said creek to the mouth of the cañon, thence west to the northeast corner of Lehi City Incorporation, thence south to Utah Lake, thence easterly and southerly along the shore of said Lake to a point directly south of the place of beginning, thence north to the place of beginning, shall be known and designated as American Fork City; and the inhabitants thereof are hereby constituted a body corporate and politic by the name aforesaid, and shall have perpetual succession, and may have and use a common seal, which they may change and alter at pleasure.

Sec. 2.—The inhabitants of said city, by the name and style aforesaid, shall have power to sue and be sued, to plead and be impleaded, to defend and be defended in all Courts of law and equity and in all actions whatsoever; to purchase, receive and hold property, real and personal, in said city, and to purchase, receive and hold real property beyond the city for burying grounds or other public purposes for the use of the inhabitants of said city; to sell, lease, convey or dispose of property, real and personal, for the benefit of said city; to improve and protect such property, and to do all other things in relation thereto, as natural persons.

Sec. 3.—There shall be a City Council to consist of a Mayor, two Aldermen and three Councilors, who shall have the qualifications of electors of said city, and shall be chosen by the qualified voters thereof, and shall hold their office for two years, and until their successors shall be elected and qualified. The City Council shall judge of the qualifications, elections and returns of their own members, and a majority of them shall form a quorum to do business; but a smaller number may adjourn from day to day, and compel the attendance of absent members, under such penalties as may be prescribed by ordinance.

Sec. 4.—The Mayor, Aldermen and Councilors, before entering upon the duties of their offices, shall take and subscribe an oath or affirmation that they will support the Constitution of the United States and the laws of this Territory, and that they will well and truly perform the duties of their offices to the best of their skill and ability.

Sec. 5.—An election, for the election of one Mayor, two Aldermen and three Councilors, shall be held on the second Monday of February, 1863; and every two years thereafter, and shall be held, conducted and returns thereof made in such manner as shall be provided for by the ordinances of the City Council.

Sec. 6.—All free white male inhabitants who are of the age of eighteen years, who are entitled to vote for Territorial officers, and who shall have been actual residents of said city sixty days next preceding said election, shall be entitled to vote for city officers.

Sec. 7.—The City Council shall have authority annually to assess, collect and expend the necessary tax for roads, streets, schools and other public purposes, and regulate and control the same within the city, and may enforce the payment of said tax by law; and the inhabitants of the city shall be exempt from all other assessments for road and school purposes, except on such property as they may possess outside of the city: Provided, that nothing herein shall be so construed as to effect, or infringe upon any tax assessed or authorized by any enactment of the Governor and Legislative Assembly.

Sec. 8.—The City Council shall have power to appoint a Recorder, Treasurer, Assessor and Collector, Marshal and Supervisor of Streets. They shall also have power to appoint all such other officers by ordinance, as may be necessary, define the duties of all city officers, and remove them from office at pleasure.

Sec. 9.—The City Council shall have power to require of all officers, appointed in pursuance of this act, bonds with penalty and security, for the faithful performance of their respective duties, such as may be deemed expedient; and also to require all officers, appointed as aforesaid, to take an oath for the faithful performance of the duties of their respective offices.

Sec. 10.—The City Council shall have power and authority to make, ordain, establish and execute all such ordinances, not repugnant to the Constitution of the United States or the laws of this Territory as they may deem necessary for the peace, benefit, good order, regulation, convenience and cleanliness of said city, for the protection of property therein, from destruction by fire or otherwise, and for the health and happiness thereof. They shall have power to fill all vacancies that may happen, by death, resignation or removal, in any of the offices herein made elective; to fix and establish all the fees of the officers of said corporation, not herein established; to impose such fines, not exceeding one hundred dollars for each offence, as they may deem just, for refusing to accept of any office in or under the Corporation, or for misconduct therein; to divide the city into Wards and specify the boundaries thereof.

Sec. 11.—To establish, support and regulate common schools; to borrow money on the credit of the city: Provided that no sum or sums of money be borrowed on a greater interest than six per cent. per annum, nor shall the interest on the aggregate of all the sums borrowed and outstanding ever exceed one half of the city revenue arising from taxes assessed on real estate within this corporation.

Sec. 12.—To make regulations to prevent the introduction of contagious diseases into the city; to make quarantine laws for that purpose and enforce the same.

Sec. 13.—To appropriate and provide for the payment and expenses and debts of the city.

Sec. 14.—To establish hospitals and make regulations for the government of the same; to make regulations to secure the general health of the inhabitants; to declare what shall be nuisances and to prevent and remove the same.

Sec. 15.—To provide the city with water; to dig wells, lay pump logs and pipes and erect pumps in the streets for the extinguishment of fires and convenience of the inhabitants; to control the water courses and mill sites in said city, and the water courses leading thereto in the immediate vicinity thereof.

Sec. 16.—To open, alter, widen, extend, establish, grade, pave or otherwise improve and keep in repair, streets, avenues, lanes and alleys; and to establish, erect and keep in repair aqueducts and bridges.

Sec. 17.—To provide for the lighting of the streets and erecting lamp posts; and establish, support and regulate night watches, to erect market houses, establish markets and market places and provide for the government and regulation thereof.

Sec. 18.—To provide for erecting all needful buildings for the use of the city, and for enclosing, improving and regulating all public grounds belonging to the city.

Sec. 19.—To license, tax and regulate auctioneers, merchants and retailers, grocers and taverns, ordinaries, hawkers, peddlers, brokers, pawn-brokers and money changers.

Sec. 20.—To license, tax and regulate hacking, carriages; wagons, carts and drays, and fix the rates to be charged for the carriage of persons and for wagonage, cartage and drayage of property; as also to license and regulate porters and fix the rates of porterage.

Sec. 21.—To license, tax and regulate theatricals and other exhibitions, shows and amusements.

Sec. 22.—To tax, restrain, prohibit and suppress tippling houses, dram shops, gaming houses, bawdy and other disorderly houses.

Sec. 23.—To provide for the prevention and extinguishment of fires; to regulate the fixing of chimneys and the flues thereof and stove pipes, and to organize and establish fire companies.

Sec. 24.—To regulate the storage of gunpowder, tar, pitch, rosin and other combustible materials.

Sec. 25.—To regulate and order parapet walls and other partition fences; to restrain, regulate or prohibit the running at large of cattle, horses, mules, sheep, swine, goats and all kinds of poultry; and to tax and regulate the keeping of dogs and to authorize the destruction of the same, when at large contrary to city ordinances.

Sec. 26.—To establish standard weights and measures and regulate the weights and measures to be used in the city, in all cases not provided for by law.

Sec. 27.—To provide for the inspection and measuring of lumber and other building materials, and for the measurement of all kinds of mechanical work.

Sec. 28.—To provide for the inspection and weighing of hay, lime and stone coal, and measuring of charcoal, firewood and other fuel to be sold or used within the city.

Sec. 29.—To license, regulate, prohibit or restrain the manufacturing, selling or giving away of spirituous vinous or fermented liquors, tavern keepers, dram or tippling shop keepers, boarding, victualing or coffee houses, restaurants, saloons or other houses or places for the selling or giving away of ardent, vinous or fermented liquors; to provide for and regulate the inspection of tobacco, beef, pork, flour and meal; also beer, whiskey, brandy and all other spirituous or fermented liquors.

Sec. 30.—To regulate the weight, quality and price of bread sold and used in the city.

Sec. 31.—To provide for taking the numeration of the inhabitants of the city.

Sec. 32.—To fix the compensation of all city officers, and regulate the fees of jurors, witnesses and others for services rendered under this or any city ordinance.

Sec. 33.—The City Council shall have exclusive power within the city, by ordinance, to license, regulate, suppress or restrain billiard tables, and from one to twenty pin alleys and every other description of gaming or gambling.

Sec. 34.—The City Council shall have exclusive power within the city, by ordinance, to regulate the police of the city; to impose fines, forfeitures and penalties for the breach of any ordinance, and provide for the recovery of such fines and forfeitures, and the enforcement of such penalties; and to pass such ordinances as may be necessary and proper to carry into effect and execution the powers specified in this act: Provided such ordinances are not repugnant to the Constitution of the United States or the laws of this Territory.

Sec. 35.—All ordinances passed by the City Council shall, within one month after they shall have been passed, be published in some newspaper, printed in said city, or certified copies thereof be posted up in three of the most public places in the city.

Sec. 36.—All ordinances of the city may be proven by the seal of the Corporation; and when published in book or pamphlet form, purporting to be printed or published by the authority of the Corporation, the same shall be received in evidence in all Courts or places without further proof.

Sec. 37.—The Mayor and Aldermen shall be Conservators of the Peace within the limits of the city, and shall have all the powers of Justices of the Peace therein, both in civil and criminal cases arising under the laws of the Territory. They shall, as Justices of the Peace, within the limits of said city perform the same duties, be governed by the same laws, give the same bonds and securities as other justices of the peace, and be commissioned, as Justices of the Peace in and for said city, by the Governor.

Sec. 38.—The Mayor and Aldermen shall have jurisdiction in all cases arising under the ordinances of the Corporation, and shall issue such process as may be necessary to carry said ordinances into execution and effect. Appeals may be had from any decision or judgment of said Mayor or Aldermen, arising under the ordinances of said city, to the Municipal Court, under such regulations as may be prescribed by ordinance; which court shall be composed of the Mayor as Chief Justice and the Aldermen as Associate Justices; and from the final judgment of the Municipal Court to the Probate Court of Utah county, in the same manner as appeals are taken from Justices of the Peace: Provided the parties litigant shall have a right to a trial by jury of twelve men, in all cases before the Municipal Court. The Municipal Court shall have power to grant writs of *habeas corpus* and try the same, in all cases arising under the ordinances of the City Council.

Sec. 39.—The Municipal Court may sit on the first Monday of every month, and the City Council at such times and places as may be prescribed by city ordinance; special meetings of which may at any time be called by the Mayor or any two Aldermen.

Sec. 40.—All process issued by the Mayor, Aldermen or Municipal Court shall be directed to the Marshal, and in the execution thereof, he shall be governed by the same laws as are or may be prescribed for the direction and compensation of Constables in similar cases. The Marshal shall also perform such other duties as may be required of him under the ordinances of said city, and shall be the principal ministerial officer.

Sec. 41.—It shall be the duty of the Recorder to make and keep accurate records of all ordinances made by the City Council and of all their proceedings in their Corporate capacity, which record shall at all times be open to the inspection of the electors of said city, and he shall perform all other duties as may be required of him by the ordinances of the City Council, and shall serve as Clerk of the Municipal Court.

Sec. 42.—When it shall be necessary to take private property for opening, widening or altering any public street, lane, avenue or alley, the Corporation shall make a just compensation therefor to the person whose property is so taken; and if the amount of such compensation cannot be agreed upon, the Mayor shall cause the same to be ascertained by a jury of six disinterested men, who shall be inhabitants of the city.

Sec. 43.—All jurors, empannelled to inquire into the amount of benefits or damages that shall happen to the owners of property so proposed to be taken, shall first be sworn to that effect, and shall return to the Mayor their inquest in writing, signed by each juror.

Sec. 44.—In case the Mayor shall, at any time, be guilty of a palpable omission of duty, or shall wilfully and corruptly be guilty of oppression, malconduct or partiality in the discharge of the duties of his office, he shall be liable to indictment in the Probate Court of Utah County; and, on conviction, he shall be liable to fine and imprisonment, and the Court shall have power on the recommend of the jury, to add to the judgment of the Court that he be removed from office.

Sec. 45.—The City Council shall have power to provide for the punishment of offenders and vagrants by imprisonment in the county or city jail, or by compelling them to labor on the streets or other public works until the same shall be fully paid, in all cases where such offenders or vagrants shall fail or refuse to pay the fines and forfeitures which may be awarded against them.

Sec. 46.—The inhabitants of American Fork City shall, from and after the first Monday in July next, be exempt from working on any road or roads beyond the limits of said city. But all taxes devoted to road purposes shall, from and after the said date, be collected and expended, by and under the direction of the Supevisor of Streets, within the limits of the city.

Approved June 4, 1853.

CHAPTER CII.

An ACT to incorporate Pleasant Grove City.

Sec. 1.—Be it enacted by the Governor and Legislative Assembly of the Territory of Utah: That all that district of Utah county embraced in the following boundaries, to wit: beginning at the southeast corner of Lake city incorporation, running in a southeasterly direction along the Lake shore to the northwest corner of the corporation of Provo city, thence east to the base of the mountain, thence along the base of the mountain to the south bank of the American creek near the mouth of the cañon; thence down the south bank of said creek to a point directly north of the northeast corner of Lake city Corporation, thence south to the place of beginning shall be known and designated as Pleasant Grove city; and the inhabitants thereof are hereby constituted a body corporate and politic, by the name aforesaid; and shall have perpetual succession, and may have and use a common seal, which they may change and alter at pleasure.

Sec. 2.—The inhabitants of said city, by the name and style aforesaid, shall have power to sue and be sued, to plead and be impleaded, defend and be defended, in all Courts of law and equity, and in all actions whatsoever; to purchase, receive and hold property, real and personal, in said city; to purchase, receive and hold real property beyond the city for burying grounds or other public purposes for the use of the inhabitants of said city; to sell, lease, convey or dispose of property, real and personal, for the benefit of said city; to improve and protect such property, and to do all other things in relation thereto, as natural persons.

Sec. 3.—There shall be a City Council, to consist of a Mayor, two Aldermen, and three Councilors, who shall have the qualifications of electors of said city, and shall be chosen by the qualified voters thereof, and shall hold their offices for two years, and until their successors be elected and qualified. The City Council shall judge of the qualifications, elections and returns of their own members, and a majority of them shall form a quorum to do business; but a smaller number may adjourn from day to day and compel the attendance of absent members, under such penalties as may be prescribed by ordinance.

Sec. 4.—The Mayor, Aldermen and Councilors, before entering upon the duties of their offices, shall take and subscribe an oath or affirmation that they will support the Constitution of the United States and the laws of this Territory, and that they will well and truly perform the duties of their offices to the best of their skill and abilities.

Sec. 5.—An election, for the election of one Mayor, two Aldermen and three Councilors, shall be held on the second Monday of February, 1863, and every two years thereafter, and shall be held, conducted and the returns thereof made in such manner as shall be provided for by the ordinances of the City Council.

Sec. 6.—All free white male inhabitants of the age of eighteen years, who are entitled to vote for Territorial officers, and who shall have been actual residents of said city sixty days next preceding said election, shall be entitled to vote for city officers.

Sec. 7.—The City Council shall have authority annually to assess, collect and expend the necessary tax for roads, streets, schools and other public purposes, and regulate and control the same within the city, and may enforce the payment of said tax by law; and the inhabitants of the city shall be exempt from all other assessments for road and school purposes, except on such property as they may possess outside of thecity: Provided that nothing herein shall be so construed as to affect or infringe upon any tax assessed or authorized by any enactment of the Governor and Legislative Assembly.

Sec. 8.—The City Council shall have power to appoint a Recorder, Treasurer, Assessor and Collector, Marshal and Supervisor of Streets. They shall also have the power to appoint all such other officers, by ordinance, as may be necessary, define the duties of all city officers, and remove them from office at pleasure.

Sec. 9.—The City Council shall have power to require of all officers, appointed in pursuance of this act, bonds with penalty and security, for the faithful performance of their respective duties, such as may be deemed expedient, and also to require of all officers, appointed as aforesaid, to take an oath for the faithful performance of the duties of their respective offices.

Sec. 10.—The City Council shall have power and authority to make, ordain, establish and execute all such ordinances not repugnant to the Constitution of the United States or the laws of this Territory, as they may deem necessary for the peace, benefit, good order, regulation, convenience and cleanliness of the city, for the protection of property therein from destruction by fire or otherwise; and for the health and happiness thereof. They shall have power to fill all vacancies, that may happen by death, resignation or removal, in any of the offices herein made elective; to fix and establish all the fees of the officers of said corporation, not herein established; to impose such fines, not exceeding one hundred dollars for each offense, as they may deem just, for refusing to accept any office in or under the Corporation, or for misconduct therein; to divide the city into Wards and specify the boundaries thereof.

Sec. 11.—To establish, support and regulate common schools; to borrow money on the credit of the city: Provided that no sum or sums of money be borrowed on a greater interest than six per cent. per annum; nor shall the interest on the aggregate of all the sums borrowed and outstanding ever exceed one half of the city revenue arising from taxes assessed on real estate, within the city.

Sec. 12.—To make regulations to prevent the introduction of contagious diseases into the city; to make quarantine laws for that purpose and enforce the same.

Sec. 13.—To appropriate and provide for the payment of the expenses and debts of the city.

Sec. 14.—To establish hospitals and make regulations for the government of the same; to make regulations to secure the general health of the inhabitants; to declare what shall be nuisances and to prevent and remove the same.

Sec. 15.—To provide the city with water, to dig wells, lay pump logs and pipes, and erect pumps in the street for the extinguishment of fires and convenience of the inhabitants.

Sec. 16.—To open, alter, widen, extend, establish, grade, pave or otherwise improve and keep in repair streets, avenues, lanes and alleys; and to establish, erect and keep in repair aqueducts and bridges.

Sec. 17.—To provide for the lighting of the streets and erecting lamp posts, and establish, support and regulate night watches; to erect market houses, establish markets and market places and provide for the government and regulation thereof.

Sec. 18.—To provide for erecting all needful buildings for the use of the city, and for inclosing, improving and regulating all public grounds belonging to the city: to regulate and control the live trees and shrubbery and the water courses and water privileges in the city and, so far as may be necessary, the water courses leading thereto in the immediate vicinity thereof.

Sec. 19.—To license, tax and regulate auctioneers, merchants, retailers, grocers and taverns, ordinaries, hawkers, peddlers, brokers, pawnbrokers and money changers.

Sec. 20.—To license, tax and regulate hacking, carriages, wagons, carts and drays, and fix the rates to be charged for the carrying of persons and for wagonage, cartage and drayage of property, as also to license and regulate porters and fix the rates of porterage.

Sec. 21.—To license, tax and regulate theatricals and other exhibitions, shows and amusements.

Sec. 22.—To tax, restrain, prohibit and restrain tippling houses, dram shops, gaming houses, bawdy and other disorderly houses.

Sec. 23.—To provide for the prevention and extinguishment of fires; to regulate the fixing of chimneys and the flues thereof and stove pipes; and to organize and establish fire companies.

Sec. 24.—To regulate the storage of gunpowder, tar, pitch, resin and other combustible materials.

Sec. 25.—To regulate and order parapet walls and other partition fences; to wall in the city or any part thereof; to restrain, regulate or prohibit the running at large of cattle, horses, mules, sheep, swine, goats and all kinds of poultry; and to tax and regulate the keeping of dogs, and to authorize the destruction of the same when running at large contrary to city ordinances.

Sec. 26.—To establish standard weights and measures and to regulate the weights and measures to be used in the city in all cases not provided for by law.

Sec. 27.—To provide for the inspecting and measuring of lumber and other building materials, and for the measurement of all kinds of mechanical work.

Sec. 28.—To provide for the inspection and weighing of hay, lime and pit coal, and the measuring of charcoal, firewood and other fuel to be sold or used within the city.

Sec. 29.—To license, regulate, prohibit or restrain the manufacturing, selling or giving away of spirituous, vinous or fermented liquors, tavern keepers, dram or tippling shop keepers, boarding, victualing or coffee houses, restaurants, saloons or other houses or places for the selling or giving away of ardent, vinous or fermented liquors; to provide for and regulate the inspection of tobacco, beef, pork, flour and meal; also beer, whisky, brandy and all other spirituous and fermented liquors.

Sec. 30.—To regulate the weights, quality and price of bread sold and used in the city.

Sec. 31.—To provide for taking the enumeration of the inhabitants of the city.

Sec. 32.—To fix the compensation of all city officers, and regulate the fees of jurors, witnesses and others for services rendered under this act or any city ordinance.

Sec. 33.—The City Council shall have exclusive power within the city, by ordinance, to license, regulate, suppress or restrain billiard tables and from one to twenty pin alleys and every other description of gaming or gambling.

Sec. 34.—The City Council shall have exclusive power within the city, by ordinance, to regulate the Police of the city; to impose fines, forfeitures and penalties for the breach of any ordinance, and provide for the recovery of such fines and forfeitures and the enforcement of such penalties; and to pass such ordinances as may be necessary and proper to carry into effect and execution the powers specified in this act: Provided, that such ordinances are not repugnant to the Constitution of the United States or the laws of this Territory.

Sec. 35.—All ordinances passed by the City Council shall, within one month after they shall have been passed, be published in some newspaper printed in the city, or certified copies thereof be posted up in three of the most public places in the city.

Sec. 36.—All ordinances of the city may be proven by the seal of the Corporation; and when published in book or pamphlet form, purporting to be printed or published by the authority of the Corporation, the same shall be received in evidence in all Courts or places without further proof.

Sec. 37.—The Mayor and Aldermen shall be Conservators of the Peace within the limits of the city, and shall have all the powers of Justices of the Peace therein, both in civil and criminal cases arising under the laws of the Territory. They shall, as Justices of the Peace, within the limits of the city, perform the same duties, be governed by the same laws, give the same bonds and securities as other Justices of the Peace, and be commissioned as Justices of the Peace in and for said city, by the Governor.

Sec. 38.—The Mayor and Aldermen shall have jurisdiction in all cases arising under the ordinances of the Corporation, and shall issue such process as may be necessary to carry said ordinances into execution and effect. Appeals may be had from any decision or judgment of said Mayor or Aldermen, arising under the ordinances of said city, to the Municipal Court, under such regulations as may be prescribed by ordinance; which Court shall be composed of the Mayor as Chief Justice and the Aldermen as Associate Justices; and from the final judgment of the Municipal Court, to the Probate Court of Utah county, in the same manner as appeals are taken from Justices of the Peace: Provided, the parties litigant shall have a right to a trial by a jury of twelve men, in all cases before the Municipal Court. The Municipal Court shall have power to grant writs of *habeas corpus* and try the same, in all cases arising under the ordinances of the City Council.

Sec. 39.—The Municipal Court may sit on the first Monday of every month, and the City Council at such times and places as may be prescribed by city ordinance; special meetings of which may at any time be called by the Mayor or any two Aldermen.

Sec. 40.—All process issued by the Mayor, Aldermen or Municipal Court shall be directed to the Marshal, and in the execution thereof he shall be governed by the same laws as are or may be prescribed for the direction and compensation of Constables in similar cases. The Marshal shall also perform such other duties as may be required of him under the ordinances of said city, and shall be the principal ministerial officer.

Sec. 41.—It shall be the duty of the Recorder to make and keep accurate records of all ordinances made by the City Council and all their proceedings in a corporate capacity, which record shall at all times be open to the inspection of the electors of said city, and he shall perform all other duties as may be required of him by the ordinances of the City Council, and shall serve as Clerk of the Municipal Court.

Sec. 42.—When it shall be necessary to take private property for opening, widening or altering any public street, lane, avenue or alley, the Corporation shall make a just compensation therefor to the person whose property is so taken; and if the amount of such compensation cannot be agreed upon, the Mayor shall cause the same to be ascertained by the jury of six disinterested men, who shall be inhabitants of the city.

Sec. 43.—All jurors empannelled to inquire into the amount of benefits or damages that shall happen to the owners of property so proposed to be taken, shall first be sworn to that effect, and shall return to the Mayor their inquest in writing, signed by each juror.

Sec. 44.—In case the Mayor shall at any time, be guilty of any palpable omission of duty, or shall wilfully or corruptly be guilty of oppression, malconduct or partiality in the discharge of the duties of his office, he shall be liable to indictment in the Probate Court of Utah county: and, on conviction, he shall be liable to fine and imprisonment; and the Court shall have power, on the recommend of the jury, to add to the judgment of the court, that he be removed from office.

Sec. 45.—The City Council shall have power to provide for the punishment of offenders and vagrants by imprisonment in the county or city jail, or by compelling them to labor upon the streets or other public works until the same shall be fully paid, in all cases where such offenders or vagrants shall fail or refuse to pay the fines and forfeitures which may be awarded against them.

Sec. 46.—The inhabitants of Pleasant Grove city shall, from and and after the first Monday in May next, be exempt from working on any road or roads beyond the limits of said city. But all taxes devoted to road purposes shall from and after said date, be collected and expended, by and under the direction of the Supervisor of Streets, within the limits of the city.

Approved Jan. 19, 1855.

——:o:——

CHAPTER CIII.

An ACT to incorporate Spanish Fork City

Sec. 1.—Be it enacted by the Governor and Legislative Assembly of the Territory of Utah: That all the district of Utah County embraced in the following boundaries, to wit: beginning at the mouth of Water cañon, thence west thirty-seven degrees north to a stake known as station 1 in J. C. Snow's survey of said line, thence west three degrees south to the center of Pond Town sloughs, thence down said sloughs to Duck creek, thence west to Peteetneet creek, thence down the main channel of said creek to Utah Lake, thence northeasterly, along the shore of said Lake to a point from which a southeast line will strike the mouth of the main sect leading into plat D, Springville survey, thence on a line of said sect to where it intersects the big slough, thence to the northeast corner of Palmyra field, thence to the southeast corner of the present Springville survey, thence east to the mountains, thence south along the base of the mountains to the place of beginning, shall be known and designated as Spanish Fork City; and the inhabitants thereof are hereby constituted a body corporate and politic, by the name aforesaid; and shall have perpetual succession, and may have and use a common seal, which they may change and alter at pleasure.

Sec. 2—The inhabitants of said city, by the name and style aforesaid, shall have power to sue and be sued, to plead and be impleaded, defend and be defended in all Courts of law and equity and in all actions whatsoever; to purchase, receive and hold property, real and personal, in said city; to purchase, receive and hold real property, beyond the city, for burying grounds or other public purposes for the use of the inhabitants of said city; to sell, lease or dispose of property real and personal, for the benefit of said city; to improve and protect such property, and to do all other things in relation thereto, as natural persons.

Sec. 3.—There shall be a City Council, to consist of a Mayor, two Aldermen and three Councilors, who shall have the qualifications of electors of said city, and shall be chosen by the qualified voters thereof, and shall hold their offices for two years, and until their successors shall be elected and qualified. The City Council shall judge of the qualifications, elections and returns of their own members; and a majority of them shall form a quorum to do business, but a smaller number may adjourn from day to day and compel the attendance of absent members, under such penalties as may be prescribed by ordinance.

Sec. 4.—The Mayor, Aldermen and Councilors, before entering upon the duties of their offices, shall take and subscribe an oath or affirmation that they will support the Constitution of the United States and the laws of this Territory, and that they will well and truly perform all the duties of their offices to the best of their skill and abilities.

Sec. 5.—An election, for the election of one Mayor, two Aldermen and three Councilors, shall be held on the second Monday of February, 1863, and every two years thereafter, and shall be held, conducted and returns thereof made in such manner as shall be provided for by the ordinances of the City Council.

Sec. 6.—All free white male inhabitants who are of the age of eighteen years, who are entitled to vote for Territorial officers, and who shall have been actual residents of said city sixty days next preceding said election shall be entitled to vote for city officers.

Sec. 7.—The City Council shall have authority annually to assess, collect and expend the necessary tax for roads, streets, schools and other public purposes, and regulate and control the same within the city, and may enforce the payment of said tax by law; and the inhabitants of the city shall be exempt from all other assessments for road or school purposes, except on such property as they may possess outside of the city: Provided, that nothing herein shall be so construed as to effect or infringe upon any tax assessed or authorized by any enactment of the Governor and Legislative Assembly.

Sec. 8.—The City Council shall have power to appoint a Recorder, Treasurer, Assessor and Collector, Marshal and Supervisors of Streets. They shall also have the power to appoint all such other officers, by ordinance, as may be necessary, define the duties of all city officers and remove them from office at pleasure.

Sec. 9.—The City Council shall have power to require of all officers, appointed in pursuance of this act, such bonds as may be deemed expedient, with penalty and security, for the faithful performance of their respective duties, and also to require of all officers, appointed as aforesaid, to take an oath for the faithful performance of the duties of their respective offices.

Sec. 10.—The City Council shall have power and authority to make, ordain, establish and execute all such ordinances, not repugnant to the Constitution of the United States or the laws of this Territory, as they may deem necessary for the peace, benefit, good order, regulation, convenience and cleanliness of said city; for the protection of property therein from destruction by fire or otherwise, and for the health and happiness thereof. They shall have power to fill all vacancies, that may happen by death, resignation or removal, in any of the offices herein made elective; to fix and establish all the fees of the officers of said Corporation not herein established; to impose such fines, not exceeding one hundred dollars for each offense, as they may deem just, for refusing to accept of any office in or under the Corporation, or for misconduct therein; to divide the city into Wards, and specify the boundaries thereof.

Sec. 11.—To establish, support and regulate common schools; to borrow money on the credit of the city: Provided, that no sum or sums of money be borrowed on a greater interest than six per cent. per annum; nor shall the interest on the aggregate of the sums borrowed and outstanding ever exceed one half of the city revenue arising from the taxes assessed on real estate within the city.

Sec. 12.—To make regulations to prevent the introduction of contagious diseases into the city; to make quarantine laws for that purpose, and enforce the same.

Sec. 13.—To appropriate and provide for the payment of the expenses and debts of the city.

Sec. 14.—To establish hospitals and make regulations for the government of the same; to make regulations to secure the general health of the inhabitants; to declare what shall be nuisances and to prevent and remove the same.

Sec. 15.—To provide the city with water; to dig wells, lay pump logs and pipes and erect pumps in the streets, for the extinguishment of fires and convenience of the inhabitants.

Sec. 16.—To open, alter, widen, extend, establish, grade, pave or otherwise improve and keep in repair streets, avenues, lanes and alleys; and to establish, erect and keep in repair aqueducts and bridges.

Sec. 17.—To provide for the lighting of the streets and erecting lamp posts; and to establish, support and regulate night watches; to erect market houses, establish markets and market places and provide for the government and regulation thereof.

Sec. 18.—To provide for erecting all needful buildings for the use of the city, and for inclosing, improving and regulating all public grounds belonging to the city; to regulate and control the live trees and shrubbery, and the water courses and water privileges in the city, and, so far as may be necessary, the water courses leading thereto in the immediate vicinity thereof.

Sec. 19.—To license, tax and regulate auctioneers, merchants, retailers, grocers and taverns, ordinaries, hawkers, peddlers, brokers, pawn-brokers and money changers.

Sec. 20.—To license, tax and regulate hacking, carriages, wagons, carts, and drays; and fix the rates to be charged for the carriage of persons and for wagonage, cartage and drayage of property; as also to license and regulate porters and fix the rates of porterage.

Sec. 21.—To license, tax and regulate theatricals and other exhibitions, shows and amusements.

Sec. 22.—To tax, restrain, prohibit and suppress tippling houses, dram shops, gaming houses, bawdy and other disorderly houses.

Sec. 23.—To provide for the prevention and extinguishment of fires: to regulate the fixing of chimneys and the flues thereof and stove pipes, and to organize and establish fire companies.

Sec. 24.—To regulate the storage of gunpowder, tar, pitch, resin and other combustible materials.

Sec. 25.—To regulate and order parapet walls and other partition fences; to wall in the city or any part thereof, to restrain, regulate or prohibit the running at large of cattle, horses, mules, sheep, swine, goats and all kinds of poultry; and to tax and regulate the keeping of dogs, and to authorize the destruction of the same when at large contrary to city ordinances.

Sec. 26.—To establish standard weights and measures and regulate the weights and measures to be used in the city, in all cases not provided for by law.

Sec. 27.—To provide for the inspection and measuring of lumber and other building materials, and for the measurement of all kinds of mechanical work.

Sec. 28.—To provide for the inspection and weighing of hay, lime and pit coal, and the measuring of charcoal, fire wood and other fuel to be sold or used within the city.

Sec. 29.—To license, regulate, prohibit or restrain the manufacturing, selling or giving away of spirituous, vinous or fermented liquors, tavern keepers, dram or tippling shop keepers, boarding, victualing or coffee houses, restaurants, saloons or other houses or places for the selling or giving away of ardent, vinous or fermented liquors; to provide for and regulate the inspection of tobacco, beef, pork, flour and meal; also beer, whisky, brandy and all other spirituous and fermented liquors.

Sec. 30.—To regulate the weights, quality and price of bread sold and used in the city.

Sec. 31.—To provide for taking the enumeration of the inhabitants of the city.

Sec. 32.—To fix the compensation of all city officers, and regulate the fees of jurors, witnesses and others for services rendered under this or any city ordinance.

Sec. 33.—The City Council shall have exclusive power within the city, by ordinance, to license, regulate, suppress or restrain billiard tables and from one to twenty pin alleys and every other description of gaming or gambling.

Sec. 34.—The City Council shall have exclusive power within the city, by ordinance, to regulate the police of the city; to impose fines, forfeitures and penalties for the breach of any ordinance, and provide for the recovery of such fines and forfeitures and the enforcement of such penalties; and to pass such ordinances as may be necessary and proper to carry into effect and execution the powers specified in this act: Provided, that such ordinances are not repugnant to the Constitution of the United States or the laws of this Territory.

Sec. 35.—All ordinances passed by the City Council shall, within one month after they shall have been passed, be published in some newspaper printed in said city, or certified copies thereof be posted up in three of the most public places in the city.

Sec. 36.—All ordinances of the city may be proven by seal of the corporation; and when published in book or pamphlet form, purporting to be printed or published by the authority of the corporation, the same shall be received in evidence in all Courts or places, without further proof.

Sec. 37.—The Mayor and Aldermen shall be Conservators of the Peace within the limits of the city, and shall have all the powers of Justices of the Peace therein, both in civil and criminal cases arising under the laws of the Territory. They shall, as Justices of the Peace within the limits of the city, perform the same duties, be governed by the same laws, give the same bonds and securities as other Justices of the Peace, and be commissioned, as Justices of the Peace in and for said city, by the Governor.

Sec. 38.—The Mayor and Aldermen shall have jurisdiction in all cases arising under the ordinances of the Corporation, and shall issue such process as may be necessary to carry said ordinances into execution and effect. Appeals may be had from any decision or judgment of said Mayor or Aldermen, arising under the ordinances of the city, to the Municipal Court under such regulations as may be prescribed by ordinance, which Court shall be composed of the Mayor as Chief Justice, and the Aldermen as Associate Justices; and from the final judgment of the Municipal Court to the Probate Court of Utah county, in the same manner as appeals are taken from Justices of the Peace: Provided the parties litigant shall have a right to a trial by a jury of twelve men, in all cases before the Municipal Court. The Municipal Court shall have power to grant writs of *habeas corpus* and try the same in all cases arising under the ordinances of the City Council.

Sec. 39.—The Municipal Court may sit on the first Monday of every month, and the City Council at such times and places as may be prescribed by city ordinance, special meetings of which may at any time be called by the Mayor or any two Aldermen.

Sec. 40.—All process issued by the Mayor, Aldermen or Municipal Court shall be directed to the Marshal; and in the execution thereof he shall be governed by the same laws as are or may be prescribed for the direction and compensation of Constables in similar cases. The Marshal shall also perform such other duties as may be required of him under the ordinances of said city, and shall be the principal ministerial officer.

Sec. 41.—It shall be the duty of the Recorder to make and keep accurate records of all ordinances made by the City Council and of all their proceedings in their Corporate capacity, which record shall at all times be open to the inspection of the electors of said city, and he shall perform all other duties as may be required of him by the ordinances of the City Council, and shall serve as Clerk of the Municipal Court.

Sec. 42.—When it shall be necessary to take private property for opening, widening or altering any public street, lane, avenue or alley, the Corporation shall make a just compensation therefor, to the person whose property is so taken; and if the amount of such compensation cannot be agreed upon, the Mayor shall cause the same to be ascertained by a jury of six disinterested men, who shall be inhabitants of the city.

Sec. 43.—All jurors, empannelled to inquire into the amount of benefits or damages that shall happen to the owners of property so proposed to be taken, shall first be sworn to that effect, and shall return to the Mayor their inquest in writing, signed by each juror.

Sec. 44.—In case the Mayor shall, at any time, be guilty of any palpable omission of duty, or shall wilfully or corruptly be guilty of oppression, malconduct, or partiality in the discharge of the duties of his office, he shall be liable to indictment in the Probate Court of Utah county: and, on conviction, he shall be liable to fine and imprisonment; and the Court shall have power, on the recommend of the jury, to add to the judgment of the Court that he be removed from office.

Sec. 45.—The City Council shall have power to provide for the punishment of offenders and vagrants by imprisonment in the county or city jail, or by compelling them to labor on the streets or other public works until the same shall be fully paid, in all cases where such offenders or vagrants shall fail or refuse to pay the fines and forfeitures which may be awarded against them.

Sec. 46:—The inhabitants of Spanish Fork City shall, from and after the first Monday in May next, be exempt from working on any road or roads beyond the limits of said city. But all taxes devoted to road purposes shall, from and after the said date, be collected and expended, by and under the direction of the Supervisor of Streets, within the limits of the city.

Approved Jan. 19, 1855.

———:o:———

CHAPTER CIV.

An ACT to incorporate Alpine City, Utah County.

Sec. 1.—Be it enacted by the Governor and Legislative Assembly of the Territory of Utah: That all that district of Utah county embraced in the following boundaries, to wit: beginning at a point one mile east of the centre of Mountainville Fort, thence south one mile, thence west two miles, thence north two miles, thence east two miles, thence south one mile to the place of beginning shall be known and designated as Alpine city; and the inhabitants thereof are hereby constituted a body corporate and politic, by the name aforesaid; and shall have perpetual succession, and may have and use a common seal, which they may change and alter at pleasure.

Sec. 2.—The inhabitants of said city, by the name and style aforesaid, shall have power to sue and be sued, to plead and be impleaded, defend and be defended in all Courts of law and equity and in all actions whatsoever; to purchase, receive and hold property, real and personal, in said city to purchase, receive and hold real property beyond the city for burying grounds or other public purposes for the use of the inhabitants of said city; to sell, lease, or dispose of property, real and personal, for the benefit of said city; to improve and protect such property, and to do all other things in relation thereto, as natural persons.

Sec. 3.—There shall be a City Council to consist of a Mayor, two Aldermen and three Councilors, who shall have the qualifications of electors of said city, and shall be chosen by the qualified voters thereof, and shall hold their offices for two years, and until their successors shall be elected and qualified. The City Council shall judge of the qualifications, elections and returns of their own members, and a majority of them shall form a quorum to do business; but a smaller number may adjourn from day to day and compel the attendance of absent members, under such penalties as may be prescribed by ordinance.

Sec. 4.—The Mayor, Aldermen and Councilors, before entering on the duties of their offices, shall take and subscribe an oath or affirmation that they will support the Constitution of the United States and the laws of this Territory, and that they will well and truly perform all the duties of their offices to the best of their skill and abilities.

Sec. 5.—An election, for the election of one Mayor, two Aldermen and three Councilors, shall be held on the second Monday of February, 1863, and every two years thereafter; and shall be held, conducted and returns thereof made in such manner as shall be provided for by the ordinances of the City Council.

Sec. 6.—All free white male inhabitants who are of the age of eighteen years, who are entitled to vote for Territorial officers and who shall have been actual residents of said city sixty days next preceding said election, shall be entitled to vote for city officers.

Sec. 7.—The City Council shall have authority annually to assess, collect and expend the necessary tax for roads, streets, schools and other public purposes, and regulate and control the same within the city, and may enforce the payment of said tax by law; and the inhabitants of the city shall be exempt from all other assessments for road and school purposes, except on such property as they may possess outside of the city: Provided that nothing herein shall be so construed as to effect or infringe upon any tax assessed or authorized by any enactment of the Governor and Legislative Assembly.

Sec. 8.—The City Council shall have power to appoint a Recorder, Treasurer, Assessor and Collector, Marshal and Supervisor of Streets. They shall also have power to appoint all such other officers, by ordinance, as may be necessary, define the duties of all city officers and remove them from office at pleasure.

Sec. 9.—The City Council shall have power to require of all officers, appointed in pursuance of this act, bonds with penalty and security for the faithful performance of their respective duties, such as may be deemed expedient; and also to require of all officers, appointed as aforesaid, to take an oath for the faithful performance of the duties of their respective offices.

Sec. 10.—The City Council shall have power and authority to make, ordain, establish and execute all such ordinances, not repugnant to the Constitution of the United States or the laws of this Territory, as they may deem necessary for the peace, benefit, good order, regulation, convenience and cleanliness of the city; for the protection of property therein from destruction by fire or otherwise, and for the health and happiness thereof. They shall have power to fill all vacancies, that may happen by death, resignation or removal, in any of the offices herein made elective; to fix and establish all the fees of the officers of said Corporation, not herein established; to impose such fines, not exceeding one hundred dollars for each offense, as they may deem just, for refusing to accept of any office in or under the Corporation, or from misconduct therein; to divide the city into Wards and specify the boundaries thereof.

Sec. 11.—To establish, support and regulate common schools; to borrow money on the credit of the city: Provided, that no sum or sums of money be borrowed on a greater interest than six per cent. per annum; nor shall the interest on the aggregate of all the sums borrowed and outstanding ever exceed one half of the city revenue arising from taxes assessed on real estate within the city.

Sec. 12.—To make regulations to prevent the introduction of contagious diseases into the city; to make quarantine laws for that purpose and enforce the same.

Sec. 13.—To appropriate and provide for the payment of the expenses and debts of the city.

Sec. 14.—To establish hospitals and make regulations for the government of the same; to make regulations to secure the general health of the inhabitants; to declare what shall be nuisances and to prevent and remove the same.

Sec. 15.—To provide the city with water; to dig wells, lay pump logs and pipes and erect pumps in the streets for the extinguishment of fires and convenience of the inhabitants.

Sec. 16.—To open, alter, widen, extend, establish, grade, pave or otherwise improve and keep in repair streets, avenues, lanes and alleys; and to establish, erect and keep in repair aqueducts and bridges.

Sec. 17.—To provide for the lighting of the streets and erecting lamp posts; and establish, support and regulate night watches; to erect market houses; establish market and market places and to provide for the government and regulation thereof.

Sec. 18.—To provide for erecting all needful buildings for the use of the city, and for inclosing, improving and regulating all public grounds belonging to the city; to regulate and control the live trees and shrubbery, and the water courses, and water privileges in the city, and, so far as may be necessary, the water courses leading thereto in the immediate vicinity thereof.

Sec. 19.—To license, tax and regulate auctioneers, merchants and retailers, grocers and taverns, ordinaries, hawkers, peddlers, brokers, pawnbrokers and money changers.

Sec. 20.—To license, tax and regulate hacking, carriages, wagons, carts and drays; and fix the rates to be charged for the carriage of persons and for wagonage, cartage and drayage of property; as also to license and regulate porters and fix the rate of porterage.

Sec. 21.—To license, tax, and regulate theatricals and other exhibitions, shows and amusements.

Sec. 22.—To tax, restrain, prohibit and suppress tippling houses, dram shops, gaming houses, bawdy and other disorderly houses.

Sec. 23.—To provide for the prevention and extinguishment of fires; to regulate the fixing of chimneys and the flues thereof and stove pipes, and to organize and establish fire companies.

Sec. 24.—To regulate the storage of gunpowder, tar, pitch, resin and other combustible materials.

Sec. 25.—To regulate and order parapet walls and other partition fences; to wall in the city or any part thereof; to restrain, regulate or prohibit the running at large of cattle, horses, mules, sheep, swine, goats and all kinds of poultry; and to tax and regulate the keeping of dogs, and to authorize the destruction of the same when at large contrary to city ordinances.

Sec. 26.—To establish standard weights and measures, and regulate the weights and measures to be used in the city, in all cases not provided for by law.

Sec. 27.—To provide for the inspecting and measuring of lumber and other building materials; and for the measurement of all kinds of mechanical work.

Sec. 28.—To provide for the inspection and weighing of hay, lime, pit coal, and measuring of charcoal, firewood and other fuel to be sold or used within the city.

Sec. 29.—To license, regulate, prohibit or restrain the manufacturing, selling or giving away of spirituous, vinous or fermented liquors, tavern keepers, dram or tippling shop keepers, boarding, victualing or coffee houses, restaurants, saloons or other houses or places for the selling or giving away of ardent, vinous or fermented liquors; to provide for and regulate the inspection of tobacco and of beef, pork, flour and meal; also beer and whisky, brandy and all other spirituous and fermented liquors.

Sec. 30.—To regulate the weights, quality and price of bread sold and used in the city.

Sec. 31.—To provide for taking the enumeration of the inhabitants of the city.

Sec. 32.—To fix the compensation of all city officers, and regulate the fees of jurors, witnesses and others for services rendered under this act or any city ordinance.

Sec. 33.—The City Council shall have exclusive power within the city, by ordinance, to license, regulate, suppress or restrain billiard tables and from one to twenty pin alleys and every other description of gaming or gambling.

Sec. 34.—The City Council shall have exclusive power within the city, by ordinance, to regulate the Police of the city; to impose fines, forfeitures and penalties for the breach of any ordinance, and provide for the recovery of such fines and forfeitures and the enforcement of such penalties; and to pass such ordinances as may be necessary and proper to carry into effect and execution the powers specified in this act: *Provided*, that such ordinances are not repugnant to the Constitution of the United States or the laws of this Territory.

Sec. 35.—All ordinances passed by the City Council shall, within one month after they shall have been passed, be published in some newspaper printed in the city, or certified copies thereof be posted up in three of the most public places in the city.

Sec. 36.—All ordinances of the city may be proven by the seal of the Corporation; and when published in book or pamphlet form, purporting to be printed or published by the authority of the Corporation, the same shall be received in evidence in all Courts or places, without further proof.

Sec. 37.—The Mayor and Aldermen shall be Conservators of the Peace within the limits of the city, and shall have all the powers of Justices of the Peace therein, both in civil and criminal cases arising under the laws of the Territory. They shall, as Justices of the Peace, within the limits of the city, perform the same duties, be governed by the same laws, give the same bonds and securities as other Justices of the Peace, and be commissioned, as Justices of the Peace in and for said city, by the Governor.

Sec. 38.—The Mayor and Aldermen shall have jurisdiction in all cases arising under the ordinances of the corporation, and shall issue such process as may be necessary to carry said ordinances into execution and effect. Appeals may be had from any decision or judgment of said Mayor or Aldermen, arising under the ordinances of said city, to the Municipal Court, under such regulations as may be prescribed by ordinance, which court shall be composed of the Mayor as Chief Justice and the Aldermen as Associate Justices; and from the final judgment of the Municipal Court to the Probate Court of Utah county, in the same manner as appeals are taken from Justices of the Peace: Provided, the parties litigant shall have a right to a trial by a jury of twelve men, in all cases before the Municipal Court. The Municipal Court shall have power to grant writs of *habeas corpus*, and try the same in all cases arising under the ordinances of the City Council.

Sec. 39.—The Municipal Court may sit on the first Monday of every month, and the City Council at such times and places as may be prescribed by city ordinance; special meetings of which may at any time be called by the Mayor or any two Aldermen.

Sec. 40.—All process issued by the Mayor, Aldermen or Municipal Court shall be directed to the Marshal, and in the execution thereof he shall be governed by the same laws as are or may be prescribed for the direction and compensation of Constables in similar cases. The Marshal shall also perform such other duties as may be required of him under the ordinances of said city, and shall be the principal ministerial officer.

Sec. 41.—It shall be the duty of the Recorder, to make and keep accurate records of all ordinances made by the City Council and of all their proceedings in their corporate capacity, which record shall at all times be open to the inspection of the electors of said city, and he shall perform such other duties as may be required of him by the ordinances of the City Council, and shall serve as Clerk of the Municipal Court.

Sec. 42.—When it shall be necessary to take private property for opening, widening, or altering any public street, lane, avenue or alley, the Corporation shall make a just compensation therefor to the person whose property is so taken; and if the amount of such compensation cannot be agreed upon, the Mayor shall cause the same to be ascertained by a jury of six disinterested men, who shall be inhabitants of the city.

Sec. 43.—All jurors, empannelled to inquire into the amount of benefits or damages that shall happen to the owners of property so proposed to be taken, shall first be sworn to that effect, and shall return to the Mayor their inquest in writing, signed by each juror.

Sec. 44.—In case the Mayor shall, at any time, be guilty of any palpable omission of duty, or shall wilfully and corruptly be guilty of oppression, malconduct or partiality in the discharge of the duties of his office, he shall be liable to indictment in the Probate Court of Utah county, and, on conviction, he shall be liable to fine and imprisonment; and the Court shall have power, on the recommend of the jury, to add to the judgment of the Court that he be removed from office.

Sec. 45.—The City Council shall have power to provide for the punishment of offenders and vagrants by imprisonment in the county or city jail, or by compelling them to labor upon the streets or other public works until the same shall be fully paid, in all cases where such offenders or vagrants shall fail or refuse to pay the fines and forfeitures which may be awarded against them.

Sec. 46.—The inhabitants of Alpine city shall, from and after the first Monday of May next, be exempt from working on any road or roads beyond the limits of said city. But all taxes devoted to road purposes shall, from and after said date, be collected and expended, by and under the direction of the Supervisor of Streets, within the limits of said city.

Approved Jan. 19, 1855.

CHAPTER CV.

An ACT to incorporate Tooele City, in Tooele County.

Sec. 1.—Be it enacted by the Governor and Legislative Assembly of the Territory of Utah: That all that portion of country situate within the following boundaries, to wit: beginning at a point half a mile southeast of the mouth of Big Creek, known also as Settlement Cañon; thence running due west three miles; thence north three miles; thence east three miles; thence south three miles, to the place of beginning, shall be known and designated by the name of Tooele City; and the inhabitants thereof are hereby constituted a body corporate and politic, by the name aforesaid; and shall have perpetual succession, and may have and use a common seal, which they may change and alter at pleasure.

Sec. 2.—The inhabitants of said city, by the name and style aforesaid, shall have power to sue and be sued, to plead and be impleaded, defend and be defended in all Courts of law and equity and in all actions whatsoever; to purchase, receive and hold property, real and personal, in said city; to purchase, receive and hold real property beyond the city for burying grounds or other public purposes for the use of the inhabitants of said city; to sell, lease, convey or dispose of property, real and personal, for the benefit of said city; to improve and protect such property, and to do all other things in relation thereto, as natural persons.

Sec. 3.—There shall be a City Council to consist of a Mayor, two Aldermen and three Councilors, who shall have the qualifications of electors of said city, and shall be chosen by the qualified voters thereof, and shall hold their offices for two years, and until their successors shall be elected and qualified. The City Council shall judge of the qualifications, elections and returns of their own members, and a majority of them shall form a quorum to do business, but a smaller number may adjourn from day to day, and compel the attendance of absent members, under such penalties as may be prescribed by ordinance.

Sec. 4.—The Mayor, Aldermen and Councilors, before entering on the duties of their offices, shall take and subscribe an oath or affirmation that they will support the Constitution of the United States and the laws of this Territory, and that they will well and truly perform all the duties of their offices, to the best of their skill and abilities.

Sec. 5.—On the first Monday of August next, and every two years thereafter, on said day, an election shall be held for the electing of a Mayor, two Aldermen and three Councilors; and at the first election under this act, two judges shall be chosen, viva voce, by the electors present. The said judges shall chose one clerk; and the judges and clerk, before entering upon their duties, shall take and subscribe an oath or affirmation, such as is now required by law to be taken by judges and clerks of other elections; and at all subsequent elections the necessary number of judges and clerks shall be appointed by the City Council. At the first election so held, the polls shall be opened at nine o'clock a. m., and closed at six o'clock p. m. At the close of the polls the votes shall be counted, and a statement thereof proclaimed at the front door of the house at which said election shall be held; and the clerks shall leave with each person elected, or at his usual place of residence, within five days after the election, a written notice of his election, and each person so notified, shall within ten days after the election, take the oath or affirmation hereinbefore mentioned; a certificate of which oath shall be deposited with the recorder, whose appointment is hereinafter provided for, and be by him preserved; and all subsequent elections shall be held, conducted, and returns thereof made, as may be provided for by ordinance of the City Council.

Sec. 6.—All free white male inhabitants who are of the age of twenty-one years, who are entitled to vote for Territorial officers and who shall be actual residents of said city sixty days next preceding said election, shall be entitled to vote for city officers.

Sec. 7.—The City Council shall have authority to levy and collect taxes, for city purposes, upon all taxable property, real and personal, within the limits of the city, not exceeding one half per cent. per annum upon the assessed value thereof; and may enforce the payment of the same in any manner to be provided by ordinance, not repugnant to the Constitution of the United States or the laws of this Territory.

Sec. 8.—The City Council shall have power to appoint a Recorder, Treasurer, Assessor and Collector, Marshal and Supervisors of Streets. They shall also have the power to appoint all such other officers, by ordinance, as may be necessary, define the duties of all city officers and remove them from office at pleasure.

Sec. 9.—The City Council shall have power to require of all officers, appointed in pursuance of this act, bonds with penalty and security for the faithful performance of their respective duties, such as may be deemed expedient, and also to require of all officers, appointed as aforesaid, to take an oath for the faithful performance of the duties of their respective offices.

Sec. 10.—The City Council shall have power and authority to make, ordain, establish and execute all such ordinances, not repugnant to the Constitution of the United States or the laws of this Territory, as they may deem necessary for the peace, benefit, good order, regulation, convenience and cleanliness of said city; for the protection of property therein from destruction by fire or otherwise, and for the health and happiness thereof. They shall have power to fill all vacancies, that may happen by death, resignation or removal, in any of the offices herein made elective; to fix and establish all the fees of the officers of said Corporation, not herein established; to impose such fines, not exceeding one hundred dollars for each offence, as they may deem just, for refusing to accept of any office in or under the Corporation, or for misconduct therein, to divide the city into Wards and specify the boundaries thereof.

Sec. 11.—All ordinances passed by the City Council shall, within one month after they shall have been passed, be published in some newspaper printed in said city, or certified copies thereof, be posted up in three of the most public places in the city.

Sec. 12.—All ordinances of the city may be proven by the seal of the Corporation; and when printed or published in book or pamphlet form, purporting to be printed or published by the authority of the Corporation, the same shall be received in evidence in all Courts and places, without further proof.

Sec. 13.—The Mayor and Aldermen shall be conservators of the peace within the limits of the city, and shall have all the powers of justices of the Peace therein, both in civil and criminal cases arising under the laws of the Territory. They shall, as Justices of the Peace, within the limits of said city, perform the same duties, be governed by the same laws, give the same bonds and securities as other Justices of the Peace and be commissioned as other Justices of the Peace in and for said city, by the Governor.

Sec. 14.—The Mayor and Aldermen shall have exclusive jurisdiction in all cases arising under the ordinances of the Corporation, and shall issue such process as may be necessary to carry said ordinances into execution and effect. Appeals may be had from any decision or judgment of said Mayor or Aldermen, arising under the ordinances of said city, to the Probate Court of Tooele County, in the same manner as appeals are taken from Justices of the Peace.

Sec. 15.—To license, regulate, prohibit or restrain the manufacturing, selling or giving away of spirituous, vinous or fermented liquors, tavern keepers, dram or tippling shop keepers, boarding, victualing or coffee houses, restaurants, saloons or other houses or places for the selling or giving away of ardent, vinous or fermented liquors.

Sec. 16.—To restrain, regulate or prohibit the running at large of cattle, horses, mules, sheep, swine, goats and all kinds of poultry; and to tax and regulate the keeping of dogs and authorize the destruction of the same when at large contrary to city ordinance.

Approved Jan. 13, 1853.

———:o:———

CHAPTER CVI.

An ACT Incorporating Ogden City.

Sec. 1.—Be it enacted by the Governor and Legislative Assembly of the Territory of Utah: That all that district of country in Weber county embraced in the following boundaries, to wit: beginning at the mouth of Burch Creek cañon, thence running due west to a point due south of the confluence of Weber and Ogden rivers, thence due north passing through the junction of Weber and Ogden rivers to the street running east between ranges five and six, North Ogden survey, thence east to the base of the mountain, thence in a southerly direction along the base of the mountain to the place of beginning, shall be known and designated by the name and style of Ogden city, and the inhabitants thereof are hereby constituted a body corporate and politic by the name aforesaid, with perpetual succession, and shall have and use a common seal, which they may change and alter at pleasure.

Sec. 2.—The inhabitants of said city, by the name and style aforesaid, shall have power to sue and be sued, to plead and be impleaded, defend and be defended in all Courts of law and equity; and in all actions whatsoever; to purchase, receive, hold, sell, lease, convey and dispose of property real and personal for the benefit of said city, both within and without its corporate boundaries; to improve and protect such property, and to do all other things in relation thereto as natural persons.

Sec. 3.—The municipal government of said city is hereby vested in a City Council, to be composed of a Mayor, three Aldermen, one from each ward, and five Councilors, who shall have the qualifications of electors in said city, and shall be chosen by the qualified voters thereof, and shall hold their office for two years, and until their successors are elected and qualified.

Sec. 4.—An election shall be held on the second Monday in February next, and every two years thereafter, on said day, at which there shall be elected, one Mayor, three Aldermen and five Councilors; and the persons respectively receiving the highest number of votes cast in the city, for said officers, shall be declared elected. When two or more candidates shall have an equal number of votes for the same office, the election shall be determined by the City Council.

Sec. 5.—The first election under this act shall be conducted in the following manner, to wit: The County Clerk of Weber county shall cause notice of the time and place, and the number and kind of officers to be chosen, to be posted up in four public places in said city, at least ten days previous to said election. Two Judges shall be selected by the Probate Judge of Weber county, at least one week previous to the day of election. Said Judges shall choose two Clerks, and the Judges and Clerks, before entering upon their duties, shall take and subscribe an oath or affirmation for the faithful discharge thereof. The poll shall be open at 8 o'clock a.m., and shall close at 6 o'clock p.m. At the close of the election the Judges shall seal up the ballot box and the list of names of the electors and transmit the same, within two days, to the County Clerk of Weber county. As soon as the returns are received, the County Clerk, in the presence of the Probate Judge, shall unseal and examine them, and furnish within five days, to each person having the highest number of votes, a certificate of his election. In case of a tie, it shall be decided by lot drawn by the County Clerk in presence of the Probate Judge.

Sec. 6—All subsequent elections held under this act shall be held, conducted, and returns thereof made as may be provided for by ordinance of the City Council.

Sec. 7.—The City Council shall be judge of the qualifications, elections and returns of their own members; and a majority of them shall form a quorum to do business, shall determine the rules of their own proceedings, and shall meet at such time and place as they may direct; the Mayor shall preside when present, and have a casting vote; and in the absence of the Mayor, any Alderman present may be appointed to preside over said meeting.

Sec. 8.—The City Council may hold stated meetings, and special meetings may be called by the Mayor, or any two Aldermen by notice to each of the members of said council, served personally or left at their usual place of abode.

Sec. 9.—The City Council shall have power to appoint a Marshal, Recorder, (who shall be the Auditor of public accounts,) Treasurer, Assessor and Collector, Supervisor of streets, Surveyor, an Attorney, a Sexton, a Sealer of weights and measures, and all such other officers as may be necessary; define their duties, remove them from office at pleasure, and fix and establish the fees of all officers, jurors and witnessess.

Sec. 10.—All officers elected in accordance with the fourth section of this act may be removed for cause from such office by a vote of two-thirds of the City Council, and shall be furnished with the charges, and have an opportunity to be heard in his defence, and the council shall have power to compel the attendance of witnesses, and the production of papers when necessary.

Sec 11.—When any vacancy shall happen by the death, resignation or removal of any officer, such vacancy may be filled by the City Council, and every person elected or appointed to any office under this act shall, before he enters upon the duties thereof, take and subscribe an oath or affirmation that he will support the Constitution of the United States, the laws of this Territory, and the ordinances of the city, and that he will well and truly perform all the duties of his office to the best of his knowledge and ability; and he may be required to give bonds as shall be prescribed by city ordinance, which oath and bond shall be filed with the City Recorder. All persons appointed under this act to any office shall be commissioned by warrant under the corporate seal signed by the City Recorder.

Sec. 12.—The City Council shall have power to divide the city into wards, and specify the boundaries thereof, and when necessary create additional wards, and add to the number of Aldermen and Councilors, and proportion them among the several wards as may be just and most conducive to the welfare of said city.

Sec. 13.—The Mayor and Aldermen shall be Conservators of the Peace within the limits of the city, and shall give bonds and qualify as other Justices of the Peace, and when so qualified shall posses the same powers and jurisdiction, both in civil and criminal cases arising under the laws of the Territory, and may be commissioned as Justices of the Peace in and for said city, by the Governor. They shall account for and pay over all fines and forfeitures arising under the ordinances of the city into the City Treasury, and all fines and forfeitures arising under the laws of the Territory into the county treasury, and shall issue such process as may be necessary to carry into effect all ordinances of said city. Appeals may be had from any decision or judgment of a Mayor or Alderman's court in the same manner as are or may be provided by statute for appeals from Justice's courts, and they shall account for, and pay over to the City Treasurer within three months all fines and forfeitures received by them, by virtue of their office, and they shall each keep a docket, subject at all times to the inspection of the City Council and all other parties interested.

Sec. 14.—All process issued by the Mayor or an Alderman shall be directed to the Marshal, or other legal officer, and in execution thereof, he shall be governed by such rules and regulation as may be provided by city ordinance.

Sec. 15.—It shall be the duty of the Recorder to make and keep accurate records of all ordinances made by the City Council, and all their proceedings in a corporate capacity, which record shall at all times be open to the inspection of the electors of the city, and all other parties interested, and audit all accounts of said incorporation. He shall have and keep a plat of all surveys within the city, and he is hereby authorized to take the acknowledgement of deeds, transfers and other instruments of writing, and shall perform such other duties as may be required of him by city ordinances.

Sec. 16.—The Treasurer shall receive all money or funds belonging to the city, and shall keep an accurate account of all receipts and expenditures in such manner as the City Council shall direct. He shall pay all funds that may come to his hand, by virtue of his office, upon orders signed by the Auditor of Public Accounts; and shall report to the City Council a true account of his receipts and disbursements, as they may require.

Sec. 17.—The City Council shall have power, within the city, by ordinance to annually levy and collect taxes on the assessed value of all property in the city made taxable by the laws of the Territory, for the following named purposes, to wit: not to exceed five mills on the dollar for contingent expenses, nor to exceed five mills on the dollar to open, improve and keep in repair the streets of the city. The City Council is further empowered to divide the city into School Districts, provide for the election of Trustees, appoint a Board of School Inspectors, annually assess and collect and expend the necessary tax for school purposes and for furnishing the city with water for irrigating and other purposes, and regulate and control the same; and furthermore, so far as may be necessary, control the water courses leading thereto in the immediate vicinity thereof.

Sec. 18.—The City Council shall have the management and control of the finances and property of said city.

Sec. 19.—To require and it is hereby made the duty of every male resident of the city, over the age of eighteen and under the age of fifty years, to labor not to exceed two days in each year upon the streets; but every person may, at his option, pay one dollar and fifty cents for the day he shall be so bound to labor: Provided it be paid within five days from the time he shall be notified by the Street Supervisor. In default of payment as aforesaid, the same may be collected as other taxes.

Sec. 20.—The Council shall have power to borrow money for city purposes, the interest of which shall not exceed one-fourth of the city revenue arising from taxes of the previous year.

Sec. 21.—The City Council shall have power by ordinance to regulate the form of the assessment rolls. The annual assessment roll shall be returned by the Assessor on or before the first Monday of April in each year, but the time may be extended or additions made thereto by order of the City Council. On the return thereof, the City Council shall fix a day for hearing objections thereto; and any person feeling aggrieved by the assessment of his property may appear at the time specified and make his objections, which shall be heard and determined upon by the City Council, and they shall have power to alter, add to, take from and otherwise correct and revise said assessment roll.

Sec. 22.—The Collector shall be furnished, within thirty days after the assessment rolls are corrected, with a list of taxes to be collected; and if not paid when demanded, the Collector shall have power to collect said taxes with interest and cost by suit in the corporate name, as may be provided by ordinance. The assessment roll shall in all cases be evidence on the part of the corporation.

Sec. 23.—To appropriate and provide for the payment of the expenses and debts of the city.

Sec. 24.—To make regulations to prevent the introduction of contagious diseases into the city; to make quarantine laws, and enforce the same within the city and around it, not exceeding twelve miles next beyond the boundaries thereof.

Sec. 25.—To establish hospitals, and make regulations for the government of the same; to make regulations to secure the general health of the inhabitants; to declare what shall be nuisances, and prevent and remove the same.

Sec. 26.—To provide the city with water; to dig wells, lay pump logs and pipes, and erect pumps in the street for the extinguishment of fires, and the convenience of the inhabitants.

Sec. 27.—To direct or prohibit the location and management of houses for the storing of gunpowder, tar, pitch, rosin or other combustible and dangerous materials within the city, and to regulate the conveying of gunpowder.

Sec. 28.—To exclusively control, regulate, repair, amend and clear the streets, alleys, bridges, sidewalks or crosswalks, and open, widen, straighten or vacate streets and alleys and put drains or ditches and sewers therein, and prevent the incumbering of the streets in any manner and protect the same from any encroachment and injury.

Sec. 29.—To provide for the lighting of the streets and erecting lamp posts; to erect market houses and establish markets and market places, and provide for the government and regulation thereof.

Sec. 30.—To provide for the erection of all needful buildings for the use of the city, and for inclosing, improving and regulating all public grounds belonging to the city.

Sec. 31.—To license, regulate, prohibit or restrain the manufacturers, sellers or venders of spirituous or fermented liquors, tavern keepers, dram or tippling shop keepers, boarding, victualling or coffee houses, restaurants, saloons or other houses or places for the selling or giving away of wines or other liquors, whether ardent, vinous or fermented.

Sec. 32.—To license, tax, and regulate auctioneers, merchants, retailers, groceries, ordinaries, hawkers, peddlers, brokers, pawnbrokers, and money changers.

Sec. 33.—To regulate the selling or giving away of any ardent spirits or other intoxicating liquors by any shopkeeper, grocer or trader, to be drank in any shop, store, grocery, outhouse, yard, garden or other place within the city, except by persons or at places duly licensed; to forbid the selling or giving away of ardent spirits or other intoxicating liquors to any child, apprentice or servant, without the consent of his or her parent, guardian; master or mistress, or to any Indian.

Sec. 34.—To regulate and license or prohibit butchers, and to revoke their license for malconduct in the course of trade; and to regulate, license and restrain the sale of fresh meat and vegetables in the city.

Sec. 35.—To license, tax, regulate, suppress or prohibit billiard tables, pin alleys, nine or ten pin alleys or table and ball alleys; to suppress or restrain all disorderly houses and groceries; to authorize the destruction and demolition of all instruments and devices used for the purpose of gaming, and all kinds of gambling; to prevent any riot, noise, disturbance or disorderly assemblage; and to restrain and punish vagrants, mendicants, street beggars and prostitutes.

Sec. 36.—To regulate, license, suppress or prohibit all exhibitions of common showmen, shows of every kind, concerts or other musical entertainments, exhibitions of natural or artificial curiosities, caravans, circuses, theatrical performances, ball rooms and all other exhibitions and amusements.

Sec. 37.—To license, tax and regulate hacking, carriages, wagons, carts and drays and fix the rates to be charged for the carriage of persons and for wagonage, cartage and drayage of property; as also to license and regulate porters and fix the rates of porterage.

Sec. 38.—To provide for the prevention and extinguishment of fires; to regulate the fixing of chimneys and flues thereof and stove pipes, and to organize and establish fire companies.

Sec. 39.—To regulate and order parapet walls and other partition fences.

Sec. 40.—To establish standard weights and measures and regulate the weights and measures to be used in the city, in all cases not provided for by law.

Sec. 41.—To provide for the inspecting and measuring of lumber and other building materials, and for the measurement of all kinds of mechanical work.

Sec. 42.—To provide for the inspection and weighing of hay, lime and stone coal, and the measuring of charcoal, firewood and other fuel to be sold or used within the city.

Sec. 43.—To provide for and regulate the inspection of tobacco, beef, pork, flour and meal; also beer, whisky and brandy and all other spirituous or fermented liquors.

Sec. 44.—To regulate the weight and quality and price of bread sold and used in the city.

Sec. 45.—The City Council shall have exclusive power within the city, by ordinance, to license, regulate or restrain the keeping of ferries and toll bridges.

Sec. 46.—To provide for the taking the enumeration of the inhabitants of the city; to regulate the burial of the dead, and registration of births and deaths; to direct the returning and keeping of bills of mortality and to impose penalties on physicians, sextons, and others for any default in the premises.

Sec. 47.—To prevent horse-racing, immoderate riding or driving in the streets, and to authorize their being stopped by any person; to punish or prohibit the abuse of animals, to provide for the putting up of posts in front of city lots to fasten their horses and other animals; to compel the fastening of horses, mules, oxen or other animals attached to vehicles, whilst standing or remaining in the streets.

Sec. 48.—To prevent the incumbering of the streets or sidewalks, lanes, alleys and public grounds with carriages, tents, wagons, carts, sleighs, horses or other animals, sleds, wheelbarrows, boxes, lumber, timber, firewood, posts, awnings, signs, adobies or any material or substance whatever.

Sec. 49.—To restrain, regulate or prohibit the running at large of cattle, horses, mules, sheep, swine, goats and all kinds of poultry; and to authorize the destraining, empounding the same and collecting penalty and cost incurred thereby, and to tax, prevent or regulate the keeping of dogs, and to authorize the destruction of the same, when at large contrary to city ordinance.

Sec. 50.—To compel the owner or occupant of any grocery, cellar, tallow chandler shop, soap factory, tannery, stable, barn, privy, sewer, or any unwholesome place to cleanse, remove or abate the same from time to time, as oft as may be necessary for the health, comfort and convenience of the inhabitants of said city.

Sec. 51.—To direct the location and management of and regulate breweries and tanneries; and to direct the location, management and construction of and restrain or prohibit within the city distilleries, slaughtering establishments and all establishments or places where nauseous, offensive or unwholesome business may be carried on.

Sec. 52.—To prevent any person from bringing, depositing or having within the limits of the city any dead carcass or any unwholesome substance, and to require the removal or destruction of the same by any person who shall have placed or caused to be placed upon or near his premises or near any of the streams of this city any such substance or any putrid or unsound beef, pork or fish, hides or skins of any kind; and, on his default, to authorize the removal or destruction of the same by any officer of said city.

Sec. 53.—To direct and regulate the planting and preserving trees in the streets and public grounds, and regulate the fencing of lots within the boundaries of the city.

Sec. 54.—To prevent the ringing of bells, the blowing of horns and bugles, the crying of goods and all other noises, performances and devices tending to disturb the peace and quiet of the said city.

Sec. 55.—To grant and issue licenses and direct the manner of issuing and registering thereof. Bonds may be taken on the granting of licenses, for the due observance of the ordinances of the City Council.

Sec. 56.—To require every merchant, retailer, trader and dealer in merchandise or property of every description, which is sold by measure or weight, to cause their weights and measures to be sealed by the City Sealer and to be subject to his inspection, the standard of which weights and measures shall be conformable to those established by law.

Sec. 57.—The City Council shall have power to make such ordinances and resolutions, not contrary to the Constitution and laws of the United States and the laws of the Territory, as may be necessary and expedient to carry into effect the powers vested in the City Council or any officer of said city by this act, and enforce observance of all ordinances and resolutions made in pursuance of this act by penalties not exceeding one hundred dollars or imprisonment not to exceed six months, or both.

Sec. 58.—The City Council shall have exclusive authority and power to establish and regulate the Police of the city; to impose fines, forfeitures and penalties for the breach of any ordinances; to provide for the recovery of such fines and forfeitures and the enforcement of such penalties, and to pass, make, ordain, establish and execute all such ordinances, not repugnant to the Constitution and laws of the United States or the laws of this Territory, as they may deem necessary for carrying into effect and execution the powers specified in this act, and for the peace, good order, regulation, convenience and cleanliness of the city, for the protection of property therein from destruction by fire or otherwise, and for the health, safety and happiness of the inhabitants thereof.

Sec. 59.—To provide for the punishment of offenders and vagrants by imprisonment in the county or city jail, or by compelling them to labor on the streets or other public works until the same shall be fully paid in all cases where such offenders or vagrants shall fail or refuse to pay the fines and forfeitures which may be awarded against them.

Sec. 60.—All ordinances passed by the City Council shall, within one month after they shall have been passed, be published in some newspaper printed in said city, or certified copies thereof be posted up in three of the most public places in the city.

Sec. 61.—All ordinances of the city may be proven by the seal of the Corporation, and, when printed or published in book form, purporting to be printed or published by the authority of the City Council, the same shall be received in evidence in all Courts or places without further proof.

Sec. 62.—When it shall be necessary to take private property for opening, widening or altering any public street, lane, avenue or alley, the Corporation shall make a just compensation therefor to the person whose property is so taken; and if the amount of such compensation cannot be agreed upon, the Mayor shall cause the same to be ascertained by a jury of six disinterested men, who shall be inhabitants of the city.

Sec. 63.—All jurors empanneled to enquire into the amounts of benefit or damages that shall happen to the owners of property so proposed to be taken shall first be sworn to that effect, and shall return to the Mayor or presiding officer of the City Council, their inquest in writing, signed by each juror.

Sec. 64.—All ordinances, resolutions and regulations now in force in Ogden city, and not inconsistent with this act, shall remain in force until altered, modified or repealed by the City Council after this act, shall take effect.

Sec. 65.—All actions, rights, fines, penalties and forfeitures, in suit or otherwise, which have accrued under the ordinance incorporating Ogden City, shall be vested in and prosecuted by the Corporation hereby created.

Sec. 66.—All plots and surveys of lands, lots or other places within said city, heretofore surveyed by the Surveyor, and all plots and surveys of lands, lots or other places that may be hereafter surveyed, and all certificates of surveys given by him shall be deemed valid by this act.

Sec. 67.—All property, now belonging to Ogden city, is hereby vested in the corporation created by this act; and the officers of said corporation now in office shall respectively continue in the same, until superseded in conformity to the provisions thereof, but shall be governed by this act.

Sec. 68.—This act shall not invalidate any act done by the present City Council of Ogden city, or by its officers, nor divest their successors under this act of any right, property or otherwise, or liability which may have accrued to or been created by said Council prior to the passage of this act.

Sec. 69.—All officers of the city, created conservators of the peace by this act, shall have power to arrest or cause to be arrested, with or without process, all persons who shall break the peace; commit for examination, and, if necessary, detain such persons in custody forty-eight hours in the city prison or other safe place; and shall have and exercise such other powers, as conservators of the peace, as the City Council may prescribe.

Sec. 70.—Nothing in this act shall be so construed as to deprive the present City Council of Ogden City of any power or authority conferred upon them by the ordinance incorporating said city, and the act amendatory thereto; but said City Council shall possess, exercise and enjoy all the powers and authority heretofore conferred upon them, except so far as such powers and authority have been expressly modified or repealed by this act, until said City Council are superseded by the election and qualification of their successors under this act.

Sec. 71.—That an ordinance to incorporate Ogden city, approved February 6th, 1851, be and is hereby repealed, and an act in relation to the assessment and collection and expenditure of a tax for road and other purposes within incorporated cities, approved January 4th, 1853, so far as the same applies to Ogden city, and is hereby repealed.

Sec. 72.—The City Council shall cause to be published in some newspaper published in Ogden city or posted up in three public places, on or before the first day of December in each year, a statement of the amount of the city revenue, specifying in said statement whence derived and for what disbursed.

Approved, January 18, 1861.

CHAPTER CVII.

An ACT to incorporate the City of Saint George in Washington County.

Sec. 1.—Be it enacted by the Governor and Legislative Assembly of the Territory of Utah: That all that portion of country situated within the following boundaries, to wit: beginning at the first point of rocks below the mouth of the Santa Clara and on the west bank of the Rio Virgin, in the County of Washington; thence, running due west two and a half miles; thence, due north five miles; thence, due east five miles; thence, due south five miles; thence, due west two and a half miles to the place of beginning shall be known and designated by the name of the "City of St. George," and the inhabitants thereof are hereby constituted a body corporate and politic by the name aforesaid; and may have and use a common seal, which they may change and alter at pleasure.

Sec. 2.—The inhabitants of said city, by the name and style aforesaid, shall have power to sue and be sued, to plead and be impleaded, defend and be defended in all Courts of law and equity and in all actions whatsoever; to purchase, receive and hold property, real and personal, in said city; to purchase, receive and hold real property beyond the city for burying grounds or other public purposes for the use of the inhabitants of said city; to sell, lease, convey or dispose of property, real and personal, for the benefit of said city; to improve and protect such property, and to do all other things in relation thereto, as natural persons.

Sec. 3.—There shall be a City Council to consist of a Mayor, two Aldermen and three Councilors, who shall have the qualifications of electors of said city, and shall be chosen by the qualified voters thereof, and shall hold their offices for two years, and until their successors shall be elected and qualified. The City Council shall judge of the qualifications, elections and returns of their own members, and a majority of them shall form a quorum to do business; but a smaller number may adjourn from day to day and compel the attendance of absent members, under such penalties as may be prescribed by ordinance.

Sec. 4.—The Mayor, Aldermen and Councilors, before entering upon the duties of their offices, shall take and subscribe an oath or affirmation that they will support the Constitution of the United States and the laws of this Territory, and that they will well and truly perform all the duties of their offices to the best of their skill and abilities.

Sec. 5.—One Mayor, two Aldermen and three Councilors shall be elected biennially, and the first election under this act shall be at such time and place as the Probate Judge of Washington County shall direct: Provided, said election shall be on or before the first Monday in August next. Said election shall be held and conducted as is now provided by law for the holding of elections for County and Territorial officers; and, at the said first election, all free white male residents, over twenty-one years of age, within said city limits, shall be entitled to vote.

Sec. 6.—The clerks of election shall leave with each person elected, or at his usual place of residence, within five days after the election, a written notice of his election, and each person so notified shall, within ten days after the election, take the oath or affirmation hereinbefore mentioned, a certificate of which oath shall be deposited with the Recorder, whose appointment is hereinafter provided for, and be by him preserved; and all subsequent elections shall be held, conducted, and returns thereof made, as may be provided for by ordinance of the City Council.

Sec. 7.—The City Council shall have authority to levy and collect taxes, for city purposes, upon all taxable property, real and personal, within the limits of the city, not exceeding one half of one per cent. per annum upon the assessed value thereof; and may enforce the payment of the same in any manner to be provided by ordinance, not repugnant to the Constitution of the United States or the laws of this Territory.

Sec. 8.—The City Council shall have power to appoint a Recorder, Treasurer, Assessor and Collector, Marshal and Supervisor of Streets. They shall also have the power to appoint all such other officers, by ordinance, as may be necessary, define the duties of all city officers and remove them from office at pleasure.

Sec. 9.—The City Council shall have power to require of all officers, appointed in pursuance of this act, bonds with security, for the faithful performance of their respective duties, and also to require of all officers, appointed as aforesaid, to take an oath for the faithful performance of the duties of their respective offices.

Sec. 10.—The City Council shall have power and authority to make, ordain, establish and execute all such ordinances, not repugnant to the Constitution of the United States or the laws of this Territory, as they may deem necessary for the peace, benefit, good order, regulation, convenience and cleanliness of said city; for the protection of property therein from destruction by fire or otherwise, and for the health and happiness thereof, and shall have control of the waters of the Santa Clara: Provided that such control shall not be exercised to the injury of any rights already acquired by actual settlers thereon, and shall have control of the water courses and mill privileges within said city. They shall have power to fill all vacancies that may happen by death, resignation or removal in any of the offices herein made elective; to fix and establish the fees of the officers of said corporation; to impose such fines, not exceeding one hundred dollars, and imprisonment not exceeding six months, for each offense, for the breach or violation of any city ordinance; to divide the city into Wards and specify the boundaries thereof.

Sec. 11.—All ordinances passed by the City Council shall, within one month after they shall have been passed, be published in some newspaper printed in said city, or certified copies thereof be posted up in three of the most public places in the city.

Sec. 12.—All ordinances of the city may be proven by the seal of the corporation: and, when printed or published in book or pamphlet form, purporting to be printed or published by the authority of the corporation, the same shall be received in evidence in all courts and places, without further proof.

Sec. 13.—The Mayor and Aldermen shall have all the powers of Justices of the Peace, both in civil and crimiual cases arising under the laws of the Territory. They shall, as Justices of the Peace within the limits of said city, perform the same duties, be governed by the same laws, give the same bonds and securities as other Justices of the Peace in and for said city, and be commissioned by the Governor.

Sec. 14.—The Mayor and Aldermen shall have exclusive jurisdiction in all cases arising under the ordinances of the corporation; and shall issue such process as may be necessary to carry said ordinances into execution and effect. Appeals may be had from any decision or judgment of said Mayor or Aldermen, arising under the ordinances of said city, to the Probate Court of Washington county, in the same manner as appeals are, or may be taken from Justices of the Peace.

Sec. 15.—The City Council shall have power to restrain, regulate or prohibit the running at large of cattle, horses, mules, sheep, swine, goats and all kinds of poultry; and to tax and regulate the keeping of dogs, and to authorize the destruction of the same when at large contrary to city ordinance.

Sec. 16.—To license, regulate, prohibit or restrain the manufacturing, selling or giving away of spirituous, vinous or fermented liquors, tavern keepers, dram or tippling shop keepers, boarding, victualing or coffee houses, restaurants, saloons or other houses or places for the selling or giving away of ardent, vinous or fermented liquors.

Sec. 17.—This act shall be in force on and after the tenth day of February, 1862, and may be amended or repealed at the pleasure of the Legislative Assembly.

Approved Jan. 17, 1862.

———:o:———

CHAPTER CVIII.

An ACT to Incorporate the City of Payson.

Sec. 1.—Be it enacted by the Governor and Legislative Assembly of the Territory of Utah: That all the Territory embraced in the following boundaries, viz: Commencing at a point on the east bank of Utah Lake due west from the center of the Public Square in the City of Payson in Utah County, thence south one mile, thence east to the mountains, thence along the base of the mountains to a spring known as "Goose nest spring," thence northerly to a point where the bridge crosses the Pondtown slough, thence down said slough to Duck creek, then west to Peeteetneet creek and down the main channel of said creek to Utah Lake, thence south along the shore of said Lake to the place of the beginning shall be known and designated as Payson; and the inhabitants thereof are hereby constituted a body corporate and politic by the name aforesaid, and shall have perpetual succession, and may have and use a common seal, which they may change and alter at pleasure.

Sec. 2.—The inhabitants of said city, by the name and style aforesaid, shall have power to sue and be sued, to plead and be impleaded, defend and be defended in all

Courts of law and equity and in all actions whatsoever; to purchase, receive, hold, sell, lease, convey and dispose of property real and personal for the benefit of said city, both within and without its corporate boundaries; to improve and protect such property, and to do all other things in relation thereto, as natural persons.

Sec. 3.—The Municipal government of said city is hereby vested in a City Council, to be composed of a Mayor, three Aldermen, one from each Ward, and five Councilors, who shall have the qualifications of electors in said city, and shall be chosen by the qualified voters thereof, and shall hold their office for two years, and until their successors are elected and qualified.

Sec. 4.—An election shall be held on the second Monday in February next, and every two years thereafter on said day, at which there shall be elected one Mayor, three Aldermen and five Councilors; and the persons respectively receiving the highest number of votes cast in the city for said officers shall be declared elected. When two or more candidates shall have an equal number of votes for the same office, the election shall be determined by the City Council.

Sec. 5.—The first election under this act shall be conducted in the following manner, to wit: The County Clerk of Utah county shall cause notice of the time and place, and the number and kind of officers to be chosen, to be posted up in four public places in said city, at least ten days previous to said election. Two Judges shall be selected by the Probate Judge of Utah county, at least one week previous to the day of election; said Judges shall choose two Clerks; and the Judges and Clerks, before entering upon their duties, shall take and subscribe an oath or affirmation for the faithful discharge thereof. The poll shall be open at eight o'clock a. m., and shall close at six o'clock p. m. At the close of the election the Judges shall seal up the ballot box and the list of names of the electors and transmit the same, within two days, to the County Clerk of Utah county. As soon as the returns are received the County Clerk, in the presence of the Probate Judge, shall unseal and examine them, and furnish, within five days, to each person having the highest number of votes, a certificate of his election. In case of a tie, it shall be decided by lot drawn by the County Clerk in presence of the Probate Judge.

Sec. 6.—All subsequent elections held under this act shall be held, conducted and returns thereof made as may be provided for by ordinance of the City Council.

Sec. 7.—The City Council shall be judge of the qualifications, elections and returns of their own members; and a majority of them shall form a quorum to do business, shall determine the rules of their own proceedings and shall meet at such time and place as they may direct; the Mayor shall preside when present, and have a casting vote; and, in the absence of the Mayor, any Aldermen present may be appointed to preside over said meeting.

Sec. 8.—The City Council may hold stated meetings; and special meetings may be called by the Mayor or any two Aldermen, by notice to each of the members of said Council, served personally or left at their usual places of abode.

Sec. 9.—The City Council shall have power to appoint a Marshal, Recorder, (who shall be the Auditor of Public Accounts,) Treasurer, Assessor and Collector, Supervisor of Streets, Surveyor and Attorney, a Sexton, a Sealer of Weights and Measures and all such other officers as may be necessary, define their duties, remove them from office at pleasure, and fix and establish the fees of all officers, jurors and witnesses.

Sec. 10.—All officers elected in accordance with the fourth section of this act may be removed for cause from such office by a vote of two-thirds of the City Council, and shall be furnished with the charges and have an opportunity to be heard in his defense; and the Council shall have power to compel the attendance of witnesses and the production of papers, when necessary.

Sec. 11.—When a vacancy shall happen by the death, resignation or removal of any officer, such vacancy may be filled by the City Council; and every person elected or appointed to any office under this act shall, before he enters upon the duties thereof, take and subscribe an oath or affirmation that he will support the Constitution of the United States, the laws of this Territory and the ordinances of the city, and that he will well and truly perform all the duties of his office to the best of his knowledge and ability; and he may be required to give bonds as shall be prescribed by city ordinances, which oath and bond shall be filed with the City Recorder.

Sec. 12.—The City Council shall have power to divide the city into Wards and specify the boundaries thereof; and, when necessary, create additional Wards and add to the number of Aldermen and Councilors and proportion them among the several Wards, as may be just and most conducive to the welfare of said city.

Sec. 13.—The Mayor and Aldermen shall be Conservators of the Peace within the limits of the city, and shall give bonds and qualify as other Justices of the Peace; and, when so qualified, shall possess the same powers and jurisdiction, both in civil and criminal cases arising under the laws of the Territory, and may be commissioned as

Justices of the Peace in and for said city by the Governor. They shall account for and pay over all fines and forfeitures arising under the ordinances of the city into the City Treasury, and all fines and forfeitures arising under the laws of the Territory into the County Treasury, and shall issue such process as may be necessary to carry into effect all ordinances of said city. Appeals may be had from any decision or judgment of a Mayor's or Alderman's court in the same manner as or may be provided by statute for appeals from Justices Courts; and they shall account for and pay over to the City Treasurer, within three months, all fines and forfeitures received by them by virtue of their office: and they shall each keep a docket, subject at all times to the inspection of the City Council and all other parties interested.

Sec. 14.—All process issued by the Mayor or an Alderman shall be directed to the Marshal or other legal officer, and in execution thereof he shall be governed by such rules and regulations as may be provided by city ordinance.

Sec. 15.—It shall be the duty of the Recorder to make and keep accurate records of all ordinances made by the City Council and all their proceedings in a corporate capacity, which record shall at all times be open to the inspection of the electors of the city and all other parties interested, and audit all accounts of said Incorporation. He shall have and keep a plat of all surveys within the city; and he is hereby authorized to take the acknowledgment of deeds, transfers and other instruments of writing, and shall perform such other duties as may be required of him by city ordinance.

Sec. 16.—The Treasurer shall receive all money or funds belonging to the city, and shall keep an accurate account of all receipts and expenditures in such manner as the City Council shall direct. He shall pay all funds that may come to hand by virtue of his office upon orders signed by the Auditor of Public Accounts, and shall report to the City Council a true account of his receipts and disbursements, as they may require.

Sec. 17.—The City Council shall have power within the city, by ordinance, to annually levy and collect taxes on the assessed value of all property in the city made taxable by the laws of the Territory, for the following named purposes, to wit: not to exceed five mills on the dollar for contingent expenses, nor to exceed five mills on the dollar to open, improve and keep in repair the streets of the city. The City Council is further empowered to divide the city into School Districts, provide for the election of Trustees, appoint a board of School Inspectors, annually assess and collect and expend the necessary tax for school purposes, and for furnishing the city with water for irrigating and other purposes, and regulate and control the same; and furthermore, so far as may be necessary, control the water courses leading thereto in the immediate vicinity thereof.

Sec. 18.—The City Council shall have the management and control of the finances and property of said city.

Sec. 19.—To require, and it is hereby made the duty of, every male resident of the city, over the age of eighteen and under the age of fifty years, to labor not to exceed two days in each year upon the streets; but every person may, at his option, pay one dollar and fifty cents for the day he shall be so bound to labor: Provided it be paid within five days from the time he shall be notified by the Street Supervisor. In default of payment as aforesaid, the same may be collected as other taxes.

Sec. 20.—The Council shall have power to borrow money for city purposes, the interest of which shall not exceed one-fourth of the city revenue arising from taxes of the previous year.

Sec. 21.—The City Council shall have power, by ordinance, to regulate the form of the assessment rolls. The annual assessment roll shall be returned by the Assessor on or before the first Monday of April in each year, but the time may be extended or additions made thereto by order of the City Council. On the return thereof, the City Council shall fix a day for hearing objections thereto, and any person feeling aggrieved by the assessment of his property may appear at the time specified and make his objections, which shall be heard and determined upon by the City Council; and they shall have power to alter, add to, take from and otherwise correct and revise said assessment roll.

Sec. 22.—The Collector shall be furnished, within thirty days after the assessment rolls are corrected, with a list of taxes to be collected; and if not paid when demanded, the Collector shall have power to collect said taxes with interest and cost, by suit in the corporate name as may be provided by ordinance. The assessment roll shall in all cases be evidence on the part of the Corporation.

Sec. 23.—To appropriate and provide for the payment of the expenses and debts of the city.

Sec. 24.—To make regulations to prevent the introduction of contagious diseases into the city; to make quarantine laws and enforce the same within the city and around it, not exceeding twelve miles next beyond the boundaries thereof.

Sec. 25.—To establish hospitals and make regulations for the government of the same; to make regulations to secure the general health of the inhabitants; to declare what shall be nuisances and remove the same.

Sec. 26.—To provide the city with water; to dig wells, lay pump logs and pipes and erect pumps in the streets for the extinguishment of fires and the convenience of the inhabitants.

Sec. 27.—To direct or prohibit the location and management of houses for the storing of gunpowder, tar, pitch, resin or other combustible and dangerous materials within the city, and to regulate the conveying of gunpowder.

Sec. 28.—To exclusively control, regulate, repair, amend and clear the streets, alleys, bridges, side-walks or cross-walks, and open, widen, straighten or vacate streets and alleys and put drains or ditches and sewers therein, and prevent the incumbering of the streets in any manner and protect the same from any incroachment and injury.

Sec. 29.—To provide for the lighting of the streets and erecting lamp posts; to erect market houses and establish markets and market places, and provide for the government and regulation thereof.

Sec. 30.—To provide for the erection of all needful buildings for the use of the city and for inclosing, improving and regulating all public grounds belonging to the city.

Sec. 31.—To license, regulate. prohibit or restrain the manufacturers, sellers or venders of spirituous or fermented liquors, tavern keepers, dram or tippling shop keepers, boarding, victualing or coffee houses, restaurants, saloons, or other houses or places for the selling or giving away of wines or other liquors, whether ardent, vinous or fermented.

Sec. 32.—To license, tax and regulate auctioneers, merchants, retailers, grocers, ordinaries, hawkers, peddlers, brokers, pawnbrokers and money changers.

Sec. 33.—To regulate the selling or giving away of any ardent spirits or other intoxicating liquors by any shopkeeper, grocer or trader, to be drank in any shop, store, grocery, outhouse, yard, garden or other place within the city, except by persons or at places duly licensed; to forbid the selling or giving away of ardent spirits or other intoxicating liquors to any child, apprentice or servant, without the consent of his or her parent, guardian, master or mistress, or to any Indian.

Sec. 34.—To regulate and license or prohibit butchers, and to revoke their license for malconduct in the course of trade; and to regulate, license or restrain the sale of fresh meat and vegetables in the city.

Sec. 35.—To license, tax, regulate, suppress or prohibit billiard tables, pin alleys, nine or ten pin alleys, or table and ball alleys; to suppress or restrain all disorderly houses and groceries; to authorize the destruction and demolition of all instruments and devices used for the purpose of gaming and all kinds of gambling; to prevent any riot, noise, disturbance or disorderly assemblage; and to restrain and punish vagrants, mendicants, street beggars and prostitutes.

Sec. 36.—To regulate, license, suppress or prohibit all exhibitions of common showmen, shows of every kind, concerts or other musical entertainments, exhibitions of natural or artificial curiosities, caravans, circuses, theatrical performances, ball rooms and all other exhibitions and amusements.

Sec. 37.—To license, tax and regulate hacking, carriages, wagons, carts, and drays, and fix the rates to be charged for the carrying of persons and for wagonage, cartage and drayage of property as also to license and regulate porters and fix the rates of porterage.

Sec. 38.—To provide for the prevention and extinguishment of fires; to regulate the fixing of chimneys and the flues thereof and stove pipes; and to organize and establish fire companies.

Sec. 39.—To regulate and order parapet walls and other partition fences.

Sec. 40.—To establish standard weights and measures and regulate the weights and measures to be used in the city, in all cases not provided by law.

Sec. 41.—To provide for the inspection and measuring of lumber and other building materials, and for the measurement of all kinds of mechanical work.

Sec. 42. To provide for the inspection and weighing of hay, lime and stone coal, and the measuring of charcoal, firewood and other fuel to be sold or used within the city.

Sec. 43.—To provide for and regulate the inspection of tobacco, beef, pork, flour and meal; also beer, whiskey, brandy and all other spirituous or fermented liquors.

Sec. 44.—To regulate the weight and quality and price of bread sold and used in the city.

Sec. 45.—The City Council shall have exclusive power within the city, by ordinance, to license, regulate or restrain the keeping of ferries and toll bridges.

Sec. 46.—To provide for the taking the enumeration of the inhabitants of the city, to regulate the burial of the dead and registration of births and deaths; to direct the returning and keeping of bills of mortality; and to impose penalties on physicians, sextons and others for any default in the premises.

Sec. 47.—To prevent horse racing and immoderate riding and driving in the streets, and to authorize their being stopped by any person; to punish or prohibit the abuse of animals; to compel persons to put up posts in front of their lots to fasten their horses and other animals; to compel the fastening of horses, mules, oxen or other animals attached to vehicles, whilst standing or remaining in the streets.

Sec. 48.—To prevent encumbering the streets or side-walks, lanes, alleys and public grounds with carriages, tents, wagons, carts, sleighs, horses or other animals, sleds, wheel-barrows, boxes, lumber, timber, firewood, posts, awnings, signs, adobies or any material or substance whatever.

Sec. 49.—To restrain, regulate or prohibit the running at large of cattle, horses, mules, sheep, swine, goats and all kinds of poultry; and to tax, prevent or regulate the keeping of dogs, and to authorize the destruction of the same when at large contrary to city ordinance.

Sec. 50.—To compel the owner or occupant of any grocery, cellar, tallow chandler shop, soap factory, tannery, stable, barn, privy, sewer or any unwholesome place, to cleanse, remove or abate the same from time to time, as oft as may be necessary for the health, comfort and convenience of the inhabitants of said city.

Sec. 51.—To direct the location and management of and regulate breweries and tanneries; and to direct the location, management and construction of and restrain or prohibit within the city distilleries, slaughtering establishments, or places where nauseous, offensive or unwholesome business may be carried on.

Sec. 52.—To prevent any person from bringing, depositing or having within the limits of the city any dead carcass or any unwholesome substance, and to require the removal or the destruction of the same by any person who shall have placed or caused to be placed upon or near his premises or near any of the streams of this city any such substance, or any putrid or unsound beef, pork, or fish, hides or skins of any kind; and on his default to authorize the removal or destruction of the same by any officer of said city.

Sec. 53.—To direct and regulate the planting and preserving trees in the streets and public grounds, and regulate the fencing of lots within the boundaries of the city.

Sec. 54.—To prevent the ringing of bells, the blowing of horns and bugles, the crying of goods and all other notices, performances and devices tending to disturb the peace and quiet of the said city.

Sec. 55.—To grant and issue licenses, and direct the manner of issuing and registering thereof. Bonds may be taken on the granting of licenses, for the due observance of the ordinances of the City Council.

Sec. 56.—To require every merchant, retailer, trader and dealer in merchandise or property of every description which is sold by measure or weight, to cause their weights and measures to be sealed by the City Sealer and to be subject to his inspection, the standard of which weights and measures shall be conformable to those established by law.

Sec. 57.—The City Council shall have power to make such ordinances and resolutions, not contrary to the Constitution and laws of the United States and the laws of the Territory, as may be necessary and expedient to carry into effect the powers vested in the City Council or any officer of said city by this act, and enforce observance of all ordinances and resolutions made in pursuance of this act, by penalties not exceeding one hundred dollars, or imprisonment not to exceed six months, or both.

Sec. 58.—The City Council shall have exclusive authority and power to establish and regulate the Police of the city; to impose fines, forfeitures and penalties for the breach of any ordinance; to provide for the recovery of such fines and forfeitures and the enforcement of such penalties: and to pass, make, ordain, establish and execute all such ordinances, not repugnant to the Constitution and laws of the United States or the laws of this Territory, as they may deem necessary for carrying into effect and execution the powers specified in this act, and for the peace, good order, regulation, convenience and cleanliness of the city, for the protection of property therein from destruction by fire or otherwise, and for the health, safety and happiness of the inhabitants thereof.

Sec. 59.—To provide for the punishment of offenders and vagrants by imprisonment in the county or city jail, or by compelling them to labor on the streets or other public works until the same shall be fully paid, in all cases where such offenders or vagrants shall fail or refuse to pay the fines and forfeitures which may be awarded against them.

Sec. 60.—All ordinances passed by the City Council shall, within one month after they shall have been passed, be published in some newspaper printed in said city, or certified copies thereof be posted up in three of the most public places in the city.

Sec. 61.—All ordinances of the city may be proven by the seal of the Corporation; and when printed or published in book form, purporting to be printed or published by the authority of the City Council, the same shall be received in evidence in all Courts or places, without further proof.

Sec. 62.—When it shall be necessary to take private property for opening, widening, or altering any public street, lane, avenue or alley, the Corporation shall make a just compensation therefor to the person whose property is so taken; and if the amount of such compensation cannot be agreed upon, the Mayor shall cause the same to be ascertained by a jury of six disinterested men, who shall be inhabitants of the city.

Sec. 63.—All jurors, empanneled to inquire into the amounts of benefits or damages that shall happen to the owners of property so proposed to be taken, shall first be sworn to that effect; and shall return to the Mayor or presiding officer of the City Council their inquest in writing, signed by each juror.

Sec. 64.—All ordinances, resolutions and regulations now in force in the city of Payson, and not inconsistent with this act, shall remain in force until altered, modified or repealed by the City Council after this act shall take effect.

Sec. 65.—All actions, rights, fines, penalties and forfeitures in suit or otherwise, which have accrued under the ordinances incorporating Payson City, shall be vested in and prosecuted by the Corporation hereby created.

Sec. 66.—All plots and surveys of lands, lots or other places within said city, heretofore surveyed by the Surveyor, and all plots and surveys of land, lots or other places that may be hereafter surveyed and all certificates of surveys given by him shall be deemed valid by this act.

Sec. 67.—All property now belonging to Payson City is hereby vested in the Corporation created by this act; and the officers of said Corporation now in office shall respectively continue in the same, until superseded in conformity to the provisions thereof, but shall be governed by this act.

Sec. 68.—This act shall not invalidate any act done by the present City Council of Payson City or by its officers, nor divest their successors under this act of any right, property or otherwise, or liability which may have accrued to or been created by said Council prior to the passage of this act.

Sec. 69.—All officers of the city, created Conservators of the peace by this act, shall have power to arrest, or cause to be arrested, with or without process, all persons who shall break the peace, commit for examination and, if necessary, detain such persons in custody forty-eight hours in the city prison or other safe place, and shall have and exercise such other powers, as Conservators of the Peace, as the City Council may prescribe.

Sec. 70.—Nothing in this act shall be so construed as to deprive the present City Council of Payson City of any power or authority conferred upon them by the ordinance incorporating said city and the act amendatory thereto; but said City Council shall possess, exercise and enjoy all powers and authority heretofore conferred upon them, except so far as such powers and authority have been expressly modified and repealed by this act, until said City Council are superseded by the election and qualification of their successors under this act.

Sec. 71.—All laws or parts of laws conflicting with the foregoing are hereby repealed.

Sec. 72.—The City Council shall cause to be published in some newspaper published in Payson City, or posted up in three public places, on or before the first day of December in each year, a statement of the amount of city revenue, specifying in said statement whence derived and for what disbursed.

Sec. 73.—This act shall be in force from and after the 24th day of January, 1865.

Approved January, 20, 1865.

——:o:——

CHAPTER CIX.

An ACT granting the City Council of Payson City the right of control of the waters of Spring Creek.

Sec. 1.—Be it enacted by the Governor and Legislative Assembly of the Territory of Utah: That the City Council of the city of Payson are hereby empowered and authorized to construct a dam or reservoir on Spring Creek, south of said city, at such place as they may deem suitable, and control the waters thereof for the use and benefit of the citizens of Payson City, and regulate and control the same.

Approved January 18, 1861.

———:o:———

CHAPTER CX.

An ORDINANCE to control the Waters of the Twin Springs and Rock Spring, in Tooele Valley and County, for Mills and Irrigating purposes.

Be it ordained by the General Assembly of the State of Deseret: That Ezra T. Benson is hereby granted the exclusive privilege of controling the waters in Tooele Valley, Tooele County, known as the Twin Springs, also the waters that issue from a spring called the Rock Spring, in said Valley and County, for mills and irrigating purposes.

Approved Dec. 9, 1850.

———:o:———

CHAPTER CXI.

An ORDINANCE concerning City Creek and Cañon.

Be it ordained by the General Assembly of the State of Deseret: That Brigham Young have the sole control of City Creek and Cañon; and that he pay into the public treasury the sum of five hundred dollars therefor.

Approved Dec. 9, 1850.

———:o:———

CHAPTER CXII.

An ORDINANCE granting the Waters of North Mill Creek Cañon, and the Waters of the next Cañon North, to Heber C. Kimball.

Sec. 1.—Be it ordained by the General Assembly of the State of Deseret: That Heber C. Kimball have the exclusive privilege of conveying the waters of North Mill Creek Cañon and the waters of the Cañon next north, to wit: about half a mile distant, to some convenient point below the mouth of the two Cañons, and of appropriating the same to the use of a saw mill, grist mill and other machinery.

Sec. 2.—Nothing herein contained shall prevent the waters aforesaid from being used, whenever and wherever it is necessary, for irrigating.

Approved Jan. 9, 1851.

CHAPTER CXIII.

An ORDINANCE in relation to the Timber in the Mountains West of Jordan.

Sec. 1.—Be it ordained by the General Assembly of the State of Deseret: That the exclusive control of the timber in the cañons on the east side of the range of mountains west of Jordan, in Great Salt Lake county, is hereby granted to George A. Smith, who is hereby authorized to control the timber in said cañons, to work roads into them and to direct when, where and by whom timber may be taken out therefrom.

Sec. 2.—Be it ordained that any person getting timber from said cañons shall be required to keep the roads clear, and to pay in labor or otherwise for the use of the private roads leading to the timber; and any person wasting, burning or otherwise destroying the timber shall be subject to all damages, and to a fine not exceeding one hundred dollars, at the discretion of the court having jurisdiction.

Sec. 3.—No person shall be allowed to cut timber in any place in these cañons without permission from the proprietor, who is hereby authorized to give directions accordingly.

Sec. 4.—Any person cutting timber or wood in the above cañons and leaving it on the ground an unreasonable time, the proprietor of said cañons shall have the privilege to remove said wood and timber and dispose of it, and the avails paid into the public treasury.

Sec. 5.—Nothing in the above ordinance shall be so construed as to prevent or hinder the citizens of said county from getting timber, wood or poles in any of said cañons for their own use, by observing the above regulations.

Approved Jan. 9, 1851.

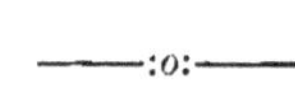

CHAPTER CXIV.

An ORDINANCE pertaining to North Cottonwood Cañon.

Be it ordained by the General Assembly of the State of Deseret: That Willard Richards have the exclusive right of working a road or roads into or through the North Cottonwood Cañon, and control the same.

Approved Jan. 18, 1851.

CHAPTER CXV.

An ACT granting waters of Mill Creek unto President Brigham Young.

Sec. 1.—Be it enacted by the Governor and Legislative Assembly of the Territory of Utah: That the privilege is hereby granted unto President Brigham Young to take the waters from the channel of Mill Creek immediately below Neff's Mill, and convey the same to the channel of Big Cañon Creek, agreeably to the provisions of the act passed in the General Assembly of the State of Deseret, Jan. 15, 1850.

Approved Feb. 5, 1852.

CHAPTER CXVI.

An ACT granting unto Brigham Young, sen., and Franklin D. Richards the control of waters from Mill Creek, in Great Salt Lake County.

Be it enacted by the Governor and Legislative Assembly of the Territory of Utah: That all the rights and privileges, as contemplated in "An Act granting the control of Waters from Mill Creek in Great Salt Lake County unto Willard Richards," approved Feb. 3, 1852, be and hereby are granted unto Brigham Young, sen., and Franklin D. Richards.

Approved Jan. 14, 1857.

——:o:——

CHAPTER CXVII.

An ACT in relation to the waters of American Creek in Utah County.

Sec. 1.—Be it enacted by the Governor and Legislative Assembly of the Territory of Utah: That the inhabitants of the settlement of Dry Creek in Utah county are hereby authorized and allowed to take out, at some convenient point, the waters of American Creek and use the same for their benefit: Provided, that no more than one-third part of said waters shall be so taken for the use of said settlement on Dry Creek.

Approved Feb. 18, 1852.

——:o:——

CHAPTER CXVIII.

PREAMBLE and ACT in relation to the construction of a Canal from Utah Lake to Great Salt Lake.

Whereas, a large portion of the citizens of Great Salt Lake county and vicinity have subscribed considerable amounts for the purpose of constructing a canal connecting Utah and Great Salt Lakes, for the purpose of navigation, machinery and irrigating the land, large bodies of which might be brought into successful cultivation if water to irrigate with could be procured; and

Whereas, the aforesaid subscribers do propose to obtain further subscriptions, and petition for the Territorial Government to adopt some system of operations and appoint an agent or commissioners, who shall be authorized to superintend and construct said canal and award land claims to the subscribers equal to the amount which they shall pay respectively:

Therefore, to aid by our influence and desiring to encourage by our acts so desirable an object:

Sec. 1.—Be it enacted by the Governor and Legislative Assembly of the Territory of Utah: That Ira Eldredge, Jesse W. Fox and Robert Wimmer are authorized to locate the route for said canal, solicit, receive, collect and disburse subscriptions, and generally do all other things necessary for the progress and completion of said work.

Sec. 2.—The aforesaid Commissioners shall proceed without delay to locate the said canal, and make an estimate of the entire cost of its construction upon the plan hereinafter indicated.

Sec. 3.—Said canal shall commence above the rapids in Jordan river, where a dam shall be constructed across said river of a sufficient height to cause slack water navigation to Utah Lake, and proceed, as near the base of the mountains on the west of Great Salt Lake Valley as practicable, to Great Salt Lake; and shall be of sufficient depth and width for the transportation of boats drawing two and a half feet of water, and twelve feet width of hull. There shall also be good and sufficient guard locks, and locks for leveling, and waste gates; as also large reservoirs, with good and sufficient embankments to contain water for irrigating purposes, at all convenient points.

Sec. 4.—The Commissioners shall survey the lands which may be benefited by the construction of said canal, upon each side thereof; likewise take into consideration the benefit arising to present holders of land claims, and apportion the land claims according to the estimated expense and cost of said canal, reserving at each terminus, and at such other convenient points along said canal, to be located by the Governor or his authorized agent, to the amount of four sections of land, to be held in reserve for future use and disposal.

Sec. 5.—The Commissioners shall then proceed and assign unto the subscribers, respectively, the possession of land claims, the right of water to irrigate, equal to the precise amount which they have paid and no more, accommodating locations already made as far as practicable; and the residue shall be held in reserve for further subscription; and it is distinctly understood that the right of water for navigation and machinery is held in reserve for future use or disposal.

Sec. 6.—The aforesaid Commissioners shall make a full and complete report of their doings herein to the Governor, on or before the first day of October in each year, and oftener if required; and they shall also notify him, when they have prepared the apportionment, that he make the reserve of land claims and possessions above mentioned.

Sec. 7.—The expense incurred by surveying the land shall be taxed upon the land claims, and be paid out of the subscriptions, and the expense incurred by locating and surveying the proposed canal shall be defrayed by the subscriptions of the Commissioners herein above appointed; and in case that the Commissioners herein appointed do not accept of their appointments, or in case of a vacancy, the Governor is hereby authorized to appoint others in their stead.

Approved Jan. 19, 1854.

———:o:———

CHAPTER CXIX.

An ACT to incorporate the Jordan Irrigation Company.

Sec. 1.—Be it enacted by the Governor and Legislative Assembly of the Territory of Utah: That Brigham Young, sen., Daniel H. Wells, George A. Smith, Alonzo H. Raleigh, Thomas Box, George B. Wallace, Enoch Reese, Jesse W. Fox and Wilford Woodruff, with their associates and successors, be and the same are hereby made and constituted a body corporate, for the purposes hereinafter specified, under the name and title of the Jordan Irrigation Company; and by that name and title they and their successors shall have succession, from and after the passage of this act, during the pleasure of the Legislature, with power to contract and be contracted with, to sue and be sued in all actions at law and equity in any Court having competent jurisdiction, to purchase and hold personal property and real estate, to sell and transfer the same, and to do and perform any and all other acts in their corporate name that any individual can or has a lawful right to do; to make and use a common seal, and to alter the same at pleasure; and to do all other acts necessary for the proper exercise of the powers conferred and the regulation of the privileges granted in this act.

Sec. 2.—The aforesaid Company shall have the right and privilege, and the same are hereby conferred, to erect and construct a dam or dams across the Jordan river and take out the waters on both sides thereof at a point about half a mile above the bridge across said river, on North Temple Street, in Great Salt Lake City, and conduct the same in a suitable canal or canals on the most practicable routes, in said City and Great Salt Lake County, as far as it may be necessary or expedient to water or irrigate lands: Provided, said Company be held responsible for any damage done thereby.

Sec. 3.—The Company shall have the entire control and management of all the waters thus taken out, and may use the same for the irrigation of lands, for mills and machinery of any kind and all other lawful purposes whatsoever; may sell, lease and dispose of the same or any portion thereof for any or all of the above purposes, on such terms and conditions as the parties may agree; and may levy and collect a per centage on all lands benefited by said waters or by the construction of the dam belonging to said Company.

Sec. 4.—The Company shall also have the right and privilege to sell and dispose of stock, in shares of twenty-five dollars each, to enable the Company to prosecute the work, and to make such improvements, with the same as may be deemed of advantage or profit for the purposes herein specified. The Company may sell stock to the amount of fifty thousand dollars. Each Stockholder shall be entitled to one vote for every share paid in, at all meetings of business requiring a vote and at all general and special election of officers of the Company: Provided, always, that each absentee shall have the right to vote by proxy in writing. Certificates of stock shall be issued by the Directors of the Company to those who have paid for shares or half shares, and shall be signed by the Secretary. The same may be transferred by registering the transfer on the Company's books, otherwise no transfer of stock shall be deemed valid.

Sec. 5.—The officers of this Company shall consist of a President, Secretary, Treasurer and five Directors, whose term of office shall be two years from the date of their election, and until their suscessors shall be duly elected and qualified. They shall take an oath of office to faithfully discharge the duties thereof, and shall file bonds of two thousand dollars each, with approved security, in the office of the Clerk of the Probate Court of the County of Great Salt Lake, which bonds shall be for the use of any person aggrieved; and shall annually present to the Stockholders a just, true and accurate balance-sheet, showing the receipts and expenditures of money and property, with a clear and explicit statement of the entire financial condition, circumstances and standing of the Company, in a plain, legible style.

Sec. 6.—By public notice being given, the aforesaid Company are hereby authorized to hold a meeting on the fourth Monday of January, one thousand eight hundred and sixty-two, to elect persons to the aforesaid offices; and every two years thereafter it shall be the duty of the board of officers then acting to call, by public notice, a similar meeting for the same purpose.

Sec. 7.—Whenever a vacancy occurs in the offices, by death, inability, removal from the Territory, resignation or any other cause, the remaining members of the Board may fill such vacancy by appointment, until the next election.

Sec. 8.—The Board of Officers are hereby authorized and empowered to make and ordain all necessary by-laws and regulations for the internal policy of the Company, and to carry out the spirit and design of this charter in good faith and virtue: Provided, that none conflict with the Constitution and laws of the United States or the laws of this Territory: and provided, also, that any by-law or ordinance may be vetoed by a vote of two-thirds of the legal voters of the Company.

Approved Jan. 17, 1862.

———:o:———

CHAPTER CXX.

An ACT to amend an ACT to Incorporate the Jordan Irrigation Company.

Sec. 1.—Be it enacted by the Governor and Legislative Assembly of the Territory of Utah: That the second section of "An Act to incorporate the Jordan Irrigation Company," approved Jan. 17, 1862, be amended to read:—The aforesaid Company shall have the right and privilege, and the same is hereby conferred, to erect and construct a dam or dams across the Jordan river and take out the waters on both sides thereof at any point not exceeding twelve miles above Jordan bridge, on north Temple Street, Great Salt Lake City, and to conduct the same in a suitable canal or canals, on the most practicable route or routes in Great Salt Lake County, as far as may be necessary, to water or irrigate lands: Provided, said Company be held responsible for any damage done thereby.

Sec. 2.—That the said Company is authorized to increase their capital stock to two hundred thousand dollars.

Approved Jan. 7, 1865.

———:o:———

CHAPTER CXXI.

An ACT granting to Brigham Young the right to make a toll road in Tooele County.

Sec. 1.—Be it enacted by the Governor and Legislative Assembly of the Territory of Utah: That Brigham Young is hereby authorized to make a road from a point in the neighborhood of what is known as the Granite Rock, on the east side of what is known as the Desert, in Tooele county, thence in a westerly direction to a point in the neighborhood of what is known as Redding's Spring, on the west side of said Desert in said county, an estimated distance of from twenty-five to thirty miles; and is further authorized, when said road is made to the acceptance of the Selectmen of Tooele county, to charge and collect toll on said road at such rates and during such time as may be allowed by the County Court of said County.

Sec. 2.—Said Brigham Young shall, during the first week in November, annually make a true report under oath, to the Territorial Treasurer, of the amount of moneys and property received for toll on said road, and pay ten per centum of the aforesaid moneys and property into the Territorial Treasury, to be held for the benefit of common schools and to be expended as may be provided by law.

Ayproved January 22, 1864.

———:o:———

CHAPTER CXXII.

An ACT granting uuto John Nelson and others the right to build a toll bridge across Bear River in Cache County.

Sec. 1.—Be it enacted by the Governor and Legislative Assembly of the Territory of Utah: That John Nelson, Crandell Dunn, George O. Pitkin, George Barber and Simpson M. Molen, citizens of Cache County, are hereby empowered to form a Company for the purpose of building a toll bridge across Bear river in Cache county, between a point on said river west of Hendrick's grist mill and where said river passes through the mountains on the west side of Cache Valley.

Sec. 2.—The within named John Nelson, C. Dunn, George O. Pitkin, George Barber and S. M. Molen are hereby authorized to take and sell stock at twenty-five dollars each share, until a sufficient amount of stock shall be taken to defray the expenses of building said bridge.

Sec. 3.—There shall be a committee of three chosen from among and by the Stockholders, whose duty it shall be to keep an accurate account of all receipts and expenditures, and report the same annually to the County Court of said County; also to superintend the building and do such other business for the Company as a majority of the Stockholders may deem expedient for the general good.

Sec. 4.—Every Stockholder shall be entitled to one vote for each share that he may hold.

Sec. 5.—The bridge shall be built to the acceptance of the County Court of Cache County.

Sec. 6.—The County Court of Cache County is hereby authorized to regulate the rates of toll for crossing said bridge, and to require said Company to pay five per cent. annually, of all receipts arising therefrom into the Territorial Treasury for the benefit of schools.

Sec. 7.—The Company thus formed may have the right to hold claim on said bridge until the net profits have amounted to one hundred per cent. over and above the first cost of the bridge, after which said bridge shall be turned over to the County Court of Cache County, in good repair, and be free to the traveling community.

Approved January 13, 1865.

——:o:——

CHAPTER CXXIII.

An ACT granting unto John L. Butler and Aaron Johnson the right of water from from Spanish Fork river, in Utah county.

Sec. 1.—Be it enacted by the Governor and Legislative Assembly of the Territory of Utah: That the privilege is hereby granted unto John L. Butler and Aaron Johnson to take one fourth of the water from the channel of Spanish Fork river, at or near the head of a slough near Spanish Fork City, and convey the same on the best possible route to a tract of land known as the Springville survey, plot D, and control the same for irrigating purposes during the pleasure of the Legislative Assembly.

Approved January 14, 1857.

——:o:——

CHAPTER CXXIV.

An ACT to incorporate the Tooele Library Association.

Sec. 1.—Be it enacted by the Governor and Legislative Assembly of the Territory of Utah: That Eli B. Kelsey, Andrew Galloway, Hugh S. Gowans, Richard Warburton, John Rowberry, Thomas Lee and John Shields, their associates and successors in office, are hereby constituted a body corporate, to be known and styled Tooele City Library Association; and shall have power to purchase, receive and hold property, real and personal; to sue and be sued, plead and be impleaded, defend and be defended in all Courts of law and equity; and to do and perform all things that may be necessary and proper to enable them to carry into effect the objects of the Association in the diffusion of knowledge, by establishing a library of books, maps, charts and scientific instruments, connecting therewith a reading room and scientific and popular lectures; and the above named persons are hereby appointed a Board of Directors of said Association, until superseded as provided in the following section.

Sec. 2.—A Board of seven Directors shall be elected by the members of said Association on the last Saturday of February annually, who shall hold their office for one year, and until their successors are duly elected; and they shall have power to appoint a President, Secretary, Treasurer, Librarian and such other officers as may be deemed necessary and define their duties; and to enact such bye-laws as may be necessary for the proper management of all business of the Association; a majority may form a quorum to do business, and they may fill any vacancy in the Board until the next regular election.

Sec. 3—This Association may raise means by the sale of shares, and may receive contributions and donations for the purchase of books, &c., and for leasing and erecting suitable buildings for the library, reading room and lectures; new members may be added on such conditions as may be prescribed in the byelaws of the Association and the library and reading rooms shall be open for the use of the public, or books loaned out under such regulations and at such times as the Board of Directors may determine.

Approved January 13, 1865.

CHAPTER CXXV.

An ACT to incorporate the Seventies' Library and Reading Room Association

Sec. 1.—Be it enacted by the Governor and Legislative Assembly of the Territory of Utah: That Joseph Young, Sen., A. P. Rockwood, H. S. Eldredge, John Van Cott, J. V. Long, Jas. W. Cummings, Robt. L. Campbell, Thos. Bullock, Wm. S. Godbe, Robt. Campbell, E. L. T. Harrison and Jas. McKnight, of G. S. L. City, and their successors in office are hereby constituted a body corporate with perpetual succession, to be known and styled the "Seventies' Library and Reading Room Association;" and shall have power to purchase, receive and hold property; to sue and be sued, to plead and be impleaded, defend and be defended in all courts of law and equity and in all actions whatsoever; and to do and perform all things that may of right pertain to their duties in the regulation, control and suitably providing for the interests and in carrying into effect the objects of this organization; and the above named persons are hereby appointed a Board of Directors of said Association, until an election shall take place.

Sec. 2.—That a Board of Directors shall be elected by the members of said Association on the fourth Monday in January, 1865, and thereafter annually. The Directors shall have power to appoint a Secretary, Treasurer and Librarian and such other officers as may be deemed necessary, also to fill any vacancy that may occur in the Board; and at the close of their term of office shall present to the Association a report of the number of books, papers and other publications on hand, the amount of moneys received and disbursed during the year, the number of books donated and by whom; also the amount incurred for services of Librarian and other incidental expenditures. A majority of the Directors shall constitute a quorum to do business; and for the proper management of the Library and Reading Room, they shall have power to frame bye-laws which, upon receiving the sanction of two-thirds of the members present at any stated meeting, shall be in full force.

Sec. 3.—That the Library and Reading Room shall be for the use and benefit of the public, subject to such regulations as may in the bye-laws be prescribed.

Sec. 4.—Conditions of membership shall be made and provided by the Directors.

Approved January 21, 1864.

——:o:——

CHAPTER CXXVI.

AN ACT to incorporate the American Fork Library Association.

Sec. 1.—Be it enacted by the Governor and Legislative Assembly of the Territory of Utah: That William Greenwood, Thomas Proctor, William Shelly, John Duncan, Washburn Chipman, Thomas Wallace and Richard Steele, their associates and successors in office, are hereby constituted a body corporate, to be known and styled American Fork Library Association; and shall have power to purchase, receive and hold property real and personal; to sue and be sued, plead and be impleaded, defend and be defended in all Courts of law and equity; and to do all things that may be proper to carry into effect the objects of the Association, by establishing a library of books, maps, charts and scientific instruments, connecting therewith a reading-room and lectures; and the above named persons are hereby appointed a Board of Directors of said Association, until superseded as provided in the following section.

Sec. 2.—A Board of seven Directors shall be elected by the members of said Association on the second Monday of February, 1865, and biennally thereafter on said day, who shall hold office two years and until their successors are duly elected; and they shall have power to appoint a President, Secretary, Corresponding Secretary, Treasurer and Librarian and define their duties; and also to enact such bye-laws as may be necessary to do all business of the Association; a majority may form a quorum to do business and may fill any vacancy in the Board, until the next regular election.

Sec. 3.—This Association may raise means by the sale of shares, by contribution and donation, for the purchase of books, maps, charts, &c., and for leasing or erecting suitable buildings for the library, reading rooms and lectures.

Sec. 4.—Conditions of membership, admission to the library, reading-room and lectures, and the loaning of books or other property shall be as provided by the bye-laws of said Association.

Approved January 14, 1865.

———:o:———

CHAPTER CXXVII.

An ACT to incorporate the Ogden City Library Association.

Sec. 1.—Be it enacted by the Governor and Legislative Assembly of the Territory of Utah: That Chauncey W. West, Aaron F. Farr, Lester J. Herrick, Francis A. Brown, James McGaw, Walter Thompson and Miles H. Jones, their associates and successors in office, are hereby constituted a body corporate to be known and styled Ogden City Library Association; and shall have power to purchase, receive and hold property real and personal; to sue and be sued, plead and be impleaded, defend and be defended in all Courts of law and equity; and to do and perform all things that may be necessary and proper to enable them to carry into effect the objects of the Association in the diffusion of knowledge by establishing a library of books, maps, charts and scientific instruments, connecting therewith a reading-room and scientific and other popular lectures; and the above named persons are hereby appointed a Board of Directors of said Association, until superseded as provided in the following section.

Sec. 2.—A Board of seven Directors may be elected by the members of said Association on the first Monday of December annually, who shall hold their office one year and until their successors are duly elected; and they shall have power to appoint a President, Secretary, Treasurer, Librarian and such other officers as may be deemed necessary and define their duties; and also to enact such bye-laws as may be necessary for the proper management of all business of the Association; a majority may form a quorum to do business, and they may fill any vacancy in the Board, until the next regular election.

Sec. 3.—This Association may raise means by shares, contribution and donation for the purchase of books, maps, charts, &c., and for leasing or erecting suitable buildings for the library, reading room and lectures. New members may be added on such conditions as may be prescribed in the bye-laws of the Association; and the library and reading room shall be open for the use of the public, or books may be loaned out under such regulations at such times as the Board of Directors may determine.

Approved January 22, 1864.

CHAPTER CXXVIII.

An ACT to incorporate the Nephi Library and Reading Room Association.

Sec. 1.—Be it enacted by the Governor and Legislative Assembly of the Territory of Utah: That Thomas Ord, Jonathan Midgley, Thomas J. Schofield, Benjamin Riches, Andrew Love, Jacob G. Bigler and George Kendall, of Nephi City, and their successors in office are hereby constituted a body corporate with perpetual succession, to be known and styled the Nephi Library and Reading Room Association; and shall have power to purchase, receive and hold property; to sue and be sued, to plead and be impleaded, defend and be defended in all Courts of law and equity and in all actions whatsoever, and to do and perform all things that may of right pertain to their duties in the regulation, control and suitably providing for the interests and in carrying into effect the objects of this organization; and the above named persons are hereby appointed a Board of Directors of said Association, until an election shall take place.

Sec. 2.—That a Board of Directors shall be elected by the members of said Association on the fourth Monday in February, 1864, and thereafter annually. The Directors shall have power to appoint a Secretary, Treasurer and Librarian and such other officers as may be deemed necessary; also to fill any vacancy that may occur in the Board; at the close of their term of office they shall present to the Association a report of the number of books, papers and other publications on hand, the amount of moneys received and disbursed during the year, the number of books donated and by whom; also the amount incurred for services of Librarian and other incidental expenditures. A majority of the Directors shall constitute a quorum to do business, and for the proper management of the library and reading room. They shall have power to frame bye-laws which, upon receiving the sanction of two-thirds of the members present at any stated meeting, shall be in full force.

Sec. 3.—That the library and reading room shall be for the use and benefit of the public, subject to such regulations as may in the bye-laws be prescribed.

Sec. 4.—Conditions of membership shall be as made and provided by the Directors.

Approved January 22, 1864.

———:o:———

CHAPTER CXXIX.

An ACT to incorporate the Saint George Library Association.

Sec. 1.—Be it enacted by the Governor and Legislative Assembly of the Territory of Utah; That Orson Pratt, sen., Erastus Snow, F. B. Woolley, A. M. Cannon, Jacob Gates, Orson Pratt, jun. and James G. Bleak, their associates and successors in office, are hereby constituted a body corporate to be known and styled Saint George Library Association; and shall have power to purchase, receive and hold property, real and personal; to sue and be sued, plead and be impleaded, defend and be defended in all Courts of law and equity; and to do and perform all things that may be necessary and proper to enable them to carry into effect the objects of the Association in the diffusion of knowledge by establishing a library of books, maps, charts and scientific instruments, connecting therewith a reading room and scientific and other popular lectures. And the above named persons are hereby appointed a Board of Directors of said Association, until superseded as provided in the following section.

Sec. 2.—A Board of seven Directors may be elected by the members of said Association on the second Monday of November annually, who shall hold their office for one year and until their successors are duly elected; and they shall have power to appoint a President, Secretary, Treasurer, Librarian and such other officers as may be deemed necessary and define their duties; and to enact such bye-laws as may be necessary for the proper management of all business of the Association. A majority may form a quorum to do business, and they may fill any vacancy in the Board, until the next regular election.

Sec. 3.—This Association may raise means by shares, contributions and donations for the purchase of books, maps, charts, &c., and for leasing and erecting suitable buildings for the library, reading room and lectures; and new members may be added on such conditions as may be prescribed in the bye-laws of the Association; and the library and reading rooms shall be opened for the use of the public, or books loaned out under such regulations and at such times as the Board of Directors may determine.

Approved January 22, 1864.

———:o:———

CHAPTER CXXX.

An ACT authorizing the Territorial Superintendent of Common Schools to Collect Certain Moneys.

Sec. 1.—Be it enacted by the Governor and Legislative Assembly of the Territory of Utah: That the Territorial Superintendent of Common Schools is hereby authorized, empowered and required to proceed against all delinquent parties on their bonds, who do not annually pay the percentage to Common Schools required by the provisions of their charters or grants.

Sec. 2.—It shall further be the duty of the said superintendent to pay over all moneys obtained under the provisions of this act, to the Territorial Treasurer, and report his doings in the premises, annually, to the Legislative Assembly.

Approved Dec. 20, 1864.

———:o:———

CHAPTER CXXXI.

An ACT to provide for the organization of new counties.

Sec. 1.—Be it enacted by the Governor and Legislative Assembly of the Territory of Utah: That the Probate Judge of any new or unorganized county, after he shall have been elected and qualified, shall proceed to organize said county by appointing three Selectmen, citizens of the said county, who shall be qualified by the Judge administering to them an oath of office; when they and the Probate Judge shall appoint all other county officers required by law, who are hereby authorized and empowered to act until the next general election, and until their successors are elected and qualified.

Approved Jan. 16, 1865.

———:o:———

CHAPTER CXXXII.

An ACT to Incorporate the Provo Cañon Road Company.

Sec. 1.—Be it enacted by the Governor and Legislative Assembly of the Territory of Utah: That William Miller and Shadrack Holdaway of Provo City, Utah

County; Joseph S. Murdock, Isaac Decker and David Van Wagoner; of Wasatch County, with their associates and successors be and they are hereby created a body corporate, to be known by the name and style of the Provo Cañon Road Company; and in their corporate name shall have power to sue and be sued, to defend and be defended in all Courts of law and equity: to hold, lease, rent, or convey real estate or personal property; and shall have perpetual succession for the term of twenty years; and may have a corporate seal, which they may use and alter at pleasure.

Sec. 2.—The capital stock of the Company shall consist of one thousand shares of fifty dollars each. Each Shareholder shall be entitled to one vote for each share, and each share shall be represented by a certificate of the same, which shall be transferable upon the books of the company in such a manner as the bye-laws may direct.

The books of the Company for the subscription of stock shall be opened on or before the first Monday in March; one thousand eight hundred and sixty-five; and when one hundred shares shall have been subscribed, the Directors may, by giving four weeks public notice in Provo and Heber cities, call an election for a President, Secretary, Treasurer and four Directors, who shall hold their office for two years, or until their successors are elected and qualified. The President, Treasurer and four Directors shall constitute a Board for the government, and control of the affairs of the Company. The Board shall have power, by a majority vote, to fill all vacancies that may occur, by the appointment of a suitable person, who is hereby authorized to act as a member of the Board, until the time of the next regular election for President and Directors; but should circumstances occur to reduce the Board to a minority, they may call a special meeting of the Shareholders, who are hereby authorized to fill a vacancy or elect a new Board. Each Shareholder may vote by person or by proxy.

Sec. 3.—The Board of Directors are hereby authorized to enact such bye-laws and regulations for the government of the Company as they may deem proper: Provided, they are not incompatable with the laws of the United States or of Utah Territory. The object of this Company is hereby declared to be the construction of a road through Provo Cañon not less than twenty feet wide, from Utah Valley, Utah County, to Provo Valley, Wasatch County; and when said road is constructed and accepted by the Selectmen of Wasatch and Utah counties, said Company are hereby authorized to collect toll thereon as provided in section 5 of this act:

In case the said road, or the bridges thereon are suffered to get out of repair, a majority of the Selectmen of the Counties of Utah and Wasatch may order the gate to be thrown open and the collection of toll stopped, until the necessary repairs are made.

Sec. 4.—The books of the Company shall be open for the inspection of the Stockholders at all reasonable hours; and an exhibit of the financial affairs of the Company, showing the receipts and expenditures of the same, shall be annually made on the first day of May in each year, for the information of the Stockholders.

Sec. 5.—That the gate shall be located in Provo Cañon; and the Company may collect toll at the following rates, which toll is for the use of said road through the aforesaid cañon, viz:

For every carriage or vehicle drawn by two animals............................	$1 00
For every additional pair of animals,..	50
For each Horse or Mule led, rode or packed,..................................	25
For Sheep, Goats and Hogs, each,...	5
For every loose animal of the horse or cattle kind,..........................	15

Sec. 6.—The aforesaid Selectmen may accept the said road when made reasonably passable, and give a reasonable time for its completion as to width, as contemplated in the third section of this act; and when so accepted, toll may be taken at the rates as specified in the fifth section of this act.

Sec. 7.—At the expiration of the aforesaid term of twenty years, said road shall become the property of the Commonwealth, in good condition as shall be accepted by the Selectmen of Utah and Wasatch counties.

Approved January 20, 1865.

CHAPTER CXXXIII.

An ACT to Incorporate Irrigation Companies.

Sec. 1.—Be it enacted by the Governor and Legislative Assembly of the Territory of Utah: That, upon the majority of the citizens of any county or part thereof representing that more water is necessary and that there are streams unclaimed which, if brought out of their natural channels and thrown upon tracts of land under cultivation or to be put under cultivation, can be of value to the interests of agriculture, the County Court having jurisdiction may proceed to organize the county or part thereof into an irrigation district; and thereafter the landholders of such district shall be equally entitled to the use of the water in or to be brought into such district, according to their several needs.

Sec. 2—The citizens of an irrigation district, when so organized for the purposes mentioned in the preceding section, may in mass meeting, after a general notice thereof has been given, proceed to the formation of a Company by electing, *viva voce*, not less than three nor more than thirteen Trustees, a Secretary and a Treasurer, and decide whether the tax to be levied shall be on all taxable property or upon the lands to be benefitted.

Sec. 3.—It shall be the duty of the Trustees so elected to locate the proposed canal or ditch, determine the amount and quality of the land to be benefitted thereby, to estimate the cost, including dams, flumes, locks, waste weirs, and all the appurtenances belonging thereto, the amount per acre or the percentage on taxable property which will be necessary to construct the same, less the value of the possession of any unoccupied lands on the line of such canal or ditch, and make a report including these items to the County Court: Provided, that if the tax to be levied is a property tax, the estimates shall be made from the latest assessment rolls in the County Assessor's office.

Sec. 4.—It shall then be the duty of the County Court, after at least six days public notice shall have been given in each precinct in the said irrigation district, to hold an election, at which the report of the Trustees, provided for in the preceding section, shall be made public; and the electors shall vote yes or no upon the following questions: First, do you mutually agree to pay   per cent. property tax or   per acre land tax, to construct the proposed ditch or canal? Second, do you approve the action of the mass meeting in the election of officers? The votes shall be polled and counted in the manner prescribed in "An Act regulating elections;" approved January 3, 1853: Provided the meaning of the word electors used in this section shall only include tax-payers, if a property tax, or land-holders, if a land tax, in the said district.

Sec. 5.—If, upon counting the votes, it shall appear that two-thirds of the votes polled have been answered in the affirmative, then the tax so levied shall be a law in the said irrigation district, and may be assessed and collected in the manner provided for Territorial revenue, and be paid over to the Treasurer of said Company on his order: Provided that not exceeding one-half of the tax so levied shall be collected at one time; the residue to be collected as the work progresses.

Sec. 6.—If less than two-thirds of the votes polled are answered in the affirmative, then all proceedings under this act shall be null and of no effect: Provided that if there are objections to the officers so elected by the mass meeting, the electors may write other names on their tickets; the persons having the most votes to be declared elected.

Sec. 7.—The officers so elected shall file bonds in the office of the Clerk of the County Court, conditioned for the faithful performance of their several duties; the amount of such bonds to be declared by the County Court having jurisdiction.

Sec. 8.—The term of office of the first Trustees, Secretary and Treasurer shall be till the next general election; and thereafter for one year, and until their successors are elected and file bonds.

Sec. 9.—The Clerk of the County Court shall give notice of and prescribe the manner of conducting all subsequent elections for Company officers; and if it should be found necessary to increase the tax already levied, such increase may be submitted to the people, upon representation of the Trustees, at any subsequent regular election for Territorial, County or Company officers; and if voted for as previously provided, shall be a law and be assessed and collected in the manner provided in the fifth section of this act.

Sec. 10.—The Trustees at their first meeting shall elect one of their number President; and it shall be their duty and they shall have power to fill any vacancy which may occur in the Board by death, change of residence or otherwise; the persons, chosen to hold office until the next annual election, to meet at such times and places as they may deem expedient; to make all bye-laws, rules and regulations necessary to carry into effect the objects of the people; to appoint agents, subordinates and officers and employ such workmen as may be requisite; to appoint Assessors and Collectors or make agreement with the County Assessor and Collector to assess and collect the tax; and notify Collectors when additional instalments of the tax will be needed to construct and complete said canal or ditch with all necessary appurtenances thereto; to cause to be kept an accurate account of all receipts and disbursements, and to make an annual report of all proceedings under this act, on or before the first day of January, to the Legislative Assembly; to complete the said canal or ditch and settle all accounts of the same; and file all books, papers and accounts in the office of the Clerk of the County Court, subject to future reference; and it shall be the duty of the Secretary to keep a record of all proceedings of the Board of Trustees, in regard to such ditch or canal.

Sec. 11.—The Trustees shall have power to sue and be sued, plead and be impleaded, to have and to hold all such real estate and personal property as may be necessary to construct the contemplated ditch or canal, including all appurtenances belonging thereto.

Sec. 12.—If any part of the lands to be benefitted by the proposed ditch or canal are not legally claimed, then such lands may be appraised by the Trustees, and shall be held and the possession of them sold by the Trustees, as opportunity may offer; and the estimated amount of funds necessary to complete such canal or ditch shall be decreased by the estimated value of such lands, previous to the levy and assessment of any tax.

Sec. 13.—Where the streams to be taken out for irrigation purposes come from counties other than the one in which the district is situated, but where there are no existing claims to the water and where no individual or settlement will be injured thereby, then the power of said irrigation district is hereby extended to said other county, insomuch as said extension may be necessary for the construction of dams to turn the waters and ditches or canals with all necessary appurtenances, as may be necessary to convey the same to where it is to be used.

Sec. 14.—Where lakes or ponds in natural basins have outlets, or where such can be made by dams across hollows, such lakes or ponds may be used as reservoirs to store water for lands lying on lower levels; and the people of any irrigation district may, under the provisions of this act, construct such artificial or use such natural basins for irrigation purposes: Provided, the waters of such lakes or ponds are in no case to be raised, by dams or otherwise, so as to interfere with or damage settlers upon the margin thereof.

Sec. 15.—Upon the completion of any canal, ditch or reservoir contemplated in this act, they shall become the property of the irrigation district; and thereafter all funds necessary for repairs upon said canal, ditch or reservoir, and for keeping the same in order, or for altering or enlarging the same may be levied by a tax upon the lands benefitted, the landholders in the district to vote upon the same in the manner heretofore provided for in this act.

Sec. 16.—All property or money belonging to any irrigation district, in the hands of Trustees to be expended by them under the provisions of this act, is hereby exempted from all City, County and Territorial taxes.

Sec. 17.—After any canal or ditch shall have been laid out under this act, or under any special charter where other provision has not been made, the Trustees or Company may agree with the owners of land through which it will pass for the purchase of so much thereof as may be necessary for the making of the canal or ditch and the appurtenances thereto belonging.

Sec. 18.—In every case where the owner of the land so required shall be absent from the County, or shall not from any case be capable in law so to agree, or shall refuse to agree, or ask an exorbitant price, the value of such land and the damages to the owner thereof shall be ascertained in the following manner: First, the occupant of or claimant to such land and the Trustees may each select referees, and in case of disagreement they two may select a third, and these referees shall proceed to determine the value of the land under controversy and assess the amount of damages, if any, which each owner of lands or improvements has sustained or will sustain in consequence thereof. Second: The appraisal with a description of the land so appraised shall be acknowledged by the referees signing it before the Clerk of the County Court in which the lands are situated; and, when so acknowledged, shall be filed in the County Clerk's office, within ten days after it shall have been made.

Sec. 19.—The Trustees, upon payment to the rightful claimant of the several sums assessed in the appraisal so made, or upon making a tender thereof when the same shall be refused, shall be entitled to enter upon the lands described in the appraisal, and have and hold the same for the use and benefit of such irrigation district for ever.

Sec. 20.—If on any parcel of the lands so described there shall be no person then living, authorized to receive payment for the damages assessed for such parcel, and such damages shall not have been lawfully demanded within ten days after the filing of such appraisal, the Board of Trustees may enter thereon without payment or tender of such damages, but subject to such payment whenever the same shall be thereafter lawfully required.

Sec. 21.—If any person shall break, injure or destroy any bank, dam, flume, waste-weir, lock or gate on said canal or ditch, or any of the appurtenances belonging thereto or in use upon the same, or take water from the said canal or ditch, except by direction of proper officers, such person so offending shall for every such offence be liable to a civil suit for the recovery of damages, to be prosecuted for, before any Court having jurisdiction, by any tax-payer in the irrigation district; and shall also be subject to indictment and, upon conviction, shall be punished by fine not exceeding one thousand dollars, or imprisonment not exceeding one year, or by both fine and imprisonment, at the discretion of the Court.

Sec. 22.—All Companies or Districts organized under the provisions of this act shall be liable for any damages which may occur by the breakage of any canal or ditch, which damages may be appraised and collected in the manner prescribed in the eighteenth and nineteenth sections of this act.

Sec. 23.—Nothing in this act shall be so construed as to interfere with the right of the Legislative Assembly to repeal, alter or amend the same at pleasure.

Approved Jan. 20, 1865.

———:o:———

CHAPTER CXXXIV.

An ACT to Incorporate the Ogden Cañon Road Company.

Sec. 1.—Be it enacted by the Governor and Legislative Assembly of the Territory of Utah: That Lorin Farr, Chauncey W. West, sen., Isaac N. Goodale, Lester I. Herrick, Aaron F. Farr, Erastus Brigham; sen., Green Taylor, and their associates and successors are hereby constituted a body corporate, to be known by the name and style of Ogden Cañon Road Company, for the purpose of making a good wagon road from the mouth of Ogden River Cañon, to Ogden Valley; and by said name and style they and their successors shall have power, from and after the passage of this act, for the term of thirty years, to contract and be contracted with, sue and be sued in all actions of law or equity in any Court having competent jurisdiction; and to do and perform any and all other acts in their corporate name that any individual can have or has a lawful right to do; to make and use a common seal and alter the same at pleasure; and to do all other acts necessary for the proper exercise of the powers and privileges conferred and granted in this act.

Sec 2.—The aforesaid Company shall have the right and privilege, and the same are hereby conferred, to build a good wagon road up the aforesaid Cañon from its mouth to Ogden Valley, to the acceptance of the County Court of Weber county, and take toll thereon at the following rates:

For every vehicle drawn by two animals, one dollar and fifty cents.

For every two additional animals, fifty cents.

For every horse or mule rode or led, twenty-five cents.

For all loose animals of horse, mule or cattle kind, ten cents each.

For sheep, goats and swine, five cents each.

Sec. 3.—Any person paying into said Company twenty-five dollars may become an Associate and Shareholder; and each Shareholder shall be entitled to a vote for each share he may hold in said Company.

Sec. 4.—The officers of said Company shall consist of a President, vice-President and five Directors who shall constitute a Board, a majority of whom shall form a quorum to do business, and shall have power to fill all vacancies that may occur in the Board by death or otherwise; said Board, before entering upon the duties of their office, shall give bond with approved security to the acceptance of the Probate Judge of Weber county, and be filed in the office of the County Clerk. The Board of Directors shall have power to appoint a Secretary, Treasurer, Superintendent of Roads and all other officers that they may deem necessary, and may require them to give bonds conditioned for the faithful performance of their duties; and shall have power to ordain and make all necessary bye-laws and regulations for the carrying into effect the provisions of this act for the building, protecting and keeping in repair said road, for the preservation of the timber in the Cañon and its tributaries, and for all other purposes whatsoever pertaining to the interest of said Company: Provided, they make no laws conflicting with the Constitution and laws of the United States or the laws of this Territory.

Sec. 5.—On the second Monday of February, 1865, and annually thereafter, there shall be an election held in Ogden City, for the purpose of electing a President, vice-President and five Directors for said Company; and for the first election under the provisions of this act the President of the present Ogden Cañon Road Company shall notify the Shareholders of said Company, by posting up notices of said election in six of the most public places in said County, at least ten days previous thereunto. Said election shall be conducted in such manner as is provided for in the bye-laws of the present Ogden Cañon Road Company; and all subsequent elections shall be held and conducted as may be provided for by the Board acting under the provisions of this act.

Sec. 6.—Any person forcibly or fraudulently passing any toll gate erected on said road shall, for each offense, be liable to a fine not exceeding one hundred dollars and costs, to be prosecuted for, in any Court having jurisdiction, by any officer, agent; servant or Stockholder, in the name of said Company.

Sec. 7.—If any person shall obstruct, break, injure or destroy any part of the road of said Company, or any work or fixture attached to or in use upon the same, the person or persons so offending shall, for every such offense, be liable to a civil suit for the recovery of damages by said Company, and shall also be subject to indictment and, upon conviction, shall be punished by fine not exceeding five hundred dollars, and imprisonment not exceeding six months, at the discretion of the Court.

Sec. 8.—Each Toll Gatherer, duly authorized by the President and Directors of said Company, may detain and prevent from passing through his gate any person riding, leading or driving animals and any carriage or other vehicle until he has received the tolls authorized by this act.

Sec. 9.—Nothing in this act shall be so construed as to deprive the present Ogden Cañon Road Company of any power or privilege conferred upon them by the grant of the County Court of Weber County, incorporating said Company; but said Company may possess, exercise and enjoy all the privileges heretofore conferred upon them, until the officers of said Company are superseded by the election and qualification of their successors under this act.

Sec. 10.—Nothing shall be so construed in this act as to prevent the Legislature from altering and amending the same at pleasure.

Approved January 20, 1865.

———:o:———

CHAPTER CXXXV.

An ACT granting to the Overland Mail Company the right to construct a graded road across Dugway Mountain and to collect Toll for the use of the same.

Sec. 1.—Be it enacted by the Governor and Legislative Assembly of the Territory of Utah: That the Overland Mail Company, through its Directors, Agents or Representatives, is hereby authorized to construct a graded road, to the acceptance of the County Court of Tooele County, across what is termed the Dugway Mountain, situated near the Mail station of that name, and distant, westerly of Salt Lake City, one hundred and five miles; and to have the privilege of erecting one toll gate at such point, at or near the eastern base of said Mountain, as may be deemed most advantageous, and to collect toll for the use of said road for the period of ten years; the rate of toll to be determined, from time to time, by the County Court of Tooele County.

Sec. 2.—The said Overland Mail Company is hereby required to make an annual report, during the first week of the Legislative Assembly, of all receipts and expenditures on said road, and to pay into the Territorial Treasury, for the use and benefit of Common Schools, five per cent. of all tolls collected thereon. And it is further required to keep said graded road in good repair and to apply all its revenue, over and above necessary expenditures for making and keeping it in repair and for the payment of the assessment heretofore named, to the general improvement of the public road now used by said Company within the Territory of Utah, and especially that portion lying between Black Rock and Cañon stations.

Sec. 3.—The said Overland Mail Company shall give bonds to the people of the Territory of Utah, in the penal sum of five thousand dollars, conditioned for their faithful compliance with the provisions of this charter, and to secure all persons for any damage that may accrue through their neglect, which bonds shall be accepted by and filed with the Probate Court of Tooele County.

Sec. 4.—The Legislature reserve the right to repeal, alter or amend all the privileges granted in this charter.

Approved January 20, 1865.

——:o:——

CHAPTER CXXXVI.

An ACT to incorporate the Uintah Road Company.

Sec. 1.—Be it enacted by the Governor and Legislative Assembly of the Territory of Utah: That William H. Hooper, Ben. Holladay and W. L. Halsey and their associates assigns are hereby constituted and declared a body politic and corporate, with succession for the term of fifteen years, to be known by the name and style of the "Uinta Road Company," by which name they may sue and be sued, plead and be impleaded, contract and be contracted with; and may have and use a common seal; and shall have power to hold and acquire real estate whereon to erect toll gates, houses, stations and bridges, and to dispose of and convey the same when no longer required for said purposes; and to make such rules and regulations for the management of its affairs and the number and appointment of its officers and workmen, as may be deemed necessary; and the said Company are hereby invested with all the powers and privileges which may be necessary to carry into effect the purpose and object of this act.

Sec. 2.—The said Company are authorized and empowered to construct a wagon road from Utah Lake eastward through Uinta Valley to the eastern boundary of this Territory, there to connect with the road running westward from Denver through Colorado Territory; and also the exclusive right to erect bridges over the streams traversed by said road and one mile above and below the crossing of said road; to erect toll gates on said road, not to exceed one to every twenty miles of road; and to erect toll gates on each of said bridges wherever the streams over which said bridges are erected exceed one hundred feet in width; and to demand and collect at each of said gates upon said road, for each wagon or vehicle passing over said road drawn by one pair of horses, mules or cattle, twenty-five cents; and for each additional pair, ten (10) cents: for each riding horse or mule, five (5) cents; for horses, mules, cattle or other animals driven loose, five (5) cents per head; and to demand and to collect the following rates of toll at each said bridges, to wit:

For a wagon drawn by two animals, one dollar,
For each additional animal, twenty-five cents,
For vehicles drawn by one animal, fifty cents,
For each horse or mule and rider, ten cents:

Provided, if the said Company shall establish and maintain a ferry over Green River at the crossing of said road, they may charge for ferriage the same rates of toll as are allowed for passing over one of the Company's bridges: And further provided, that five per cent. of all tolls collected on the said road and bridges, within this Territory, shall be paid annually to the Territorial Treasurer for the use and benefit of common schools.

Sec. 3.—Any person passing over said road, who shall refuse to pay the toll herein required, shall forfeit and pay to said Company, for each and every such offence, the sum of twenty-five dollars, to be recovered by action of debt by said Corporation.

Sec. 4.—Upon complaint being made to any Justice of the Peace in any county through which said road is located, that any portion of said road or any of said bridges are not in reasonably good condition for wagons or vehicles to pass, the said Justice may summon the gate keeper nearest to the defective bridge or portion of the road to appear before him on a certain day, not more than five (5) from the day of complaint;

and if it shall appear to the Justice that the complaint is true, judgment shall be rendered against the Corporation as defendant for the costs of the proceedings; and thereafter no tolls shall be collected by said gate keeper, until the said road or bridge is repaired: Provided, that if by reason of snow or high water it shall not be possible for any person with reasonable expense to repair said road or bridge, a reasonable time shall be allowed for repairing the same, before any judgments of costs shall be rendered.

Sec. 5.—No toll shall be levied upon the citizens of Utah Territory for travel on said road for local purposes, for the distance intervening between the point where the road begins in Utah County and the summit of the dividing ridge between the waters of the Great Basin and the Colorado.

Sec. 6.—It shall be the duty of the Uinta Road Company to make an annual report to the Legislative Assembly, during the first week of its session; said report to be to the thirty-first of the next preceding October, and to show all receipts and expenditures on said road and from what source and for what purpose.

Sec. 7.—Nothing in this act shall be so construed as to prevent the Legislature from amending, altering or repealing the same when they think the public good requires it.

Approved Jan. 20, 1865.

——:o:——

CHAPTER CXXXVII.

An ACT for the organization of the Militia of the Territory of Utah.

Sec. 1.—Be it enacted by the Governor and Legislative Assembly of the Territory of Utah: That the present acting Lieutenant General of the Nauvoo Legion, aided by six or more commissioned officers of the line or staff, to be selected by him, is hereby authorized and empowered to draft and adopt a system of laws and regulations for the militia of the Territory of Utah, and create and fill such offices as are or may be necessary for its organization; which system of regulations shall be subject to the revision of the Legislative Assembly when in session, and shall be in force from and after their publication, unless annulled by legislative enactments.

Sec. 2.—That the Lieutenant General shall hereafter be elected by the people, at such time and place as shall be directed by the Governor.

Sec. 3.—All laws and parts of laws conflicting with this act are hereby repealed: Provided, that the present laws shall continue in force until superseded as herein provided for.

Approved Jan. 15, 1857.

——:o:——

CHAPTER CXXXVIII.

Organization of the Militia of Utah.

Agreebly to the provisions of "An act for the organization of the Militia of the Territory of Utah," approved January 15th, 1857, the Board of Officers appointed by and associated with the Lieutenant General, for that purpose, have adopted the following:—

SYSTEM OF REGULATIONS FOR THE PRESENT ORGANIZATION AND GOVERNMENT OF THE MILITIA OF THE TERRITORY OF UTAH.

Sec. 1.—The Militia of the Territory of Utah, under the Governor of the Territory as Commander-in-Chief, shall be commanded by a Lieutenant General and formed into an independent military body called the Nauvoo Legion, and shall be organized into Platoons, Companies, Battalions, Regiments, Brigades, Divisions and Departments, as hereinafter provided for.

Sec. 2.—All able-bodied white male persons, between the ages of eighteen and forty-five years, resident in the Territory, are liabe to military duty, except such as are or may be exempt by law. Commanders of districts will be held responsible for the enrolment of all persons in their districts liable to military duty. All persons voluntarily enrolling in any corps, though under the age of eighteen or over the age of forty-five years, shall be equally subject to military duty with those enrolled by virtue of the foregoing regulation: Provided, That such persons may on application be discharged by a published order from the Commanders of their respective districts.

Sec. 3.—A Division shall consist of two Brigades, and be commanded by a Major General.

A Brigade shall consist of one thousand rank and file, and be commanded by a Brigadier General.

A Regiment shall consist of five Battalions, five hundred rank and file and be commanded by a Colonel.

A Battalion shall consist of one hundred rank and file, two Companies, and be commanded by a Major.

A Company shall consist of fifty rank and file, five Platoons, and be commanded by a Captain.

A Platoon shall consist of ten men, commanded by a Second Lieutenant who, with one Sergeant, shall be elected by the platoon and of their number, and shall be included in the rank and file.

Sec. 4.—The Lieutenant General may, at his discretion, organize one or more Bands of Music, to be proportioned with officers as any other corps of the Legion, and assign them for duty where necessary. Bands of Divisions, Brigades, Regiments or independent Battalions shall be composed of the Company music of such commands.

Sec. 5.—The staff of the Lieutenant General shall consist of an Adjutant General with the rank of Brigadier General of Light Artillery; one Aide-de Camp with the rank of Brigadier General of Cavalry; a Quartermaster General with the rank of Brigadier General of Heavy Artillery; a Commissary General of Subsistence with the rank of Brigadier General of Infantry; a Chief of Topographical Engineers with the rank of Colonel; a Chief of Ordnance with the rank of Colonel of Light Artillery; one Aide-de-Camp with the rank of Colonel of Cavalry; a Paymaster General with the rank of Colonel of Cavalry; a Judge Advocate with the rank of Colonel of Heavy Artillery; one Aide-de-Camp with the rank of Colonel of Infantry; two Chaplains with the rank of Colonels of Infantry; a Surgeon General with the rank of Colonel of Infantry; a Chief of Music with the rank of Colonel of Infantry; a Military Secretary with the rank of Lieutenant Colonel of Infantry; one Color Bearer General with the rank of Major of Cavalry; one Color Bearer General with the rank of Captain of Cavalry; and such assistants in the various departments as the good of the service may require, with the ranks corresponding, to be designated by the Lieutenant General.

Sec. 6.—The Staff of a Major General shall consist of a Division Adjutant with the rank of Colonel of Light Artillery; a Division Commissary, who also shall discharge the duties of Division Quartermaster, with the rank of Colonel of Heavy Artillery; a Surgeon of Division with the rank of Lieutenant Colonel of Infantry; a Chaplain with the rank of Lieutenat Colonel of Infantry; and two Aides-de-Camp with the rank of Majors of Infantry.

Sec. 7.—The Staff of a Brigadier General shall consist of a Brigade Adjutant with the rank of Lieutenant Colonel of Light Artillery; a Brigade Quartermaster, who shall also discharge the duties of Brigade Commissary, with the rank of Lieutenant Colonel of Infantry, and a Surgeon of Brigade with the rank of Major of Infantry.

Sec. 8.—The Staff of a Colonel shall consist of an Adjutant with the rank of Major, who shall command the regiment in the absence of the Colonel; a Surgeon with the rank of Captain; and a principal Musician with the rank of Second Lieutenant.

Sec. 9.—The Staff of a Major, commanding a separate Battalion, shall consist of an Adjutant with the rank of Captain, who shall be entitled to command the battalion in the absence of the Major.

Sec. 10.—To each Company there shall be a Company Adjutant with the rank of a First Lieutenant and two Musicians.

Sec. 11.—Staff officers shall be appointed by their respective commandants from within the limits of their commands.

Sec. 12.—Staff officers shall take precedence according to the rank held by virtue of their staff appointment. When a vacancy occurs in any command in the line, the Lieutenant General may appoint a staff officer, holding suitable rank, to fill such vacancy, until superseded in regular course of election or the return of the absent officer: Provided, That the officer next in rank, present at the time the vacancy occurs, may assume command, until the action of the Lieutenant General on the subject.

Sec. 13.—All officers shall be commissioned by the Governor, when the commands to which they are elected are filled.

Sec. 14.—Precedence of corps shall be as follows, viz:—1st Light artillery; 2nd Cavalry; 3d Heavy Artillery; 4th Infantry. Platoons in Companies; Companies in Battalions; Battalions in Regiments; Brigades or Districts; and Regiments in Brigades or Districts; of one corps, shall take precedence from right to left, unless temporarily changed for manœuvring. This arrangement shall be conductedunder the supervision of their immediae commanders. The numbers and titles of Divisions, Brigades, Regiments and independent Battalions shall be given by the Lieutenant General. Precedence of officers shall be:—First, according to the corps named in their commission, when of the same grade and corps, according to the date of commission; and when of the same grade, corps and date of commission, reference shall be had to the rank of the Platoon, Company, Battalion, Regiment, Brigade, Division, District, Department or Staff in which such officers serve, and the rank decided accordingly. Staffs shall take precedence according to the rank of their commanding officers, Departments according to the rank of their respective chiefs, as designated in the Staff of the Lieutenant General.

Sec. 15.—The Lieutenant General shall organize Military Districts at his discretion, appoint the times of District Musters, and create and fill, by appointment, any Staff offices not herein provided for, that he may deem necessary.

Sec. 16.—Subordinate Commanders in districts are required to furnish the ranking officer of each district with correct returns and muster rolls of district musters and courts martial, with a full account of the arms, ammunition, equipage, &c., on hand, who shall forward the same to the Adjutant General within twenty days after each muster and court martial. Each commanding officer, from the Lieutenant of a platoon to the General of a Division, shall keep constantly on hand a correct record of the strength, condition and doings of his command.

Sec. 17.—It shall be the duty of the Lieutenant of each platoon to inspect his platoon once a month, for the purpose of ascertaining the condition of the arms, ammunition and equipage of his platoon.

Voluntary Company, Battalion or Regimental musters and drills may be held at the discretion of the several corps, and the fines for such controlled by them for their benefit.

Sec. 18.—On the publication of orders for musters, the Lieutenant of each platoon shall proceed at once to notify his men.

Sec. 19.—Fines for neglecting to appear at district musters shall be assessed by courts martial, composed of not exceeding five commissioned officers to each, detailed by District Commanders, at the rate of not more than five dollars for non-commissioned officers, musicians and privates, and not exceeding ten dollars for commissioned officers. District Commanders shall be held responsible, and demand from subordinate Commanders a similar responsibility to them, that such fines are collected and paid into the Territorial Treasury.

Sec. 20.—Any person enrolled and failing to provide arms, accoutrements and ammunition suitable to his corps, where he has had an opportunity of so doing, shall be fined as a delinquent for non-attendance. Any person having disposed of his arms, accoutrements or ammunition, so as to leave himself unprovided, shall, upon conviction before a court martial, be fined in twice the amount of the value of such, which amount shall be paid into the Territorial Treasury.

Sec. 21.—Courts Martial, detailed by district Commanders, shall take cognizance of and punish by fine all breaches of good dicipline within their jurisdiction.

Sec. 22.—Commissioned officers shall not be dismissed the service, except by the sentence of a General Court Martial, but may be suspended by their commanding officers until the decision of a General Court Martial, or release from such suspension by the Lieutenant General. Disrespect to a superior officer, immoral conduct, neglect of duty and incompetency are each sufficient cause for the dismissal of an officer.

Sec. 23.—General Courts Martial shall be detailed by the Lieutenant General; and shall have jurisdiction in all cases arising under the military laws of the Territory, and to try any officer when the President of the Court ranks the officer on trial.

Sec. 24.—Resignation of officers shall be forwarded through the Commander of the District to the Lieutenant General, but no officer shall be permitted to vacate his office until his resignation is accepted. All vacancies, hosowever they may occur, shall be reported to the Adjutant General's office, and the filling of such vacancies determined by the Lieutenant General.

Sec. 25.—Courts Martial are hereby empowered to make provisions for enforcing their decisions in the collection of fines. Commanding officers, ordering Courts Martial, shall have power to mitigate or repeal their decisions. Such mitigation or repeal must be through a published order assigning the reason.

Sec. 26.—Elections for all commissioned officers shall be as ordered by the Lieutenant General.

Sec. 27.—All military orders shall be numbered, to commence and terminate with the year or with the compaign. Those issued by the Lieutenant General shall be in two series, general and special. General orders are such as pertain to the Legion generally; special orders pertain to particular corps, districts, departments or individuals, and may be addressed to such by the Lieutenant direct. Orders issued from the Head Quarters of Divisions, Brigades, Regiments, separate Battalions or Districts shall be simply styled "Orders," copies of which shall be filed in the Adjutant General's office.

Sec. 28.—The publication of orders from the Lieutenant General, in any public newspaper of the Territory, shall be a lawful notice.

Sec. 29.—An Ordnance department is hereby created, under the charge of the Chief of Ordnance. It shall consist of one Lieutenant Colonel, one Major, three Captains and five First Lieutenants.

Sec. 30.—The corps of Topographical Engineers, under the charge of the Chief of the corps, shall consist of two Lieutenant Colonels, three Majors, five Captains, five First Lieutenants and five Second Lieutenants.

Sec. 31.—The Lieutenant General shall appoint the officers who shall constitute the Ordnance and Topographical corps, and may increase or lessen the number of either at discretion.

Sec. 32.—The Adjutant General shall keep his offices in Great Salt Lake City, until otherwise directed by the Lieutenant General, and shall preserve therein reports of the doings of the various departments of the Legion, and may call on the proper officers for their reports, when necessary. He shall also furnish to the Governor a report of the strength and condition of the forces of the Territory, on or before the first day of December in each year.

Sec. 33.—The Lieutenant General is authorized to adopt, through general orders, any regulations not contravening any provision herein contained, that he may deem essential to the good of the service.

DANIEL H. WELLS, Lieutenant General.
JAMES FERGUSON, Adjt. Gen'l.
A. P. ROCKWOOD, Com'y Gen'l.
GEO. D. GRANT, Brig'r Gen'l. Cav.
H. B. CLAWSON, Aid-de-Camp.
L. W. HARDY, Division Com'y.
W. H. KIMBALL, Lt. Col. Cavalry.
WILLIAM HYDE, Lt. Col. Infantry.
R. T. BURTON, Major Life Guards.
HOSEA STOUT, Attorney General, U. T.
} Nauvoo Legion.

July, 1857.

———:o:———

CHAPTER CXXXIX.

An ACT to repeal an Act entitled "An Act creating an agent to receive and manage the Agricultural Fund of the Territory.

Be it enacted by the Governor and Legislative Assembly of the Territory of Utah: That "an act creating an agent to receive and manage the Agricultural Fund of the Territory," approved January 20, 1865, is hereby repealed.

Approved December 18, 1865.

CHAPTER CXL.

An ACT defining the Judicial Districts for the Territory of Utah, prescribing the times and places of holding the Supreme and District Courts and assigning the Chief Justice and the two Associate Justices.

Sec. 1.—Be it enacted by the Governor and Legislative Assembly of the Territory of Utah: That Millard, Piute, Sevier, Sanpete, Juab, Utah and Wasatch Counties are the First Judicial District; that Kane, Washington; Iron and Beaver Counties are the Second Judicial District; and that Great Salt Lake, Tooele, Summit, Green River, Davis, Morgan, Weber, Box Elder, Cache and Richland Counties are the Third Judicial District.

Sec. 2.-That a term of the Supreme Court shall each year be held in Great Salt Lake City, Great Salt Lake County, commencing on the second Monday in November, at ten o'clock a. m.; that a term of the District Court in the First Judicial District shall each year be held in Manti, Sanpete County, commencing on the third Monday in October; that a term of the District Court in the Second Judicial District shall each year be held in St. George, Washington County, commencing on the first Monday of February; and that a term of the District Court in the Third Judicial District shall each year be held in Great Salt Lake City, Great Salt Lake County, commencing on the second Monday in March.

Sec. 3.—That Chief Justice John Titus is hereby assigned to the Third Judicial District; that Associate Justice Thomas J. Drake is hereby assigned to the First Judicial District; and that Associate Justice Solomon P. McCurdy is hereby assigned to the Second Judicial District.

Sec. 4.—All matters and proceedings now pending in the District Courts of the First and Second Judicial Districts shall be deemed pending in said Courts at the times and places herein specified.

Approved December 27, 1865.

———:o:———

CHAPTER CXLI.

An ACT to Incorporate the Lehi Library Association.

Sec. 1.—Be it enacted by the Governor and Legislative Assembly of the Territory of Utah:—That Israel Evans, William H. Winn, Canute Peterson, James Taylor and William S. S. Willis and their associates and successors in office are hereby constituted a body corporate, to be known and styled Lehi Library Association; and shall have power to purchase, receive and hold property real and personal; to sue and be sued, plead and be impleaded, defend and be defended in all Courts of law and equity; and to do all or any thing that may be proper to carry into effect the objects of the Association, by establishing a library of books, maps, charts and scientific instruments, connecting therewith a reading room and lectures. And the above named persons are hereby appointed a Board of Directors of said Association, until superseded as provided in the following section.

Sec. 2.—A Board of five Directors shall be elected by the members of said Association on the first Monday of March, eighteen hundred and sixty-six, and annually thereafter on said day, who shall hold their office for one year and until their successors are duly elected; and they shall have power to appoint a President, Secretary, Corresponding Secretary, Treasurer and Librarian, and define their duties; and also to enact such bye-laws as may be necessary to do all business of the Association. A majority may form a quorum to do business and fill any vacancy in the Board, until the next regular election.

Sec. 3.—This Association may raise means by the sale of shares and by contributions and donations for the purchase of books, maps, charts, &c., and for leasing or erecting suitable buildings for the library, reading room and lectures.

Sec. 4.—Conditions of membership, admission to the library, reading room and lectures and the loaning of books or other property shall be as provided by the bye-laws of said Association.

Approved December 27, 1865.

CHAPTER CXLII.

An ACT to incorporate Logan City.

Sec. 1.—Be it enacted by the Governor and Legislative Assembly of the Territory of Utah: That all that district of country embraced in the following boundaries in Cache County, to wit: commencing at the south bank of Logan River, at the mouth of Logan, Cañon, thence in a northerly direction along the base of the mountains three miles; thence west to the west bank of little Bear river; thence south along said bank to the mouth of Logan river; thence in an easterly direction along the bank of said river to the place of beginning; shall be known and designated under the name and style of Logan City; and the inhabitants thereof are hereby constituted a body corporate and politic, by the name aforesaid; and shall have perpetual succession, and may have and use a common seal, which they may change and alter at pleasure.

Sec. 2.—The inhabitants of said city, by the name and style aforesaid, shall have power to sue and be sued, to plead and be impleaded, defend and be defended in all Courts of law and equity; and in all actions whatsoever; to purchase, receive, hold, sell, lease, convey and dispose of property real and personal for the benefit of said city, both within and without its corporate boundaries; to improve and protect such property, and to do all other things in relation thereto as natural persons.

Sec. 3.—The municipal government of said city is hereby vested in a City Council, to be composed of a Mayor, three Aldermen, one from each ward, and five Councilors, who shall have the qualifications of electors in said city, and shall be chosen by the qualified voters thereof, and shall hold their office for two years, and until their successors are elected and qualified.

Sec. 4.—An election shall be held on the first Monday of March next, and every two years thereafter, on said day, at which there shall be elected, one Mayor, three Aldermen and five Councilors and two Justices of the Peace; and the persons respectively receiving the highest number of votes cast in the city, for said officers, shall be declared elected. When two or more candidates shall have an equal number of votes for the same office, the election shall be determined by the City Council.

Sec. 5.—The first election under this act shall be conducted in the following manner, to wit: The County Clerk of Cache county shall cause notice of the time and place, and the number and kind of officers to be chosen, to be posted up in four public places in said city, at least ten days previous to said election. Two Judges shall be selected by the Probate Judge of Cache county, at least one week previous to the day of election. Said Judges shall choose two Clerks, and the Judges and Clerks, before entering upon their duties, shall take and subscribe an oath or affirmation before the County Court for the faithful performance of said duties. The poll shall be open at 8 o'clock a.m., and shall close at 6 o'clock p.m. At the close of the election the Judges shall seal up the ballot box and the list of names of the electors and transmit the same, within two days from the time of holding such election, to the County Clerk of Cache county. As soon as the returns are received, the County Clerk, in the presence of the Probate Judge, shall unseal and examine them, and furnish within five days, to each person having the highest number of votes, a certificate of his election. In case of a tie, it shall be decided by lot drawn by the County Clerk in presence of the Probate Judge.

Sec. 6—All subsequent elections held under this act shall be held, conducted, and returns thereof made as may be provided for by ordinance of the City Council.

Sec. 7.—The City Council shall be judge of the qualifications, elections and returns of their own members; and a majority of them shall form a quorum to do business, shall determine the rules of their own proceedings, and shall meet at such time and place as they may direct; the Mayor shall preside when present, and have a casting vote; and in the absence of the Mayor, any Alderman present may be appointed to preside over said meeting.

Sec. 8.—The City Council may hold stated meetings, and special meetings may be called by the Mayor, or any two Aldermen by notice to each of the members of said council, served personally or left at their usual place of abode.

Sec. 9.—The City Council shall have power to appoint a Marshal, Recorder, (who shall be the Auditor of public accounts,) Treasurer, Assessor and Collector, Supervisor of streets, Surveyor, an Attorney, a Sexton, a Sealer of weights and measures, and all such other officers as may be necessary; define their duties, remove them from office at pleasure, and fix and establish the fees of all city officers.

Sec. 10.—All officers elected in accordance with the fourth section of this act may be removed for cause from such office by a vote of two-thirds of the City Council, and shall be furnished with the charges, and have an opportunity to be heard in their defense, and the council shall have power to compel the attendance of witnesses, and the production of papers when necessary.

Sec 11.—When any vacancy shall happen by the death, resignation or removal of any officer, such vacancy may be filled by the City Council, and every person elected or appointed to any office under this act shall, before he enters upon the duties thereof, take and subscribe an oath or affirmation that he will support the Constitution of the United States, the laws of this Territory, and the ordinances of the city, and that he will well and truly perform all the duties of his office to the best of his knowledge and ability; and he shall be required to give bonds as shall be prescribed by the city ordinances, which oath and bond shall be filed with the City Recorder.

Sec. 12.—The City Council shall have power to divide the city into wards, and specify the boundaries thereof, and when necessary create additional wards, and add to the number of Aldermen and Councilors, and proportion them among the several wards as may be just and most conducive to the welfare of said city.

Sec. 13.—The Justices of the Peace shall be Conservators of the Peace within the limits of the city, and shall give bonds and qualify as other Justices of the Peace, and when so qualified shall posses the same powers and jurisdiction, both in civil and criminal cases arising under the laws of the Territory, and may be commissioned as Justices of the Peace in and for said city, by the Governor. They shall account for and pay over all fines and forfeitures arising under the ordinances of the city into the City Treasury, and all fines and forfeitures arising under the laws of the Territory into the county treasury, and shall issue such process as may be necessary to carry into effect all ordinances of said city. Appeals may be had from any decision or judgment of a Justice's court in the same manner as are or may be provided by statute for appeals from Justice's courts, and they shall account for, and pay over to the City Treasurer within three months all fines and forfeitures received by them, by virtue of their office, and they shall keep a docket, subject at all times to the inspection of the City Council and all other parties interested.

Sec. 14.—All process issued by the Justices of the Peace shall be directed to the Marshal, or other legal officer, and in execution thereof, he shall be governed by such rules and regulation as may be provided by city ordinance.

Sec. 15.—It shall be the duty of the Recorder to make and keep accurate records of all ordinances made by the City Council, and all their proceedings in a corporate capacity, which record shall at all times be open to the inspection of the electors of the city, and all other parties interested, and audit all accounts of said incorporation. He shall have and keep a plat of all surveys within the city, and he is hereby authorized to take the acknowledgements of deeds, transfers and other instruments of writing, and shall perform such other duties as may be required of him by city ordinance.

Sec. 16.—The Treasurer shall receive all money or funds belonging to the city, and shall keep an accurate account of all receipts and expenditures in such manner as the City Council shall direct. He shall pay all funds that may come to his hand, by virtue of his office, upon orders signed by the Auditor of Public Accounts; and shall report to the City Council a true account of his receipts and disbursements, as they may require.

Sec. 17.—The City Council shall have power, within the city, by ordinance to annually levy and collect taxes on the assessed value of all property in the city made taxable by the laws of the Territory, for the following named purposes, to wit: not to exceed five mills on the dollar for contingent expenses, nor to exceed five mills on the dollar to open, improve and keep in repair the streets of the city. The City Council is further empowered to divide the city into School Districts, provide for the election of Trustees, appoint a Board of School Inspectors, annually assess and collect and expend the necessary tax for school purposes and for furnishing the city with water for irrigating and other purposes, and regulate and control the same; and furthermore, so far as may be necessary, control the water courses leading thereto.

Sec. 18.—The City Council shall have the management and control of the finances and property of said city.

Sec. 19.—To require and it is hereby made the duty of every able-bodied male resident of the city, over the age of eighteen and under the age of fifty years, to labor not to exceed two days in each year upon the streets; but every person may, at his option, pay two dollars for the day he shall be so bound to labor: Provided it be paid within five days from the time he shall be notified by the Street Supervisor. In default of payment as aforesaid, the same may be collected as other taxes.

Sec. 20.—The Council shall have power to borrow money for city purposes, the interest of which shall not exceed one-fourth of the city revenue arising from taxes of the previous year.

Sec. 21.—The City Council shall have power by ordinance to regulate the form of the assessment rolls. The annual assessment roll shall be returned by the Assessor on or before the first Monday of June in each year, but the time may be extended or additions made thereto by order of the City Council. On the return thereof, the City Council shall fix a day for hearing objections thereto; and any person feeling aggrieved by the assessment of his property may appear at the time specified and make his objections, which shall be heard and determined upon by the City Council, and they shall have power to alter, add to, take from and otherwise correct and revise said assessment roll.

Sec. 22.—The Collector shall be furnished, within thirty days after the assessment rolls are corrected, with a list of taxes to be collected; and if not paid when demanded, the Collector shall have power to collect said taxes with interest and cost by suit in the corporate name, as may be provided by ordinance. The assessment roll shall in all cases be evidence on the part of the corporation.

Sec. 23.—To appropriate and provide for the payment of the expenses and debts of the city.

Sec. 24.—To make regulations to prevent the introduction of contagious diseases into the city; to make quarantine laws, and enforce the same within the city and around it, not exceeding ten miles next beyond the boundaries thereof.

Sec. 25.—To examine, license and regulate the practice of Surgeons and Physicians; to prohibit, prevent and punish, by fine and imprisonment, the imposition of quacks and other medical pretenders; to establish hospitals and infirmaries, and make regulations for the government of the same; to make regulations to secure the general health of the inhabitants; to declare what shall be nuisances, and prevent and remove the same.

Sec. 26.—To provide the city with water; to dig wells, lay pump logs and pipes, and erect pumps in the streets for the extinguishment of fires, and the convenience of the inhabitants.

Sec. 27.—To direct or prohibit the location and management of houses for the storing of gunpowder, tar, pitch, resin or other combustible and dangerous materials within the city, and to regulate the conveying of gunpowder.

Sec. 28.—To exclusively control, regulate, repair, amend and clear the streets, alleys, bridges, sidewalks or crosswalks, and open, widen, straighten or vacate streets and alleys and put drains or ditches and sewers therein, and prevent the incumbering of the streets in any manner and protect the same from any encroachment and injury.

Sec. 29.—To provide for the lighting of the streets and erecting lamp posts; to erect market houses and establish markets and market places, and provide for the government and regulation thereof.

Sec. 30.—To provide for the erection of all needful buildings for the use of the city, and for inclosing, improving and regulating all public grounds belonging to the city.

Sec. 31.—To license, regulate, prohibit or restrain the manufacturers, sellers or venders of spirituous or fermented liquors, tavern keepers, dram or tippling shop keepers, boarding, victualling or coffee houses, restaurants, saloons or other houses or places for the selling or giving away of wines or other liquors, whether ardent, vinous or fermented.

Sec. 32.—To license, tax, and regulate auctioneers, merchants, retailers, groceries, ordinaries, hawkers, peddlers, brokers, pawnbrokers, and money changers.

Sec. 33.—To regulate the selling or giving away of any ardent spirits or other intoxicating liquors by any shopkeeper, grocer or trader, to be drank in any shop, store, grocery, outhouse, yard, garden or other place within the city, except by persons or at places duly licensed; to forbid the selling or giving away of ardent spirits or other intoxicating liquors to any child, apprentice or servant, without the consent of his or her parent, guardian, master or mistress, or to any Indian.

Sec. 34.—To regulate and license or prohibit butchers, and to revoke their license for malconduct in the course of trade; and to regulate, license and restrain the sale of fresh meat and vegetables in the city.

Sec. 35.—To license, tax, regulate, suppress or prohibit billiard tables, pin alleys, nine or ten pin alleys or table and ball alleys; to suppress or restrain all disorderly houses and groceries; to authorize the destruction and demolition of all instruments and devices used for the purpose of gaming, and all kinds of gambling; to prevent any riot, noise, disturbance or disorderly assemblages; and to restrain and punish vagrants, mendicants, street beggars and prostitutes.

Sec. 36.—To regulate, license, suppress or prohibit all exhibitions of common showmen, shows of every kind, concerts or other musical entertainments, exhibitions of natural or artificial curiosities, caravans, circuses, theatrical performances, ball rooms and all other exhibitions and amusements.

Sec. 37.—To license, tax and regulate hacking, carriages, wagons, carts and drays and fix the rates to be charged for the carriage of persons and for wagonage, cartage and drayage of property; as also to license and regulate porters and fix the rates of porterage.

Sec. 38.—To provide for the prevention and extinguishment of fires; to regulate the fixing of chimneys and flues thereof and stove pipes, and to organize and establish fire companies.

Sec. 39.—To regulate and order parapet walls and other partition fences.

Sec. 40.—To establish standard weights and measures and regulate the weights and measures to be used in the city, in all cases not provided for by law.

Sec. 41.—To provide for the inspecting and measuring of lumber and other building materials, and for the measurement of all kinds of mechanical work.

Sec. 42.—To provide for the inspection and weighing of hay, lime and stone coal, and the measuring of charcoal, firewood and other fuel to be sold or used within the city.

Sec. 43.—To provide for and regulate the inspection of tobacco, beef, pork, flour and meal; also beer, whisky and brandy and all other spirituous or fermented liquors.

Sec. 44.—To regulate the weight and quality of bread sold and used in the city.

Sec. 45.—The City Council shall have exclusive power within the city, by ordinance, to license, regulate or restrain the keeping of ferries and toll bridges.

Sec. 46.—To provide for taking the enumeration of the inhabitants of the city; to regulate the burial of the dead, and registration of births and deaths; to direct the returning and keeping of bills of mortality and to impose penalties on physicians, sextons, and others for any default in the premises.

Sec. 47.—To prevent horse-racing, immoderate riding or driving in the streets, and to authorize their being stopped by any person; to punish or prohibit the abuse of animals, to provide for the putting up of posts in front of city lots to fasten horses and other animals; to compel the fastening of horses, mules, oxen or other animals attached to vehicles, whilst standing or remaining in the streets.

Sec. 48.—To prevent the incumbering of the streets or sidewalks, lanes, alleys and public grounds with carriages, tents, wagons, carts, sleighs, horses or other animals, sleds, wheelbarrows, boxes, lumber, timber, firewood, posts, awnings, signs, adobies or any material or substance whatever.

Sec. 49.—To restrain, regulate or prohibit the running at large of cattle, horses, mules, sheep, swine, goats and all kinds of poultry; and to tax, prevent or regulate the keeping of dogs, and to authorize the destruction of the same, when at large contrary to city ordinance.

Sec. 50.—To compel the owner or occupant of any grocery, cellar, tallow chandler shop, soap factory, tannery, stable,barn,privy, sewer or any unwholesome place to cleanse, remove or abate the same from time to time, as oft as may be necessary for the health, comfort and convenience of the inhabitants of said city.

Sec. 51.—To direct the location and management of and regulate breweries and tanneries; and to direct the location, management and construction of and restrain or prohibit within the city distilleries, slaughtering establishments and all establishments or places where nauseous, offensive or unwholesome business may be carried on.

Sec. 52.—To prevent any person from bringing, depositing or having within the limits of the city any dead carcass or any unwholesome substance, and to require the removal or destruction of the same by any person who shall have placed or caused to be placed upon or near his premises or near any of the streams of this city any such substance or any putrid or unsound beef, pork or fish, hides or skins of any kind; and, on his default, to authorize the removal or destruction of the same by any officer of said city.

Sec. 53.—To direct and regulate the planting and preserving trees in the streets and public grounds, and regulate the fencing of lots within the boundaries of the city.

Sec. 54.—To prevent the ringing of bells, the blowing of horns and bugles, the crying of goods and all other noises, performances and devices tending to disturb the peace and quiet of the city.

Sec. 55.—To grant and issue licenses and direct the manner of issuing and registering thereof. Bonds may be taken on the granting of licenses, for the due observance of the ordinances of the City Council.

Sec. 56.—To require every merchant, retailer, trader and dealer in merchandise or property of every description, which is sold by measure or weight, to cause their weights and measures to be sealed by the City Sealer and to be subject to his inspection, the standard of which weights and measures shall be conformable to those established by law.

Sec. 57.—The City Council shall have power to make such ordinances and resolutions, not contrary to the Constitution and laws of the United States and the laws of the Territory, as may be necessary and expedient to carry into effect the powers vested in the City Council or any officer of said city by this act, and enforce observance of all ordinances and resolutions made in pursuance of this act by penalties not exceeding one hundred dollars or imprisonment not to exceed six months, or both.

Sec. 58.—The City Council shall have exclusive authority and power to establish and regulate the Police of the city; to impose fines, forfeitures and penalties for the breach of any ordinances; to provide for the recovery of such fines and forfeitures and the enforcement of such penalties, and to pass, make, ordain, establish and execute all such ordinances, not repugnant to the Constitution and laws of the United States or the laws of this Territory, as they may deem necessary for carrying into effect and execution the powers specified in this act, and for the peace, good order, regulation, convenience and cleanliness of the city, for the protection of property therein from destruction by fire or otherwise, and for the health, safety and happiness of the inhabitants thereof.

Sec. 59.—To provide for the punishment of offenders and vagrants by imprisonment in the county or city jail, or by compelling them to labor on the streets or other public works until the same shall be fully paid in all cases where such offenders or vagrants shall fail or refuse to pay the fines and forfeitures which may be awarded against them.

Sec. 60.—All ordinances passed by the City Council shall, within one month after they shall have been passed, be published in some newspaper printed in said city, or certified copies thereof be posted up in three of the most public places in the city.

Sec. 61.—All ordinances of the city may be proven by the seal of the Corporation, and, when printed or published in book form, purporting to be printed or published by authority of the City Council, the same shall be received in evidence in all Courts or places without further proof.

Sec. 62.—When it shall be necessary to take private property for opening, widening or altering any public street, lane, avenue or alley, the Corporation shall make a just compensation therefor to the person whose property is so taken; and if the amount of such compensation cannot be agreed upon, a Justice of the Peace shall cause the same to be ascertained by a jury of six disinterested men, who shall be inhabitants of the city.

Sec. 63.—All jurors empanneled to enquire into the amount of benefit or damage that shall happen to the owners of property so proposed to be taken shall first be sworn to that effect, and shall return to the Mayor or presiding officer of the City Council, their inquest in writing, signed by each juror.

Sec. 64.—All officers of the city, created conservators of the peace by this act, shall have power to arrest or cause to be arrested, with or without process, all persons who shall break the peace; commit for examination, and, if necessary, detain such persons in custody forty-eight hours in the city prison or other safe place; and shall have and exercise such other powers, as conservators of the peace, as the City Council may prescribe.

Sec. 65.—The City Council shall cause to be published in some newspaper published in Logan city or posted up in three public places, on or before the first day of December in each year, a statement of the amount of the city revenue, specifying in said statement whence derived and for what disbursed.

Approved, January 17, 1866.

———:o:———

CHAPTER CXLIII.

An ACT to incorporate the City of Wellsville.

Sec. 1.—Be it enacted by the Governor and Legislative Assembly of the Territory of Utah: That all that district of country embraced in the following boundaries in Cache County, to wit: Commencing at the mouth of Wellsville City Cañon, thence in a northerly direction along the base of the mountains to a parallel line running through Clayton's Spring, thence east on said line four miles, thence south four miles, thence in a westerly direction to the place of beginning, shall be known and designated under the name and style of the City of Wellsville, and the inhabitants thereof are hereby constituted a body corporate and politic by the name aforesaid, and shall have perpetual succession, and may have and use a common seal, which they may change and alter at pleasure.

Sec. 2.—The inhabitants of said city, by the name and style aforesaid, shall have power to sue and be sued, to plead and be impleaded, defend and be defended in all Courts of law and equity and in all actions whatsoever; to purchase, receive, hold, all property for Cemeteries, Public Squares, City buildings, Water Works, Canals, streams of water and for all other purposes for the benefit and use of said city, both within and without its corporate boundaries, to improve and protect such property, and do all other things in relation thereto, as natural persons.

Sec. 3.—The Municipal government of said city is hereby vested in a City Council, to be composed of a Mayor, six Councilors, who shall have the qualifications of electors in said city, and shall hold their office for two years, and until their successors are elected and qualified.

Sec. 4.—An election shall be held on the first Monday of March next, and every two two years thereafter on said day, at which there shall be elected one Mayor, six Councilors and two Justices of the Peace for said city; and the persons receiving the highest number of votes cast in the city for said offices shall be declared elected. When two or more candidates shall have an equal number of votes for the same office, the election shall be determined by the City Council.

Sec. 5.—The first election under this act shall be conducted in the following manner, to wit: The County Clerk of Cache county shall cause notice of the time and place, and the number and kind of officers to be elected, to be posted up in four public places in said city, at least ten days previous to said election. Two Judges shall be chosen by the Probate Judge of Cache county, at least one week previous to the day of election; said Judges shall choose two Clerks; and the Judges and Clerks, before entering upon their duties, shall take and subscribe an oath or affirmation before the Clerk of the County Court for the faithful performance of said duties. The polls shall be open at eight a. m., and close at six p. m. At the close of said election the Judges shall seal up the ballot box and the list of names of the electors, and transmit the same, within two days from the time of holding such election to the County Clerk of Cache county. As soon as the returns are received the County Clerk, in the presence of the Probate Judge, shall unseal and examine them, and furnish, within five days, to each person having the highest number of votes, a certificate of his election. In case of a tie, it shall be decided by lot drawn by the County Clerk in the presence of the Probate Judge.

Sec. 6.—All subsequent elections held under this act shall be held, conducted and returns thereof made as may be provided for by ordinance of the City Council.

Sec. 7.—The City Council shall be judge of the qualifications, elections and returns of their own members; and a majority of them shall form a quorum to do business, shall determine the rules of their own proceedings and shall meet at such time and place as they may direct; the Mayor shall preside when present, and have a casting vote; and, in the absence of the Mayor, any Councillor present may be appointed to preside over said meeting.

Sec. 8.—The City Council may hold stated meetings; and special meetings may be called by the Mayor or any two Councilors, by notice to each of the members of said Council, served personally or left at their usual places of abode.

Sec. 9.—The City Council shall have power to appoint a Marshal, Recorder, (who shall be the Auditor of Public Accounts,) Treasurer, Assessor and Collector, Supervisor of Streets, Surveyor and Attorney, a Sexton, a Sealer of Weights and Measures and all such other officers as may be necessary, define their duties, remove them from office at pleasure, and fix and establish the fees of all city officers.

Sec. 10.—All officers elected in accordance with the fourth section of this act may be removed for cause from such office by a vote of two-thirds of the City Council, and shall be furnished with the charges and have an opportunity to be heard in their defense; and the Council shall have power to compel the attendance of witnesses and the production of papers, when necessary.

Sec. 11.—When a vacancy shall happen by the death, resignation or removal of any officer, such vacancy may be filled by the City Council; and every person elected or appointed to any office under this act shall, before he enters upon the duties thereof, take and subscribe an oath or affirmation that he will support the Constitution of the United States, the laws of this Territory and the ordinances of the city, and that he will well and truly perform all the duties of his office to the best of his knowledge and ability; and shall be required to give bonds as shall be prescribed by city ordinances, which oath and bond shall be filed with the City Recorder.

Sec. 12.—The City Council shall have power to divide the city into Wards and specify the boundaries thereof; and, when necessary, create additional Wards and add to the number of Councilors and proportion them among the several Wards, as may be just and most conducive to the welfare of said city.

Sec. 13.—The Justices of the Peace shall be Conservators of the Peace within the limits of the city, and shall give bonds and qualify as other Justices of the Peace; and, when so qualified, shall possess the same powers and jurisdiction, both in civil and criminal cases arising under the laws of the Territory, and may be commissioned as Justices of the Peace in and for said city by the Governor. They shall account for and pay over all fines and forfeitures arising under the ordinances of the city into the City Treasury, and all fines and forfeitures arising under the laws of the Territory into the County Treasury, and shall issue such process as may be necessary to carry into effect all ordinances of said city.

Sec. 14.—It shall be the duty of the Recorder to make and keep accurate records of all ordinances made by the City Council and all their proceedings in a corporate capacity, which record shall at all times be open to the inspection of the electors of the city and all other parties interested, and audit all accounts of said Incorporation. He shall have and keep a plat of all surveys within the city; and he is hereby authorized to take the acknowledgment of deeds, transfers and other instruments of writing, and shall perform such other duties as may be required of him by city ordinance.

Sec. 15.—The Treasurer shall receive all money or funds belonging to the city, and shall keep an accurate account of all receipts and expenditures in such manner as the City Council shall direct. He shall pay all funds that may come to hand by virtue of his office upon orders signed by the Auditor of Public Accounts, and shall report to the City Council a true account of his receipts and disbursements, as they may require.

Sec. 16.—The City Council shall have power within the city, by ordinance, to annually levy and collect taxes on the assessed value of all property in the city made taxable by the laws of the Territory, for the following named purposes, to wit: not to exceed five mills on the dollar for contingent expenses, nor to exceed five mills on the dollar to open, improve and keep in repair the streets of the city. The City Council is further empowered to divide the city into School Districts, provide for the election of Trustees, appoint a board of School Inspectors, annually assess and collect and expend the necessary tax for school purposes, and for furnishing the city with water for irrigating and other purposes, and regulate and control the same; and furthermore, so far as may be necessary, control the water courses leading thereto.

Sec. 17.—The City Council shall have the management and control of all the finances and property of said city.

Sec. 18.—To require, and it is hereby made the duty of every able-bodied male resident of the city, over the age of eighteen and under the age of fifty years, to labor not to exceed two days in each year upon the streets; but every person may, at his option, pay two dollars for the day he shall be so bound to labor: Provided it be paid within five days from the time he shall be notified by the Street Supervisor. In default of payment as aforesaid, the same may be collected as other taxes.

Sec. 19.—The Council shall have power to borrow money for city purposes, the interest of which shall not exceed one-fourth of the city revenue arising from taxes of the previous year.

Sec. 20.—The City Council shall have power, by ordinance, to regulate the form of the assessment rolls. The annual assessment roll shall be returned by the Assessor on or before the first Monday of June in each year, but the time may be extended or additions made thereto by order of the City Council. On the return thereof, the City Council shall fix a day for hearing objections thereto, and any person feeling aggrieved by the assessment of his property may appear at the time specified and make his objections, which shall be heard and determined upon by the City Council; and they shall have power to alter, add to, take from and otherwise correct and revise said assessment roll.

Sec. 21.—The Collector shall be furnished, within thirty days after the assessment rolls are corrected, with a list of taxes to be collected; and if not paid when demanded, the Collector shall have power to collect said taxes with interest and cost, by suit in the corporate name as may be provided by ordinance. The assessment roll shall in all cases be evidence on the part of the Corporation.

Sec. 22.—To appropriate and provide for the payment of the expenses and debts of the city.

Sec. 23.—To make regulations to prevent the introduction of contagious diseases into the city; to make quarantine laws and enforce the same within the city and around it, not exceeding ten miles next beyond the boundaries thereof.

Sec. 24.—To examine licences and regulate the practice of Surgeons and Physicians; to prohibit, prevent and punish, by fine and imprisonment, the imposition of quacks and other medical pretenders; to establish hospitals and infirmaries, and make regulations for the government of the same; to make regulations to secure the general health of the inhabitants; to declare what shall be nuisances and prevent and remove the same.

Sec. 25.—To provide the city with water; to dig wells, lay pump logs and pipes and erect pumps in the streets for the extinguishment of fires and the convenience of the inhabitants.

Sec. 26.—To direct or prohibit the location and management of houses for the storing of gunpowder, tar, pitch, resin or other combustible and dangerous materials within the city, and to regulate the conveying of gunpowder.

Sec. 27.—To exclusively control, regulate, repair, amend and clear the streets, alleys, bridges, side-walks or cross-walks, and open, widen, straighten or vacate streets and alleys and put drains or ditches and sewers therein, and prevent the incumbering of the streets in any manner and protect the same from any incroachment or injury.

Sec. 28.—To provide for the lighting of the streets and erecting lamp posts; to erect market houses and establish markets and market places, and provide for the government and regulation thereof.

Sec. 29.—To provide for the erection of all needful buildings for the use of the city and for inclosing, improving and regulating all public grounds belonging to the city.

Sec. 30.—To license, regulate, prohibit or restrain the manufacturers, sellers or venders of spirituous or fermented liquors, tavern keepers, dram or tippling shop keepers, boarding, victualing or coffee houses, restaurants, saloons, or other houses or places for the selling or giving away of wines or other liquors, whether ardent, vinous or fermented.

Sec. 31.—To license, tax and regulate auctioneers, merchants, retailers, grocers, ordinaries, hawkers, peddlers, brokers, pawnbrokers and money changers.

Sec. 32.—To regulate the selling or giving away of any ardent spirits or other intoxicating liquors by any shopkeeper, grocer or trader, to be drank in any shop, store, grocery, outhouse, yard, garden or other place within the city, except by persons or at places duly licensed; to forbid the selling or giving away of ardent spirits or other intoxicating liquors to any child, apprentice or servant, without the consent of his or her parent, guardian, master or mistress, or to any Indian.

Sec. 33.—To regulate and license or prohibit butchers, and to revoke their license for malconduct in the course of trade; and to regulate, license or restrain the sale of fresh meat and vegetables in the city.

Sec. 34.—To license, tax, regulate, suppress or prohibit billiard tables, pin alleys, nine or ten pin alleys, or table and ball alleys; to suppress or restrain all disorderly houses and groceries; to authorize the destruction and demolition of all instruments and devices used for the purpose of gaming; to prevent any riot, noise, disturbance or disorderly assemblage; and to restrain and punish vagrants, mendicants, street beggars and prostitutes.

Sec. 35.—To regulate, license, suppress or prohibit all exhibitions of common showmen, shows of every kind, concerts or other musical entertainments, exhibitions of natural or artificial curiosities, caravans, circuses, theatrical performances, ball rooms and all other exhibitions and amusements.

Sec. 36.—To license, tax and regulate hacking, carriages, wagons, carts, and drays, and fix the rates to be charged for the carrying of persons and for wagonage, cartage and drayage of property as also to license and regulate porters and fix the rates of porterage.

Sec. 37.—To provide for the prevention and extinguishment of fires; to regulate the fixing of chimneys and the flues thereof and stove pipes; and to organize and establish fire companies.

Sec. 38.—To regulate and order parapet walls and other partition fences.

Sec. 39.—To establish standard weights and measures and regulate the weights and measures to be used in the city, in all cases not provided by law.

Sec. 40.—To provide for the inspection and measuring of lumber and other building materials, and for the measurement of all kinds of mechanical work.

Sec. 41. To provide for the inspection and weighing of hay, lime and stone coal, and the measuring of charcoal, firewood and other fuel to be sold or used within the city.

Sec. 42.—To provide for and regulate the inspection of tobacco, beef, pork, flour and meal; also beer, whiskey, brandy and all other spirituous or fermented liquors.

Sec. 43.—To regulate the weight and quality of bread sold and used in the city.

Sec. 44.—The City Council shall have exclusive power within the city, by ordinance, to license, regulate or restrain the keeping of ferries and toll bridges.

Sec. 45.—To provide for taking the enumeration of the inhabitants of the city, to regulate the burial of the dead and registration of births and deaths; to direct the returning and keeping of bills of mortality; and to impose penalties on physicians, sextons and others for any default in the premises.

Sec. 46.—To prevent horse racing and immoderate riding and driving in the streets, and to authorize their being stopped by any person; to punish or prohibit the abuse of animals; to compel persons to put up posts in front of their lots to fasten their horses and other animals; to compel the fastening of horses, mules, oxen or other animals attached to vehicles, whilst standing or remaining in the streets.

Sec. 47.—To prevent encumbering the streets or side-walks, lanes, alleys and public grounds with carriages, tents, wagons, carts, sleighs, horses or other animals, sleds, wheel-barrows, boxes, lumber, timber, firewood, posts, awnings, signs, adobies or any material or substance whatever.

Sec. 48.—To restrain, regulate or prohibit the running at large of cattle, horses, mules, sheep, swine, goats and all kinds of poultry; and to tax, prevent or regulate the keeping of dogs, and to authorize the destruction of the same when at large contrary to city ordinance.

Sec. 49.—To compel the owner or occupant of any grocery, cellar, tallow chandler shop, soap factory, tannery, stable, barn, privy, sewer or any unwholesome place, to cleanse, remove or abate the same from time to time, as oft as may be necessary for the health, comfort and convenience of the inhabitants of said city.

Sec. 50.—To direct the location and management of and regulate breweries and tanneries; and to direct the location, management and construction of and restrain or prohibit within the city distilleries, slaughtering establishments, and all establishments or places where nauseous, offensive or unwholesome business may be carried on.

Sec. 51.—To prevent any person from bringing, depositing or having within the limits of the city any dead carcass or any unwholesome substance, and to require the removal or the destruction of the same by any person who shall have placed or caused to be placed upon or near his premises or near any of the streams of this city any such substance, or any putrid or unsound beef, pork, or fish, hides or skins of any kind; and on his default to authorize the removal or destruction of the same by any officer of said city.

Sec. 52.—To direct and regulate the planting and preserving of trees in the streets and public grounds, and regulate the fencing of lots within the boundaries of the city.

Sec. 53.—To prevent the ringing of bells, the blowing of horns and bugles, the crying of goods and all other noises, performances and devices tending to disturb the peace and quiet of the said city.

Sec. 54.—To grant and issue licenses, and direct the manner of issuing and registering thereof. Bonds may be taken on the granting of licenses, for the due observance of the ordinances of the City Council.

Sec. 55.—To require every merchant, retailer, trader and dealer in merchandise or property of every description which is sold by measure or weight, to cause their weights and measures to be sealed by the City Sealer and to be subject to his inspection, the standard of which weights and measures shall be conformable to those established by law.

Sec. 56.—The City Council shall have power to make such ordinances and resolutions, not contrary to the Constitution and laws of the United States and the laws of the Territory, as may be necessary and expedient to carry into effect the powers vested in the City Council or any officer of said city by this act, and enforce observance of all ordinances and resolutions made in pursuance of this act, by penalties not exceeding one hundred dollars, or imprisonment not to exceed six months, or both.

Sec. 57.—The City Council shall have exclusive authority and power to establish and regulate the Police of the city; to impose fines, forfeitures and penalties for the breach of any ordinance; to provide for the recovery of such fines and forfeitures and the enforcement of such penalties: and to pass, make, ordain, establish and execute all such ordinances, not repugnant to the Constitution and laws of the United States or the laws of this Territory, as they may deem necessary for carrying into effect and execution the powers specified in this act, and for the peace, good order, regulation, convenience and cleanliness of the city, for the protection of property therein from destruction by fire or otherwise, and for the health, safety and happiness of the inhabitants thereof.

Sec. 58.—To provide for the punishment of offenders and vagrants by imprisonment in the county or city jail, or by compelling them to labor on the streets or other public works until the same shall be fully paid, in all cases where such offenders or vagrants shall fail or refuse to pay the fines and forfeitures which may be awarded against them.

Sec. 59.—All ordinances passed by the City Council shall, within one month after they shall have been passed, be published in some newspaper printed in said city, or certified copies thereof be posted up in three of the most public places in the city.

Sec. 60.—All ordinances of the city may be proven by the seal of the Corporation; and when printed or published in book form, purporting to be printed or published by the authority of the City Council, the same shall be received in evidence in all Courts or places, without further proof.

Sec. 61.—When it shall be necessary to take private property for opening, widening, or altering any public street, lane, avenue or alley, the Corporation shall make a just compensation therefor to the person whose property is so taken; and if the amount of such compensation cannot be agreed upon, the Justices of the Peace shall cause the same to be ascertained by a jury of six disinterested men, who shall be inhabitants of the city.

Sec. 62.—All jurors, empanneled to inquire into the amounts of benefits or damages that shall happen to the owners of property so proposed to be taken, shall first be sworn to that effect; and shall return to the Mayor or presiding officer of the City Council their inquest in writing, signed by each juror.

Sec. 63.—All officers of the city, created Conservators of the peace by this act, shall have power to arrest, or cause to be arrested, with or without process, all persons who shall break the peace, commit for examination and, if necessary, detain such persons in custody forty-eight hours in the city prison or other safe place, and shall have and exercise such other powers, as Conservators of the Peace, as the City Council may prescribe.

Sec. 64.—The City Council shall cause to be published in some newspaper printed in the city of Wellsville, or posted up in three public places, on or before the first day of December in each year, a statement of the amount of city revenue, specifying in said statement whence derived and for what disbursed.

Approved January, 19, 1866.

———:0:———

CHAPTER CXLIV.

An ACT to incorporate the City of Moroni, in Sanpete County.

Sec. 1.—Be it enacted by the Governor and Legislative Assembly of the Territory of Utah: That all that portion of country situated within the following boundaries, to wit: beginning at the north end of the bridge South of Moroni crossing Sanpitch river, running west two miles from said bridge, thence north four miles, thence east four miles, thence south four miles, thence west two miles to Sanpitch bridge, the place of beginning, shall be known and designated by the name of Moroni City, and the inhabitants thereof are hereby constituted a body corporate and politic by the name aforesaid; and may have and use a common seal, which they may change and alter at pleasure.

Sec. 2.—The inhabitants of said city, by the name and style aforesaid, shall have power to sue and be sued, to plead and be impleaded, defend and be defended in all Courts of law and equity and in all actions whatsoever; to purchase, receive and hold property, real and personal, in said city; to purchase, receive and hold real property beyond the city for burying grounds or other public purposes for the use of the inhabitants of said city; to improve and protect such property, and to do all other things in relation thereto, as natural persons.

Sec. 3.—There shall be a City Council to consist of a Mayor and five Councilors, who shall have the qualifications of electors of said city, and shall be chosen by the qualified voters thereof, and shall hold their offices for two years, and until their successors shall be elected and qualified. The City Council shall judge of the qualifications, elections and returns of their own members, and a majority of them shall form a quorum to do business; but a smaller number may adjourn from day to day and compel the attendance of absent members, under such penalties as may be prescribed by ordinance; there shall also be elected in like manner two Justices of the Peace who shall have the qualifications of voters, be commissioned by the Governor and have jurisdiction in all cases arising under the ordinances of the City.

Sec. 4.—The Mayor and Councilors, before entering upon the duties of their offices, shall take and subscribe an oath or affirmation that they will support the Constitution of the United States and the laws of this Territory, and that they will well and truly perform all the duties of their offices to the best of their skill and abilities.

Sec. 5.—One Mayor and five Councilors shall be elected biennially and the first election under this act shall be at such time in said city as the Probate Judge of Sanpete County shall direct: Provided, said election shall be on or before the first Monday in August next. Said election shall be held and conducted as is now provided by law for the holding of elections for County and Territorial officers; and, at the said first election, all free white male residents, over twenty-one years of age, within said city limits, shall be entitled to vote.

Sec. 6.—The clerks of election shall leave with each person elected, or at his usual place of residence, within five days after the election, a written notice of his election, and each person so notified shall, within ten days after the election, take the oath or affirmation hereinbefore mentioned, a certificate of which oath shall be deposited with the Recorder, whose appointment is hereinafter provided for, and be by him preserved; and all subsequent elections shall be held, conducted, and returns thereof made, as may be provided for by ordinance of the City Council.

Sec. 7.—The City Council shall have authority to levy and collect taxes, for city purposes, upon all taxable property, real and personal, within the limits of the city, not exceeding one half of one per cent. per annum upon the assessed value thereof; and may enforce the payment of the same to be provided for by ordinance, not repugnant to the Constitution of the United States or to the laws of this Territory.

Sec. 8.—The City Council shall have power to appoint a Recorder, Treasurer, Assessor and Collector, Marshal and Supervisor of Streets. They shall also have the power to appoint all such other officers, by ordinance, as may be necessary, define the duties of all city officers and remove them from office at pleasure.

Sec. 9.—The City Council shall have power to require of all officers, appointed in pursuance of this act, bonds with security, for the faithful performance of their respective duties, and also to require of all officers, appointed as aforesaid, to take an oath for the faithful performance of the duties of their respective offices.

Sec. 10.—The City Council shall have power and authority to make, ordain, establish and execute all such ordinances, not repugnant to the Constitution of the United States or the laws of this Territory, as they may deem necessary for the peace, benefit, good order, regulation, convenience and cleanliness of said city; for the protection of property therein from destruction by fire or otherwise, and for the health and happiness of the inhabitants thereof, and shall have control of the water of the Santpitch river: Provided that such control shall not be exercised to the injury of any rights already acquired by actual settlers thereon, and shall have control of the water courses and mill privileges within said city, but in no case shall they interfere with the natural rights of others heretofore acquired in relation to water. They shall have power to fill all vacancies that may happen by death, resignation or removal of any of the officers herein made elective; to fix and establish the fees of the officers of said corporation. The City Council shall have power to divide the city into Wards and specify the boundaries thereof.

Sec. 11.—All ordinances passed by the City Council shall, within ten days after they shall have been passed, be published in some newspaper printed in said city, or certified copies thereof be posted up in three of the most public places in the city. They shall not be in force until thus published or posted up.

Sec. 12.—All ordinances of the city may be proven by the seal of the corporation affixed thereto; and, when printed or published in book or pamphlet form, purporting to be printed or published by the authority of the corporation, the same shall be received in evidence in all courts and places, without further proof.

Sec. 13.—The Justices of the Peace of said city shall have all the powers of other Justices of the Peace, both in civil and criminal cases arising under the laws of the Territory. They shall perform the same duties, be governed by the same laws, give the same bonds and securities as other Justices of the Peace. They shall have exclusive jurisdiction in all cases arising under the ordinances of the Corporation, and shall issue such process as may be necessary to carry such ordinance into execution. Appeals may be had from any decision or judgment of said Justices arising under the ordinances of said City, or laws of the Territory, to the Probate Court of said Sanpete County, in the same manner as appeals are or may be taken from other Justices of the Peace.

Sec. 14.—The Mayor shall be the chief executive officer of said Corporation, he shall preside in the City Council, and shall have power to veto any ordinance when not passed by four-fifths majority, and it shall be his duty to sign all city ordinances.

Sec. 15.—This act shall be in force on and after the tenth day of February, 1866, and may be amended or repealed at the pleasure of the Legislative Assembly.

Approved Jan. 17, 1866.

CHAPTER CXLV.

An ACT creating the office of Selectmen and prescribing their duties, also the duties of the County Courts.

Sec. 1.—Be it enacted by the Governor and Legislative Assembly of the Territory of Utah: That there shall be three Selectmen in each organized county within the Territory, whose term of office shall be three years. And at the organization of new counties there shall be elected, at the first general election, three Selectmen, as follows, to wit: The senior shall hold his office for three years, the second for two years and the junior for one year; and thereafter one shall be elected each year, who shall hold his office for the term of three years and until his successor is elected and qualified: Provided that in each county now organized the Selectmen shall be elected in the same manner as provided for the continuation of the election of Selectmen in new counties.

Sec. 2.—Said Selectmen shall be sworn before the Clerk of the Probate Court and give such bonds as the Clerk shall approve, and the same shall be filed in the Clerk's office, who shall give them a certificate of office under the seal of the Probate Court.

Sec. 3.—The Probate Judge in connection with the Selectmen shall be known as the County Court, any three of whom shall form a quorum to do business; and they are invested with such powers and jurisdiction as are or may be conferred by law. The Clerk of the Probate Court shall be the Clerk of this Court, shall keep his office at the County Seat and shall attend himself or by deputy all sessions of the Court, and keep the records, papers and seal of the Court. The office of the County Clerk is to be kept open during usual business hours.

Sec. 4.—This Court is authorized and required to take the management of all County business and the care and custody of all the County property, except such as is by it placed in the custody of another; and shall have the control of all books, papers and instruments pertaining to their office. Said Court shall audit all claims against the county, and cause the county seal to be affixed to all warrants or orders on the Treasurer for money to be paid out of the County treasury: shall audit and settle the accounts of the Treasurer and those of any other officer or receiver of County revenue, taxes or other dues payable into the County treasury, and those of any person entrusted to expend any money of the county, and to require them to render their accounts as directed by law.

Sec. 5.—Said Court shall keep a book to be known as the County Book, in which shall be recorded all orders and decisions made by them, except those relating to roads and Probate affairs. Orders for the allowance of money from the County Treasury shall state on what account and to whom the allowance is made, dating and numbering the drawing on the Treasury each order; and said Court are to superintend the fiscal affairs of the county and secure their management in the best possible manner.

Sec. 6.—The County Court shall also keep a separate book for the entries of all proceedings and adjudications relating to the establishment, change or discontinuance of roads; and also separate books for probate business. They shall keep an account of the receipts and expenditures of the county and annually on the first Monday of June, cause a minute statement of them for the preceding year to be made, with an account of all debts payable to and by the county and the assets of the county; have a copy of the same posted up, one at the County Seat, at the usual place of holding Courts, and at each of two other public places in the county, or published in some newspaper having general circulation in the county, and shall cause the original to be filed in their office.

Sec. 7.—The County Courts shall district their respective counties into road districts, precincts, school districts or such other subdivisions as may become necessary or proper; locate sites for public buildings and erect the same; have the control of all timber, water privileges or any watercourse or creek; to grant mill sites and exercise such powers as in their judgment shall best preserve the timber and subserve the interest of the settlements in the distribution of water for irrigation or other purposes. Grants or rights held under Legislative authority shall not be interfered with.

Sec. 8.—It shall further be the duty of said Courts to oversee the poor and provide for their maintenance; to take care, custody and management of insane persons, who are incapable of conducting their own affairs, and of their estate both real and personal, and to provide for the safe keeping of such insane persons, their maintenance and the maintenance of their families and the education of their children.

Sec. 9.—The Selectmen may transact business separately, subject to the approval of the County Courts, relating to the poor, insane persons, orphans and minors; and may have authority to bind out vicious, idle or vagrant children or orphans and minors, until they shall attain the age of legal majority. They shall also have power to appoint guardians for minors who are orphans, for the persons and property of the insane, where they shall be found incapable of managing their own affairs, and generally to do and perform such other duties pertaining to their office, as shall be required by law or by the Probate Court in their respective counties.

Sec. 10.—Said Selectmen shall make a report of all their proceedings to the County Court at their next regular session, as also a true report of all the affairs and situation of the poor or destitute and insane within their respective counties, and make such suggestions and recommendations as to them shall appear necessary for the action of the Court.

Sec. 11.—The sessions of the County Courts shall be held quarterly on the first Monday in March, June, September and December in each year, and oftener if they deem it necessary.

Sec. 12.—It is hereby made the duty of all County officers to deliver to their successors in office all books, papers, seals, or other public property in their possession.

Sec. 13.—The County Courts are hereby authorized and required to appoint all county and precinct officers not made elective by law, and to fill all vacancies of county and precinct officers, not otherwise provided for, that may occur between elections in their respective counties; and any person, so elected or appointed, failing to qualify within ten days after receiving notice of his election, unless he shall previously notify the County Clerk that he does not accept the office, or, after qualifying, shall fail or neglect to fulfil the duties thereof, may be fined in any sum not less than five dollars nor more than one hundred dollars before any Court having jurisdiction.

Sec. 14.—An Act entitled "An Act creating the office of Selectmen and prescribing their duties," approved February 5, 1852, and sections 34 to 42, inclusive, of "An Act in relation to the Judiciary," approved February 4, 1852, are hereby repealed.

Approved January 8, 1866.

——:o:——

CHAPTER CXLVI.

An ACT defining the boundaries of Counties and locating County Seats.

Sec. 1.—Be it enacted by the Governor and Legislative Assembly of the Territory of Utah: That all that portion of Utah Territory bounded north by a line running due east from a point four miles north of the northeast corner of Fort Harmony, east by Colorado Territory, south by Arizona and west by a line running due north from the southern boundary of Utah Territory, passing through the largest mineral spring at the mouth of the Rio Vergen Cañon, until it reaches the summit of the dividing ridge bewcen the Leverkin and Ash creeks, and thence northeasterly along the summit of said dividing ridge to its intersection with the line first above mentioned is hereby made and named Kane County, with County Seat at Grafton.

Sec. 2.—All that portion of the Territory bounded north by a line running due west from the northern boundary of Kane County, east by Kane County, south by Arizona and west by Nevada is hereby made and named Washington County, with County Seat at Saint George.

Sec. 3.—All that portion of the Territory bounded south by Washington and Kane Counties, west by Nevada, north by a due west and west line crossing the military road on the summit of the ridge dividing Little Salt Lake and upper Beaver Valleys, and east by Colorado Territory is hereby made and named Iron County, with County Seat at Parowan.

Sec. 4.—All that portion of the Territory bounded south by Iron County, west by Nevada, north by a line running due east and west through a point two miles due south from the south side of Fort Wilden on Cove creek and east by the range of mountains dividing Beaver and Pauvan Valleys from the Valley of the Sevier is hereby made and named Beaver County, with County Seats at Beaver.

Sec. 5.—All that portion of the Territory bounded south by Iron County, west by Beaver County, north by an east and west line crossing the road on the summit of the dividing ridge between Mary's Vale and Alma, and east by Colorado Territory is hereby made and named Piute County, with County Seat at Circleville.

Sec. 6.—All that portion of the Territory bounded south by beaver County, west by Nevada; east by the summit of the mountains separating the Sevier from Pauvan and Round Valleys, following said summit east of the lake in Round Valley and north of Round Valley to its intersection with the Sevier river, thence down the channel of said river to the mouth of its lower cañon, thence due west to Nevada is hereby made and named Millard County, with County Seat at Fillmore.

Sec. 7.—All that portion of the Territory bounded south by Piute County, west by Millard County, north by an east and west line crossing the road at the fork of Willow creek between Gunnison and Salina, and east by Colorado is hereby made and named Sevier County, with County Seat at Richfield.

Sec. 8.—All that portion of the Territory bounded south by Millard County, west by a line drawn due north from the north line of Millard County to the most western peak in the range of mountains between Tintic Valley and Meadow creek, thence along the summit of said range to its intersection with the range between Tintic and Rush valleys, north by the summit of the range between Tintic and Rush valleys, and the summit of the range between Tintic valley and Cedar and Goshen valleys and the summit of the range between Goshen and Juab valleys and the summit of the high ground and range between Utah and Juab valleys, and east by the summit of the Nebo range of mountains to the highest southern peak of said range of mountains, thence on a straight line southwesterly to the north boundary of Millard County, crossing the Sevier river at the Upper Bluff Rock at the south end of Cedar Ridge, is hereby made and named Juab County, with a County Seat at Nephi.

Sec. 9.—All that portion of the Territory bounded south by Sevier County, west by Juab County, north by the summit of the range of mountains between Sanpete Valley and Spanish Fork river and along the summit of said range until it intersects Green river, thence by a line drawn due east from said intersection to the thirty-second meridian west from Washington City, and east by said meeidian is hereby made and named Sanpete County, with County Seat at Manti: Provided, that the hay ground of Thistle Valley shall be included in Sanpete County.

Sec. 10.—All that portion of the Territory bounded south by Juab and Sanpete Counties, west by the summit of the range between Cedar and Rush Valleys, north by the summit of the cross range between the Oquirh and Wasatch mountains, east by the summit of the range passing around the head of Dry American Fork, Battle, Hobble, and Spanish Fork creeks and a line drawn due north and south across Provo river, at a point one-fourth of a mile above the north fork of Deer creek of said river, to intersect of each extremity of said line the summit of the last named range, is hereby made and named Utah County, with County Seat at Provo.

Sec. 11.—All that portion of the Territory bounded south by Utah and Sanpete Counties, west by Utah and Great Salt Lake Counties, north by the summit of the range of mountains south of the head waters of East Cañon and Silver creeks, following said summit to the points where the road leading to Great Salt Lake City and Rhode's Valley crosses, thence south to Provo river at the high bluff below Goddard's ranch, thence along the channel of said river to its head waters, thence easterly to the summit of the range of mountains north of Uinta Valley, thence along the last named summit and south of Brown's Hole to the thirty-second meridian west from Washington City and east by said meridian is hereby made and named Wasatch County, with County Seat at Heber City.

Sec. 12.—All that portion of the Territory bounded south by Utah County, west by the summit of the range of mountains between Great Salt Lake and Tooele Valleys and a line running from the northern termination of said summit through Black Rock on the south shore of Great Salt Lake, north by the shore of said Lake easterly to the mouth of Jordan river, thence by the centre of the channel of said river to a point due west from the Hot Springs north of Great Salt Lake City, thence by a line running due east to said Hot Springs, thence by the summit of the spur range terminating at such Hot Springs to its intersection with the summit of the Wasatch mountains, and east by the summit of said mountains is hereby made and named Great Salt Lake County, with County Seat at Great Salt Lake City.

Sec. 13.—All the Islands in Great Salt Lake are hereby attached to Great Salt Lake County for election, revenue and judicial purposes; and judicial jurisdiction of all acts and transactions done or entered into on the waters of Great Salt Lake and on so much of its beach as is not included in any county is hereby given to Great Salt Lake County and the Judicial District to which said County at the time belongs.

Sec. 14.—All that portion of the Territory bounded south by Great Salt Lake County, west by the eastern shore of Great Salt Lake, north by a line running due east from a point on said shore to a point in the centre of the channel of Weber river due north from the northwest corner of Kingston's Fort, thence up the centre of said channel to a point opposite the summit of the Wasatch mountains, and east by the summit of said mountains is hereby made and named Davis County, with County Seat at Farmington.

Sec. 15.—All that portion of the Territory bounded south by Davis County and the dividing ridge between Ogden Hole and Weber Valley, west by the eastern shore of Great Salt Lake, north by a line drawn due east from a point in said shore to the Hot Springs by the Territorial road north of Ogden City, thence by the summit of the spur range terminating at said Hot Springs to its intersection with the summit of the Wasatch mountains, east by the summit of said mountains, passing around the head waters of Ogden river, is hereby made and named Weber County, with County Seat at Ogden City.

Sec. 16.—All that portion of Territory bounded south by Weber County, thence by the shore of Great Salt Lake, following said shore around the head of Bear River Bay, Promontory Point and the north end of said Lake, and thence southeasterly to a point where it is intersected by latitude forty-one degrees north, thence by said latitude to the summit of Pilot Peak, thence due south thirty minutes of latitude, thence by latitude forty degrees and thirty minutes north, west by Nevada, north by latitude forty-two degrees and east by the summit of the range of mountains east of Malad Valley, crossing Bear river at the centre of its lower cañon, and thence southerly along the summit of the Wasatch mountains and passing around the head waters of Box Elder and Willow creeks, is hereby made and named Box Elder County, with County Seat at Brigham City.

Sec. 17.—All that portion of the Territory bounded south by Juab and Millard Counties, west by Nevada, north by Box Elder County, and east by the west and south shores of Great Salt Lake and Great Salt Lake and Utah Counties is hereby made and named Tooele County, with County Seat at Tooele City.

Sec. 18.—All that portion of the Territory bounded south by Wasatch County, west by Great Salt Lake County, north by the summit of the range of mountains forming the upper cañon of East Cañon creek, thence northerly along the summit of the range of mountains between said creek and Weber river; thence across said river to, and along the summit of the high land between Plumbar or Lost and Echo Cañon creeks, thence to, and along the summit next north of Yellow creek to Bear river, thence easterly across said river to the summit of the divide between Bear river and the tributaries of Green river, and east by the summit of said range is hereby made and named Summit County, with County Seat at Wanship.

Sec. 19.—All that portion of the Territory bounded south and east by Summit County, west by Great Salt Lake, Davis and Weber Counties, and north by Weber County and a line running from a point in the eastern boundary of Weber County nearest the most eastern head waters of Ogden river along the summit of the high lands or ranges passing around the head waters of Plumbar or Lost creek, easterly to the point where the north boundary of Summit County crosses Bear river is hereby made and named Morgan County, with County Seat at Littleton.

Sec. 20.—All that portion of the Territory bounded south by Morgan, Weber and Box Elder Counties, west by Box Elder County, north by latitude forty-two degrees north, and east by the summit of the ridge mountains between Cache and Bear Lake Valleys is hereby made and named Cache County, with the County Seat at Logan City.

Sec. 21.—All that portion of the Territory bounded south by Summit and Morgan Counties, west by Cache County, north by latitude forty-two degrees north, and east by the summit of the divide between the waters of Bear river and the tributaries of Green river is hereby made and named Richland County, with the County Seat at St. Charles.

Sec. 22.—All that portion of the Territory bounded south by Wasatch County, west by Summit and Richland Counties, north by latitude forty-two degrees north, and east by Colorado and Dakota Territories is hereby made and named Green River County, with the County Seat at Fort Bridger.

Sec. 23.—When any uncertainty or dispute arises as to what county an act or transaction has transpired in, either of the counties in which it is fairly presumable such act or transaction has occurred is hereby authorized to have jurisdiction in the case.

Sec. 24.—All laws in relation to the boundaries of counties and locating county seats, conflicting with this Act, are hereby repealed.

Approved Jan. 10, 1866.

CHAPTER CXLVII.

An ACT to amend certain City Charters.

Be it enacted by the Governor and Legislative Assembly of the Territory of Utah: That section seventeen of the charters of Ogden, Provo and Payson Cities be amended so as to read in the fifth line of said section, between the words "to wit" and "not," "not to exceed five mills on the dollar for contingent expenses;" and that the word "not" in the same line be made to read "nor."

Approved January 11, 1866.

——:o:——

CHAPTER CXLVIII.

An ACT repealing "An ACT granting unto Charles Hopkins and others the right to build a bridge across the river Jordan."

Be it enacted by the Governor and Legislative Assembly of the Territory of Utah: That an Act entitled "An Act granting unto Charles Hopkins and others the right to build a bridge across the river Jordan," "Approved January 21, 1853," is hereby repealed.

Approved January 12, 1866.

——:o:——

CHAPTER CXLIX.

An ACT in relation to Marks and Brands.

Sec. 1.—Be it enacted by the Governor and Legislative Assembly of the Territory of Utah: That a general office for recording marks and brands shall be kept at the Seat of Government, and a Recorder for the same shall be elected by the Legislative Assembly, whose term of office shall be one year and until his successor is elected and qualified.

Sec. 2.—There shall also be an auxiliary office in every county other than that in which the general office is located, and the duties thereof are hereby devolved on the Clerks of the County Courts respectively.

Sec. 3.—Whenever any person wishes to obtain a recorded mark or brand, application therefor may be made to the General Recorder direct or through the auxiliary office of the county in which the applicant resides; and it shall be the duty of the General Recorder to designate the particular mark or brand to be used by such applicant and define the place and position it shall occupy on the animal, consulting always the choice or convenience of applicants, so far as may be without interfering with previously recorded marks or brands: Provided, if a character is wanted for which there is no type, the applicant shall pay the extra expense thereof.

Sec. 4.—The General Recorder shall keep a record of all marks and brands, with the name and residence of the person owning the same, in a book suitable for the purpose, which shall be free to the inspection of all persons interested; and he shall furnish to the owners certified copies of all marks or brands, which certificates shall be deemed evidence in law.

Sec. 5.—The General Recorder shall once a year, or as often as he may deem expedient, furnish the Public Printer a list of all recorded marks or brands which have not been previously published, and cause to be printed, at the public expense, one thousand copies, either in pamphlet or other convenient form, for reference and preservation; and shall, immediately after publication, gratuitously distribute to each Auxilary Office a sufficient number of copies to supply the County Clerks, Sheriffs, Probate Judges, Selectmen, City Recorders, Justices, Constables, and Poundkeepers in their respective counties; and one copy each to like officers in his own county, and the residue he may dispose of at not exceeding twenty five cents a copy. He may also charge and receive, from each person applying for a mark or brand, the fee of one dollar for each mark or brand so recorded.

Sec. 6.—Clerks of Auxilary Office shall receive and forward to the General Recorder all applications for recording marks and brands, and shall furnish each applicant the Recorder's certificate of the mark or brand designated and recorded for him, for which service they may receive fifty cents each in addition to the Recorder's fee: Provided, that they shall gratuitously distribute the printed copies in their respective counties, as contemplated in the fifth section. All such printed copies shall be deemed the property of the several officers respectively, and shall be delivered by them to their successors in office.

Sec. 7.—Any person, using a like brand in the position and place recorded to another, shall be deemed guilty of a misdemeanor, and shall be liable to a fine in any sum not exceeding one hundred dollars for each offense.

Sec. 8.—After the expiration of one year from the publication of this Act, any stock, over eighteen months old, running at large without a recorded mark or brand, shall be deemed estrays, and may be taken into custody by the Poundkeeper and disposed of as other estrays.

Sec. 9.—"An Act in relation to marks and brands," "Approved March 1, 1852," is hereby repealed: Provided, that nothing in this repeal shall be construed to invalidate marks and brands already recorded.

Approved January 13, 1866.

——:o:——

CHAPTER CL.

An ACT granting to Alvin Nichols and William S. Godbe the right to establish a toll bridge across Bear River, in Box Elder County, and a bridge across the Malad.

Sec. 1.—Be it enacted by the Governor and Legislative Assembly of the Territory of Utah: That Alvin Nichols and William S. Godbe are hereby authorized and required to erect, within one year from the passage of this Act, a good and substantial bridge across Bear river, in Box Elder County, at or near the place where the Territorial road from Great Salt Lake City to Montana and Idaho Territories crosses Bear river at the old California and Fort Hall ford; and also a good and substantial bridge across the Malad, in said county, at or near where the present traveled road to California crosses said river; and they shall keep the same in good repair, and may take toll at the Bear river bridge during eight years, not to exceed the following rates:

For each vehicle drawn by two animals,	$2,00
For each vehicle drawn by four animals,	2,50
For each vehicle drawn by six animals,	3,00
For each vehicle drawn by one animal,	1,00
For each pack animal,	50
For each horseman,	50
For each footman,	10
For each loose horse, mule, jack, camel, ox, cow or bull,	15
For each colt, calf, sheep, goat, or swine,	5

Necessary drivers and assistants in driving herds or teams may pass toll free The foregoing rates shall be kept posted up at each end of the bridge during the season of taking toll; and if the said Nichols and Godbe shall fail to post up the rates of toll as required, or shall collect above the rates specified, they shall be liable to a fine not exceeding one hundred dollars for each offense.

Sec. 2.—After the completion of said bridge, if any person shall take toll upon any bridge or ferry within one and a half miles up the channel of said river or within six miles down the channel from the location of Nichols and Godbe's bridge, he shall forfeit and pay to the parties injured the sum of five thousand dollars annually, so long as said bridge or ferry shall be used.

Sec. 3.—The said Nichols and Godbe, before receiving toll as herein provided, shall execute sufficient bonds, to be approved by the Probate Judge of Box Elder County and filed in his office, in the sum of ten thousand dollars, conditioned for the indemnifying of all persons against losses they may sustain by reason of the insufficiency and unsafe condition of said bridge while toll is being received thereon, to be recovered as in action of debt before any Court having jurisdiction.

Sec. 4.—As there are new settlements being formed for agricultural and herding purposes in Box Elder County, westerly and northerly of said bridge, therefore the rates of toll for crossing said bridge, by persons engaged in the aforesaid employments, shall be established by the County Court of Box Elder County.

Sec. 5.—The said Nichols and Godbe, at the expiration of eight years from the passage of this Act, shall transfer said bridge in good condition to the Territorial Road Commissioner, as the property of the Territory.

Sec. 6.—Said Alvin Nichols and William S. Godbe are hereby required to make an annual report, during the first week of the Legislative Assembly, of all receipts of toll received on said bridge, and pay into the Territorial Treasury, for the benefit of common schools, five per cent. of all toll collected thereon.

Sec. 7.—Be it further enacted that all the rights and privileges granted to Joseph Young, senior, in "An Act concerning a ferry or ferries across Bear river and a bridge across the Malad," "approved January 22, 1864," are hereby transferred to the said Alvin Nichols and William S. Godbe.

Approved January 13, 1866.

——:o:——

CHAPTER CLI.

An ACT Regulating Estray Pounds and for other purposes.

Sec. 1.—Be it enacted by the Governor and Legislative Assembly of the Territory of Utah: That the County Court of each county is hereby authorized and required to provide and keep in constant repair a good and substantial pound in each precinct, and at the County Seat of each county, and furnish suitable blank books for the use of the Poundkeepers.

Sec. 2.—There shall be elected, at the general election, a County Poundkeeper for each county, who shall take an oath of office and file sufficient bonds, with approved security, conditioned for the faithful performance of the duties thereof; the amount of bond and approval of securities shall be determined by the County Court, and the bond shall be filed with the County Clerk. Said Poundkeeper's term of office shall be for two years, and until his successor is elected and qualified; he shall also be a resident of the County Seat and shall have the disposal of all estrays within said county, as hereinafter provided.

Sec. 3.—There shall be elected, at the general election in each precinct, a Precinct Poundkeeper, whose term of office shall be for two years, and until his successor is elected and qualified; he shall take an oath of office and give bonds as provided for the County Poundkeeper, and shall take charge of all estrays found within his precinct and forward the same, if unclaimed, to the County Poundkeeper: Provided, that the County Poundkeeper shall be the Precinct Poundkeeper for the precinct in which the County Pound is kept.

Sec. 4.—Each precinct Poundkeeper shall receive and take good care of all animals committed to his charge, and use due diligence to find the owner or owners thereof, by record of brands or otherwise, and shall deliver to his successor in office all books, papers and other property belonging to his office.

Sec. 5.—Any animal remaining unclaimed two days from the time of commitment shall be registered in the Pound Book, in which shall be set forth when received, from whom, where found, amount of damage done, if any, kind of animal, approximate age, color, stripes, marks, brands and such other description as may aid the owner to find his animal, true copies of which the Precinct Poundkeeper shall post up, within four days from the time of its being impounded, in three of the most conspicuous places in his precinct, stating that, if it be not claimed and taken away within ten days days thereafter, said anmial will be forwarded to the County Poundkeeper.

Sec. 6.—Each Precinct Pounkeeper shall receive and file all bills of damage duly presented and enter the amounts in the Pound Book, which shall be open to the inspection of the public; he shall not deliver any animal to the owner until all costs and damages are paid or satisfactorily arranged for; he shall forward to the County Poundkeeper all animals remaining unclaimed or not taken away within fourteen days from commitment, with the bill of costs and damages on each animal, and shall semi-annually collect and forward all strays within his precinct to the County Poundkeepers.

Sec. 7.—The County poundkeeper is to receive and receipt for all animals delivto him by Precinct Poundkeepers or other persons, to enter upon his registry when said animal or animals were received, from what pound or person, amount of damages and costs, together with a full and complete description of each animal, including approximate age, marks and brands.

Sec. 8.—Each County Poundkeeper shall provide forage or pasturage, or place said animals in the care of a responsible person, and forthwith advertise them for sale in three consecutive numbers of some newspaper having a general circulation, which advertisement shall be posted up in three public places in the county, and shall contain the description of each animal, as recorded in his registry, stating the time and place of sale and that, if not claimed and taken away within thirty days from the date of advertisement, he will expose them at public sale and sell them to the highest responsible bidder; the proceeds of said sale, after deducting costs and damage, he shall pay into the County Treasury, subject to the orders of the owners of said animals, if applied for within six months from the date of sale; if not applied for by the owners within that time, the Treasurer shall pass the same to the credit of the Common Schools in his county, to be drawn and applied under the direction of the County School Superintendent.

Sec. 9.—The County Poundkeeper shall register the disposal of all animals and the amount sold for, the total amount of cost and damage, and report his proceedings to the County Court semi-annually, or oftener if required by said Court, and shall deliver to his successor in office all books, papers and other property belonging to his office and take duplicate receipts therefor, one of which shall be deposited with the County Clerk.

Sec. 10.—All damages done by any animal trespassing shall be forthwith appraised by any disinterested voter, who may make a reasonable charge for his services. Said appraisal shall set forth, in writing, the time and place of the damage, the name of the person aggrieved and, if known, the name of the owner of the animal, and, so far as may be, the kind and decription of the animal, which amount, if not paid or satisfactorily arranged for by the owner, or if, the owner be not known, shall, together with the animal, be placed in the charge of the Precinct Poundkeeper: Provided, that the owner, if he deems the appraisal too high, may choose another appraiser who, with the first, may make a new appraisal; or, when they cannot agree, they two may choose a third appraiser, and an appraisal by the two or by the three, as the case may be, shall be final.

Sec. 11.—Any animal found trespassing may be taken up by any person, and if the owner cannot be found, or, if found, shall refuse to pay all cost and damage, said animal shall be forthwith taken to the precinct or County Pound and delivered to the keeper thereof.

Sec. 12.—Any person, other than a Poundkeeper, taking up an animal under the provisions of this Act and retaining it more than three days, shall be liable to a fine not exceeding one hundred dollars for each animal so retained, and to lose all damages that may have accrued thereon.

Sec. 13.—Any person taking his own stock or that of any other person out of the custody of any person holding the same for damage done by it, or out of any pound by stealth or by force, or shall interrupt or hinder any one while in the discharge of his duty under this Act, may be fined in any sum not exceeding one hundred dollars at the discretion of any court having jurisdiction.

Sec. 14.—Fees for impounding shall not exceed one dollar a head for horses, mules, cattle, swine, or goats, nor ten cents for sheep, one half of which shall be paid into the County Treasury; fees for registry shall not exceed twenty-five cents a head for horses or cattle kind, and not more than ten cents for sheep, goats or swine; fees for advertising may be charged twenty-five per cent. additional to the price charged by the publisher; fees for keeping animals shall be governed by the price of forage at the time and place, as well as the price that may be demanded for pasturage or herding; fees for making inquiries for owners and driving and delivering animals to the County Poundkeeper may be charged at the discretion of said Poundkeeper, but shall not exceed a fair compensation for time and expenses.

Sec. 15.—Each County and Precinct Poundkeeper is hereby required to keep a book in which he shall keep an account of all funds paid to him, showing the amount paid for poundage and damages, and pay into the County Treasury all funds belonging to the county, once in six months, or oftener; if required by the County Court.

Sec. 16.—"An Ordinance for the establishment and regulation of Stray Pounds," "Approved Feb. 12, 1851," and sections 2, 3, 4, 5 and 6 of "An Act pertaining to damage done by animals," "Approved Jan. 19, 1865," are hereby repealed.

Approved Jan. 17, 1866.

———:o:———

CHAPTER CLII.

An ACT concerning Notaries Public.

Sec. 1.—Be it enacted by the Governor and Legislative Assembly of the Territory of Utah: That there shall be elected, by the joint vote of the Legislative Assembly, one or more Notaries Public for each organized county, whose term of office shall be one year, and until their successors are elected and qualified.

Sec. 2.—Each Notary Public shall, before entering upon his official duties, take the oath of office and give a bond, with sufficient sureties, to the Territory of Utah, in the penal sum of five hundred dollars, conditioned that he will faithfully perform the duties of his office; said bond to be approved by the Probate Judge of the county in which the Notary Public resides:

Sec. 3.—The commission and oath shall be recorded in the office of the Probate Judge of the county in which the Notary Public resides; and such bond shall be filed in said office, and may be sued on by any person injured through the unfaithful performance of said Notary's duties: Provided, that no suit shall be so instituted after three years from the time the cause of such action occurred.

Sec. 4.—Notaries Public are hereby authorized to administer all oaths provided for by law; to acknowledge powers of attorney and all instruments of writing conveying or effecting property in any part of this Territory, and elsewhere so far as may be lawful; to take affidavits and depositions; to make declarations and protests, and to do all other acts usually done by Notaries Public in other States and Territories.

Sec. 5.—It is hereby made the duty of a Notary Public, whenever any instrument in writing is by him protested for non-payment or non acceptance, to give written notice thereof, as soon as practicable, to the maker and each endorser or security of of said instrument; and to personally serve such notice, when the person protested against resides in the same town or city with the Notary, otherwise he may forward said notice by mail or other safe conveynce.

Sec. 6.—Each Notary Public shall keep a fair record of his official acts, including such notices, the time and manner in which they have been served and the names of all the parties to whom they were directed, and the description and amount of the instrument protested, which record shall be competent evidence to legally prove such notices; and, when required and the fees are paid, he shall give a certified copy of any official record or paper in his office.

Sec. 7.—When the office of a Notary Public becomes vacant, the records of said Notary and all the papers relating to his office shall be deposited in the office of the Clerk of the Probate Court in the county in which the said Notary Public resided; and if said records and papers are not so delivered within thirty days after said vacancy occurs, said Clerk of the Probate Court is hereby authorized and required to take and deposit them as aforesaid; and in either case said Clerk shall safely keep the said records and papers, and, when requested and the fees are paid, shall give a certified copy of any portion thereof, which copy is hereby made as valid as if it had been given by the aforesaid Notary Public.

Sec. 8.—In case a Notary Public uses an official seal, it shall contain the name of the county in which he resides, and he shall therewith attest all his official acts.

Sec. 9.—This act shall be in force from the date of its approval, and all laws and parts of laws conflicting therewith are hereby repealed.

Approved January 17, 1866.

CHAPTER CLIII.

An ACT to Incorporate the Deseret City Library Association.

Sec. 1.—Be it enacted by the Governor and Legislative Assembly of the Territory of Utah: That Thomas Memmott, John Rowell, Henry Roper, Isaac W. Pierce, Martin Littlewood and their associates and successors are hereby constituted a body corporate, to be known and styled Deseret City Library Association, and shall have power to purchase, receive and hold property real and personal, to sue and be sued, plead and be impleaded, defend and be defended in all Courts of law and equity, and to do all things that may be proper to carry into effect the objects of the Association, by establishing a library of books, maps, charts and scientific instruments, connecting therewith a reading room and lectures. And the above named persons are hereby appointed a Board of Directors of said Association, until superseded as provided in the following section.

Sec. 2.—A Board of seven Directors shall be elected by the members of said Association on the second Monday of March, eighteen hundred and sixty-six, and biennially thereafter on said day, who shall hold office two years, and until their successors are duly elected; and they shall have power to appoint a President, Secretary, Corresponding Secretary, Treasurer and Librarian and define their duties, and also to enact such bye-laws as may be necessary to do all business of the Association. A majority may form a quorum to do business, and may fill any vacancy in the Board, until the next regular election.

Sec. 3.—This Association may raise means by the sale of shares and by contribution and donation, for the purchse of books, maps, charts, &c., and for leasing or erecting suitable buildings for the library, reading rooms and lectures.

Sec. 4.—Conditions of membership, admission to the library, reading rooms and lectures and the loaning of books or other property shall be as provided by the byelaws of said Association.

Approved Jan. 17, 1866.

———:o:———

CHAPTER CLIV.

An ACT to amend "An Act to Incorporate Irrigation Companies."

Be it enacted by the Governor and Legislative Assembly of the Territory of Utah: That persons who have constructed canals, ditches, or dams, and taken out water for irrigation purposes before the passage of the Act to which this Act is amendatory, are hereby authorized to organize under the provisions of said Act, and to enjoy all the rights, powers and privileges guaranteed therein: Provided, they shall proceed in the same manner as is provided for the organization of new companies.

Approved January 17, 1866.

———:o:———

CHAPTER CLV.

An ACT amending "An ACT to provide for the appointment of a Territorial Treasurer, and Auditor of Public Accounts."

Be it enacted by the Governor and Legislative Assembly of the Territory of Utah: That "An Act to provide for the appointment of a Territorial Treasurer and

Auditor of Public Accounts," approved January 20, 1852, is hereby amended as follows: In section four, for "on or before the first day of November," read, on or before the first day of December; and change the seventh section so as to read: It shall be the duty of all Territorial officers handling public funds, either in collecting or disbursing the same, unless otherwise provided for by law, to make a report to the Auditor of Public Accounts on or before the thirtieth day of November in each year.

Approved January 17, 1866.

———:o:———

CHAPTER CLVI.

An ACT authorizing the Attorney General and the District and Prosecuting Attorneys to appoint Deputies.

Be it enacted by the Governor and Legislative Assembly of the Territory of Utah: That the Attorney General and District and County Attorneys are hereby authorized to appoint Deputies, to revoke such appointments, and to perform their official duties either by or with said Deputies.

Approved, Jan. 19, 1866.

———:o:———

CHAPTER CLVII.

An ACT to amend "An Act concerning costs and fees of Courts, and for other purposes," Approved January 21, 1859.

Sec. 1.—Be it enacted by the Governor and Legislative Assembly of the Territory of Utah: That "An Act concerning costs and fees of courts, and for other purposes," "Approved January 21, 1859," is hereby amended as follows: In the third section all the fees shall be increased one hundred per cent., except those for collecting and paying over monies. In the eighth section all the fees shall be increased one hundred per cent., except the per cent. on sums collected and paid over on executions. In the ninth section the fees shall be increased one hundred per cent.; and in the sixteenth section the fees shall be increased one hundred per cent.

Sec. 2.—This Act shall continue in force but one year from and after February 1, 1866; and sections three, eight, nine and sixteen of said Act are hereby made inoperative until the amendments made in this Act shall expire by limitation, after which time they shall remain in full force and virtue.

Approved January 19, 1866.

———:o:———

CHAPTER CLVIII.

An ACT amending "An Act entitled an Act to incorporate the Weber Cañon Road Company.

Be it enacted by the Governor and Legislative Assembly of the Territory of Utah: That "An Act to incorporate the Weber Cañon Road Company," "approved January

20, 1865," be amended as follows: In the first section, in lieu of William H. Hooper, Horace S. Eldredge and Ben Holladay, of New York," read John W. Hess and Christopher Layton. In the third section, first line, before "any," read, The capital stock shall be fifty thousand dollars, and." In the fifth section, fifth line, in lieu of "by the Company," read, by this act. And in the ninth section, fifth line, in lieu of "ten," read, five.

Approved January 19, 1866.

——:o:——

CHAPTER CLIX.

An ACT amending "An Act prescribing the manner of assessing and collecting Territorial and County Taxes, and for other purposes," "approved January 20, 1865."

Sec. 1.—Be it enacted by the Governor and Legislative Assembly of the Territory of Utah: That "An Act prescribing the manner of assessing and collecting Territorial and County taxes, and for other purposes," "approved January 20, 1865," be amended as follows: In the first section strike out the first proviso, and the word "further" in the second proviso.

Sec. 2.—The second section of said Act is hereby repealed, and the following substituted in its place as Section 2: An annual assessment shall be made on all taxable property in the several Counties of the Territory, between the first day of January and the first Monday in June. Property shall be assessed at a fair cash value, and such assessment, when so made, shall constitute a lien on the property assessed, until such tax is paid, or remitted by the County Court: Provided, That the Assessor and Collector shall assess and collect a tax upon all taxable property brought into this Territory and offered for sale after the assessment list is completed, at the rates of the regular assessment for the current year. And further provided: That where money may have been assessed and afterwards sent outside the Territory for the purchase of merchandize or any articles whatever, then the assessment on the cash value of such merchandize or articles shall be decreased by the amount of such purchase money.

Sec. 3.—The sixth section of said Act, fifth line, is amended by striking out the word "finally;" and in the eight section, third line, strike out the words, "the same" after the word "requiring;" and append to the end of the section the words, the proceeds of such fines to be divided equally between the Territorial and County Treasuries.

Sec. 4.—In section fourteen of said Act, fourteenth line, for "thirty first day of October" read, thirtieth day of November; and at the end of the section strike out the words "not beyond the thirty-first day of December;" and in section fifteen, seventh line, for "thirty-first day of October," read, thirtieth day of November; and at the end of the section strike out the words "in accordance with said notice, or sooner if required by the Collector."

Sec. 5.—Section eighteen of said Act is hereby repealed, and the provisions for taxation in the several city charters are revived and declared to be in full force.

Approved January 19, 1866.

CHAPTER CLX.

An ACT changing the boundaries of Manti City, in Sanpete County.

Sec. 1.—Be it enacted by the Governor and Legislative Assembly of the Territory of Utah: That the boundaries of Manti City Incorporation shall be and are hereby extended as follows, to wit: Commencing at the mouth of Six Mile Creek Cañon, thence west along the south bank of said creek to the base of mountain at its mouth, thence north along the base of West Mountain to Ax-helve Cañon, thence on an easterly line to the northeast corner of Manti meadow, connecting with the southeast corner of Ephraim meadow, thence continuing on an easterly line to where the county road leading from Manti to Ephraim crosses Willow creek, thence along the centre of the channel of said creek to the mouth of the cañon, giving one-half of the waters of said creek to Manti City and the other half to the settlement of Fort Ephraim, thence due south to a parallel line due east of the aforesaid mouth of Six Mile Creek Cañon, thence west to the place of beginning shall, from and after the passage of this Act, be known as the boundaries of Manti City.

Approved January 19, 1866.

———:o:———

CHAPTER CLXI.

An Act to incorporate the Logan Cañon Road Company.

Sec. 1.—Be it enacted by the Governor and Legislative Assembly of the Territory of Utah: That William Hyde, Thomas E. Ricks, William Budge, George L. Farrel and Thomas Tarbitt with their associates and assigns are hereby created a body corporate in law, with succession for fourteen years, to be known by the name and style of the Logan Cañon Road Company; which Company shall have power to sue and be sued and to plead and be impleaded in all Courts having jurisdiction; to receive by gift or purchase and to hold so much real estate and personal property as may be necessary for carrying into effect the provisions of this Act; and to pass, by vote of the stockholders, all needful bye-laws for the government of said Company; and the Company may have and use a common seal, which they may alter at pleasure.

Sec. 2.—The capital stock of said Company shall be fifty thousand dollars, in shares of twenty-five dollars each, which shares shall be assignable and transferable in such manner as may be prescribed in the bye-laws of said Company; and any of the aforementioned persons are hereby authorized, immediately after the passage of this Act, to open books and receive subscriptions to the same, until the Company shall be organized.

Sec. 3.—Within thirty days next after the publication of this Act, the Stockholders shall meet and proceed to organize the Company by electing the following officers: a President, five Directors, a Secretary and a Treasurer, a majority of whom shall form a Board to transact the business of the Company; and they shall hold their office for two years, and until their successors are elected and qualified; and they shall give bonds to the acceptance of the County Court of Cache County, to be filed in the office of the County Clerk, conditioned for the faithful performance of their several duties. Subsequent meetings for the election of officers may be provided for in the bye-laws of said Company; and at every election for Company officers, each Stockholder shall be entitled to one vote for each share of capital stock he holds, and may vote in person or by proxey.

Sec. 4.—It shall be the duty of the President and Directors of said Company to keep or cause to be kept in good repair the road specified in this Act; and they shall have power to fill all vacancies which may occur, in the Board of Directors, by death or otherwise, until the next election of officers; and to appoint such assistants as they may need; to decide the time, manner and proportions in which payments shall be made on shares; and to declare forfeited to the use of the Company the share or shares of any person who shall fail to make any payment so required to be paid, after not less than forty days notice shall have been given; and they shall cause to be issued to each

Stockholder a certificate of the number of shares he holds, signed by the President, countersigned by the Secretary, and sealed with the seal of said Company; and no transfer of stock will be valid, until recorded by the Secretary of said Company.

Sec. 5.—It shall also be the duty of the Company to locate and construct a good wagon road, to the acceptance of the County Court of Cache County, within two years from the publication of this Act, commencing at the present location of William Hyde's carding machine in Logan City, thence up the Logan Cañon to the summit of the range of mountains dividing Cache and Richland Counties; and upon the completion of six miles of said road from the place of beginning, the Company are hereby authorized and empowered to erect a toll gate and take toll thereon, the rates to be specified and regulated by the County Court of Cache County.

Sec. 6.—The Secretary shall keep a record of the transactions of all business, and also an account of the receipts and expenditures of the Company, which shall at all times be open to the inspection of the Stockholders. The President and Board of Directors shall make an annual report to the County Court of Cache County, at its December term, of all receipts and expenditures.

Sec. 7.—The Company shall be liable for all damages to persons and property, which may occur through negligence or failure on their part to comply with the conditions and specifications of this Act, Provided, That, in case of floods or severe storms, the Company shall be allowed a reasonable time to repair damages to the road.

Sec. 8.—Any person forcibly or fraudulently passing the toll gate erected on said road shall, for each offense, be liable to a fine, not exceeding one hundred dollars, and costs, to be prosecuted for in any Court having jurisdiction, by any officer, agent, servant or Stockholder, in the name of said Company.

Sec. 9.—If any person shall obstruct, break, injure or destroy any part of the road of said Company, or any work or fixture attached to or in use upon the same, the person so offending shall, for every such offense, be liable to a civil suit for the recovery of damages by said Company; and shall also be subject to indictment, and, upon conviction, shall be punished by fine not exceeding five hundred dollars, or imprisonment not exceeding six months, or both at the discretion of the Court.

Sec. 10.—The toll gatherer duly authorized by the President and Directors of said Company, may prevent from passing through his gate any person riding, leading or driving animals, and any carriage or other vehicles, until he has received the tolls authorized by the County Court.

Sec. 11.—Nothing shall be so construed in this Act as to prevent the Legislature from altering and amending the same at pleasure.

Approved January 19, 1866.

CHAPTER CLXII.

An ACT providing for the establishment and support of Common Schools.

Sec. 1.—Be it enacted by the Governor and Legislative Assembly of the Territory of Utah: That any School District heretofore established pursuant to any law of this Territory, shall remain as it now exists, until altered as hereinafter provided.

Sec. 2.—The County Courts, at their regular or special sessions, shall divide their respective counties into School Districts, where not already done, and number the same, and prescribe such limits as will promote education and the convenience of the people.

Sec. 3.—The County Courts are hereby empowered to change the boundaries of School Districts, or consolidate two or more into one, if the public good require: Provided, That where School Districts have built school houses by a tax on the whole District, said District shall not be divided, until equitable provision has been made for school houses in the new Districts to be organized. Settlers on or near county lines of two or more counties, may be formed into a School District, by the mutual agreement of the County Courts of such counties.

Sec. 4.—In each School District there shall be three Trustees, residents and householders in their Districts, who shall be elected by a majority of the votes given at a meeting held for that purpose; and shall have power to appoint a Clerk, an Assessor, Collector and Treasurer, who may be of their own number or be selected from citizens of the District.

Sec. 5.—The Trustees now in office, or who shall be elected or appointed, shall qualify, by taking an oath of office and giving bonds to the County Court of the county where they reside, in such sums and with such securities as the Clerk of the County Court may approve, conditioned for the faithful performance of their duties; and shall continue in office for two years, and until their successors are elected and qualified.

Sec. 6.—The Trustees shall be elected by the voters, residents and owners of taxable property in their respective School Districts. For the election of Trustees and for the vote on the rate per cent. on the taxes to be assessed, notice shall be given, at least one week before the time appointed, by notifying each tax-payer, either in person or by leaving a written notice at his residence, of the time, place and object of the meeting; said notice shall be given by at least five permanent residents of the District; but if the District be organized, then said notice shall be given by the Trustees. At such meeting Trustees may be elected or a tax levied viva voce, or by ballot, as the meeting may determine.

Sec. 7.—The Trustees shall provide a suitable school house or school houses and keep the same in repair, for which purpose they are hereby empowered to assess and collect annually a tax on all taxable property within their District, not exceeding one-fourth of one per cent.; should more than one-fourth of one per cent. be needed per annum to build and repair school houses, or for other school purposes, an estimate of the approximate cost thereof shall be made by the Trustees, and the rate may be increased to any sum not exceeding three per cent., as shall be decided by a vote of two-thirds of the tax payers voting at a meeting called for that purpose, which tax shall be levied upon the taxable property in the District; and by a similar vote a tax may be assessed and collected, of any sum not exceeding one per cent. per annum, to pay Teachers and furnish fuel, books, maps and other suitable articles for school purposes. The Trustees shall have power to remit taxes, to prescribe the manner in which schools shall be conducted, to establish out-houses, play grounds and other appurtenances.

Sec. 8.—The Assessor shall, within such time as the Trustees may direct, make an assessment of the taxable property in his District and report the same to the Trustees, and when appealed to, the Trustees shall have power to examine said assessment and, if necessary, correct the same; and their decision shall be final.

Sec. 9.—The Collector shall pay all moneys or property, received on taxes, to the Trustees or to the Treasurer, as the Trustees may direct; and the Assessor, Collector and Treasurer, before entering upon the duties of their office, shall respectively qualify and give bonds, conditioned for the faithful performance of their duties, to the acceptance of the County Court, to be filed with the Clerk of said Court.

Sec. 10.—Whenever taxes shall have been assessed in accordance with this Act and the taxpayers shall have been duly notified of the amount due, the Board of Trustees, or any one of its members, or the qualified Collector, shall have power to commence suits at law, in any Court having jurisdiction, against any taxpayer who shall neglect or refuse to pay said tax, or levy upon and sell his property, as upon executions at law; and any conveyance of such property made by the Trustees shall be valid. There shall be no appeal from any judgment rendered as prescribed in this section, unless the amount exceeds twenty dollars, when sued in the Courts of the Justices of the Peace, or fifty dollars, when sued in the Probate or District Courts.

Sec. 11.—The County Court of each County shall appoint, in their respective counties, where not already done, a Board of Examination, to consist of three competent persons, who shall judge of the qualifications of School Teachers applying for schools; and all applicants of a good moral character, considered competent, shall receive a suitable certificate signed by the Board.

Sec 12.—The Trustees shall visit, officially, each school in their respective districts at least once during each term; and, on or before the second Monday in October in each year, take a census of the children between the ages of four and sixteen years, residing in their Districts; and, within ten days thereafter, shall make a report to the County Superintendent, stating the condition of the school or schools under their supervision, and particularly the items contained in the following form:

FORM FOR SCHOOL TRUSTEES.

Annual Report of School District, No. in the County of, U. T., ending, 186— Trustees.

	No. of district.	No. of schools.	Grade of schools.	Branches taught.	No. of male teachers.	No. of female teachers.	No. of male children in the district between the ages of 4 and 16 years.	No. of female children in the district between the ages of 4 and 16 years.	No. of male scholars enrolled.	No. of female scholars enrolled.	Average daily attendance.	Amount paid to teachers.	To male.	To female.	No. of months schools have been taught during the year.	No. of school libraries.	No. of volumes in each.	Present condition of school buildings, &c.	Amount of building funds raised.	Amount of taxes appropriated to the use of schools.	REMARKS

Sec. 13.—Teachers of schools shall furnish their respective Trustees with a quarterly report of their schools, in the following form:

FORM OF SCHOOL TEACHER'S REPORT.

Quarterly Report of School No. , District No. , County of , U. T., ending , 186—. Teacher.

NAMES OF PUPILS	Age.	Total number of males.	Total number of females.	Daily attendance.	Average daily attendance.	BRANCHES TAUGHT.																SCHOOL BOOKS USED	CERTIFICATE AND REMARKS
						Alphabet.	Spelling.	Reading.	Writing.	Geography.	Grammar.	Arithmetic.	Book-keeping.	Algebra.	Geometry.	Astronomy.	History.	Languages.	Music.	Drawing.	Painting.		

Sec. 14.—There shall be elected annually, by a vote of the Legislative Assembly of the Territory of Utah, a Superintendent of Common Schools for said Territory; and said Superintendent shall make his report annually to the Legislative Assembly, during the first week of its session; before entering upon the duties of his office, he shall qualify, by taking and subscribing an oath to faithfully perform the duties of his office.

Sec. 15.—The Territorial Superintendent shall keep a record of the condition of common schools throughout this Terrritory, as reported to him by the County Superintendents; and he shall furnish each County Superintendent with a blank record headed according to form for Trustees' reports, and also forms of said reports, together with forms of School Teachers' reports, as contemplated in this Act; and he shall cause to be printed such a number of blanks, after the forms described in this Act, as will be necessary for distribution to the Trustees and Teachers throughout the Territory, and distribute the same.

Sec. 16.—The Territorial and County Superintendents shall decide what text books shall be adopted in the schools; and the County Superintendents, with the Trustees in their respective Districts, may regulate in their respective counties the school terms, allowing such holidays and vacations as may be advisable.

Sec. 17.--At the general election held on the first Monday of August, each county shall elect, for the term of two years, a County Superintendent of Common Schools, who shall hold his office until his successor is elected and qualified; and he shall qualify, by taking and subscribing an oath to faithfully perform the duties of his office.

Sec. 18.—The duties of the County Superintendent shall be: First, to take the general supervision of schools in his county, and visit officially, at least once in each year, the schools under his supervision, and see that the School Trustees are diligent in the discharge of their duties: Second, to superintend, in the manner and to the extent to be prescribed by law, all business matters connected with Public School Domain within his jurisdiction: Third, to keep a correct account, with the County Treasurer and with the Trustees of School Districts, of all funds received or disbursed for school purposes, arising from the General Government or by Legislative enactment of the Territory: Fourth, to audit all school accounts against the County Treasury, and deliver his warrants for the payment thereof: Fifth, to make an annual report to the Territorial Superintendent of Common schools, on or before the first Monday in November in each year, and said report shall be in the following form:

FORM FOR COUNTY SUPERINTENDENTS.

Annual report of County, ending first Monday in November, 188—. County Superintendent.

NAMES OF DISTRICTS.	No. of Districts in county.	No. of Districts reported.	No. of schools.	Grade of schools.	No. of male Teachers.	No. of female Teachers.	No. of boys in county between 4 and 16 years.	No. of girls in county between 4 and 16 years.	Total children between 4 and 16 years.	No. of male scholars enrolled.	No. of female scholars enrolled.	Total enrolled.	Per centage of names enrolled.	Average daily attendance.	Per centage of school population actually attending school.	Amount paid to male Teachers.	Amount paid to female Teachers.	Total paid to Teachers.	No. of months schools have been taught during the year.	Present condition of school buildings.	Amount of building funds raised.	Amount of taxes appropriated to the use of schools.	REMARKS.

Sec. 19.—The County Superintendent shall enter in his records every official return made to him by School Trustees and Teachers, and keep the same in his office, subject to the inspection of the Territorial Superintendent and the County Court of his County.

Sec. 20.—A majority of the Board of Trustees shall have power to transact business; and in case of a vacancy in the Board in any School District, by death, resignation or otherwise, the remaining Trustees shall have power to fill such vacancy, until the next general election.

Sec. 21.—The Territorial Superintendent of Common Schools is hereby authorized and required to proceed against all delinquent parties, on their bonds, who fail to pay the per centage to common schools prescribed by their grants or charters; and the said Superintendent shall pay all moneys obtained under the provisions of this Act to the Territorial Treasurer, and annually report his doings to the Legislative Assembly.

Sec. 22.—Nothing in this act shall be so construed as to interfere with any assessment heretoforemade or contract entered into by parties under the former law, or suits pending that have originated under any former Acts of this Legislature.

Sec. 23.—"An Act authorizing the Territorial Superintendent of Common Schools to collect certain moneys," "approved Dec. 20, 1864," and any provision in "An Act consolidating and amending the school laws," "approved Jan. 18, 1865," conflicting with this Act, are hereby repealed.

Approved Jan. 19, 1866.

——:o:——

CHAPTER CLXIII.

An ACT establishing a Territorial Road from Great Salt Lake City to Wanship, Summit County.

Sec. 1.—Be it enacted by the Governor and Legislative Assembly of the Territory of Utah: That the sum of six thousand dollars be and is hereby appropriated, to be drawn and expended by the Territorial Road Commissioner on the Territorial road leading from Great Salt Lake City, via Big Cañon creek, over the summit of the Wasatch range of mountains to Parley's Park and across East Cañon creek near Ferguson's settlement, thence through Parley's Park to Kimball's ranch, thence over the Summit and down Silver Creek Cañon to Wanship, Summit County.

Sec. 2.—The said road, when completed, shall be twenty feet wide, where practicable, and is hereby divided into four Sections; that part of the road lying between Charles Decker's residence and Hardy's station to be the First Section; from Hardy's station to the crossing of East Cañon creek, near Ferguson's settlement, the Second Section; from the crossing of East Cañon creek to the summit of the divide between East Cañon and Silver creeks, the Third Section; and from the divide to Wanship, Summit County, the Fourth Section.

Sec. 3.—The Territorial Road Commissioner is hereby authorized and required to proceed, as soon as practicable, to examine the route herein contemplated and direct the expenditure of the said six thousand dollars; and upon the completion of said road or any Section thereof, he is further authorized and empowered to erect not exceeding one toll-gate to the Section, and for each Section to demand and receive not exceeding the following rates of toll; For any vehicle drawn by one or two animals, twenty-five cents; for each additional pair of animals, fifteen cents; for every horse or mule and rider or led horse or mule, ten cents; for every score of meat cattle, loose horses or mules, fifty cents; for every score of sheep, twenty-five cents: Provided, that persons hauling fuel or produce from within sixty miles of Great Salt Lake City shall pay but one way, being entitled to a return ticket free; and that no traveler shall be compelled to pay toll for a greater distance than one Section of the road at any one toll-gate.

Sec. 4.—The said Road Commissioner is further authorized to appoint a Superintendent for said road and the necessary toll gatherers, for whose acts he shall require sufficient bonds filed with the Clerk of the Probate Court of Great Salt Lake County, conditioned for the faithful performance of the duties of their offices.

Sec. 5.—The said Superintendent shall keep an accurate account of all receipts and disbursements by him made, and report the same through the Territorial Road Commissioner, to the Legislative Assembly annually, during the first week of its session.

Sec. 6.—The toll herein contemplated shall be expended by said Superintendent, under the direction of the Road Commissioner, in making, repairing, and other incidental expenses of said road.

Sec. 7.—The present road is hereby divided into four sections, in the same manner as provided for the new road in the second section of this Act, except that for the "crossing of East Cañon creek, near Ferguson's settlement," in the second and third sections of the road, read Ferguson's settlement, and it shall be the duty of the Territorial Road Superintendent, within eight months from and after the approval of this Act, to put the present traveled road in good repair, from Charles Decker's residence on Big Cañon creek, to Wanship in Summit County; to establish toll-gates, and demand and collect not to exceed the rates of toll prescribed in the third section of this act.

Sec. 8.—The Superintendent shall keep a person constantly on duty at each toll-gate between the hours of six a.m. and nine p.m., and from the hours of nine p.m. to six a.m. travelers shall be delayed only a reasonable time.

Sec. 9.—Any person forcibly or fraudulently passing any toll-gate erected on said road shall, for each offence, be liable to a fine not exceeding one hundred dollars and costs, to be prosecuted for in any Court having jurisdiction by any officer or agent thereof in the name of the people of the Territory.

Sec. 10.—If any person shall obstruct, break, injure or destroy any part of the said road or any work or fixture attached to or in use upon the same, the person so offending shall, for every such offense, be liable to a civil suit for the recovery of damages, and shall also be subject to indictment, and upon conviction, shall be punished by fine not exceeding five hundred dollars or imprisonment not exceeding six months, or both, at the discretion of the Court.

Sec. 11.—Each toll-gatherer, duly authorized by the Road Commissioner, may detain and prevent from passing through his gate any person riding, leading or driving animals, and any carriage or other vehicles, until he has received the tolls authorized by this Act.

Sec. 12.—Any captain, proprietor, agent, wagon-master or teamster in charge of any train, wagon or wagons obstructing the common travel on said road by camping therein, or otherwise unnecessarily causing delay, shall be liable to a fine of not more than five hundred dollars, and be liable for all damages and costs, at the discretion of any Court having jurisdiction, which fines shall be paid into the Territorial Treasury, subject to the order of the Territorial Road Commissioner to be expended on said road:

Sec. 13.—Nothing shall be so construed in this Act as to prevent the Legislature from altering and amending the same at pleasure.

Approved January 19, 1866.

——:o:——

CHAPTER CLXIV.

Territorial Appropriation Bill.

Sec. 1.—Be it enacted by the Governor and Legislative Assembly of the Territory of Utah: That there be paid, out of any money in the Territorial Treasury not otherwise appropriated, the following amounts, viz:—

To William Clayton, for services for the year 1865, as Auditor of Public Accounts, four hundred dollars,........	$400 00
To David O. Calder, for services for the year 1865, as Territorial Treasurer, four hundred dollars,........	400 00
To Theodore McKean, for services as Territorial Road Commissioner for the year 1865, four hundred dollars; for books and stationery, ten dollars,........	410 00
To J. D. T. McAllister, for services rendered as Territorial Marshal, also for fuel and stationery furnished,........	496 90
To J. D. T. McAllister, for rent of rooms and fuel furnished for the Third District Court, five hundred and sixty dollars,........	560 00
To Franklin B. Woolley, for services rendered as Deputy Territorial Marshal,........	13 00
To William Clayton, Recorder of Marks and Brands, to supply deficiency and print brand sheets,........	300 00
To Auditor's Office, to close an account towards paying for the secretary in the Office,........	14 00
To Seth M. Blair, for four years' services as Territorial Attorney-General,......	200 00

To Seth M. Blair, for services as Territorial Attorney-General in the year 1865,	$50 00
To Patrick Lynch, for services as Clerk of the Third Judicial District, one hundred and fifty-two dollars and seventy-five cents	152 75
To Jesse W. Fox, for assistance rendered the Territorial Road Commissioner, ten dollars,	10 00
To Jesse W. Fox, for drawing new plots and maps of Great Salt Lake, Tooele, Davis, Weber, Box Elder and Cache counties,	500 00
For rent of office for the Attorney-General, Territorial Marshal and Clerk of the Third Judicial District, for the years 1864 and 1865, one hundred dollars each,	300 00
To enable the Territorial Librarian to purchase a few works and to replace missing volumes, with the amount appropriated for the binding of books by the Legislative Assembly of 1864–5, one hundred and fifty dollars,	150 00
To R. V. Morris, for services as Clerk after close of last Session, fifteen dollars,	15 00
To reimburse Archibald Gardner for material furnished to build a bridge across Jordan river in Great Salt Lake county, nine hundred and twenty-eight dollars and forty-eight cents,	928 48
To reimburse Edward Stratton, of Weber County, for a part of his farm used for the Territorial Road, one hundred and fifty dollars,	150 00
To reimburse John Taylor for team-work and rock to secure the Weber bridge, Weber County, four hundred and three dollars and seventy-nine cents,	403 79
To cover amounts overdrawn by the Territorial Road Commissioner for labor on Great Salt Lake and Weber road, sixty dollars,	60 00
To pay the Warden for convict labor, seventy-four dollars and fifty cents,	74 50
For roads in Washington County, three hundred and sixty-eight dollars and eighty-three cents,	368 83
To cover amounts unappropriated, for which the Auditor has issued warrants, for repairing and changing the road between Tokerville, Washington County, and Grafton, Kane County, one thousand dollars,	1,000 00
On account of roads, sixteen dollars and six cents, drawn by Territorial Road Commissioner,	16 06
On account of secretary for Surveyor-General's Office, forty-five dollars and forty cents,	45 40
For stationery for Auditor's Office, 1865, eighty dollars,	80 00
For stationery for Auditor's Office, 1866, sixty-seven dollars and twenty-five cents,	67 25
For printing and binding order book for Auditor's Office, ten dollars,	10 00
For services of John Kay as Deputy Marshal, thirty dollars,	30 00
For services of John Sharp as Deputy Marshal, thirty dollars,	30 00
For a secretary for the Auditor's Office, one hundred and thirty-six dollars,	136 00
To defray expenses of the Penitentiary for the year 1866, two thousand dollars,	2,000 00
To be expended on the road from St. George to old Fort Harmony, Washington County,	800 00
On the road from St. George to Cedar City, by way of Pine Valley,	1,200 00
To make a road between St. George and the settlements on the Lower Muddy, by way of the Beaver Dam Wash,	800 00
To make roads in Kane county, to be expended under the direction of the County Court	1,200 00
To make a road from Circleville, in Piute county, up the west fork of the Sevier river, to the mouth of Bear creek, thence up Bear Creek Cañon and down Little creek to Little Salt Lake Valley, eight hundred dollars,	800 00
To make a road over the mountain dividing Sevier and Piute Counties, one thousand dollars,	1,000,00
To improve the Territorial Road over the Sevier mountain, between the Sevier bridge and Cedar Springs, one hundred and sixty dollars,	160,00
To be expended on the road between Gunnison and Manti, Sanpete County, four hundred dollars	400,00
To repair the road in Salt Creek Cañon, Juab County; two hundred and forty dollars	240,00
To be expended on the road in Lower Salt Creek Cañon, Juab county, two hundred and forty dollars	240,00
To assist Utah county in building a bridge across the northwest branch of Provo river, Utah county, eight hundred dollars,	800,00
To be expended on the road around the point of the mountain in Great Salt Lake and Utah counties, eight hundred dollars,	800,00

To be expended on the road between Great Salt Lake City and the valley of the Weber, via Big Cañon creek, six thousand dollars, being the amount incorporated in an Act establishing a Territorial Toll Road from Great Salt Lake City to Wanship, Summit county,............ 6,000,00

To improve the road in Chalk Creek Cañon, Summit county, when the citizens or others expend a similar amount, eight hundred dollars,............ 800,00

To improve and Protect the Territorial Road running west from Jordan bridge, Great Salt Lake county, one thousand six hundred dollars, ... 1600,00

To improve North Temple Street, Great Salt Lake city, two thousand four hundred dollars, to be drawn and expended under the direction of the Mayor of Great Salt Lake City, ... 2,400,00

To improve the State Road running south of Great Salt Lake City Corporation, eight hundred dollars,............ 800,00

To secure the abutments, and turnpike and levee on the west side of the Weber bridge, Weber county, eight hundred dollars, ... 800,00

To assist in building a bridge across Ogden river, on the Territorial Road in Weber county, three thousand dollars,............ 3,000,00

To improve the Territorial road north of Brigham City, Box Elder county, four hundred dollars,............ 400,00

To be expended on the road from Huntsville, Weber county, to Ithica, Richland county, two thousand dollars, ... 2,000,00

To the Territorial Road Commissioner, for a contingent fund, one thousand two hundred dollars, ... 1,200,00

To provide and furnish an Office for the Adjutant General, with furniture, books, stationary, blanks, reports and whatever may be necessary, to be drawn on the order of the Lieutenant General, three thousand dollars,...... 3,000,00

To be expended on the road from Ogden Valley to Paradise, in Cache Valley, one hundred and twenty dollars, ... 120,00

To Orson Hyde, for moneys expended in running the boundary line between Utah and California, in 1855, and to compensate him for three months services in running said line, five hundred dollars, ... 500,00

To Thomas Bullock, for postal map of Utah and Memorial with accompanying schedules, &c., fifty dollars, ... 50,00

To A. P. Rookwood, Warden of the Penitentiary, for his services for 1865, twelve hundred dollars 1,200

To making a dugway from Glenwood to Selina, under the direction of the County Court of Sevier county, eight hundred dollars,............ 800,00

The following sums, to be drawn on the order of the the Territorial Superintendent of Common Schools: For services, for the year 1865, two hundred and fifty dollars, ... 250,00

To enable said Superintendent to visit the County Superintendents and advise with them in relation to school interests, statistics, &c., in 1866, two hundred and fifty dollars, ... 250,00

For forms for Teachers, Trustees and County Superintendents, fifty dollars ... 50,00

To. R. V. Morris, for fourteen days services as Engrossing Clerk to the Council during its present session, forty two dollars,............ 42,00

To repairing bridges on the Blacksmith Fork, and making roads through the Logan bottoms, sixteen hundred dollars, ... 1,600,00

To assist Spanish Fork, Pondtown and Payson to build a bridge across the Spanish Fork; fifteen hundred dollars, ... 1,500,00

To open a road from St. George to Panacca, Meadow Valley, eight hundred dollars, ... 800,00

To assist Springville to pay for building a bridge across Hobble creek, two hundred and forty dollars,............ 240,00

To be drawn on the order of Joseph F. Smith, for services of Engrossing Clerk for the House, eighty-eight dollars, ... 88,00

To Warren S. Snow, to reimburse him for services rendered the Territory, two hundred and fifty dollars, ... 250,00

To R. V. Morris, for twenty-four days services as Clerk of the Committee of Revision and Compilation, seventy-two dollars, ... 72,00

All sums herein appropriated to be expended on roads and bridges, shall be drawn and expended under the direction of the Territorial Road Commissioner, where other provision has not been made.

Approved January 19, 1866.

CHAPTER CLXV.

An ACT to provide for Printing and Distributing the Digest of Laws and the Laws and Journals of the Fifteenth Annual Session of the Legislative Assembly.

Be it enacted by the Governor and Legislative Assembly of the Territory of Utah: That the Public Printer for this Legislative Assembly is hereby authorized and required to print and publish, in book form, three thousand copies of the Digest of Laws as prepared and reported by the Joint Committee on Revision and Compilation, together with the Acts, Resolutions and Memorials passed and adopted during this Fifteenth Annual Session of said Assembly, with Index; and five hundred copies of the Journals in pamphlet form, including the Governor's Message and reports of the Treasurer, Auditor, Superintendent of Schools and Directors of Penitentiary, with such other matter, as has been or may be ordered to be included of this the Fifteenth Annual Session of the Legislative Assembly; and the Secretary of the Territory is hereby required to furnish the President of the United States and each of his Cabinet, the President of the Senate, the Speaker of the House of Representatives and the Governor of each State and Territory of the United States with one copy each of the Laws and Journals, and the Governor of Utah with five copies each; one copy of the Laws and Journals to each Member and Officer of the present Legislative Assembly; one copy of the Laws to the Judges and Clerks of the Supreme, District and Probate Courts, to the United States and Territorial Marshals, to the United States District Attorney and Attorney-General, and to each additional civil officer in the Territory, including the Mayor, Aldermen, Recorder and Marshal for each Incorporated City; one copy of the Laws to the Commandant of the Nauvoo Legion, the Commandants of each Division, Brigade, Regiment, Battalion and Company, also to their Adjutants and respecteve Staff Officers, and two copies of the Laws and Journals to each public Library in the Territory.

Approved January 19, 1866.

———:o:———

CHAPTER CLXVI.

An ACT prescribing the term of certain Officers, and designating where their bonds shall be filed.

Sec. 1.—Be it enacted by the Governor and Legislative Assembly of the Territory of Utah: That the term of all officers made elective by joint vote of the Legislative Assembly, including the officers elected during the present session, shall be four years, and until their successors are elected and qualified, unless sooner superseded by Legislative election; and shall give bonds, with approved security, to the acceptance of the Auditor of Public Accounts, which bonds shall be filed in his office: Provided, that the Auditor of Public Accounts shall give his bonds, with approved security, to the acceptance of the Probate Judge of Great Salt Lake County, to be filed in his office.

Sec. 2.—All county and precinct officers made elective at the general election, who are required by law to file bonds, shall give bonds with approved security, to the acceptance of the Probate Judge of their respective counties, which shall be filed in his office.

Sec. 3.—All laws or parts of laws conflicting with this Act are hereby repealed.

Approved January 19, 1866.

CHAPTER CLXVII.

An ACT to amend "an act to incorporate the Ogden Cañon Road Company," "approved January, 20, 1865."

Sec. 1.—Be it enacted by the Governor and Legislative Assembly of the Territory of Utah: That the means yet undrawn by said Company shall become capital stock, subject to be increased to fifty thousand dollars. Each share shall be transferable only on the Company's books, in such a manner as the bye-laws shall regulate.
Approved January 19, 1866.

———:o:———

CHAPTER CLXVIII.

Am ACT to more clearly authorize the Surveyor General to give certificates of his surveys, and to further legalize the certificates he has given.

Sec. 1.—Be it enacted by the Governor and Legislative Assembly of the Territory of Utah: That the Surveyor General is hereby authorized and required to give, to the person for whom he makes a survey, a certificate thereof, describing the tract, block, or lot, and specifying its area; and such certificate shall be title of possession to the person holding it.
Sec. 2.—Certificates of surveys, given by the Surveyor General, previous to this Act taking effect, are hereby made valid.
Approved January 19, 1866.

———:o:———

CHAPTER CLXIX.

RESOLUTION authorizing the Deseret Agricultural and Manufacturing Society to collect statistics.

Be it resolved by the Governor and Legislative Assembly of the Territory of Utah: That the President and Board of Directors of the Deseret Agricultural and Manufacturing Society are hereby authorized and required to collect, during the year 1866, agricultural, horticultural and irrigation statistics of the settlements in this Territory, and report to the Legislative Assembly during the first week of its next annual session.
Approved January 17, 1866.

———:o:———

CHAPTER CLXX.

RESOLUTION authorizing the Auditor to close certain accounts.

Whereas there are certain accounts standing open on the Auditor's books, amounting, in the aggregate, to nine thousand three hundred and eighty dollars and seventy-two cents, where auditors warrants were issued, during 1854 and following years, to pay expense of State House, Territorial Library, public roads, &c., which have not heretofore been provided for by Legislative action:

Therefore, Be it resolved by the Governor and Legislative Assembly of the Territory of Utah: That the Auditor of Public Accounts be hereby authorized and instructed to settle with parties interested, and to enter credits to correspond with the footing of each and every open account embraced in the said aggregate of nine thousand three hundred and eighty dollars and seventy-two cents.

Approved January 19, 1866.

——:o:——

CHAPTER CLXXI.

RESOLUTION to cancel the account against Alexander McRae.

Be it resolved by the Governor and Legislative Assembly of the Territory of Utah: That the Directors of the Penitentiary are hereby authorized to cancel the account against Alexander McRae, of one hundred and fifty-two dollars.

Approved January 19, 1866.

——:o:——

CHAPTER CLXXII.

RESOLUTION concerning the Sixteenth Annual Session of the Legislative Assembly.

Resolved by the Governor and Legislative Assembly of the Territory of Utah: That the next annual session of the Legislative Assembly shall convene in the State House (commonly called Council House) in Great Salt Lake City, and that said session shall begin at one o'clock p.m. of the second Monday in December next.

Approved January 19, 1866.

——:o:——

CHAPTER CLXXIII.

RESOLUTION pertaining to the Penitentiary.

Sec. 1.—Be it resolved by the Legislative Assembly of the Territory of Utah: That it shall be the duty of the Directors of the Penitentiary to ascertain where land can be purchased, at some point in Great Salt Lake City, suitable for a site to erect a Penitentiary building thereon, and make conditional contract therefor.

Sec. 2.—The said Directors shall employ a competent Architect, to prepare plans and specifications for the said Penitentiary building; and, having decided upon the plan for said building, shall thereupon advertise, at least five consecutive weeks, for sealed proposals for the erection of said Prison upon such plan, in the *Deseret News* and *Telegraph* printed in Great Salt Lake City; and all proposals received by the said

Directors shall be returned, under seal, to the next Legislative Assembly, during the first week of its session, with the plan of said building, stating where such site can be located, the price therefor, together with a bill of expenses accrued in carrying into effect the requirements of the foregoing, which expenses, properly certified by said Directors, shall be paid out of the Territorial funds.

Approved January 19, 1866.

———:o:———

CHAPTER CLXXIV.

RESOLUTION concerning an appropriation for Weber Cañon Road.

Be it resolved by the Governor and Legislative Assembly of the Territory of Utah: That the Territorial Road Commissioner is authorized to expend the fifteen hundred dollars that was appropriated to be expended on the road in Lower Weber Cañon, "approved January 22, 1864," in assisting to build a bridge across the Weber river, at or near Weber city, in Morgan county.

Approved January 19, 1866.

———:o:———

CHAPTER CLXXV.

MEMORIAL to Congress for the establishment of certain Mail Routes.

To the Honorable the Senate and House of Representatives of the United States, in Congress assembled:

Gentlemen:—Your Memorialists, the Governor and Legislative Assembly of the Territory of Utah, respectfully ask your Honorable Body to establish a mail route from Gunnison, Sanpete county, via Salina, Glenwood, Richfield, County Seat of Sevier county, Alma, Marysville, Circleville, County Seat of Piute county, Pangwitch, Berryville, Wanab, Pipe Spring, Short Creek, Grafton, Gould and Washington, to St. George, the County Seat of Washington county, a distance of about two hundred and sixty miles; also a route from St. George, Washington county, via Santa Clara, Clover Valley, Meadow Valley and Pannacca, to Pahranuaget, a distance of about one hundred and forty miles; also a route from Kanarra, in Iron county, to Harmony, in Washington county, distance ten miles; also a route from Huntsville, in Weber county, via Ithica, Swan Creek, Fish-haven, St. Charles, County Seat of Richland county, Bloomington, Paris, Ovid, Liberty and Montpelier to Bennington, in Richland county, a distance of one hundred and thirty miles; also a route from Logan, County Seat of Cache county, via Clarkston to Weston, distance twenty-eight miles; also a route from Franklin, Cache county, to Oxford, distance twenty-five miles.

The rapidly increasing population of these settlements, extreme portions of our Territory, urges us to solicit your early and favorable action on this our Memorial, and, as in duty bound, your Memorialists will ever pray.

GEORGE A. SMITH, President of the Council.
JOHN TAYLOR, Speaker of the House of Representatives.
CHARLES DURKEE, Governor.

CHAPTER CLXXVI.

MEMORIAL to Congress for an appropriation to increase the Territorial Library.

To the Honorable, the Senate and House of Representatives of the United States, in Congress assembled:

Your memorialists, the Governor and Legislative Assembly of the Territory of Utah, respectfully represent that:

Whereas, your honorable body did, in the year eighteen hundred and fifty, appropriate five thousand dollars, for the purchase of a Library for the use of the Federal and Territorial officers and inhabitants of this Territory; and

Whereas, that sum was expended and the basis of a good and valuable Library was obtained; and

Whereas, during the fifteen years which have elapsed said appropriation was expended, many standard works on almost every branch of knowledge have been published, which are necessary for reference, and the want of which is greatly felt:

Therefore, we, your memorialists, respectfully pray your honorable body to appropriate the further sum of ten thousand dollars for the extension of said Library, to be expended, by our Delegate in Congress, in procuring the latest and most reliable standard works as will be useful for purposes of reference and improvement, and such productions of art and science as will aid in the progress of enlightenment in the Territory of Utah. And your memorialists, as in duty bound, will ever pray.

GEORGE A. SMITH, President of the Council.
JOHN TAYLOR, Speaker of the House of Rep's.

CHARLES DURKEE, Governor.

———:o:———

CHAPTER CLXXVII.

MEMORIAL to the Hon. James Harlan, Secretary of the Interior.

Your Memorialists, the Governor and Legislative Assembly of the Territory of Utah, would respectfully represent that the Indian Reservation, on Corn creek, in Millard county, and on Twelve Mile creek, in the county of Sanpete, located by Indian Agent Dr. Garland Hurt, previous to the development of any settlements in their immediate vicinity, have by recent alterations and extension of their lines, been made to embrace the following named settlements: Petersburg and Meadow Creek, in Millard county, and Gunnison and Warm Creek, in the county of Sanpete, together with their farms, gardens and orchards, all of which are situated on lands redeemed from their desert condition through the industry of the hardy pioneers, by artificial irrigation.

Your memorialists would further represent that, in consequence of the before mentioned extension of the lines of reservation, and the lands they embrace being surveyed and exposed for sale in a manner that precludes the possessors of said lands from availing themselves of the right of pre-emption, or the advantages of the homestead law, great injustice is done to the citizens whose interests are involved in the transaction:

Therefore, your Memorialists would respectfully ask your Honor to institute such action as you may of right do, to counteract the injustice of the before mentioned encroachments upon the rights of the parties aggrieved, and thus open to them all the privileges that the Parent Government has so beneficently extended to its citizens. And, as in duty bound, your Memorialists will ever pray.

GEORGE A. SMITH, President of the Council.
JOHN TAYLOR, Speaker of the House of Rep's.

CHARLES DURKEE, Governor.

CHAPTER CLXXVIII.

MEMORIAL to the Honorable William Dennison, Postmaster General.

Your Memorialists, the Governor and Legislative Assembly of the Territory of Utah, in view of the rapid development of settlements in the northern and southern portions of this Territory, and a corresponding increase and extent of business relations, would respectfully ask for increase and change of mail service, as named in this memorial: From Great Salt Lake City, in Great Salt Lake county, to St. George in Washington county, a tri-weekly service, a distance of 330 miles, via Fort Union and Drapersville in Great Salt Lake county, and Lehi, American Fork, Pleasant Grove, Provo, Springville, Spanish Fork, Payson and Santaquin, in Utah county, Mona, Nephi, and Chicken Creek, in Juab County, and Scipio, Cedar Springs, Fillmore, Meadow Creek, Petersburg and Cove Creek, in Millard county, and Pine Creek, Indian Creek and Beaver, in Beaver county, Paragoona, Parowan; Summit Creek, Cedar City, Kanarra, in Iron county, Tokerville, Harrisburg, Washington, Middleton and St. George, County Seat of Washington county.

Your Memorialists ask for a weekly instead of a semi-monthly service on the route between St. George and Los Angelos, California, via Millersburg and St. Joseph to St. Thomas on the Muddy, distance 100 miles; mail to leave St. George, Thursday, 7 o'clock a. m.

Also on the following new routes we need weekly service: From St. George, via Santa Clara, Clover Valley and Pannacca, to Pahranagat, distance 140 miles; mail to leave St. George, Thursday at 6 o'clock a. m., and Pahranagat, Monday, 6 a. m.

Also weekly service from Logan, in Cache county, via Clarkston, to Weston, distance twenty-eight miles; and from Franklin, Cache county, to Oxford, distance twenty-five miles; to leave Logan on Saturday, at seven o'clock a.m., to arrive at Clarkston at one o'clock p.m., thence to Weston, to arrive at five o'clock p.m., same day; to leave Weston at seven o'clock a.m., on Sunday, each week, via Clarkston, to arrive at Logan at five o'clock p.m., same day; to leave Franklin at seven o'clock a.m., on Sunday, each week, to arrive at Oxford at five o'clock, same day; to leave Oxford at seven o'clock a.m., Monday, each week, to arrive at Franklin at five o'clock p.m., same day.

Also semi-weekly service on route from Gunnison, in Sanpete county, via Salina, Glenwood, Richfield, County Seat of Sevier county, Alma, Marysvale, Circleville, County Seat of Piute county, Pangwitch, Berryville, Kanab, Pipe Spring, Shirt Creek, Grafton, County Seat of Kane county, Duncan, Dalton, Virgen City and Baker's Spring and Washington, to St. George, 275 miles; mail to leave Gunnison and St. George every Monday and Thursday, at six a.m.

Also semi-weekly mail from Nephi, Juab county, to Manti, Sanpete county, via Fountain Green, Moroni and Ephraim, to Manti, 43 miles, leaving Nephi every Wednesday and Saturday, at six a.m.; and to leave Manti every Thursday and Monday at six a.m.

Also semi-weekly service to be put upon the route from Huntsville, in Weber county, via Ithica, Swan Creek, Fish-haven, St. Charles, Bloomington, Paris, Liberty, Ovid, Montpelier and Bennington, in Richland county.

For Postmasters on said routes the following names are suggested:

For Ithica,............................Joseph Moore.
" Swan Creek,..................Phineas W. Cook.
" Fish-haven, ...Preston Thomas.
" St. Charles,....................Richard R. Hopkins.
" Bloomington, ...James H. Hart.
" Paris,.............................Joseph C. Rich.
" Liberty, ...Solomon Hale.
" Ovid, ...Neils Ch. Edlefsen.
" Montpelier,.......................Morris Phelps.
" Bennington,.......................Edward Merrill.

Your prompt and kind consideration of the subject matter of the foregoing Memorial is most respectfully solicited, and, as in duty bound, your Memorialists will ever pray.

GEORGE A. SMITH, President of the Council.
JOHN TAYLOR, Speaker of the House of Representatives.
CHARLES DURKEE, Governor.

CHAPTER CLXXIX.

MEMORIAL to Congress for a donation of Town Sites, in aid of a Common School Fund.

To the Honorable the Senate and House of Representatives of the United States, in Congress assembled:

Your Memorialists, the Governor and Legislative Assembly of the Territory of Utah, respectfully pray your Honorable Body to donate to this Territory the lands included in the recorded plots of the several Cities, Towns, and Villages of this Territory, to aid in laying the foundation for a Common School Fund for the benefit of the Territory and future State; said lands to be disposed of under such regulations as the Legislature may provide.

GEORGE A. SMITH, President of the Council.
JOHN TAYLOR, Speaker of the House of Representatives.
CHARLES DURKEE, Governor.

---:o:---

CHAPTER CLXXX.

MEMORIAL to Congress for appropriations for Roads.

To the Honorable the Senate and House of Representatives of the United States, in Congress assembled.

Your Memorialists, the Governor and Legislative Assembly of the Territory, of Utah in view of the great increase of trafic between the Rocky Mountain Territories and the States east and west, respectfully ask your Honorable Body to appropriate one hundred thousand dollars, for making a good wagon road and brirdging streams between the Missouri River and Great Salt Lake City.

Also fifty thousand dollars, for making a good wagon road between Great Salt Lake City and Callville, the head of navigation on the Colorado River.

GEORGE A. SMITH, President of the Council.
JOHN TAYLOR, Speaker of the House of Rep's.
CHARLER DURKEE, Governor.

FORMS.

---:o:---

1.—*Certificate of acknowledgement by party known to the Officer.*

County, ss.

On this day of , in the year of our Lord one thousand eight hundred and , before me personally came A. B., to me known to be the individual described in, and who executed the within [or, above, or, annexed,] conveyance [or, bond, or, letter of attorney, or, instrument in writing,] and acknowledged that he executed the same, for the purposes therein mentioned.

[To be here officially signed by officer.]

---:o:---

2.—*Certificate by husband and wife known to the Officer.*

County, ss.

On this day of , &c., before me personally came A. B. and Mary his wife, to me known to be the individuals described in, and who executed the within conveyance, [or, above, or, annexed letter of attorney, or, other instrument in writing,] and acknowledged that they executed the same; and the said Mary acknowledged, in a private conversation with me had, apart from her husband, that she executed the said conveyance [or, other instrument] freely, and without any fear or compulsion from him.

[To be here officially signed by officer.]

---:o:---

3.—*General form of agreement—damages fixed.*

This agreement made the day of , A. D., one thousand eight hundred and , by and between A. B. of the town of , in the county of , of the first part, and C. D., of , of the second part, witnesseth: The said party of the second part covenants and agrees, to and with the party of the first part, to [here state the subject matter of agreement.] And the said party of the first part covenants and agrees to pay unto the said party of the second part, for the same, the sum of dollars, lawful money of the United States, as follows: the sum of dollars, on the day of , 18 , and the sum of dollars, on the day of , 18 , with the interest on the amount due, payable at the time of each payment.

And for the true and faithful performance of all and every of the covenants and agreements above mentioned, the parties to these presents bind themselves, each unto the other, in the penal sum of dollars, as fixed and settled damages, to be paid by the failing party.

In witness whereof the parties to these presents have hereunto set their hands and seals, the day and year first above written.

Signed, sealed and delivered in the presence of
E. F.
G. H.

A. B. [L. S.]
C. D. [L. S.]

———:o:———

4. *Agreement to cultivate land on shares.*

This agreement, made the day of, (&c.), between A. B., of, (&c.), and C. D. of, (&c.), witnesseth: That the said A. B. agrees that he will break up, properly prepare, and sow with wheat, all that field belonging to the said C. D., lying immediately north of the dwelling-house and garden of the said C. D., in the town of, aforesaid, and containing twenty acres or thereabouts, on or before the twenty-fifth day of September next; that when the said crop, to be sown as aforesaid, shall be in fit condition, he will cut, harvest and safely house it in the barn of said C. D.; and that he will properly thrash and clean the same, and deliver one-half, being the produce thereof, to the said C. D., at the granery near his dwelling-house, as aforesaid, on or before the day of , in the year 18 .

It is understood between the parties, that one-half of the seed wheat is to be found by the said C. D.; that the said A. B. is to perform all the work and labor necessary in the premises, or cause it to be done; and that the straw is to be equally divided between the parties, within ten days after the wheat shall have been thrashed as aforesaid.

In witness, &c., as in 3.

———:o:———

5. *Protest of bill for non-acceptance.*

United States of America, }
Territory of Utah, } ss:

On the day of , 18 , at the request of A. B., [insert the name of the holder, or endorser, or endorsee], I, D. E., a Notary Public, duly admitted and sworn, dwelling in the of , in the Territory aforesaid, did present the original bill of exchange, hereunto annexed, to F. G., the drawee therein named, for acceptance, who refused to accept the same: Whereupon I, the said Notary, at the request aforesaid, did protest, and by these presents do publicly and solemnly protest, as against all others whom it doth or may concern, for exchange, re-exchange, and all costs, damages and interest already incurred and to be hereafter incurred, for want of acceptance of the same.

Thus done and protested in the of aforesaid.

In testimony of the truth,

D. E., Notary Public.

[L. S.]

6. *Protest of bill or note, for non-payment.*

United States of America, } ss:
Territory of Utah, }

On the day of , 18 , at the request of A. B., [insert the name of the holder, endorser, endorsee, or cashier] I, D. E., a Notary Public, duly admitted and sworn, dwelling in the of , in the Territory aforesaid, did present the original bill of exchange, [or, note,] hereunto annexed, to F. G., the acceptor [or, maker] of said bill, [or, note;] and demanded payment, who refused to pay the same: [or, did present the original note [or, check,] hereunto annexed, at the Bank where the same is made payable, [or, at the place of business of E. F., the acceptor [or, maker] of the said bill, [or, note,] he being absent therefrom, [or, at the dwelling-house of E. F., &c., his place of business being closed; and he being absent from his said dwelling-house,] and demanded payment of the same, which was refused:] [or, did make diligent inquiry for the said E. F., and his place of business, or dwelling-house in the said of , where the said bill [or, note] was made payable, [or, purported to be drawn,] but was unable to find the said E. F., or his place of business, or dwelling-house, in said , in order to demand payment of the said bill [or note:] whereupon I, the said Notary Public, at the request aforesaid, did protest, and by these presents do solemnly and publicly protest, as well against the drawer and endorsers of the said bill, [or, note, or, check,] as against all others whom it doth or may concern, for exchange, re-exchange, and all costs, damages and interest already incurred and to be hereafter incurred, for want of payment of the same.

Thus done and protested in the of . aforesaid.

In testimony of the truth,

[L. S.] D. E., Notary Public.

———:o:———

7. *Notice of protest for non-acceptance.*

Mr. A. B.: Sir—You will take notice that your bill for , at thirty days from sight, dated , 18 , drawn on C. D., has this day been protested for non-acceptance.

Dated

D. E., Notary Public.

———:o:———

8.—*Notice of protest for non-payment.*

Mr. A. B.: Sir—You will take notice that your bill for at days from sight, dated , 18 , has this day been protested for non-payment; [or, that the bill of A. B. for at days from sight, dated , 18 , endorsed by you, [or, by C. D., E. F., &c.,] and drawn on and accepted by G. H., has, &c., as above; or, that the note of A. B. for , dated , 18 , payable at the Bank, days after date, and endorsd by E. F. and G. H., has, &c., as above.]

Dated , , 18 .

J. S., Notary Public.

9.—*General form of a Notarial certificate.*

United States of America, } ss:
Territory of Utah, }

By this public instrument be it known, to all whom the same doth or may in anywise concern, that I, A. B., a Notary in and for the Territory of Utah, duly sworn and commissioned, dwelling in , do hereby certify that [here state the subject matter of the certificate.]

In testimony whereof I have subscribed my name, and caused my notarial [L.S.] seal of office to be hereunto affixed, the day of A. D. 18 .

A. B., Notary Public.

———:o:———

10.—*Common bill of sale.*

Know all men by these presents: That I, A.B.; of the [town, or, city,] of , in the county of , and Territory of Utah, of the first part, for and in consideration of the sum of dollars, lawful money of the United States, to me paid by C. D., of &c., of the second part, the receipt whereof is hereby acknowledged, have bargained and sold, and by these presents do grant and convey, unto the said party of the second part, his executors, administrators and assigns, [the one undivided half of six acres of wheat, now growing on the farm of E. F., in the town of , aforesaid, one chesnut colored horse, &c., &c.,] to have and to hold the same unto the said party of the second part, his executors, administrators and assigns, for ever. And I do, for myself, my heirs, executors and administrators, covenant and agree, to and with the said party of the second part, his executors, administrators and assigns, to warrant and defend the sale of the said property, hereby made, unto the said party of the second part, his executors, administrators and assigns, against all and every person and persons whomsoever.

In witness whereof, I have hereunto set my hand and seal this day of , A. D. 18 .

Signed, sealed and de- } A. B. [L.S.]
livered in presence of }
G. H.
J. K.

NOTE.—If the property conveyed consists of a great number of articles, it is as well to refer to them, in the bill of sale, as "all the goods, wares and merchandise, chattels and effects, mentioned and described in the schedule hereto annexed, marked "schedule A;" " and they should be particularly enumerated in the schedule.

———:o:———

11.—*Common chattel mortgage.*

This indenture, made the day of , &c., between A. B., of, &c., of the first part, and C. D., of, &c., of the second part, witnesseth: That said party of the first part, in consideration of the sum of dollars, to him duly paid, hath sold, and by these presents doth grant and convey, to the said party of the second part, and his assigns, the following described goods, chattels and property, [describe them particularly, or refer to them in the schedule, as directed in the note to number 10,] now in my possession, at the , of , aforesaid, together with the appurtenances, and all the estate, title and interest, of the said party of the first part therein.

This grant is intended as security for [here state what].

In witness whereof, the said party of the first part hath hereunto set his hand and seal, the day and year first above written.

Signed, sealed and de- } A. B. [L.S.]
livered in presence of }
G. H.
J. K.

12.—*Chattel mortgage to secure a debt.*

Whereas I, A. B., of the town of , in the county of , and Territory of Utah, am justly indebted unto C. D., of, &c., in the sum of dollars, [on account, or, note, or otherwise, as the case may be,] to be paid on or before the day of next, with [or, without,] interest from this date: Now, therefore, in consideration of such indebtedness, and in order to secure the payment of the same, as aforesaid, I do hereby sell, assign, transfer and set over, unto the said C.D., the property mentioned and described in the schedule hereinunder written: Provided, however, that if the said debt and interest be paid, as above specified, this sale and transfer shall be void; and this grant is also subject to the following conditions:

The property hereby sold and transferred is to remain in my possession until default be made in the payment of the debt and interest aforesaid, or some part thereof, unless I shall sell, or attempt to sell, assign or dispose of, the said property, or any part thereof, or suffer the same unreasonably to depreciate in value; in which case the said C. D. may take the said property, or any part thereof, into his possession.

Upon taking said property, or any part thereof, into his possession, either in case of default, or as above provided, the said C. D. shall sell the same at public or private sale; and after satisfying the aforesaid debt and interest thereon, and all necessary and reasonable costs, charges and expenses, incurred by him, out of the proceeds of such sale, he shall return the surplus to me or my representatives.

Witness my hand and seal this day of , 18 .

Signed, sealed and delivered in presence of
G. H.
J. K.

A. B. [L.S.]

Schedule above referred to.

[Insert the articles, and let the mortgagor sign his name at the end of the list.]

———:o:———

13.—*Common bond, with conditions.*

Know all men by these presents: That I, A. B., of the town [or, city] of , in the county of , and Territory of Utah, am held and firmly bound unto C. D., of, &c., in the sum of dollars, lawful money of the United States, to be paid to the said C. D., his executors, administrators or assigns; for which payment, well and truly to be made, I bind my heirs, executors and administrators firmly by these presents.

Sealed with my seal. Dated the day of , one thousand eight hundred and .

The condition of the above obligation is such, that if the above bounden A. B., his heirs, executors or administrators, shall well and truly pay, or cause to be paid, unto the above named C. D., his executors, administrators or assigns, the just and full sum of dollars, in [here state the number of payments,] from the date hereof, with [or, without] annual interest, then the above obligation to be void; otherwise to remain in full force and virtue.

Signed, sealed and delivered in presence of
G. H.
J. K.

A. B. [L.S.]

14. *Indemnity bond to Sheriff.*

Know all men by these presents: That we, A. B., C. D. and H. R. are held and firmly bound unto F. G., Sheriff of the county of , &c., in the sum of , lawful money of the United States, to be paid to the said F. G., his executors, administrators, or assigns; for which payment, well and truly to be made, we bind ourselves, our and each of our heirs, executors, and administrators, jointly and severally, firmly by these presents.

Sealed with our seals, Dated this day of , one thousand eight hundred and .

Whereas the above bounden A. B. did obtain a judgment in the Court of , on the day of , 18 , against E. F., for dollars and cents, damages and costs, whereupon execution has been issued, directed, and delivered to F. G., Sheriff, as aforesaid, commanding him that, of the goods and chattels of the said E. F., he should cause to be made the damages and costs aforesaid. And whereas certain goods and chattels that appear to belong to the said E. F. are claimed by L. M., of, &c.: Now, therefore, the condition of this obligation is such that if the bounden A. B. shall well and truly keep and bear harmless, and indemnify the said F. G., Sheriff as aforesaid, and all and every person and persons aiding and assisting him in the premises, of and from all harm, let, trouble, damages, costs, suits, actions, judgments, and executions that shall, or may, at any time arise, come, or be brought against him, them, or any of them, as well for the levying and making sale, under and by virtue of such execution, of all or any goods and chattels which he or they shall or may judge to belong to the said E. F., as for entering any shop, store, building, or other premises, for the taking of any such goods and chattels, then this obligation to be void; else to remain in full force and virtue.

Sealed and delivered in presence of
G. N.
M. S.

A. B. [L. S.]
C. D. [L. S.]
H. R. [L. S.]

———:o:———

15. *Oath of the Foreman of a Grand Jury.*

You, as foreman of this grand inquest, shall diligently inquire, and true presentment make, of all such matters and things as shall be given to you in charge; the counsel of the people, of your fellows, and your own, you shall keep secret: you shall present no one from envy, hatred, or malice; nor leave any one unpresented, for fear, favor, affection, reward, or the hope of reward; but you shall present all things truly, as they come to your knowledge, according to the best of your understanding. So help you God.

———:o:———

16. *Oath of Grand Jurors.*

The same oath your foreman has taken on his part, you and each of you shall truly observe and keep on your part. So help you God.

17. *Oath of Petit Jurors in civil causes.*

You, and each of you, shall well and truly try the several issues which you shall have in charge at this Court, and true verdicts give in them, respectively, according to evidence. So help you God.

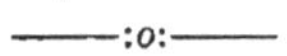

18. *Oath of witnesses in a civil cause.*

The evidence you shall give in this issue, joined between A. B., plaintiff, and C. D., defendant, shall be the truth, the whole truth, and nothing but the truth. So help you God.

19. *Oath of Interpreter.*

You shall truly interpret between the Court, the jury, the council, and the witness, in the issue joined between A. B., plaintiff, and C. D., defendent. So help you God.

20. *Voire Dire.*

You shall true answers make to such questions as shall be put to you, touching your interest in the event of this cause. So help you God.

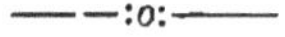

21. *Simple Deed.*

This indenture, made the day of , in the year of our Lord one thousand eight hundred and , between A. B., of, &c., of the first part, and C. D., of, &c., of the second part, witnesseth: That the said party of the first part, for and in consideration of the sum of dollars, to him in hand paid by the said party of the second part, the receipt whereof is hereby acknowledged, hath bargained and sold, and by these presents doth bargain and sell, unto the said party of the second part, and to his heirs and assigns, forever, all and singular, [here describe the premises]; together with all and singular hereditaments and appurtenances thereunto belonging, or in any wise appertaining; and the reversion and reversions, remainder and remainders, rents, issues and profits thereof; and also all the estate, right, title, interest, claim, or demand whatsoever, of him, the said party of the first part, either in law or equity, of, in and to, the above bargained premises, and every part and parcel thereof.

In witness whereof, the said party of the first part has hereunto set his hand and seal, the day and year first above written.

Sealed and delivered } A. R. [L. S.]
in presence of }
N. S.
O. M.

———:o:———

22.—*Deed by Administrator, empowered to sell by Judge.*

To all to whom these presents shall come: I, A. B., of , in the county of , Territory of Utah, administrator of the goods and estate which were of C. D., late of , &c., deceased, intestate, send greeting: Whereas, by an order of the Probate Judge of the county of , made at a Probate Court held at , within the county of , on the day of last past, I, the said A. B., was licensed and empowered to sell and pass deeds, to convey the real estate of the said C. D, hereinafter described; and whereas I, the said A. B., having given public notice of the intended sale, by causing a notification thereof to be printed and inserted weeks, successively, in the newspaper called the , printed in , [or posted up in places, in the county of ,] agreeably to the order and direction of said Court, and having given the bond and taken the oath, by law in such cases required, previous to fixing the time and place of sale, did, on the day of instant, pursuant to the license and notice aforesaid, sell, by public auction, the real estate of the said C. D., hereinafter described, to E. F., of , in the county of , for the sum of dollars, he being the highest bidder therefor: Now, therefore, know ye that I, A. B., by virtue of the power and authority in me vested, as aforesaid, and in consideration of the aforesaid sum of dollars, to me paid by the said E. F., the receipt whereof is hereby acknowledged, do hereby grant, bargain, sell and convey, unto the said E. F., his heirs and assigns, all and singular, the [here describe the property:] To have and to hold the above granted premises, to the said E. F., his heirs and assigns, to his and their use and behoof forever. And I, the said A B., for myself, my heirs, executors and administrators, do hereby coveuant with the said E. F., his heirs and assigns, that, in pursuance of the license aforesaid, I took the oath and gave the bond by law required, and gave public notice of said sale, as above set forth.

In witness whereof, I, the said A. B., have hereunto set my hand and seal, the day of , in the year one thousand eight hundred and .

Sealed and delivered } A. B. [L. S.
in presence of }
M. N.
O. P.

———:o:———

23.—*Sheriff's certificate of the sale of real estate on an execution.*

Court,

A. B. } I, A. P., Sheriff of the county of , do hereby certify that, by virtue
against } of an execution in the above cause, tested the day of , in
C. D. } the year , by which I was commanded to make, of the goods and

s

chattels of E. D., within my official jurisdiction, dollars, which A. B. had recovered against him in the said Court, for damages which he had sustained, as well by reason of the not performing certain promises, [or, for the detention of certain debt; or, as the cause of action may be,] as for his costs and charges; and if sufficient goods and chattels could not be found, that then I should cause the said damages to be made of the real estate which the said E. D. had on the day of in the year , or at any time afterwards, in whose hands soever the same might be; as by the said writ of execution, reference being thereunto had, more fully appears; I have levied on, and this day sold, at public auction, to E. F., who was the highest bidder, for the sum of dollars, which was the whole consideration of such sale, the real estate described as follows, to wit: All and singular the [here describe the property:] And that the sale will become absolute at the expiration of . calendar months from this day, to wit, on the day of A. D. 18 , and E. F., or his assigns, be entitled to a conveyance, pursuant to law, unless the said lands shall be redeemed.

Given under my hand, this day of , 18 .

A. P., Sheriff of the county of

——:o:——

24.—*Sheriff's deed, where land is sold under an execution.*

This indenture, made the day of in the year of , between A. P., Sheriff, [or, late Sheriff,] of the county of , of the first part, and E. F., of, &c., of the second part: Whereas, by virtue of a certain execution issued out of and under the seal of the Court of the Territory of Utah, tested the day of , in the year 18 , at the suit of A. B., plaintiff, against C. D., defendant, directed and delivered to the said Sheriff, commanding him that, of the goods and chattels of the said defendant, he should cause to be made certain moneys in the said writ specified, and, if sufficient goods and chattels could not be found, that then he should cause the amount so specified to be made of the real estate which the said defendant had on a day in the said writ mentioned, or at any time afterwards, in whose hands soever the same might be, the said Sheriff did levy on and seize all the estate, right, title and interest, which the said defendant so had, of, in and to, the premises hereinafter conveyed and described; and on the day of , in the year one thousand eight hundred and , sold the said premises at public vendue, at the house of , in the town of in the said county; having first given public notice of the time and place of such sale, according to law; at which sale the said premises were struck off to E. F., for the sum of dollars, he being the highest bidder, and that being the highest sum bidden for the same.* And whereas, the said premises, after the expiration of months from the time of said sale, remained unredeemed, and no creditor of the said C. D. hath acquired the right and title of the said purchaser, according to law.* [If the deed is given to redeeming creditor, substitute the name of such creditor for E. F., as aforesaid, and instead of the words between the two *s, say: And whereas, the said premises, after the expiration of months from the time of said sale, remained unredeemed, by any person entitled to make such redemption within that time: And whereas, L. M., a creditor of the said C. D., having in his own name [or, as assignee; or, representative; or, trustee] a judgment in the Court, &c., against the said C. D., for the sum of dollars, in an action of , rendered before the expiration of months from the time of such sale, and which is a lien and charge on the premises so sold, hath acquired all the rights of the said E. F., the original purchaser, to said premises, within the time and in the manner and form prescribed by law; and no other creditor of the said C. D. hath acquired the said rights from or against the said E. F.] Now this indenture witnesseth: That the said party of the first part, by virtue of the said writ, and pursuance of law, and in consideration of the sum of money so bidden as aforesaid, hath sold, and by these presents doth grant and convey, unto the said party of the second part, all the estate, right, title and interest, which the said defendant had on said day of , one thousand eight hundred and , or at any time afterwards, of, in and to, all and singular [here describe the premises:] to have and to hold the said above mentioned premises, unto the said party of the second part, his heirs and assigns, forever, as fully and absolutely as the said party of the first part, as Sheriff aforesaid can, or ought to, by virtue of the said writ and the law relating thereto.

In witness whereof, the said Sheriff has hereunto set his hand and seal, the day and year first above written.

Sealed and delivered
in presence of
M. N.
O. P.

A. P., Sheriff of .

———:o:———

25.—*Summons.*

Town of , County, } ss.

To any Constable of the said county, greeting.

The people of the Territory of Utah command you to summon A. B. to appear before me, the undersigned, one of the Justice sof the Peace [or, Judge] of the town aforesaid, at my office, [or, as the case may be,] in the said county, on the day of , at o'clock, in the noon, to answer C. D., in an action arising on contract, [or, in any action for damages for an injury to the person of the said C. D., or, as the cause of action may be,] to his damage dollars or under. And have you then and there this precept.

Witness my hand, the day of , 18 .

H. B., Justice of the Peace. [or, Judge.]

———:o:———

26.—*Attachment.*

County, Town of , } ss.

To any Sheriff [or, Constable] of the said county, greeting:

Whereas, C. D. has appiled for an attachment against the property of A. B., against whom he has a claim for a debt of dollars, and produced satisfactory proof that the said A. B. is about to depart from the said county of , where he last resided, [or, as the case may be,] with intent to defraud his creditors: Therefore, the people of the Territory of Utah command you to attach so much of the goods and chattels of the said A. B., as will be sufficient to satisfy the said claim, and safely to keep the same, to satisfy any judgment that may be recovered on this attachment; and that you make return of your proceedings thereon to me, on the day of , at o'clock in the noon, at my office in the said town.

Dated the day of , 18 .

G. H., Judge. [or, Justice of the Peace.

27. *Subpœna.*

Town of County, } ss:

The people of the Territory to E. F., H. M., &c., greeting:

We command you, and each of you, that, all business and excuses being laid aside, you and each of you be and appear, in your proper persons, before the undersigned, Judge, [or, Justice of the Peace,] of county, [or, district, or, precinct,] at his office in , in the said county, on the day of , at o'clock in the noon, then and there to testify those things which you or either of you know, in a certain action now pending before the said Judge, [or, Justice,] between C. D., plaintiff, and A. B., defendant, on the part of the defendant [or, plaintiff.] [If a witness is required to produce some paper or other evidence, insert here:] And you, E. F., are further commanded to bring with you, and then and there produce in evidence, a certain agreement in writing, &c., [as the case may be, describing the paper.] Hereof fail not, at your peril.

Witness my hand, this day of , 18 .

G. H., Judge. [or, Justice.]

———:o:———

28. *Venire.*

Town of County, } ss:

To any Sheriff [or, Constable; or, Marshal,] of the said county, [or, town; or, district,] greeting:

The people of the Territory of Utah command you to summon good and lawful men, in the county of , [or, town; or, district,] qualified to serve as jurors, and not exempt from serving on juries, in the Courts of this Territory, to appear before me, Judge [or, Justice,] of the said County, (or, town, or, district,] at my office in said town, on the day of , 18 , at o'clock in the noon, to make a jury for the trial of an action arising on contract, [or, as the cause of action may be,] between C. D., plaintiff, and A. B., defendant: And you are also required to make a list of the persons summoned, which you will certify and annex to this venire, and make return thereof to me.

Witness my hand, this day of, 18 .

G. H., Judge. [or, Justice.]

———:o:———

29. *Execution.*

Town of County, } ss:

To any Sheriff of said county, [or, Marshal; or, Constable, as the case may be,] greeting: Whereas, judgment has been rendered before me, Judge of the said county, [or, of said district; or, of Justice of precinct, naming it,] against A. B., defendant, in favor of C. D., plaintiff, for dollars and cents: Therefore, the people of the Territory of Utah command you to levy the amount of the said judgment, with interest from the day of , 18 , on which day judgment was rendered, until received, of the goods and chattels of the said defendant, (except such goods and chattels as are by law exempted from [execution,) and bring the money before me days from the date hereof to render to the said plaintiff: and have you then and there this precept.

Witness my hand, the day of , 18 .

G. H., Judge. [or, Justice.]

——:o:——

30.—*General form of Power of Attorney.*

Know all men by these presents: That I, A. B., of , in the county of , and Territory of Utah, have made, constituted and appointed, and by these presents do make, constitute and appoint, C. D., of, &c.. my true and lawful attorney, for me, and in my name, place, stead,* [here set forth the subject matter of the power,] giving and granting unto my said attorney *full power and authority to do and perform all and every act and thing whatsoever, requisite and necessary to be done, in and about the premises, as fully, to all intents and purposes, as I might or could do if personally present, with full power of substitution and revocation, hereby ratifying and confirming all that my said attorney, or his substitute, shall lawfully do, or cause to be done, by virtue thereof.

In witness whereof, I have hereunto set my hand and seal, the day of , in the year one thousand eight hundred and .

Sealed and delivered in the presence of
G. H.
M. N.

A. B. [L.S.]

——:o:——

31.—*Power of Attorney to collect debts.*

Know all men by these presents: &c. [as in number 30, to the *, then add,] and to my use, to ask, demand, sue for, collect and receive all such sums of money, debts, rents, dues, accounts and other documents whatsoever, which are or shall be due, owing, payable and belonging to me, or detained from me, in any manner whatsoever, by E. F., of, &c., his heirs, executors and administrators, or any of them, [or, by any person or persons residing or being in the State; or, Territory; or, Kingdom of ;] giving and granting, unto my said attorney, &c., [as number 30, from the last * to end of that number.]

——:o:——

32.—*Power of Attorney to collect rents.*

Know all men by these presents, &c., [as in number 30, to the *, then add,] and for my use to ask, demand, [insert, distrain for, if necessary,] collect and receive all such rents and arrears of rents as now are or may be, or shall hereafter grow due, or owing to me, from E. F., R. F. &c., of &c., or any of them, or occupiers of any lands, tenements or hereditaments, belonging to, or claimed by me, situate in the county of

, in the Territory of Utah, [or, elsewhere,] or which may be due from, or payable by, any other person or persons whomsoever, as tenants, occupiers, lessees or assignees, of any term or terms, of such lands, tenements or hereditaments, or any of them, or any part or parcel of them; and, upon receipt thereof, to give proper acquittances and sufficient discharge thereof; giving and granting unto my said attorney, &c., [as in number 30, from the last * to the end.]

——:o:——

33. *General Power to Transact Business.*

Know all men by these presents: That whereas, I, A. B., of , have this day leased the premises known as No. in the of , for the term of years next ensuing after the day of next, for the purpose of conducting, carrying on and transacting, at the place and number aforesaid, the business of a general commission merchant, and more particularly, the receiving, selling and vending, on commission, all kinds of dry and wet groceries: Now, therefore, I, the said A. B., have made, constituted and appointed, and by these presents do make, constitute and appoint, C. D., of , aforesaid, my true and lawful attorney, for me and in my name, place and stead, to conduct, carry on and transact, the business aforesaid, at the place and number aforesaid; to receive on commission, sell and vend, all and every such goods, wares and merchandize, appertaining to the business aforesaid, as my said attorney may deem meet and proper; to make and execute, sign, seal and deliver, for me and in my name, all bills, bonds, notes, specialties, or other instruments in writing whatsoever, which shall be necessary to the proper conducting, carrying on and transacting, the business aforesaid; and to do and perform all and every act and deed, of whatsoever name or nature, legally appertaining to the same, binding me as firmly and irrevocably by such deed or performance, as if I were myself present thereto consenting; hereby ratifying, confirming and allowing, whatever my said attorney shall lawfully do in the premises.

In witness, &c., [as in 30.]

——:o:——

34. *Power to Sell and Convey Real Estate.*

Know all men by these presents, &c., [as in 30 to the *, and then add:] to enter into and take possession of all such lands, tenements, hereditaments, and real estate whatever, in the State of to or in which I am or may be in any way entitled or interested; and to grant, bargain and sell the same or any part or parcel thereof, for such sum or price, and on such terms, as to him shall seem meet; and for me, and in my name, to make, execute, acknowledge and deliver, good and sufficient deeds and conveyances for the same, either with or without covenants and warranty; and until the sale thereof, to let and demise the said real estate, for the best rent that can be procured for the same; and to ask, demand, [insert distrain for, if necessary,] collect, recover, and receive, all sums of money which shall become due and owing to me, by means of such bargain and sale, or lease and demise; giving and granting unto my said attorney, &c., [as in 30, to the end.]

35. *Will of Real and Personal Estate.*

In the name of God, amen: I, A. B, of the town of , in the county of , and State [or, Territory] of , of the age of years, and being of sound mind and memory, do make, publish and declare, this my last will and testament, in manner following, that is to say:

First, I give and bequeath to my wife, E. B., the sum of , to be accepted and received by her in lieu of dower; to my son, C. B., the sum of ; to my daughter, M. B., the sum of ; to my daughter-in-law, S. B., widow of my son, R. B., deceased, the sum of ; which said several legacies or sums of money, I direct and order to be paid to the said respective legatees, within one year after my decease.

Second, I give and devise to my son, C. B., aforesaid, his heirs and assigns, all that tract or parcel of land, situate, &c., [describe the premises,] together with all the hereditaments and appurtenances thereunto belonging or in any wise appertaining: To have and to hold the premises above described to the said C. B., his heirs and assigns, forever.

Third, I give and devise all the rest, residue and remainder, of my real estate, of every name and nature whatsoever, to my said daughter, M. B., and my said daughter-in-law, S. B., to be divided equally between them, share and share alike.

And lastly, I give and bequeath all the rest, residue and remainder, of my personal estate, goods and chattels, of what nature or kind soever, to my said wife, E. B., whom I hereby appoint sole executrix of this my last will and testament; hereby revoking all former wills by me made.

In witness whereof, I have hereunto set my hand and seal, this day of , in the year of our Lord one thousand eight hundred and .

A. B. [L. S.]

The above instrument, consisting of one sheet, [or, two sheets,] was, at the date thereof, signed, sealed, published and declared, by the said A. B., as and for his last will and testament, in presence of us, who, at his request and in his presence, and in the presence of each other, have subscribed our names as witnesses thereto. [Or, The above instrument, consisting of one sheet, was, at the date thereof, declared to us by A. B., the testator therein mentioned, to be his last will and testament; and he at the same time acknowledged to us, and each of us, that he had signed and sealed the same; and we thereupon, at his request, and in his presence, and in the presence of each other, signed our names thereto as attesting witnesses.]

C. D., residing at , in county.
G. H., residing at , in county.

www.ingramcontent.com/pod-product-compliance
Lightning Source LLC
Chambersburg PA
CBHW020849270326
41928CB00006B/623